PVP™ PLAYER VS. PLAYER

LEVELS UP

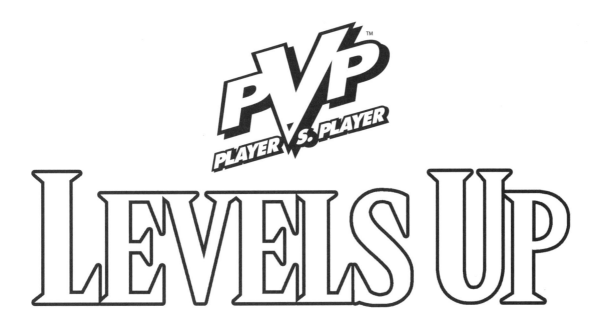

PvP: Levels Up
©2010 Scott R. Kurtz. All Rights Reserved.

Read *PvP* five days a week at
www.pvponline.com

Collecting all strips from 2007.
First printing
ISBN: 978-1-60706-180-9

Cover design by **Scott Kurtz**
Back cover design by **Mary Cagle**

For information regarding promotions, licensing and advertising please email:
kurtz@pvponline.com

Published by Image Comics
www.imagecomics.com

Chief Operating Officer - Robert Kirkman
Chief Financial Officer - Erik Larsen
President - Todd McFarlane
Chief Executive Officer - Marc Silvestri
Vice President - Jim Valentino
Publisher - ericstephenson
PR & Marketing Coordinator - Joe Keatinge
Accounts Manager - Branwyn Bigglestone
Administrative Assistant - Sarah deLaine
Production Manager - Tyler Shainline
Art Director - Drew Gill
Production Artist - Jonathan Chan
Production Artist - Monica Howard
Production Artist - Vincent Kukua

International Rights Representative - Christine Jensen (christine@gfloystudio.com)
Printed in Canada

foreword

Mildly like him or intensely believe he's the worst human being on the planet, you have to admit Scott is one hell of a businessman. Masterfully drawing upon old ensemble sitcoms such as Night Court and Newsradio, Scott has built a deft carbon copy of television in the mid-1980s.

As to his cartooning ability I can present no opinion. But 350,000 readers can't be wrong, as the expression leads one to believe. I have no reason to disbelieve, yet.

PVP inspired my own decision to enter the world of webcomics, and I'm pleased to say "the student has eclipsed the master," so to speak! -- by which I mean without Scott's successes, my own much-greater successes would not have been possible.

Well, that's putting it kindly given that my ascension was inevitable -- let's compromise by saying I didn't know you could put comics on the internet before I saw PVP.

I've only read a handful of them but I can say with certainty: they are getting better.

So give PVP a try. Who knows, you might just find yourself calling Scott one hell of a businessman.

Kris Straub
Los Angeles, CA
Oct 2009

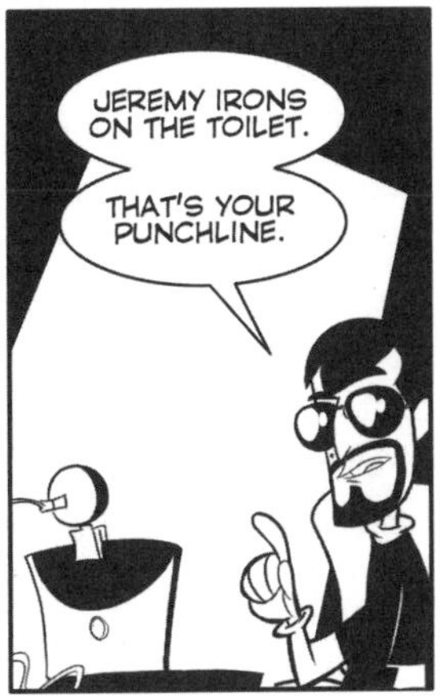
JEREMY IRONS ON THE TOILET.
THAT'S YOUR PUNCHLINE.

Kris Straub is the author of such webcomics as chainsawsuit (www.chainsawsuit.com) and Starslip (www.starslip.com)

for Khoo

CHOOSE YOUR PLAYER

Meet the staff of Player vs. Player Magazine; the 11th worst selling popular-culture review periodical in the country. They watch, read and play everything so you don't have to.

1 Cole Richards:
The glue that holds PvP Magazine together, Cole tries to retain a small semblance of sanity amongst the chaos of his employees. This makes him an obvious target.

2 Brent Sienna:
Pretentious and pompous, Brent is the master of the inappropriate comment. Brent loves three things: Apple Computers, Starbucks Coffee and Jade Fontaine. But not necessarily in that order.

3 Jade Fontaine:
Jade Fontaine fancies herself a writer. It's just too bad that she's stuck reviewing books, games and comics when she could be writing her novel. It's a good thing she loves what she does.

4 Francis Ray Ottoman:
Francis is the random 16 year old jerk-hole you meet playing xbox live. He knows this and is gleefully waiting to make your acquaintance.

5 Skull The Troll:
The heart of PvP Magazine lies deep within the chest of this gentle giant. Skull goes where he is needed and the staff of PvP need him right now. Especially since he makes such a great mascot for tee-shirts and toys.

Panel 1: HAPPY NEW YEAR, BUDDY. / HAPPY NEW YEAR, BRENT.

Panel 2: I JUST WANT YOU TO KNOW THAT MY NEW YEAR'S RESOLUTION IS TO NOT START BEING SO CONVERSELY UNKIND TO YOU IN 2007.

Panel 3: WOW! THAT'S AWESOME. THANKS, BRENT.

Panel 4: YOU AND ME IN 2007, PAL. / STINK BUTT

Panel 5: HAPPY PIXMAS ONE AND ALL! / PIXMAS? WHAT THE HELL IS PIXMAS?

Panel 6: PIXMAS IS THE MOST IMPORTANT RELIGIOUS HOLIDAY FOR GAMERS. IT'S A TIME TO CELEBRATE VIDEO GAMES AND REFLECT ON THE TRUE MEANING OF GAMING.

Panel 7: THIS TRADITIONAL GARB HARKENS BACK TO A TIME WHEN CHILDREN WOULD LEAVE BLANK FLOPPIES OUT ON PIXMAS EVE IN THE HOPES THAT SAINT PIXOLAS WOULD SPAWN IN THEIR HOMES AND FILL THEM WITH SOFTWARE.

Panel 8: NO, FRANCIS. YOU DON'T GET A HOLIDAY TO CELEBRATE GAMING. YOU ALREADY DO THAT ENOUGH YEAR ROUND. / WAY TO DISCRIMINATE, COLE.

Panel 9: SO, BRENT. WHAT GAMES DO YOU HOPE SAINT PIXOLAS LEAVES YOU THIS YEAR? / I'M NEWBISH, DUDE.

Panel 10: COME ON, MAN. WHY WON'T YOU CELEBRATE PIXMAS WITH ME? / BECAUSE I'M ORTHODOX NEWBISH, FRANCIS. I DON'T BELIEVE IN PIXIANITY LIKE YOU DO.

Panel 11: PEOPLE OF THE NEWBISH FAITH BELIEVE IN GAMING, BUT WE DON'T BELIEVE THAT YOUR PIXIAN SAVIOR IS THE TRUE LEETNESS.

Panel 12: BOY... WHEN ARE YOU PIXIANS GOING TO REALIZE THAT YOU'RE NOT THE ONLY GAMING RELIGION ON THE PLANET?

Panel 13: HAPPY PIXMAS, REGGIE! / COME ON, MAN...YOU KNOW I CELEBRATE PWONZAA.

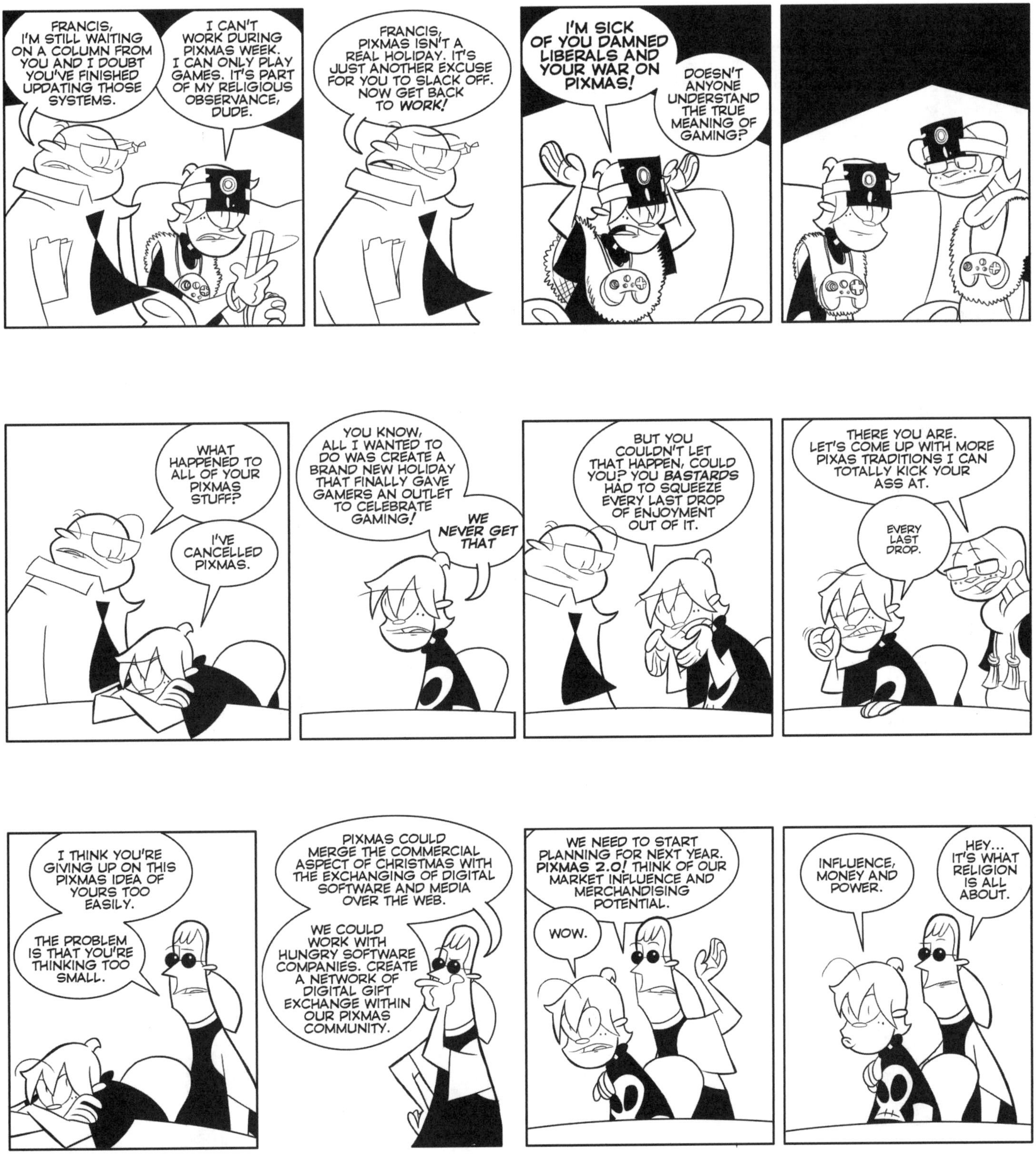
FRANCIS, I'M STILL WAITING ON A COLUMN FROM YOU AND I DOUBT YOU'VE FINISHED UPDATING THOSE SYSTEMS.
I CAN'T WORK DURING PIXMAS WEEK. I CAN ONLY PLAY GAMES. IT'S PART OF MY RELIGIOUS OBSERVANCE, DUDE.
FRANCIS, PIXMAS ISN'T A REAL HOLIDAY. IT'S JUST ANOTHER EXCUSE FOR YOU TO SLACK OFF. NOW GET BACK TO WORK!
I'M SICK OF YOU DAMNED LIBERALS AND YOUR WAR ON PIXMAS!
DOESN'T ANYONE UNDERSTAND THE TRUE MEANING OF GAMING?
WHAT HAPPENED TO ALL OF YOUR PIXMAS STUFF?
I'VE CANCELLED PIXMAS.
YOU KNOW, ALL I WANTED TO DO WAS CREATE A BRAND NEW HOLIDAY THAT FINALLY GAVE GAMERS AN OUTLET TO CELEBRATE GAMING!
WE NEVER GET THAT
BUT YOU COULDN'T LET THAT HAPPEN, COULD YOU? YOU BASTARDS HAD TO SQUEEZE EVERY LAST DROP OF ENJOYMENT OUT OF IT.
THERE YOU ARE. LET'S COME UP WITH MORE PIXAS TRADITIONS I CAN TOTALLY KICK YOUR ASS AT.
EVERY LAST DROP.
I THINK YOU'RE GIVING UP ON THIS PIXMAS IDEA OF YOURS TOO EASILY.
THE PROBLEM IS THAT YOU'RE THINKING TOO SMALL.
PIXMAS COULD MERGE THE COMMERCIAL ASPECT OF CHRISTMAS WITH THE EXCHANGING OF DIGITAL SOFTWARE AND MEDIA OVER THE WEB.
WE COULD WORK WITH HUNGRY SOFTWARE COMPANIES. CREATE A NETWORK OF DIGITAL GIFT EXCHANGE WITHIN OUR PIXMAS COMMUNITY.
WE NEED TO START PLANNING FOR NEXT YEAR. PIXMAS 2.0! THINK OF OUR MARKET INFLUENCE AND MERCHANDISING POTENTIAL.
WOW.
INFLUENCE, MONEY AND POWER.
HEY... IT'S WHAT RELIGION IS ALL ABOUT.

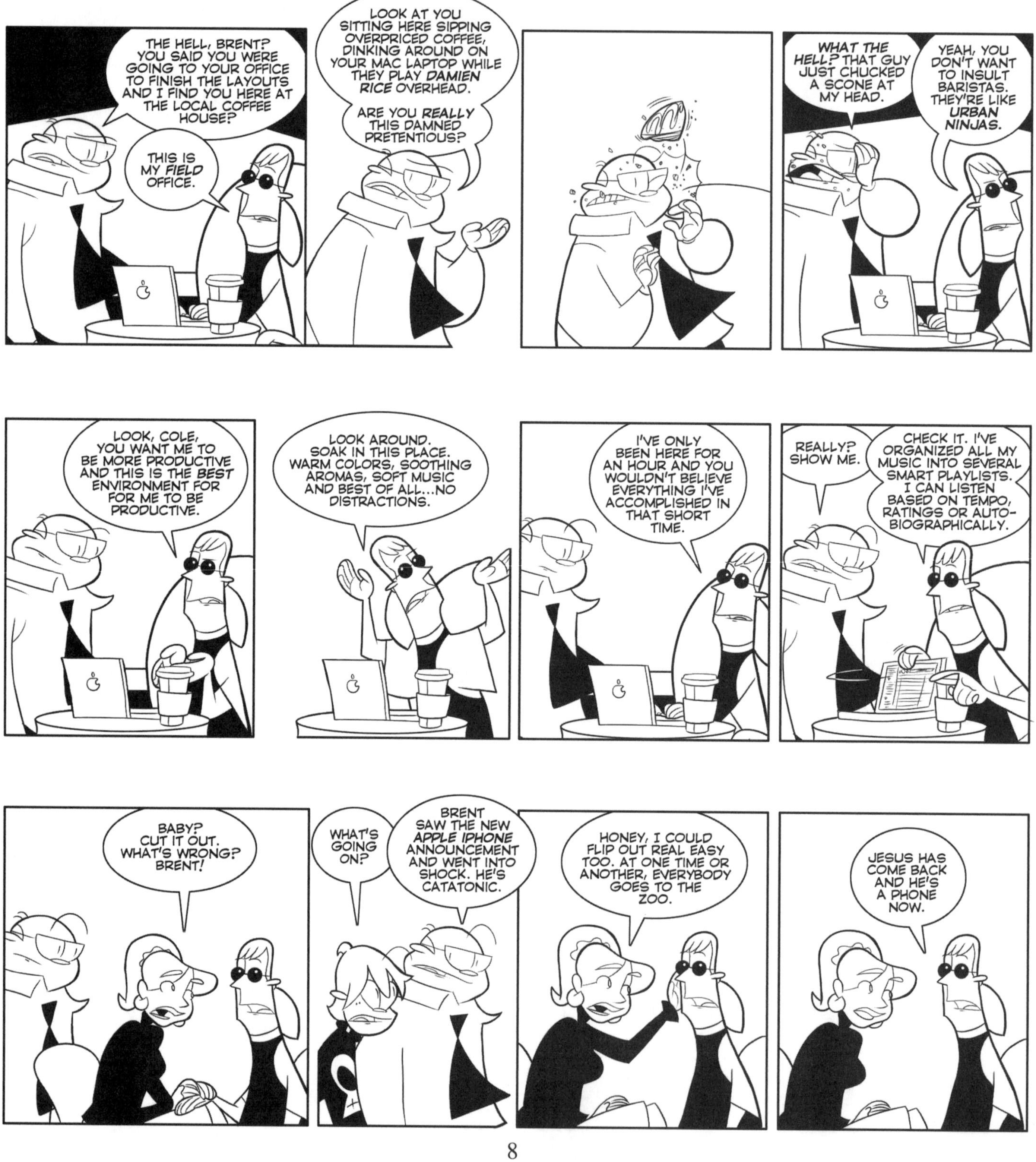
THE HELL, BRENT? YOU SAID YOU WERE GOING TO YOUR OFFICE TO FINISH THE LAYOUTS AND I FIND YOU HERE AT THE LOCAL COFFEE HOUSE?
THIS IS MY *FIELD* OFFICE.
LOOK AT YOU SITTING HERE SIPPING OVERPRICED COFFEE, DINKING AROUND ON YOUR MAC LAPTOP WHILE THEY PLAY *DAMIEN RICE* OVERHEAD.
ARE YOU *REALLY* THIS DAMNED PRETENTIOUS?
WHAT THE HELL? THAT GUY JUST CHUCKED A SCONE AT MY HEAD.
YEAH, YOU DON'T WANT TO INSULT BARISTAS. THEY'RE LIKE *URBAN NINJAS.*
LOOK, COLE, YOU WANT ME TO BE MORE PRODUCTIVE AND THIS IS THE *BEST* ENVIRONMENT FOR FOR ME TO BE PRODUCTIVE.
LOOK AROUND. SOAK IN THIS PLACE. WARM COLORS, SOOTHING AROMAS, SOFT MUSIC AND BEST OF ALL...NO DISTRACTIONS.
I'VE ONLY BEEN HERE FOR AN HOUR AND YOU WOULDN'T BELIEVE EVERYTHING I'VE ACCOMPLISHED IN THAT SHORT TIME.
REALLY? SHOW ME.
CHECK IT. I'VE ORGANIZED ALL MY MUSIC INTO SEVERAL SMART PLAYLISTS. I CAN LISTEN BASED ON TEMPO, RATINGS OR AUTO-BIOGRAPHICALLY.
BABY? CUT IT OUT. WHAT'S WRONG? BRENT!
WHAT'S GOING ON?
BRENT SAW THE NEW *APPLE IPHONE* ANNOUNCEMENT AND WENT INTO SHOCK. HE'S CATATONIC.
HONEY, I COULD FLIP OUT REAL EASY TOO. AT ONE TIME OR ANOTHER, EVERYBODY GOES TO THE ZOO.
JESUS HAS COME BACK AND HE'S A PHONE NOW.

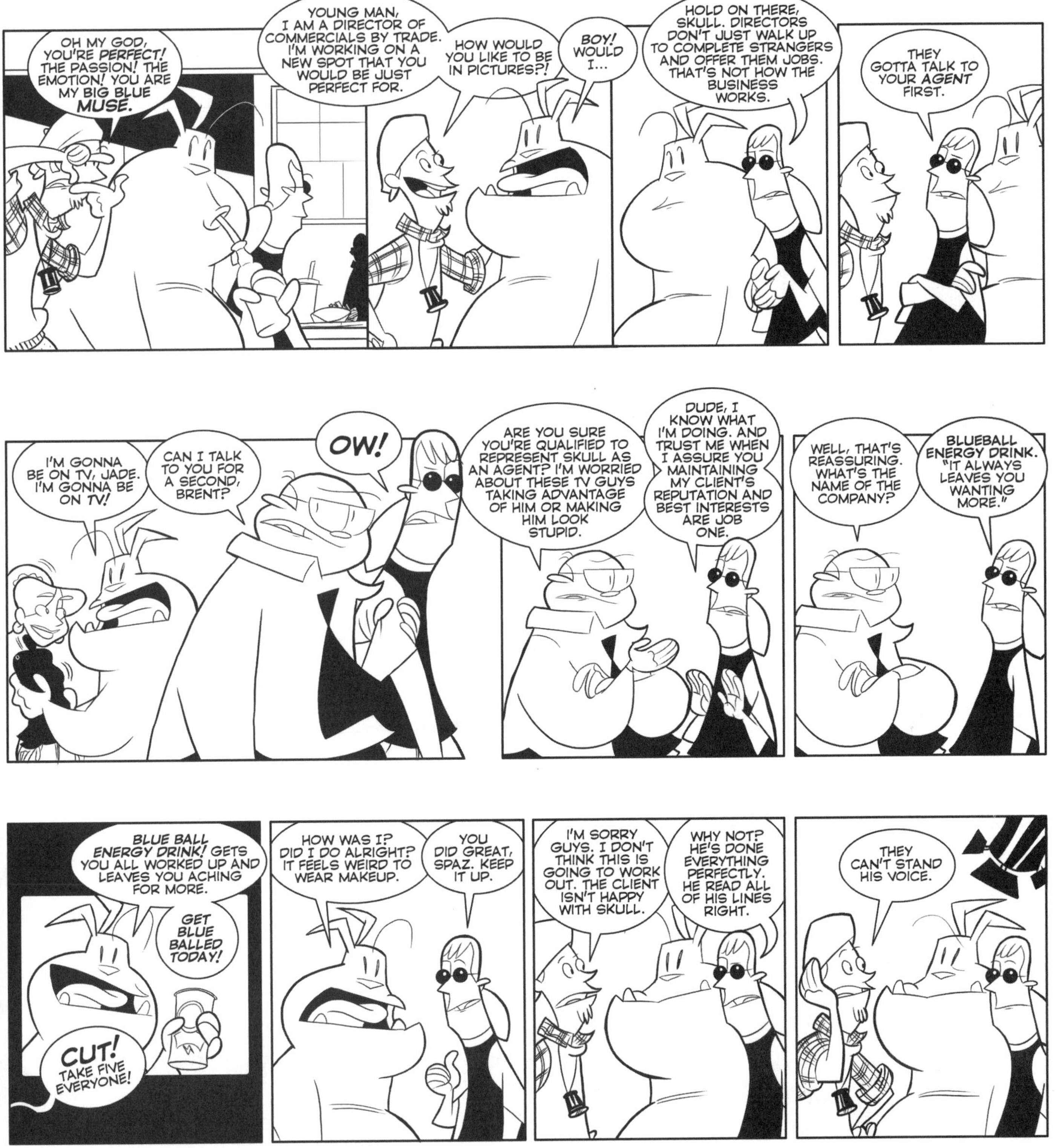
OH MY GOD, YOU'RE PERFECT! THE PASSION! THE EMOTION! YOU ARE MY BIG BLUE MUSE.
YOUNG MAN, I AM A DIRECTOR OF COMMERCIALS BY TRADE. I'M WORKING ON A NEW SPOT THAT YOU WOULD BE JUST PERFECT FOR.
HOW WOULD YOU LIKE TO BE IN PICTURES?!
BOY! WOULD I...
HOLD ON THERE, SKULL. DIRECTORS DON'T JUST WALK UP TO COMPLETE STRANGERS AND OFFER THEM JOBS. THAT'S NOT HOW THE BUSINESS WORKS.
THEY GOTTA TALK TO YOUR AGENT FIRST.
I'M GONNA BE ON TV, JADE. I'M GONNA BE ON TV!
CAN I TALK TO YOU FOR A SECOND, BRENT?
OW!
ARE YOU SURE YOU'RE QUALIFIED TO REPRESENT SKULL AS AN AGENT? I'M WORRIED ABOUT THESE TV GUYS TAKING ADVANTAGE OF HIM OR MAKING HIM LOOK STUPID.
DUDE, I KNOW WHAT I'M DOING. AND TRUST ME WHEN I ASSURE YOU MAINTAINING MY CLIENT'S REPUTATION AND BEST INTERESTS ARE JOB ONE.
WELL, THAT'S REASSURING. WHAT'S THE NAME OF THE COMPANY?
BLUEBALL ENERGY DRINK. "IT ALWAYS LEAVES YOU WANTING MORE."
BLUE BALL ENERGY DRINK! GETS YOU ALL WORKED UP AND LEAVES YOU ACHING FOR MORE.
GET BLUE BALLED TODAY!
CUT! TAKE FIVE EVERYONE!
HOW WAS I? DID I DO ALRIGHT? IT FEELS WEIRD TO WEAR MAKEUP.
YOU DID GREAT, SPAZ. KEEP IT UP.
I'M SORRY GUYS. I DON'T THINK THIS IS GOING TO WORK OUT. THE CLIENT ISN'T HAPPY WITH SKULL.
WHY NOT? HE'S DONE EVERYTHING PERFECTLY. HE READ ALL OF HIS LINES RIGHT.
THEY CAN'T STAND HIS VOICE.

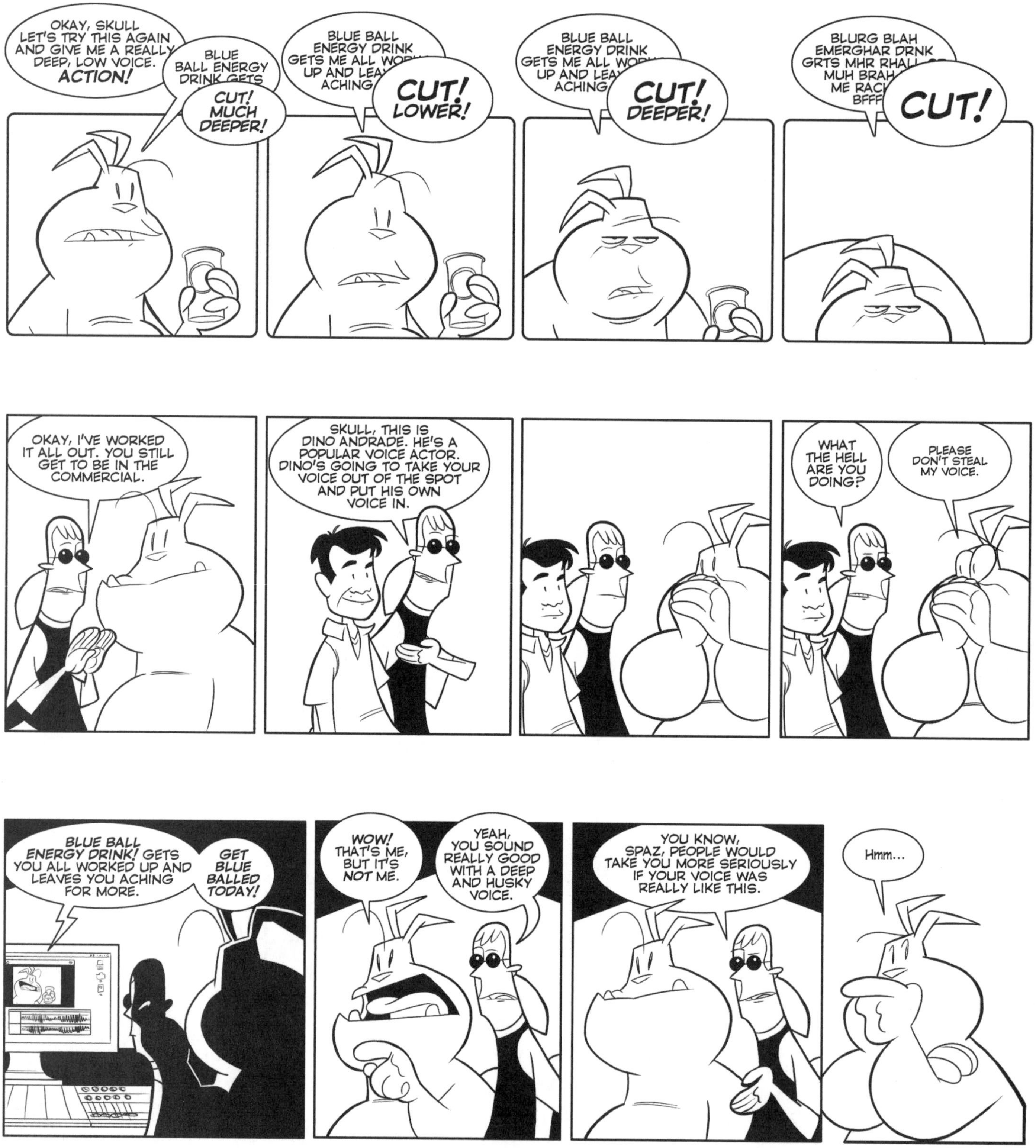

OKAY, SKULL LET'S TRY THIS AGAIN AND GIVE ME A REALLY DEEP, LOW VOICE. ACTION!
BLUE BALL ENERGY DRINK GETS
CUT! MUCH DEEPER!
BLUE BALL ENERGY DRINK GETS ME ALL WOR UP AND LEA ACHING
CUT! LOWER!
BLUE BALL ENERGY DRINK GETS ME ALL WOR UP AND LEA ACHING
CUT! DEEPER!
BLURG BLAH EMERGHAR DRNK GRTS MHR RHALL MUH BRAH ME RAC BFF
CUT!
OKAY, I'VE WORKED IT ALL OUT. YOU STILL GET TO BE IN THE COMMERCIAL.
SKULL, THIS IS DINO ANDRADE. HE'S A POPULAR VOICE ACTOR. DINO'S GOING TO TAKE YOUR VOICE OUT OF THE SPOT AND PUT HIS OWN VOICE IN.
WHAT THE HELL ARE YOU DOING?
PLEASE DON'T STEAL MY VOICE.
BLUE BALL ENERGY DRINK! GETS YOU ALL WORKED UP AND LEAVES YOU ACHING FOR MORE.
GET BLUE BALLED TODAY!
WOW! THAT'S ME, BUT IT'S NOT ME.
YEAH, YOU SOUND REALLY GOOD WITH A DEEP AND HUSKY VOICE.
YOU KNOW, SPAZ, PEOPLE WOULD TAKE YOU MORE SERIOUSLY IF YOUR VOICE WAS REALLY LIKE THIS.
Hmm...

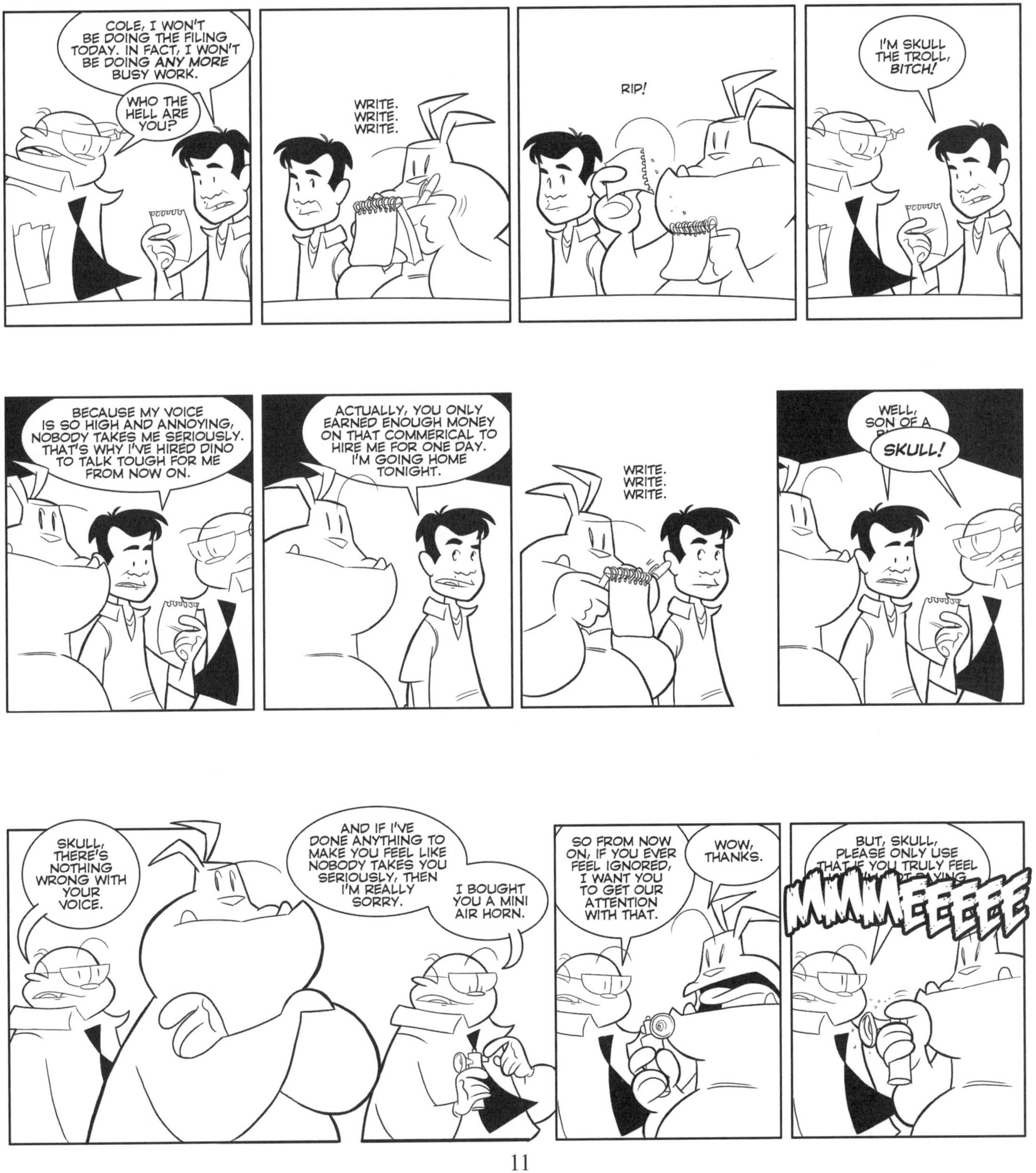

COLE, I WON'T BE DOING THE FILING TODAY. IN FACT, I WON'T BE DOING ANY MORE BUSY WORK.
WHO THE HELL ARE YOU?
WRITE. WRITE. WRITE.
RIP!
I'M SKULL THE TROLL, BITCH!
BECAUSE MY VOICE IS SO HIGH AND ANNOYING, NOBODY TAKES ME SERIOUSLY. THAT'S WHY I'VE HIRED DINO TO TALK TOUGH FOR ME FROM NOW ON.
ACTUALLY, YOU ONLY EARNED ENOUGH MONEY ON THAT COMMERICAL TO HIRE ME FOR ONE DAY. I'M GOING HOME TONIGHT.
WRITE. WRITE. WRITE.
WELL, SON OF A
SKULL!
SKULL, THERE'S NOTHING WRONG WITH YOUR VOICE.
AND IF I'VE DONE ANYTHING TO MAKE YOU FEEL LIKE NOBODY TAKES YOU SERIOUSLY, THEN I'M REALLY SORRY.
I BOUGHT YOU A MINI AIR HORN.
SO FROM NOW ON, IF YOU EVER FEEL IGNORED, I WANT YOU TO GET OUR ATTENTION WITH THAT.
WOW, THANKS.
BUT, SKULL, PLEASE ONLY USE THAT IF YOU TRULY FEEL
MMMEEEEE

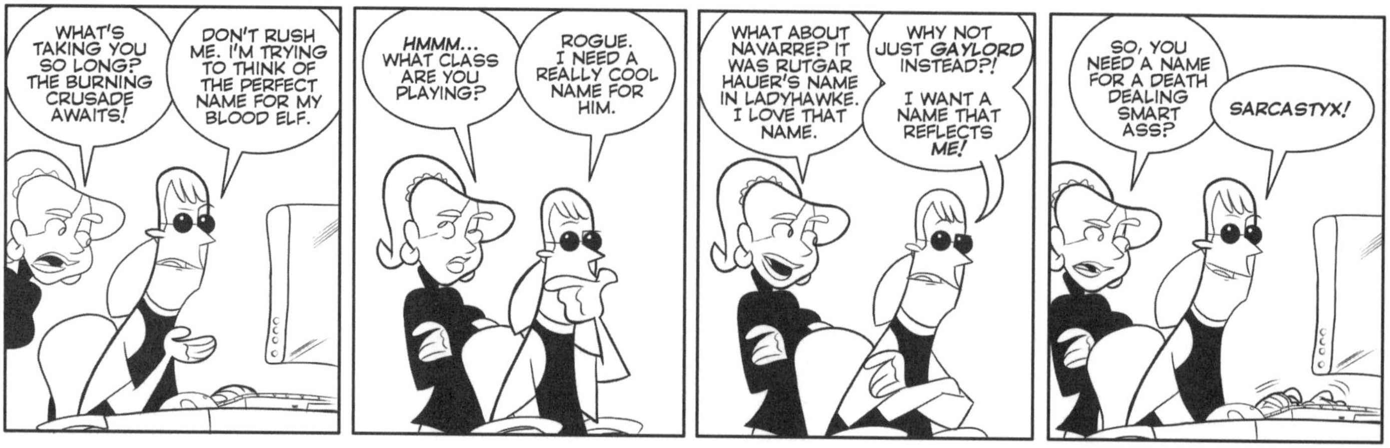
WHAT'S TAKING YOU SO LONG? THE BURNING CRUSADE AWAITS!
DON'T RUSH ME. I'M TRYING TO THINK OF THE PERFECT NAME FOR MY BLOOD ELF.
HMMM... WHAT CLASS ARE YOU PLAYING?
ROGUE. I NEED A REALLY COOL NAME FOR HIM.
WHAT ABOUT NAVARRE? IT WAS RUTGAR HAUER'S NAME IN LADYHAWKE. I LOVE THAT NAME.
WHY NOT JUST GAYLORD INSTEAD?!
I WANT A NAME THAT REFLECTS ME!
SO, YOU NEED A NAME FOR A DEATH DEALING SMART ASS?
SARCASTYX!

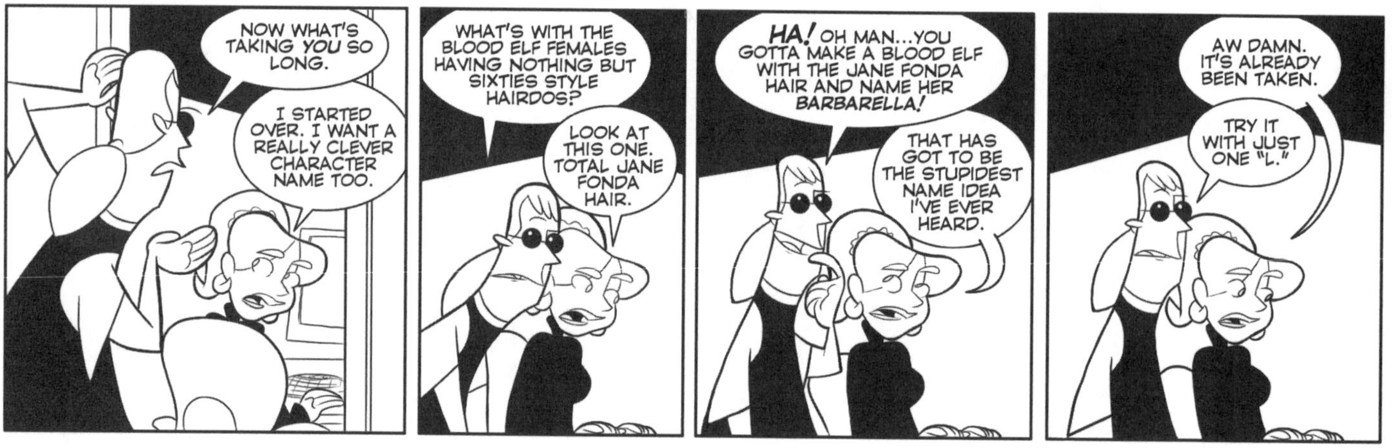
NOW WHAT'S TAKING YOU SO LONG.
I STARTED OVER. I WANT A REALLY CLEVER CHARACTER NAME TOO.
WHAT'S WITH THE BLOOD ELF FEMALES HAVING NOTHING BUT SIXTIES STYLE HAIRDOS?
LOOK AT THIS ONE. TOTAL JANE FONDA HAIR.
HA! OH MAN...YOU GOTTA MAKE A BLOOD ELF WITH THE JANE FONDA HAIR AND NAME HER BARBARELLA!
THAT HAS GOT TO BE THE STUPIDEST NAME IDEA I'VE EVER HEARD.
AW DAMN. IT'S ALREADY BEEN TAKEN.
TRY IT WITH JUST ONE "L."

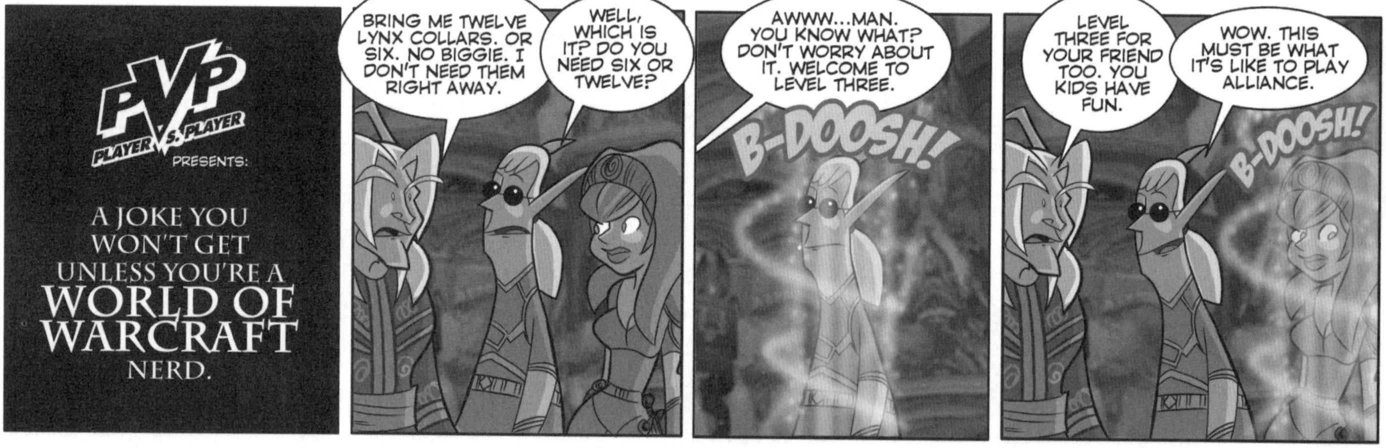
PVP PLAYER VS. PLAYER
PRESENTS:
A JOKE YOU WON'T GET UNLESS YOU'RE A WORLD OF WARCRAFT NERD.
BRING ME TWELVE LYNX COLLARS. OR SIX. NO BIGGIE. I DON'T NEED THEM RIGHT AWAY.
WELL, WHICH IS IT? DO YOU NEED SIX OR TWELVE?
AWWW...MAN. YOU KNOW WHAT? DON'T WORRY ABOUT IT. WELCOME TO LEVEL THREE.
B-DOOSH!
LEVEL THREE FOR YOUR FRIEND TOO. YOU KIDS HAVE FUN.
WOW. THIS MUST BE WHAT IT'S LIKE TO PLAY ALLIANCE.
B-DOOSH!

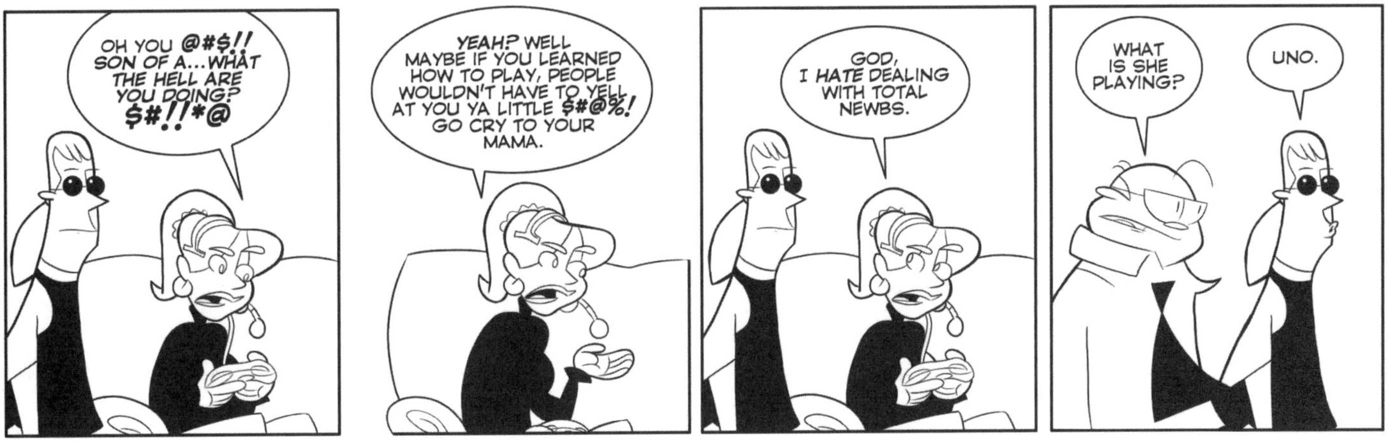
OH YOU @#$!! SON OF A...WHAT THE HELL ARE YOU DOING? $#!!*@
YEAH? WELL MAYBE IF YOU LEARNED HOW TO PLAY, PEOPLE WOULDN'T HAVE TO YELL AT YOU YA LITTLE $#@%! GO CRY TO YOUR MAMA.
GOD, I HATE DEALING WITH TOTAL NEWBS.
WHAT IS SHE PLAYING?
UNO.

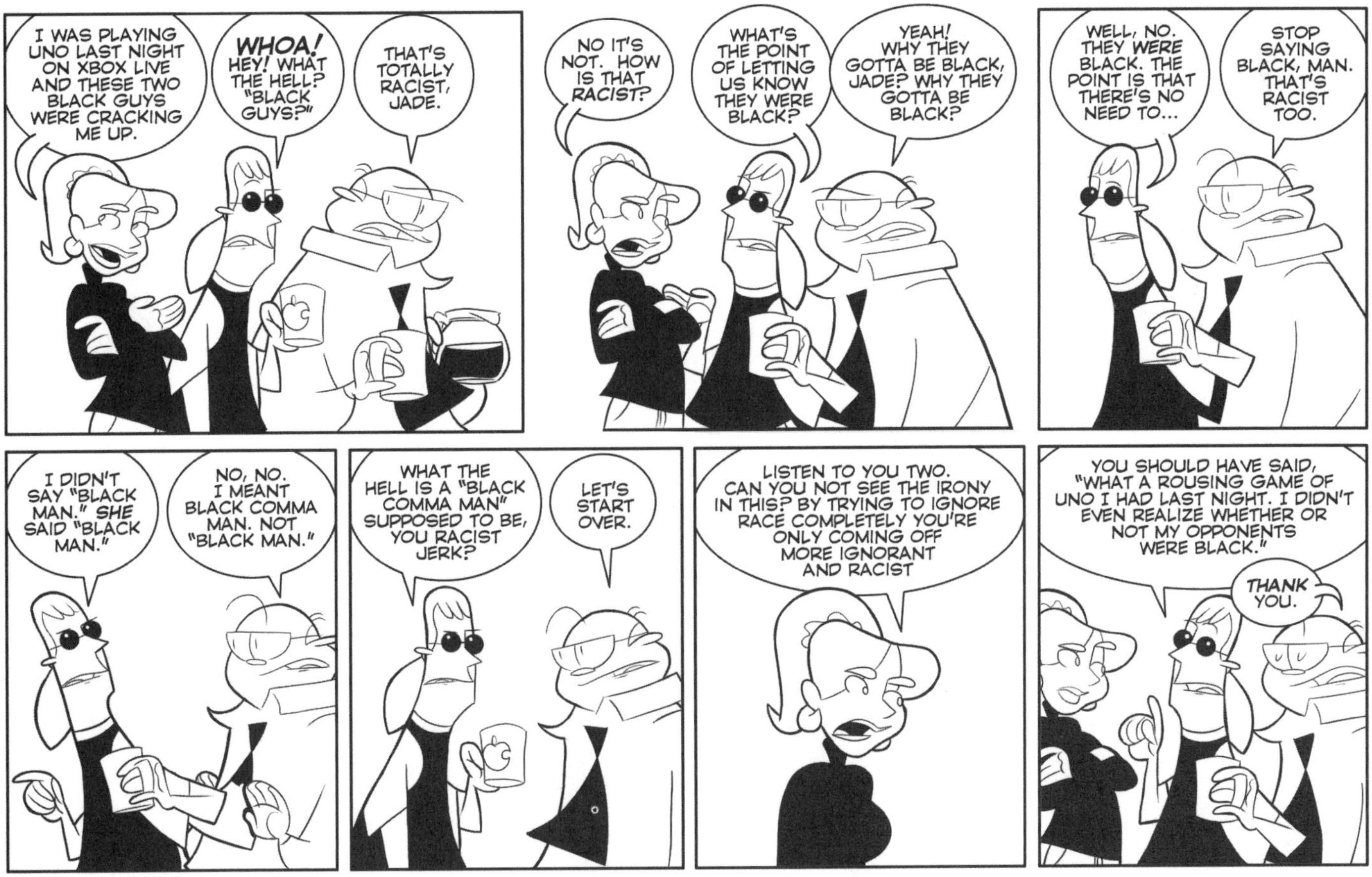
I WAS PLAYING UNO LAST NIGHT ON XBOX LIVE AND THESE TWO BLACK GUYS WERE CRACKING ME UP.
WHOA! HEY! WHAT THE HELL? "BLACK GUYS?"
THAT'S TOTALLY RACIST, JADE.
NO IT'S NOT. HOW IS THAT RACIST?
WHAT'S THE POINT OF LETTING US KNOW THEY WERE BLACK?
YEAH! WHY THEY GOTTA BE BLACK, JADE? WHY THEY GOTTA BE BLACK?
WELL, NO. THEY WERE BLACK. THE POINT IS THAT THERE'S NO NEED TO...
STOP SAYING BLACK, MAN. THAT'S RACIST TOO.
I DIDN'T SAY "BLACK MAN." SHE SAID "BLACK MAN."
NO, NO. I MEANT BLACK COMMA MAN. NOT "BLACK MAN."
WHAT THE HELL IS A "BLACK COMMA MAN" SUPPOSED TO BE, YOU RACIST JERK?
LET'S START OVER.
LISTEN TO YOU TWO. CAN YOU NOT SEE THE IRONY IN THIS? BY TRYING TO IGNORE RACE COMPLETELY YOU'RE ONLY COMING OFF MORE IGNORANT AND RACIST
YOU SHOULD HAVE SAID, "WHAT A ROUSING GAME OF UNO I HAD LAST NIGHT. I DIDN'T EVEN REALIZE WHETHER OR NOT MY OPPONENTS WERE BLACK."
THANK YOU.

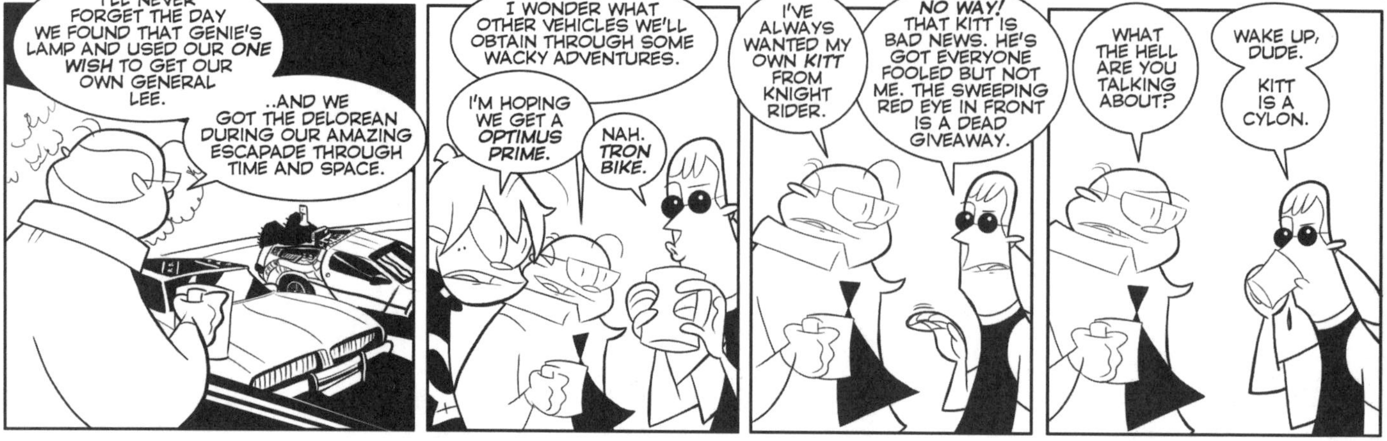
I'LL NEVER FORGET THE DAY WE FOUND THAT GENIE'S LAMP AND USED OUR ONE WISH TO GET OUR OWN GENERAL LEE.
..AND WE GOT THE DELOREAN DURING OUR AMAZING ESCAPADE THROUGH TIME AND SPACE.
I WONDER WHAT OTHER VEHICLES WE'LL OBTAIN THROUGH SOME WACKY ADVENTURES.
I'M HOPING WE GET A OPTIMUS PRIME.
NAH. TRON BIKE.
I'VE ALWAYS WANTED MY OWN KITT FROM KNIGHT RIDER.
NO WAY! THAT KITT IS BAD NEWS. HE'S GOT EVERYONE FOOLED BUT NOT ME. THE SWEEPING RED EYE IN FRONT IS A DEAD GIVEAWAY.
WHAT THE HELL ARE YOU TALKING ABOUT?
WAKE UP, DUDE.
KITT IS A CYLON.

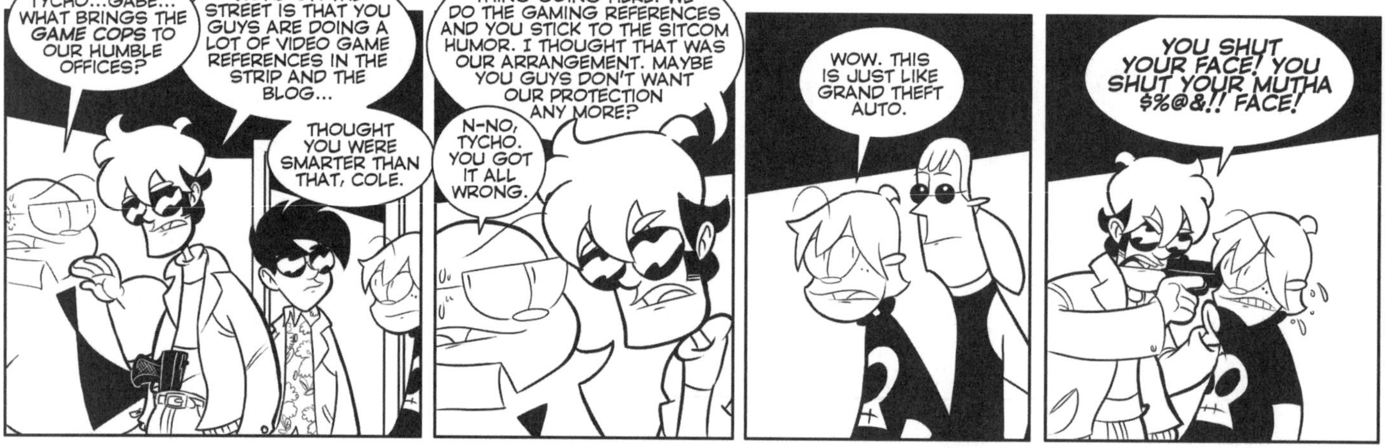
TYCHO...GABE... WHAT BRINGS THE GAME COPS TO OUR HUMBLE OFFICES?
WORD ON THE STREET IS THAT YOU GUYS ARE DOING A LOT OF VIDEO GAME REFERENCES IN THE STRIP AND THE BLOG...
THOUGHT YOU WERE SMARTER THAN THAT, COLE.
WE HAVE A GOOD THING GOING HERE. WE DO THE GAMING REFERENCES AND YOU STICK TO THE SITCOM HUMOR. I THOUGHT THAT WAS OUR ARRANGEMENT. MAYBE YOU GUYS DON'T WANT OUR PROTECTION ANY MORE?
N-NO, TYCHO. YOU GOT IT ALL WRONG.
WOW. THIS IS JUST LIKE GRAND THEFT AUTO.
YOU SHUT YOUR FACE! YOU SHUT YOUR MUTHA $%@&!! FACE!

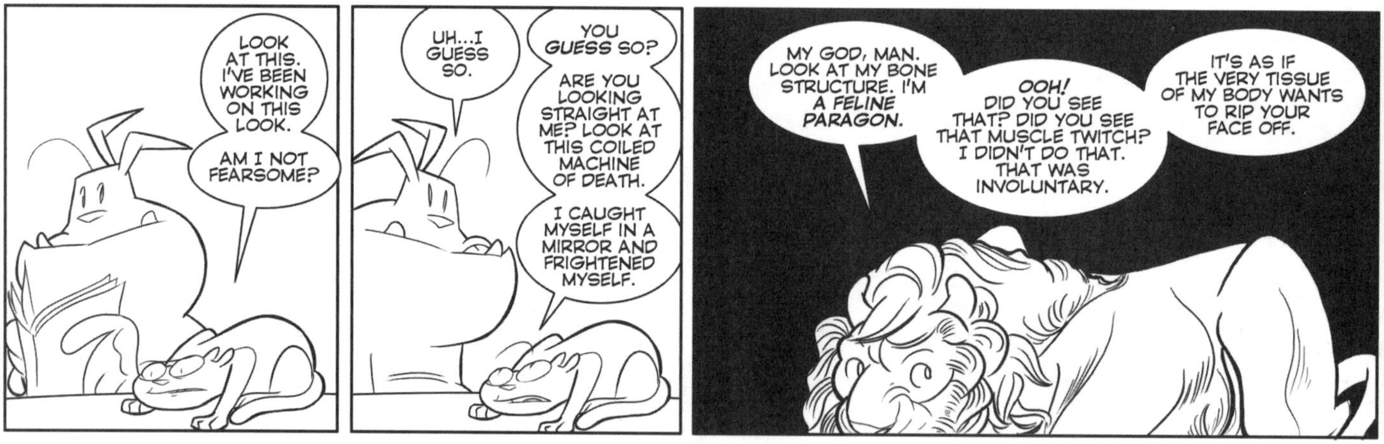
LOOK AT THIS. I'VE BEEN WORKING ON THIS LOOK.
AM I NOT FEARSOME?
UH...I GUESS SO.
YOU GUESS SO?
ARE YOU LOOKING STRAIGHT AT ME? LOOK AT THIS COILED MACHINE OF DEATH.
I CAUGHT MYSELF IN A MIRROR AND FRIGHTENED MYSELF.
MY GOD, MAN. LOOK AT MY BONE STRUCTURE. I'M A FELINE PARAGON.
OOH! DID YOU SEE THAT? DID YOU SEE THAT MUSCLE TWITCH? I DIDN'T DO THAT. THAT WAS INVOLUNTARY.
IT'S AS IF THE VERY TISSUE OF MY BODY WANTS TO RIP YOUR FACE OFF.

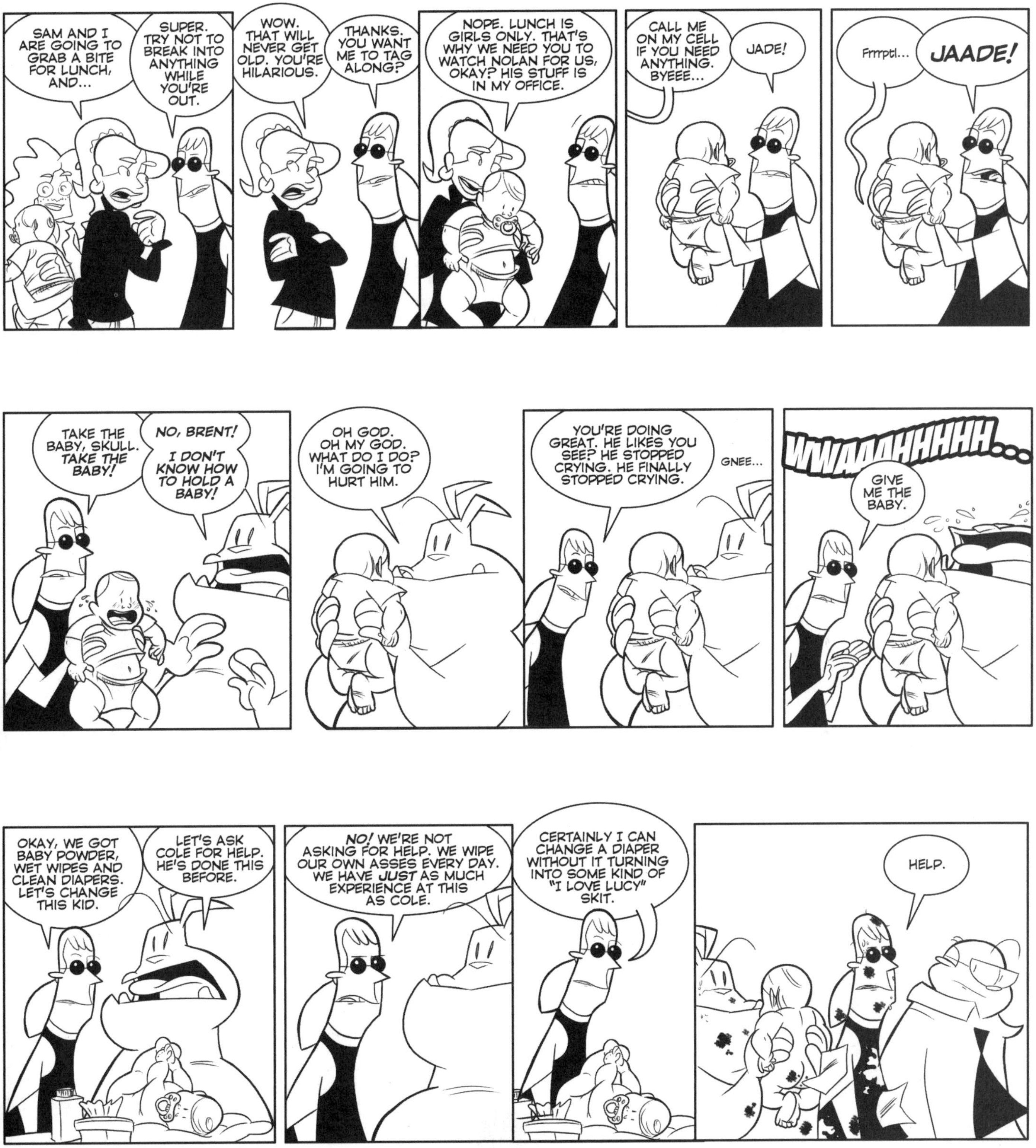
SAM AND I ARE GOING TO GRAB A BITE FOR LUNCH, AND...
SUPER. TRY NOT TO BREAK INTO ANYTHING WHILE YOU'RE OUT.
WOW. THAT WILL NEVER GET OLD. YOU'RE HILARIOUS.
THANKS. YOU WANT ME TO TAG ALONG?
NOPE. LUNCH IS GIRLS ONLY. THAT'S WHY WE NEED YOU TO WATCH NOLAN FOR US, OKAY? HIS STUFF IS IN MY OFFICE.
CALL ME ON MY CELL IF YOU NEED ANYTHING. BYEEE...
JADE!
Frrrptl...
JAADE!
TAKE THE BABY, SKULL. TAKE THE BABY!
NO, BRENT! I DON'T KNOW HOW TO HOLD A BABY!
OH GOD. OH MY GOD. WHAT DO I DO? I'M GOING TO HURT HIM.
YOU'RE DOING GREAT. HE LIKES YOU SEE? HE STOPPED CRYING. HE FINALLY STOPPED CRYING.
GNEE...
WWAAAHHHHH...
GIVE ME THE BABY.
OKAY, WE GOT BABY POWDER, WET WIPES AND CLEAN DIAPERS. LET'S CHANGE THIS KID.
LET'S ASK COLE FOR HELP. HE'S DONE THIS BEFORE.
NO! WE'RE NOT ASKING FOR HELP. WE WIPE OUR OWN ASSES EVERY DAY. WE HAVE JUST AS MUCH EXPERIENCE AT THIS AS COLE.
CERTAINLY I CAN CHANGE A DIAPER WITHOUT IT TURNING INTO SOME KIND OF "I LOVE LUCY" SKIT.
HELP.

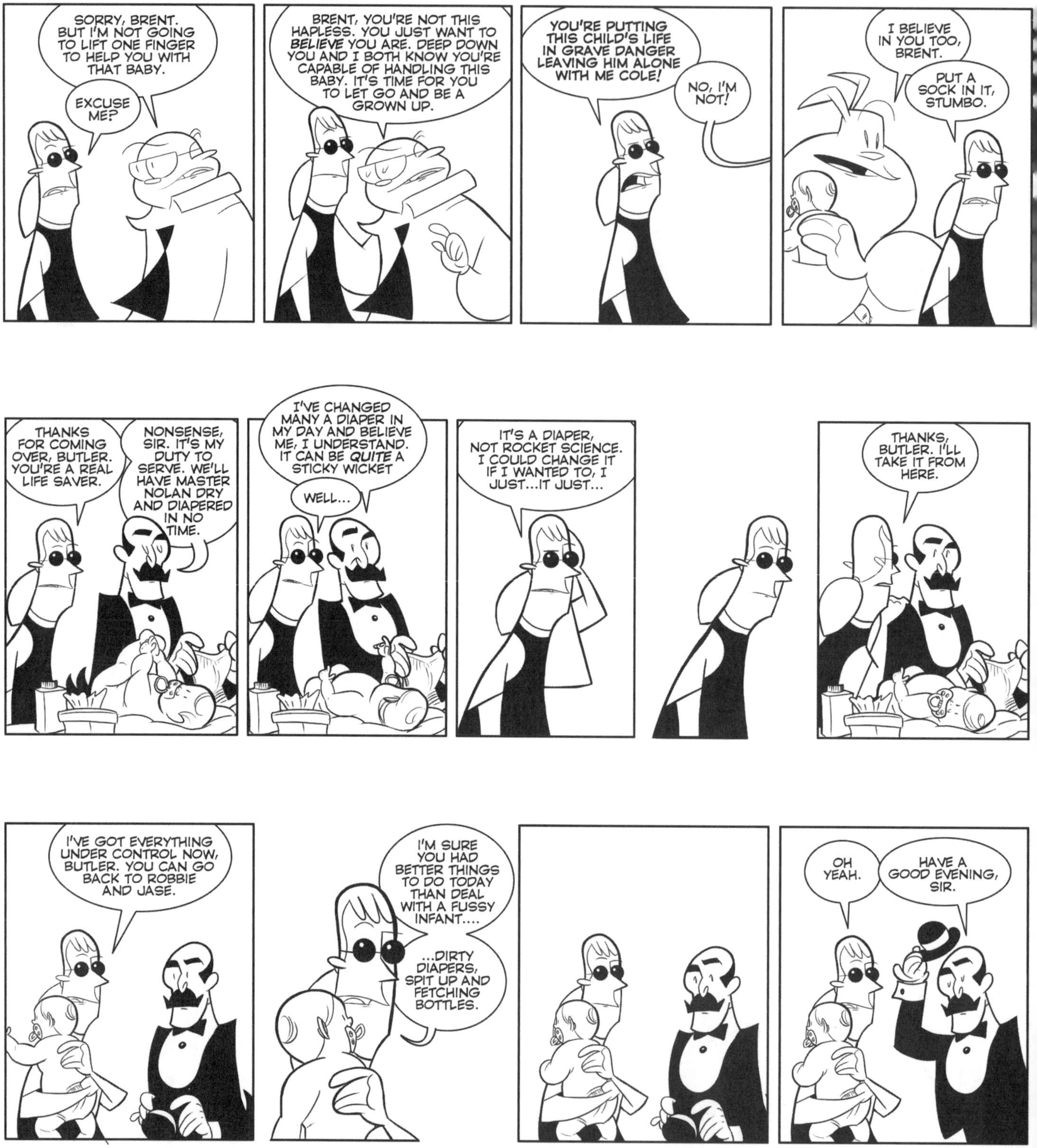
SORRY, BRENT. BUT I'M NOT GOING TO LIFT ONE FINGER TO HELP YOU WITH THAT BABY.
EXCUSE ME?
BRENT, YOU'RE NOT THIS HAPLESS. YOU JUST WANT TO *BELIEVE* YOU ARE. DEEP DOWN YOU AND I BOTH KNOW YOU'RE CAPABLE OF HANDLING THIS BABY. IT'S TIME FOR YOU TO LET GO AND BE A GROWN UP.
YOU'RE PUTTING THIS CHILD'S LIFE IN GRAVE DANGER LEAVING HIM ALONE WITH ME COLE!
NO, I'M NOT!
I BELIEVE IN YOU TOO, BRENT.
PUT A SOCK IN IT, STUMBO.
THANKS FOR COMING OVER, BUTLER. YOU'RE A REAL LIFE SAVER.
NONSENSE, SIR. IT'S MY DUTY TO SERVE. WE'LL HAVE MASTER NOLAN DRY AND DIAPERED IN NO TIME.
I'VE CHANGED MANY A DIAPER IN MY DAY AND BELIEVE ME, I UNDERSTAND. IT CAN BE *QUITE* A STICKY WICKET
WELL...
IT'S A DIAPER, NOT ROCKET SCIENCE. I COULD CHANGE IT IF I WANTED TO, I JUST...IT JUST...
THANKS, BUTLER. I'LL TAKE IT FROM HERE.
I'VE GOT EVERYTHING UNDER CONTROL NOW, BUTLER. YOU CAN GO BACK TO ROBBIE AND JASE.
I'M SURE YOU HAD BETTER THINGS TO DO TODAY THAN DEAL WITH A FUSSY INFANT....
...DIRTY DIAPERS, SPIT UP AND FETCHING BOTTLES.
OH YEAH.
HAVE A GOOD EVENING, SIR.

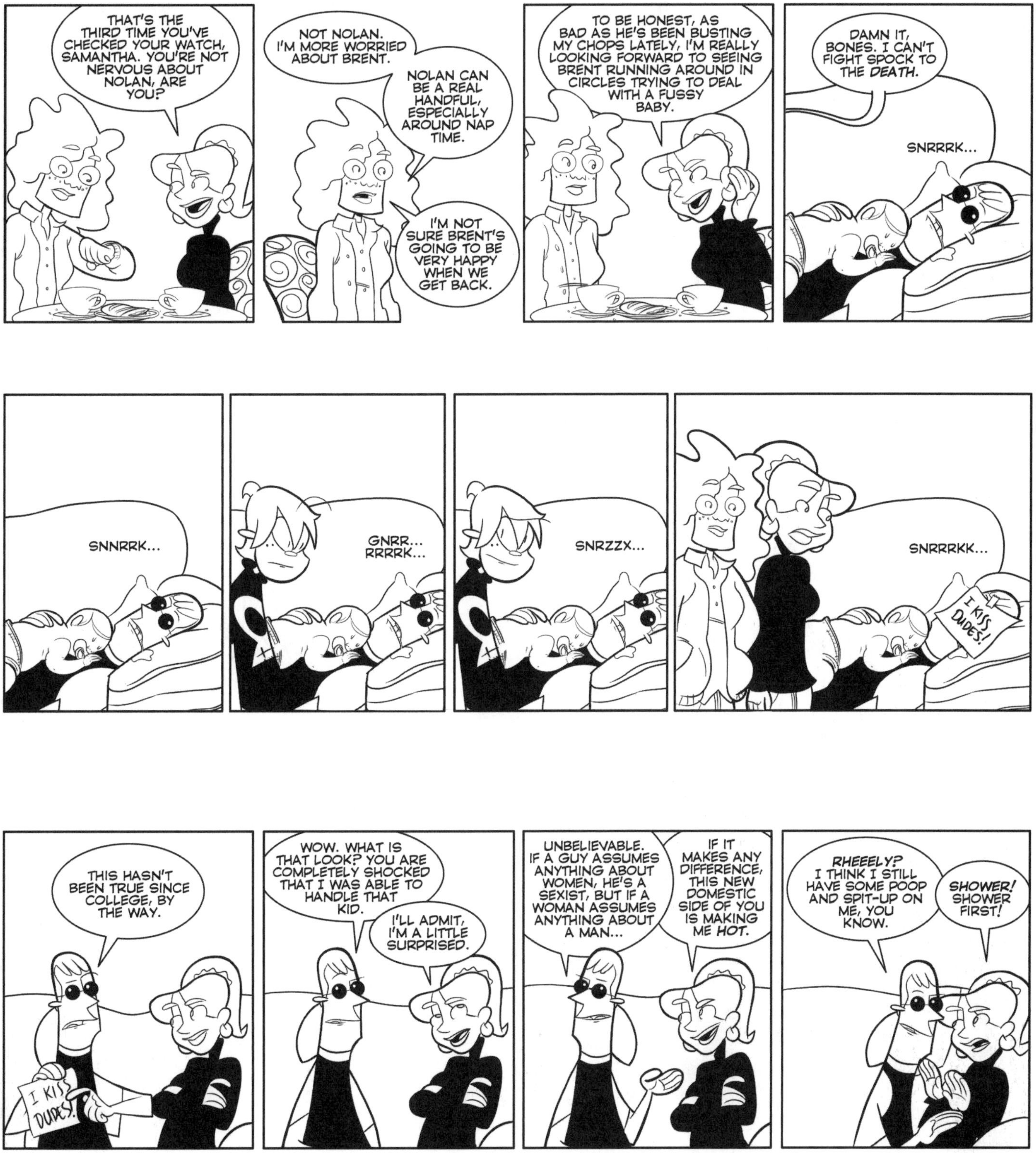
THAT'S THE THIRD TIME YOU'VE CHECKED YOUR WATCH, SAMANTHA. YOU'RE NOT NERVOUS ABOUT NOLAN, ARE YOU?
NOT NOLAN. I'M MORE WORRIED ABOUT BRENT.
NOLAN CAN BE A REAL HANDFUL, ESPECIALLY AROUND NAP TIME.
I'M NOT SURE BRENT'S GOING TO BE VERY HAPPY WHEN WE GET BACK.
TO BE HONEST, AS BAD AS HE'S BEEN BUSTING MY CHOPS LATELY, I'M REALLY LOOKING FORWARD TO SEEING BRENT RUNNING AROUND IN CIRCLES TRYING TO DEAL WITH A FUSSY BABY.
DAMN IT, BONES. I CAN'T FIGHT SPOCK TO THE *DEATH*.
SNRRRK...
SNNRRK...
GNRR... RRRRK...
SNRZZX...
SNRRRKK...
I KISS DUDES!
THIS HASN'T BEEN TRUE SINCE COLLEGE, BY THE WAY.
I KISS DUDES!
WOW. WHAT IS THAT LOOK? YOU ARE COMPLETELY SHOCKED THAT I WAS ABLE TO HANDLE THAT KID.
I'LL ADMIT, I'M A LITTLE SURPRISED.
UNBELIEVABLE. IF A GUY ASSUMES ANYTHING ABOUT WOMEN, HE'S A SEXIST, BUT IF A WOMAN ASSUMES ANYTHING ABOUT A MAN...
IF IT MAKES ANY DIFFERENCE, THIS NEW DOMESTIC SIDE OF YOU IS MAKING ME *HOT*.
RHEEELY? I THINK I STILL HAVE SOME POOP AND SPIT-UP ON ME, YOU KNOW.
SHOWER! SHOWER FIRST!

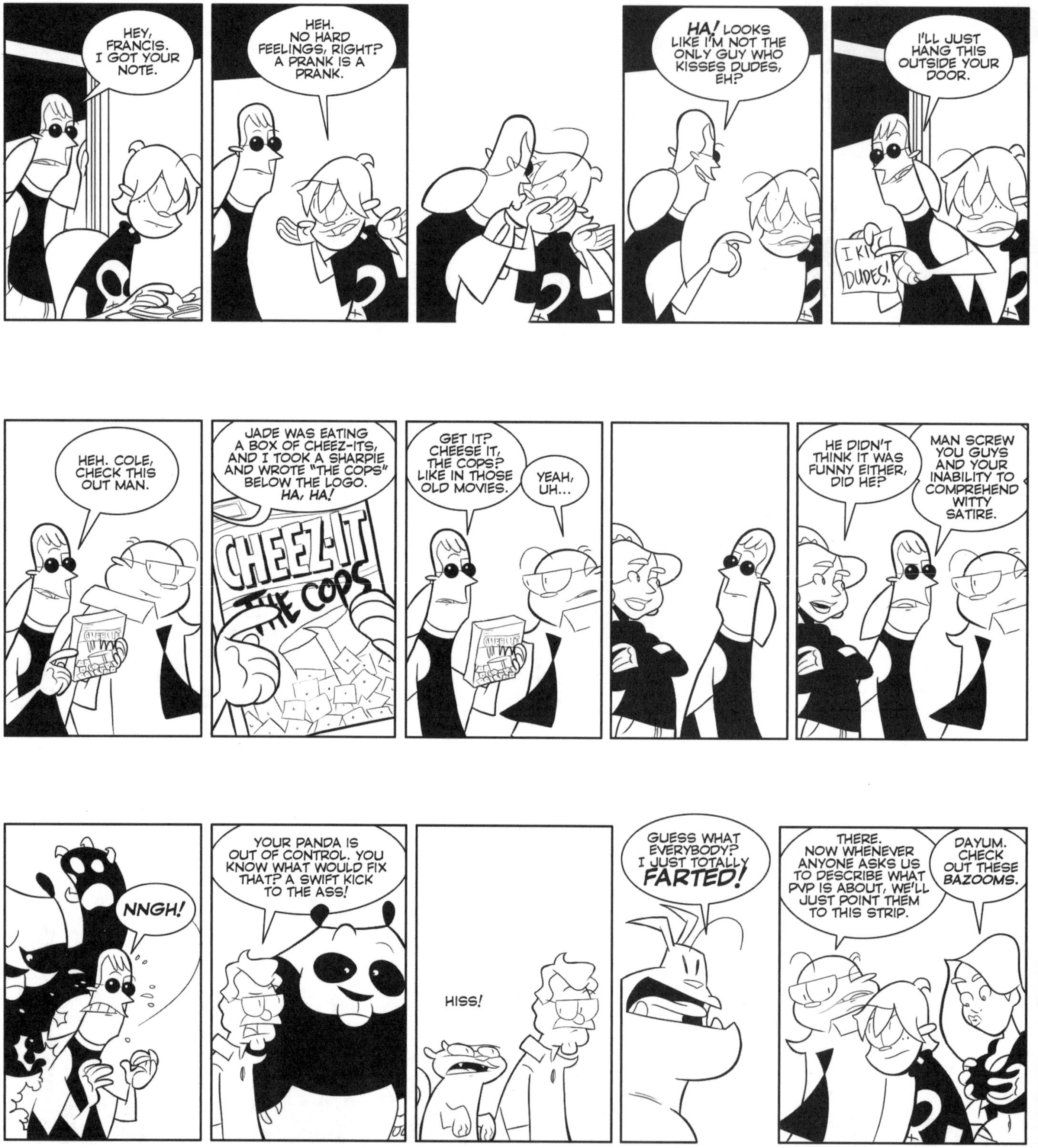
HEY, FRANCIS. I GOT YOUR NOTE.
HEH. NO HARD FEELINGS, RIGHT? A PRANK IS A PRANK.
HA! LOOKS LIKE I'M NOT THE ONLY GUY WHO KISSES DUDES, EH?
I'LL JUST HANG THIS OUTSIDE YOUR DOOR.
DUDES!
HEH. COLE, CHECK THIS OUT MAN.
JADE WAS EATING A BOX OF CHEEZ-ITS, AND I TOOK A SHARPIE AND WROTE "THE COPS" BELOW THE LOGO. HA, HA!
CHEEZ-IT
THE COPS
GET IT? CHEESE IT, THE COPS? LIKE IN THOSE OLD MOVIES.
YEAH, UH...
HE DIDN'T THINK IT WAS FUNNY EITHER, DID HE?
MAN SCREW YOU GUYS AND YOUR INABILITY TO COMPREHEND WITTY SATIRE.
NNGH!
YOUR PANDA IS OUT OF CONTROL. YOU KNOW WHAT WOULD FIX THAT? A SWIFT KICK TO THE ASS!
HISS!
GUESS WHAT EVERYBODY? I JUST TOTALLY FARTED!
THERE. NOW WHENEVER ANYONE ASKS US TO DESCRIBE WHAT PVP IS ABOUT, WE'LL JUST POINT THEM TO THIS STRIP.
DAYUM. CHECK OUT THESE BAZOOMS.

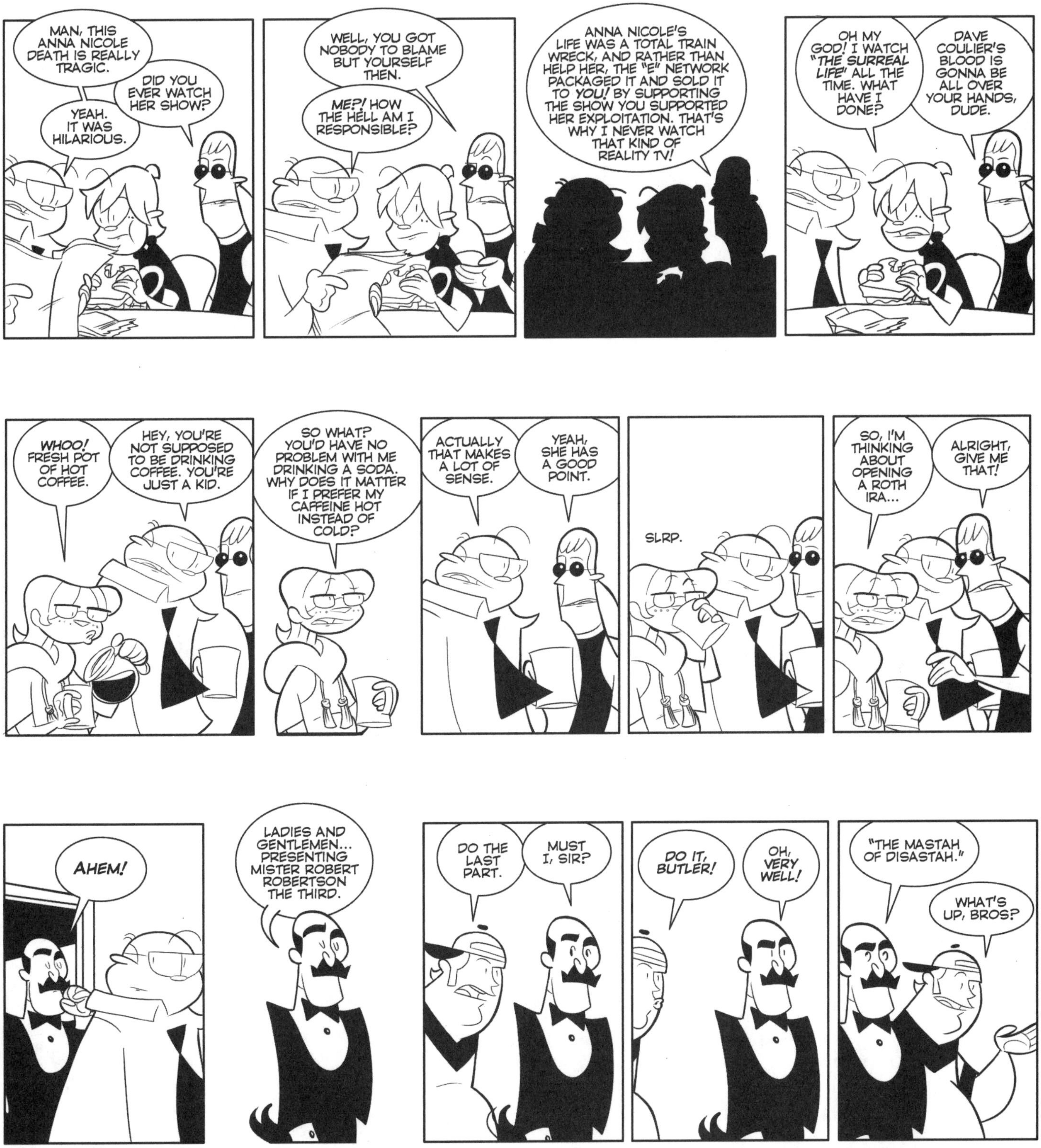
MAN, THIS ANNA NICOLE DEATH IS REALLY TRAGIC.
DID YOU EVER WATCH HER SHOW?
YEAH. IT WAS HILARIOUS.
WELL, YOU GOT NOBODY TO BLAME BUT YOURSELF THEN.
ME?! HOW THE HELL AM I RESPONSIBLE?
ANNA NICOLE'S LIFE WAS A TOTAL TRAIN WRECK, AND RATHER THAN HELP HER, THE "E" NETWORK PACKAGED IT AND SOLD IT TO YOU! BY SUPPORTING THE SHOW YOU SUPPORTED HER EXPLOITATION. THAT'S WHY I NEVER WATCH THAT KIND OF REALITY TV!
OH MY GOD! I WATCH "THE SURREAL LIFE" ALL THE TIME. WHAT HAVE I DONE?
DAVE COULIER'S BLOOD IS GONNA BE ALL OVER YOUR HANDS, DUDE.
WHOO! FRESH POT OF HOT COFFEE.
HEY, YOU'RE NOT SUPPOSED TO BE DRINKING COFFEE. YOU'RE JUST A KID.
SO WHAT? YOU'D HAVE NO PROBLEM WITH ME DRINKING A SODA. WHY DOES IT MATTER IF I PREFER MY CAFFEINE HOT INSTEAD OF COLD?
ACTUALLY THAT MAKES A LOT OF SENSE.
YEAH, SHE HAS A GOOD POINT.
SLRP.
SO, I'M THINKING ABOUT OPENING A ROTH IRA...
ALRIGHT, GIVE ME THAT!
AHEM!
LADIES AND GENTLEMEN... PRESENTING MISTER ROBERT ROBERTSON THE THIRD.
DO THE LAST PART.
MUST I, SIR?
DO IT, BUTLER!
OH, VERY WELL!
"THE MASTAH OF DISASTAH."
WHAT'S UP, BROS?

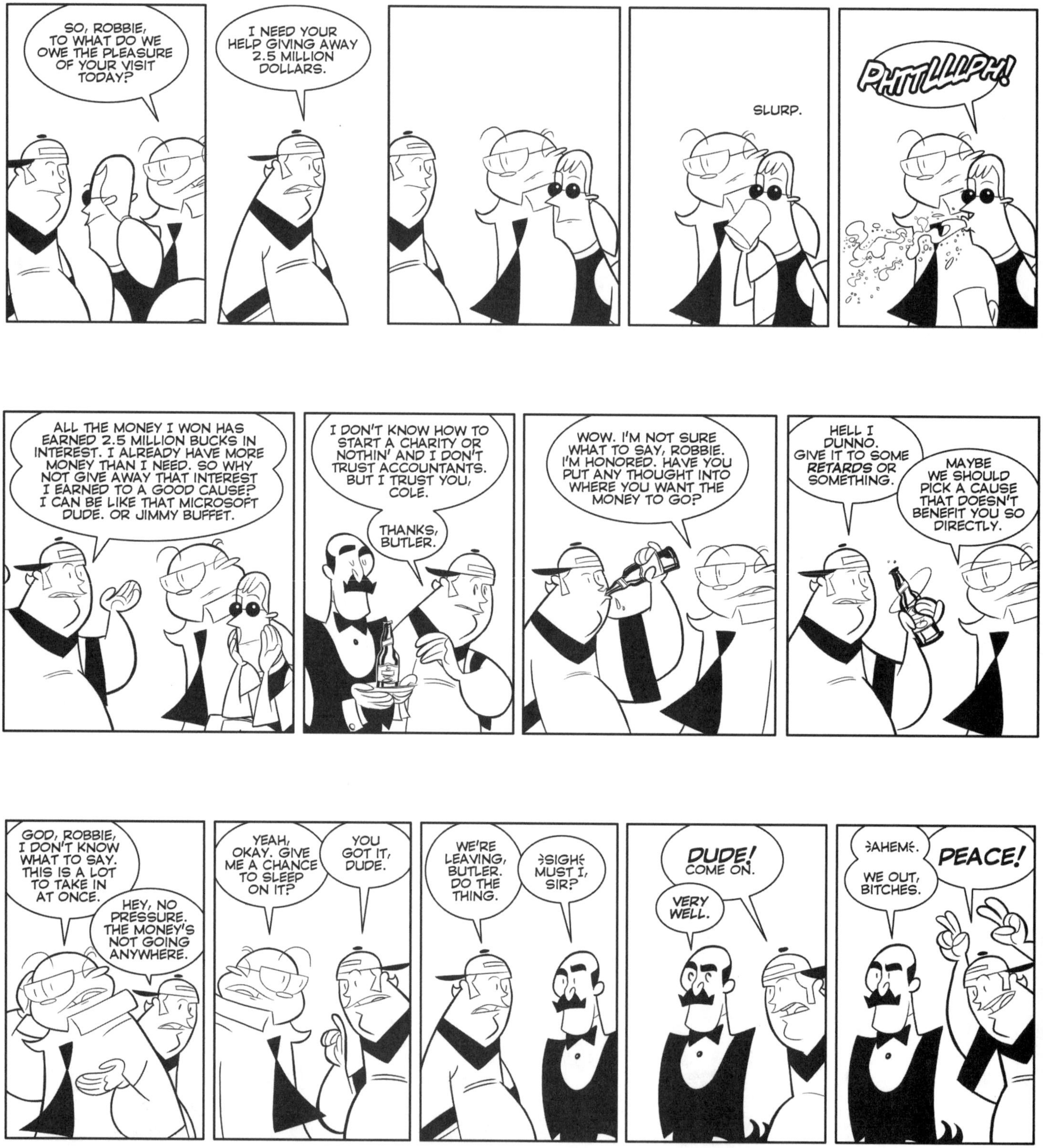
SO, ROBBIE, TO WHAT DO WE OWE THE PLEASURE OF YOUR VISIT TODAY?
I NEED YOUR HELP GIVING AWAY 2.5 MILLION DOLLARS.
SLURP.
PHTTLLLPH!
ALL THE MONEY I WON HAS EARNED 2.5 MILLION BUCKS IN INTEREST. I ALREADY HAVE MORE MONEY THAN I NEED. SO WHY NOT GIVE AWAY THAT INTEREST I EARNED TO A GOOD CAUSE? I CAN BE LIKE THAT MICROSOFT DUDE. OR JIMMY BUFFET.
I DON'T KNOW HOW TO START A CHARITY OR NOTHIN' AND I DON'T TRUST ACCOUNTANTS. BUT I TRUST YOU, COLE.
THANKS, BUTLER.
WOW. I'M NOT SURE WHAT TO SAY, ROBBIE. I'M HONORED. HAVE YOU PUT ANY THOUGHT INTO WHERE YOU WANT THE MONEY TO GO?
HELL I DUNNO. GIVE IT TO SOME *RETARDS* OR SOMETHING.
MAYBE WE SHOULD PICK A CAUSE THAT DOESN'T BENEFIT YOU SO DIRECTLY.
GOD, ROBBIE, I DON'T KNOW WHAT TO SAY. THIS IS A LOT TO TAKE IN AT ONCE.
HEY, NO PRESSURE. THE MONEY'S NOT GOING ANYWHERE.
YEAH, OKAY. GIVE ME A CHANCE TO SLEEP ON IT?
YOU GOT IT, DUDE.
WE'RE LEAVING, BUTLER. DO THE THING.
SIGH MUST I, SIR?
DUDE! COME ON.
VERY WELL.
AHEM.
WE OUT, BITCHES.
PEACE!

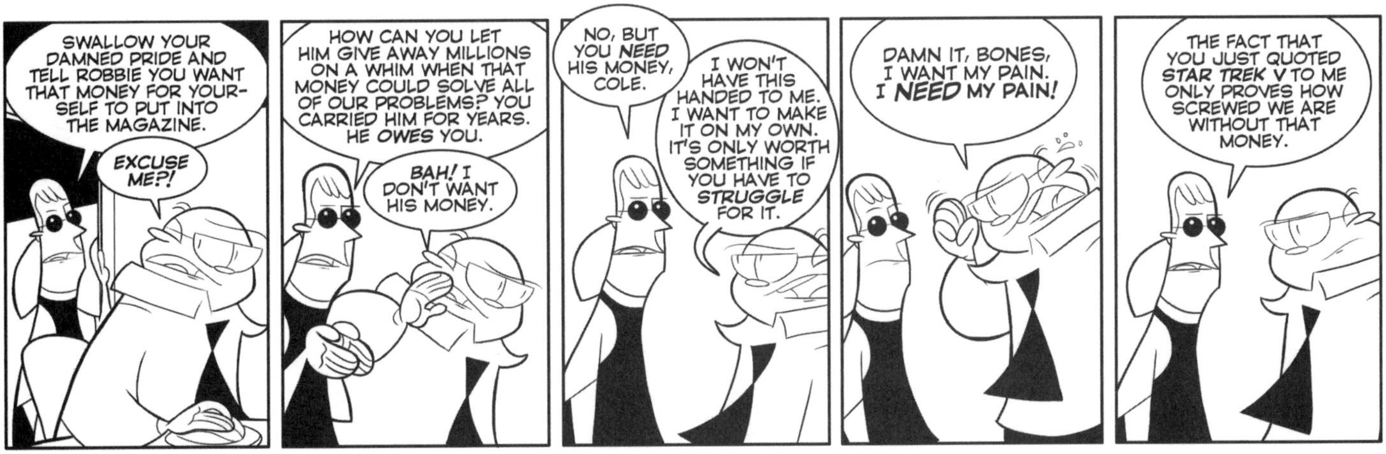
SWALLOW YOUR DAMNED PRIDE AND TELL ROBBIE YOU WANT THAT MONEY FOR YOURSELF TO PUT INTO THE MAGAZINE.
EXCUSE ME?!
HOW CAN YOU LET HIM GIVE AWAY MILLIONS ON A WHIM WHEN THAT MONEY COULD SOLVE ALL OF OUR PROBLEMS? YOU CARRIED HIM FOR YEARS. HE OWES YOU.
BAH! I DON'T WANT HIS MONEY.
NO, BUT YOU NEED HIS MONEY, COLE.
I WON'T HAVE THIS HANDED TO ME. I WANT TO MAKE IT ON MY OWN. IT'S ONLY WORTH SOMETHING IF YOU HAVE TO STRUGGLE FOR IT.
DAMN IT, BONES, I WANT MY PAIN. I NEED MY PAIN!
THE FACT THAT YOU JUST QUOTED STAR TREK V TO ME ONLY PROVES HOW SCREWED WE ARE WITHOUT THAT MONEY.

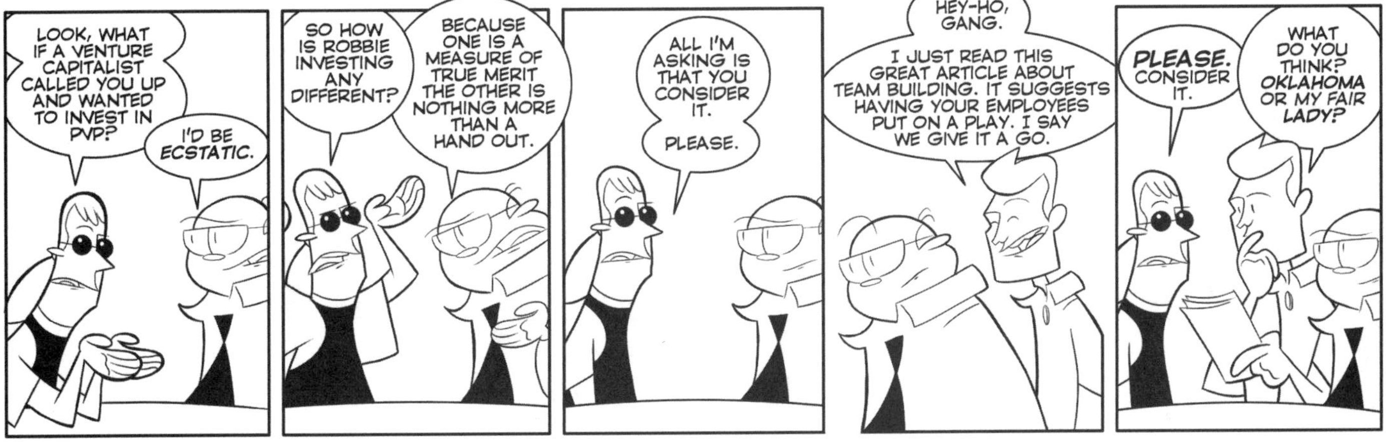
LOOK, WHAT IF A VENTURE CAPITALIST CALLED YOU UP AND WANTED TO INVEST IN PVP?
I'D BE ECSTATIC.
SO HOW IS ROBBIE INVESTING ANY DIFFERENT?
BECAUSE ONE IS A MEASURE OF TRUE MERIT THE OTHER IS NOTHING MORE THAN A HAND OUT.
ALL I'M ASKING IS THAT YOU CONSIDER IT.
PLEASE.
HEY-HO, GANG.
I JUST READ THIS GREAT ARTICLE ABOUT TEAM BUILDING. IT SUGGESTS HAVING YOUR EMPLOYEES PUT ON A PLAY. I SAY WE GIVE IT A GO.
PLEASE. CONSIDER IT.
WHAT DO YOU THINK? OKLAHOMA OR MY FAIR LADY?

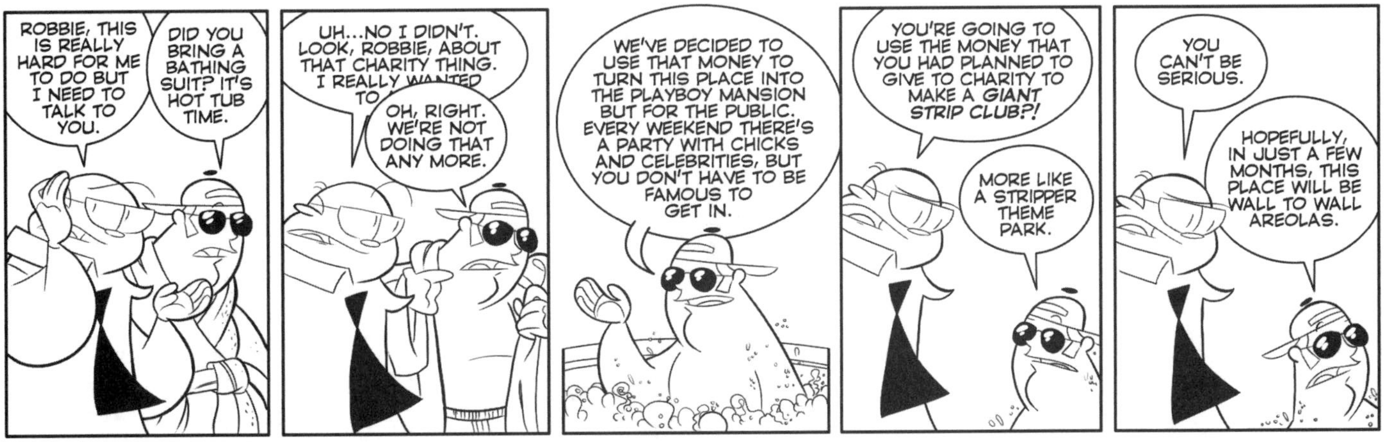
ROBBIE, THIS IS REALLY HARD FOR ME TO DO BUT I NEED TO TALK TO YOU.
DID YOU BRING A BATHING SUIT? IT'S HOT TUB TIME.
UH...NO I DIDN'T. LOOK, ROBBIE, ABOUT THAT CHARITY THING. I REALLY WANTED TO
OH, RIGHT. WE'RE NOT DOING THAT ANY MORE.
WE'VE DECIDED TO USE THAT MONEY TO TURN THIS PLACE INTO THE PLAYBOY MANSION BUT FOR THE PUBLIC. EVERY WEEKEND THERE'S A PARTY WITH CHICKS AND CELEBRITIES, BUT YOU DON'T HAVE TO BE FAMOUS TO GET IN.
YOU'RE GOING TO USE THE MONEY THAT YOU HAD PLANNED TO GIVE TO CHARITY TO MAKE A GIANT STRIP CLUB?!
MORE LIKE A STRIPPER THEME PARK.
YOU CAN'T BE SERIOUS.
HOPEFULLY, IN JUST A FEW MONTHS, THIS PLACE WILL BE WALL TO WALL AREOLAS.

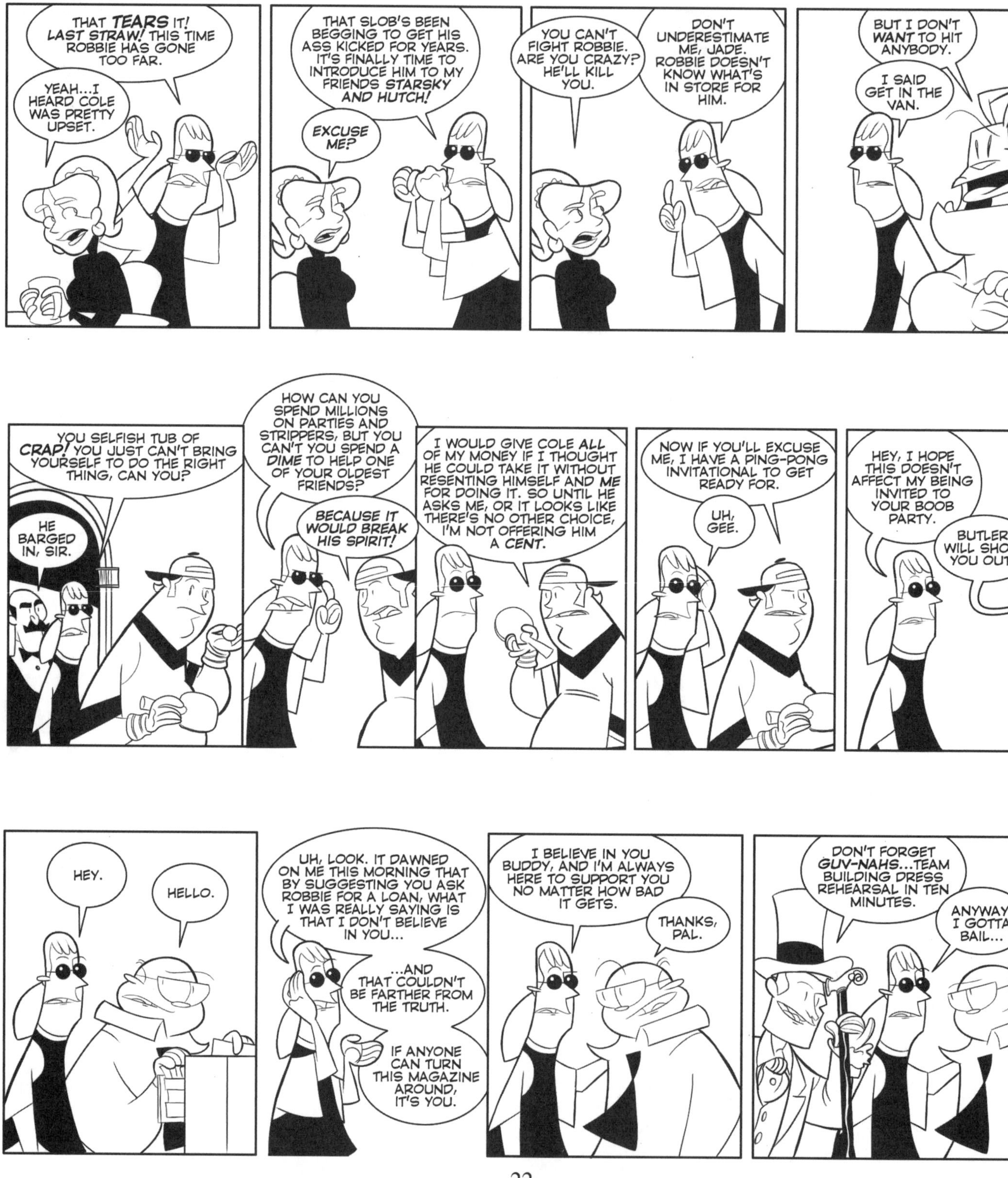
THAT TEARS IT! LAST STRAW! THIS TIME ROBBIE HAS GONE TOO FAR.
YEAH...I HEARD COLE WAS PRETTY UPSET.
THAT SLOB'S BEEN BEGGING TO GET HIS ASS KICKED FOR YEARS. IT'S FINALLY TIME TO INTRODUCE HIM TO MY FRIENDS STARSKY AND HUTCH!
EXCUSE ME?
YOU CAN'T FIGHT ROBBIE. ARE YOU CRAZY? HE'LL KILL YOU.
DON'T UNDERESTIMATE ME, JADE. ROBBIE DOESN'T KNOW WHAT'S IN STORE FOR HIM.
BUT I DON'T WANT TO HIT ANYBODY.
I SAID GET IN THE VAN.
YOU SELFISH TUB OF CRAP! YOU JUST CAN'T BRING YOURSELF TO DO THE RIGHT THING, CAN YOU?
HE BARGED IN, SIR.
HOW CAN YOU SPEND MILLIONS ON PARTIES AND STRIPPERS, BUT YOU CAN'T YOU SPEND A DIME TO HELP ONE OF YOUR OLDEST FRIENDS?
BECAUSE IT WOULD BREAK HIS SPIRIT!
I WOULD GIVE COLE ALL OF MY MONEY IF I THOUGHT HE COULD TAKE IT WITHOUT RESENTING HIMSELF AND ME FOR DOING IT. SO UNTIL HE ASKS ME, OR IT LOOKS LIKE THERE'S NO OTHER CHOICE, I'M NOT OFFERING HIM A CENT.
NOW IF YOU'LL EXCUSE ME, I HAVE A PING-PONG INVITATIONAL TO GET READY FOR.
UH, GEE.
HEY, I HOPE THIS DOESN'T AFFECT MY BEING INVITED TO YOUR BOOB PARTY.
BUTLER WILL SHOW YOU OUT.
HEY.
HELLO.
UH, LOOK. IT DAWNED ON ME THIS MORNING THAT BY SUGGESTING YOU ASK ROBBIE FOR A LOAN, WHAT I WAS REALLY SAYING IS THAT I DON'T BELIEVE IN YOU...
...AND THAT COULDN'T BE FARTHER FROM THE TRUTH.
IF ANYONE CAN TURN THIS MAGAZINE AROUND, IT'S YOU.
I BELIEVE IN YOU BUDDY, AND I'M ALWAYS HERE TO SUPPORT YOU NO MATTER HOW BAD IT GETS.
THANKS, PAL.
DON'T FORGET GUV-NAHS...TEAM BUILDING DRESS REHEARSAL IN TEN MINUTES.
ANYWAY, I GOTTA BAIL...

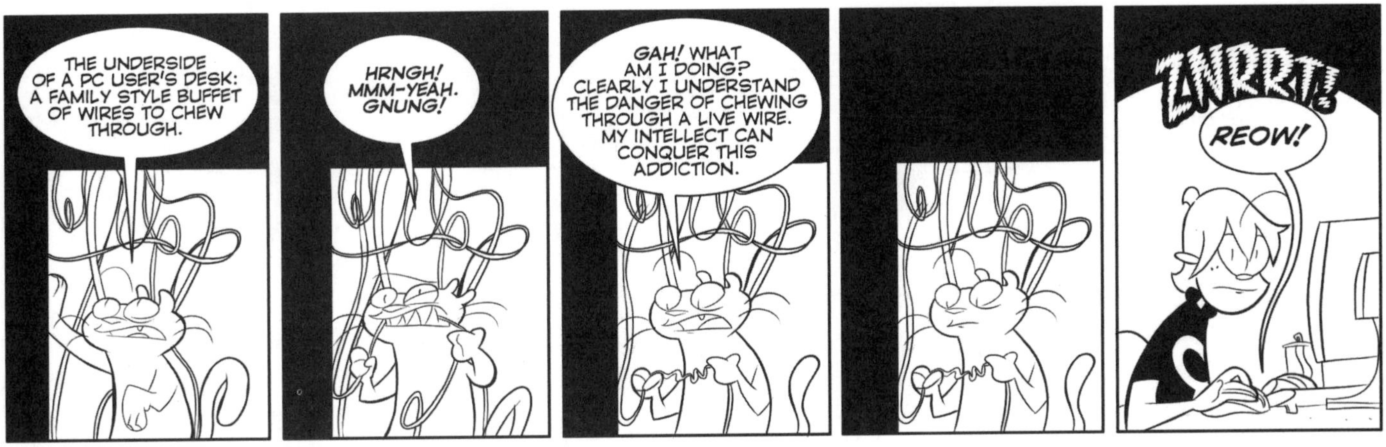
THE UNDERSIDE OF A PC USER'S DESK: A FAMILY STYLE BUFFET OF WIRES TO CHEW THROUGH.
HRNGH! MMM-YEAH. GNUNG!
GAH! WHAT AM I DOING? CLEARLY I UNDERSTAND THE DANGER OF CHEWING THROUGH A LIVE WIRE. MY INTELLECT CAN CONQUER THIS ADDICTION.
ZNRRT!
REOW!

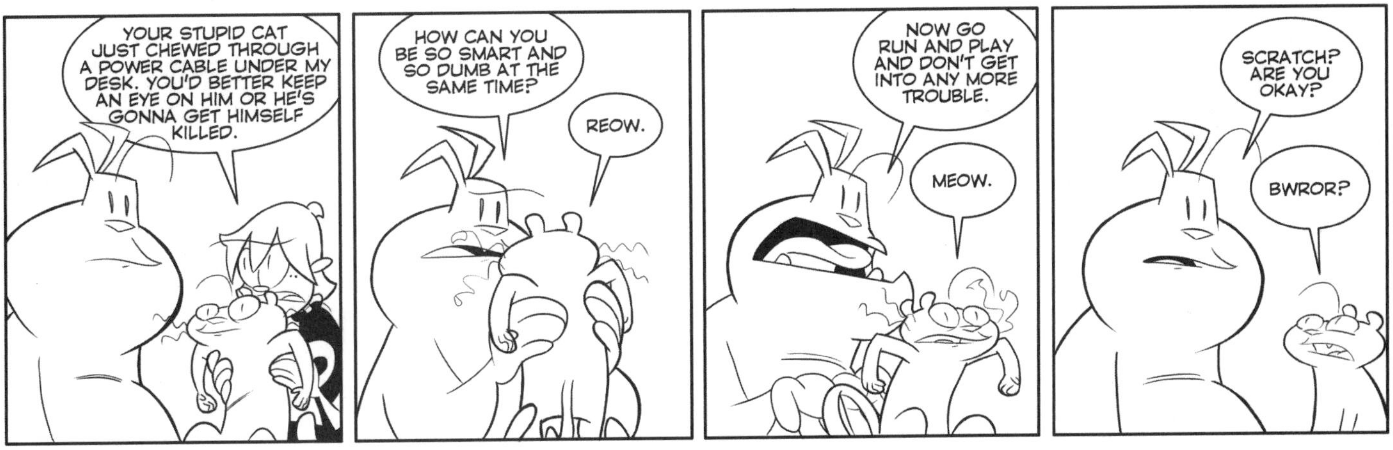
YOUR STUPID CAT JUST CHEWED THROUGH A POWER CABLE UNDER MY DESK. YOU'D BETTER KEEP AN EYE ON HIM OR HE'S GONNA GET HIMSELF KILLED.
HOW CAN YOU BE SO SMART AND SO DUMB AT THE SAME TIME?
REOW.
NOW GO RUN AND PLAY AND DON'T GET INTO ANY MORE TROUBLE.
MEOW.
SCRATCH? ARE YOU OKAY?
BWROR?

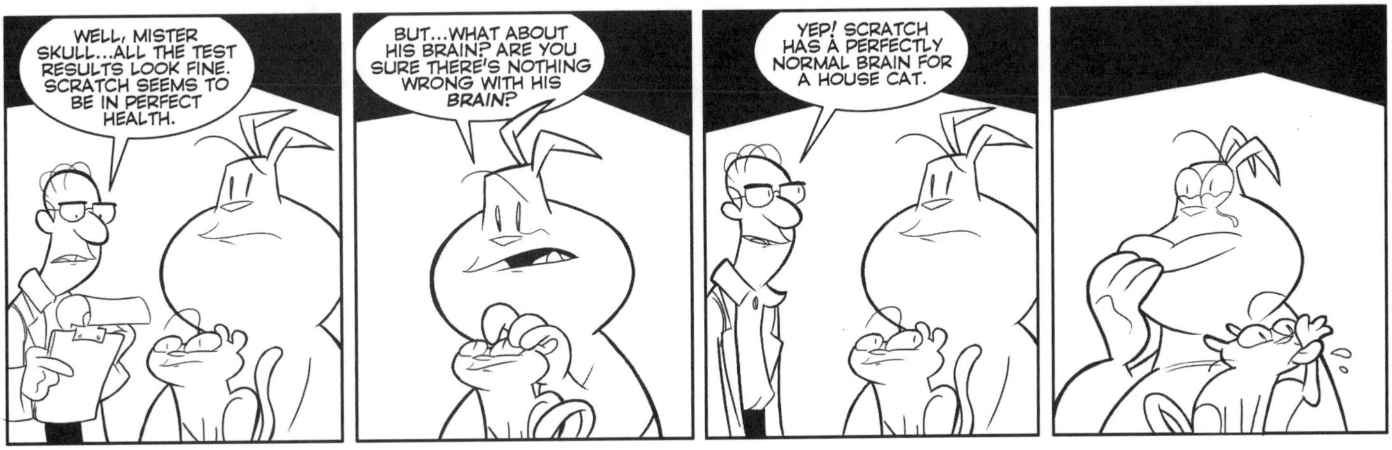
WELL, MISTER SKULL...ALL THE TEST RESULTS LOOK FINE. SCRATCH SEEMS TO BE IN PERFECT HEALTH.
BUT...WHAT ABOUT HIS BRAIN? ARE YOU SURE THERE'S NOTHING WRONG WITH HIS BRAIN?
YEP! SCRATCH HAS A PERFECTLY NORMAL BRAIN FOR A HOUSE CAT.

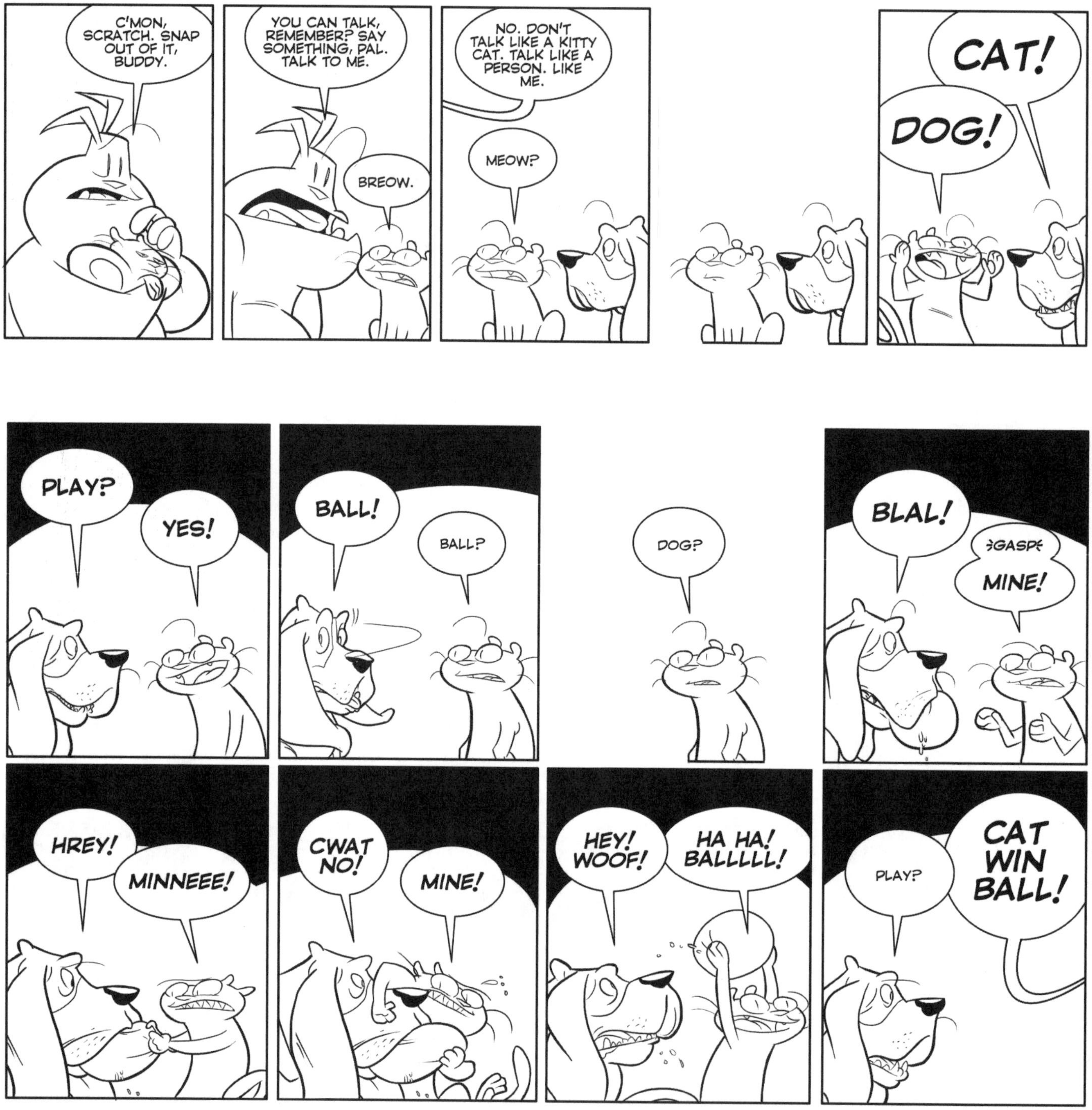
C'MON, SCRATCH. SNAP OUT OF IT, BUDDY.
YOU CAN TALK, REMEMBER? SAY SOMETHING, PAL. TALK TO ME.
BREOW.
NO. DON'T TALK LIKE A KITTY CAT. TALK LIKE A PERSON. LIKE ME.
MEOW?
CAT!
DOG!
PLAY?
YES!
BALL!
BALL?
DOG?
BLAL!
GASP
MINE!
HREY!
MINNEEE!
CWAT NO!
MINE!
HEY! WOOF!
HA HA! BALLLLL!
PLAY?
CAT WIN BALL!

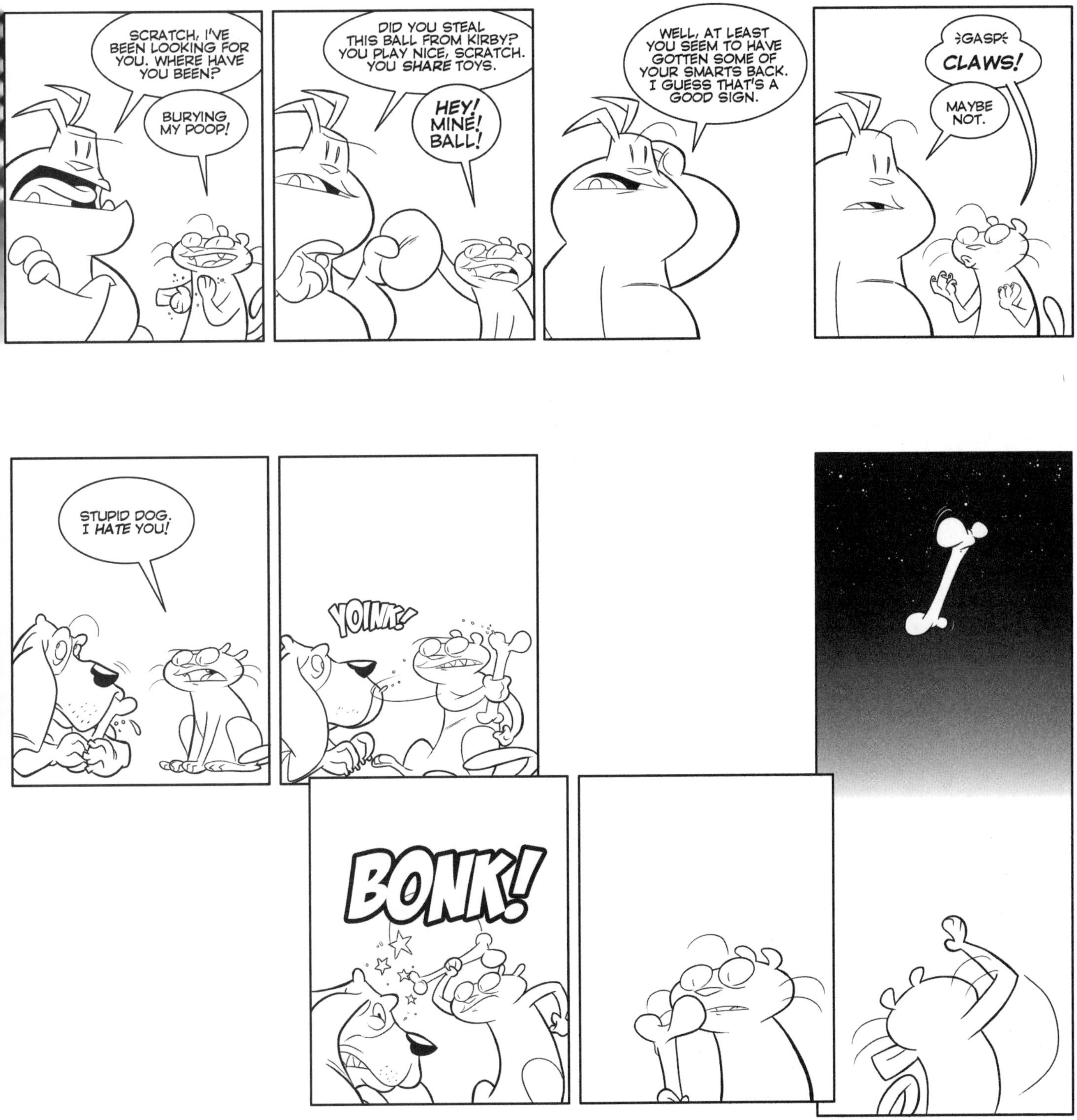
SCRATCH, I'VE BEEN LOOKING FOR YOU. WHERE HAVE YOU BEEN?
BURYING MY POOP!
DID YOU STEAL THIS BALL FROM KIRBY? YOU PLAY NICE, SCRATCH. YOU SHARE TOYS.
HEY! MINE! BALL!
WELL, AT LEAST YOU SEEM TO HAVE GOTTEN SOME OF YOUR SMARTS BACK. I GUESS THAT'S A GOOD SIGN.
GASP
CLAWS!
MAYBE NOT.
STUPID DOG. I HATE YOU!
YOINK!
BONK!

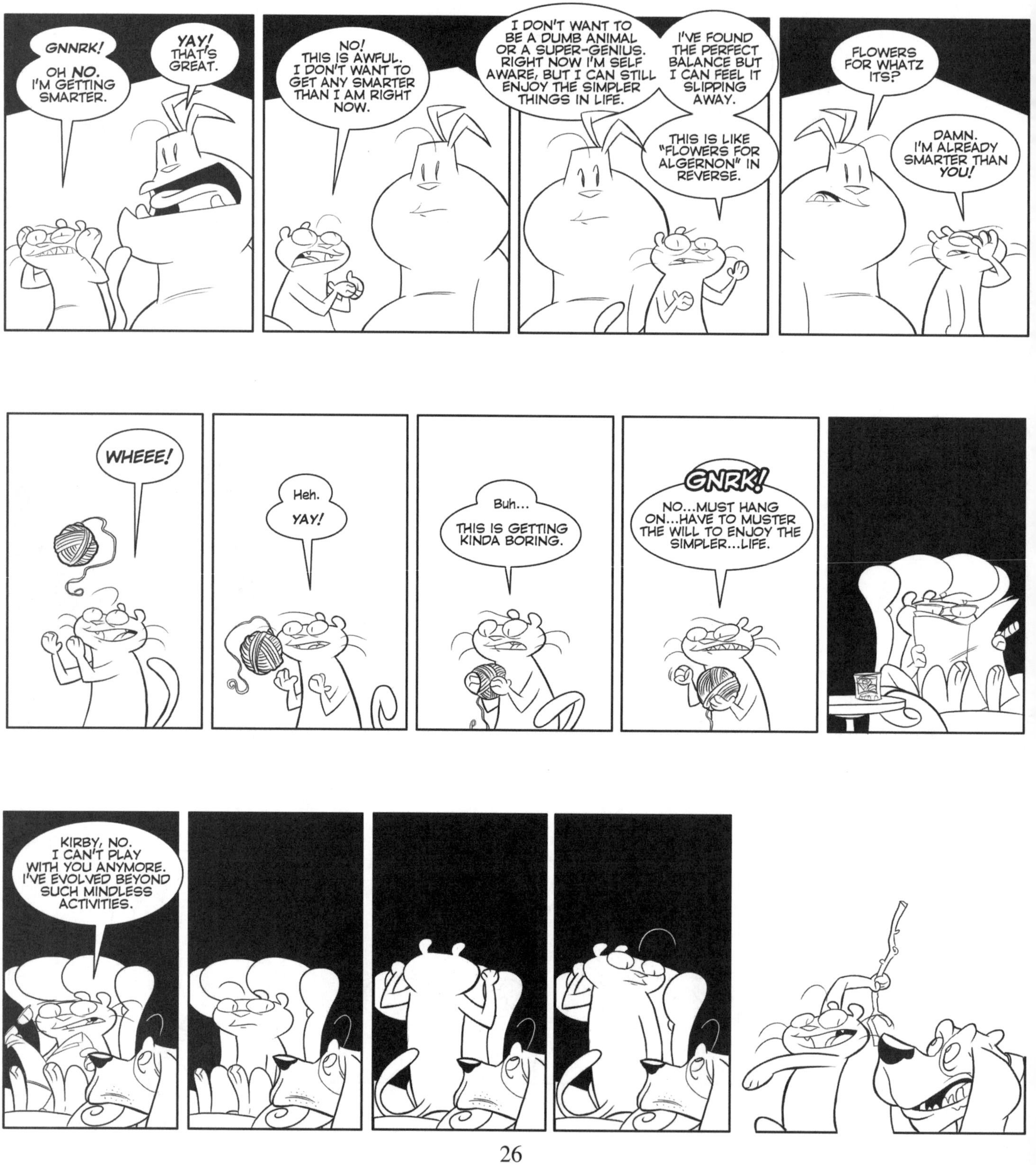
GNNRK!
OH NO. I'M GETTING SMARTER.
YAY! THAT'S GREAT.
NO! THIS IS AWFUL. I DON'T WANT TO GET ANY SMARTER THAN I AM RIGHT NOW.
I DON'T WANT TO BE A DUMB ANIMAL OR A SUPER-GENIUS. RIGHT NOW I'M SELF AWARE, BUT I CAN STILL ENJOY THE SIMPLER THINGS IN LIFE.
I'VE FOUND THE PERFECT BALANCE BUT I CAN FEEL IT SLIPPING AWAY.
THIS IS LIKE "FLOWERS FOR ALGERNON" IN REVERSE.
FLOWERS FOR WHATZ ITS?
DAMN. I'M ALREADY SMARTER THAN YOU!
WHEEE!
Heh.
YAY!
Buh...
THIS IS GETTING KINDA BORING.
GNRK!
NO...MUST HANG ON...HAVE TO MUSTER THE WILL TO ENJOY THE SIMPLER...LIFE.
KIRBY, NO. I CAN'T PLAY WITH YOU ANYMORE. I'VE EVOLVED BEYOND SUCH MINDLESS ACTIVITIES.

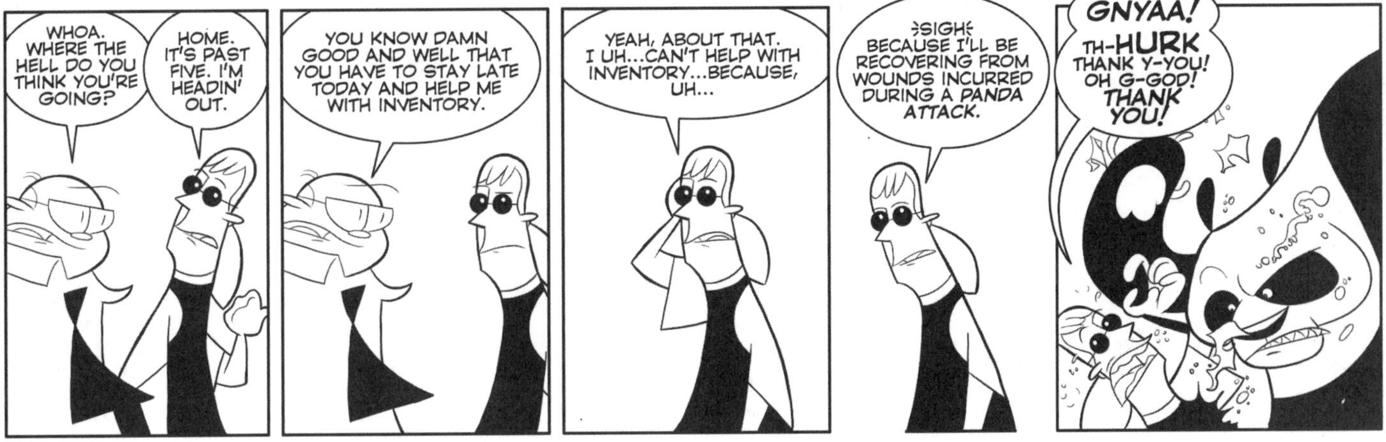
WHOA. WHERE THE HELL DO YOU THINK YOU'RE GOING?
HOME. IT'S PAST FIVE. I'M HEADIN' OUT.
YOU KNOW DAMN GOOD AND WELL THAT YOU HAVE TO STAY LATE TODAY AND HELP ME WITH INVENTORY.
YEAH, ABOUT THAT. I UH...CAN'T HELP WITH INVENTORY...BECAUSE, UH...
SIGH
BECAUSE I'LL BE RECOVERING FROM WOUNDS INCURRED DURING A PANDA ATTACK.
GNYAA!
TH-HURK
THANK Y-YOU! OH G-GOD! THANK YOU!

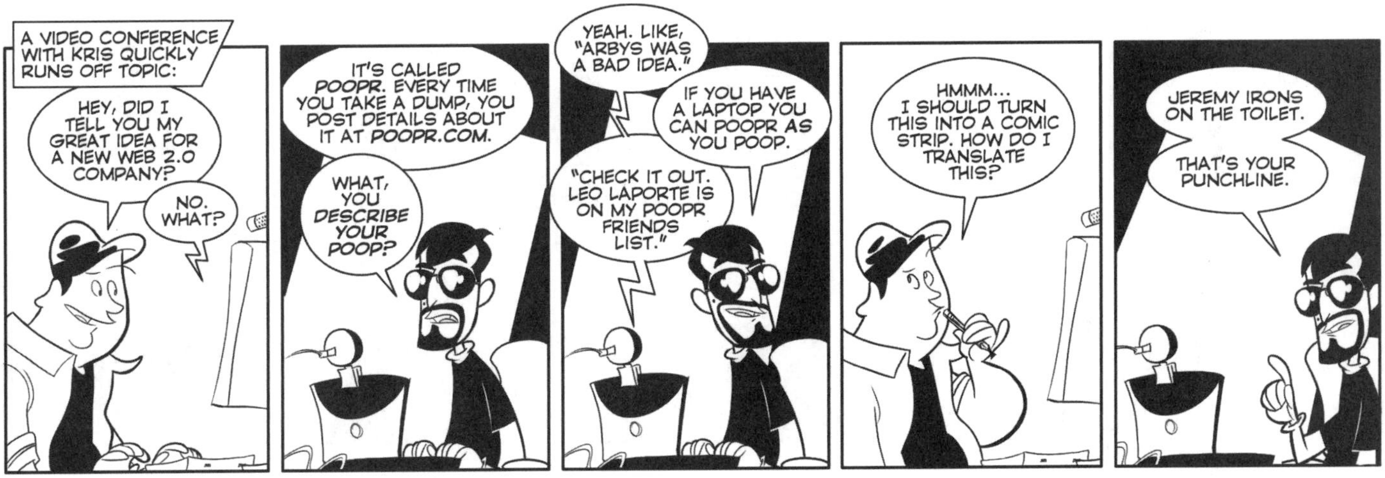
A VIDEO CONFERENCE WITH KRIS QUICKLY RUNS OFF TOPIC:
HEY, DID I TELL YOU MY GREAT IDEA FOR A NEW WEB 2.0 COMPANY?
NO. WHAT?
IT'S CALLED POOPR. EVERY TIME YOU TAKE A DUMP, YOU POST DETAILS ABOUT IT AT POOPR.COM.
WHAT, YOU DESCRIBE YOUR POOP?
YEAH. LIKE, "ARBYS WAS A BAD IDEA."
IF YOU HAVE A LAPTOP YOU CAN POOPR AS YOU POOP.
"CHECK IT OUT. LEO LAPORTE IS ON MY POOPR FRIENDS LIST."
HMMM... I SHOULD TURN THIS INTO A COMIC STRIP. HOW DO I TRANSLATE THIS?
JEREMY IRONS ON THE TOILET.
THAT'S YOUR PUNCHLINE.

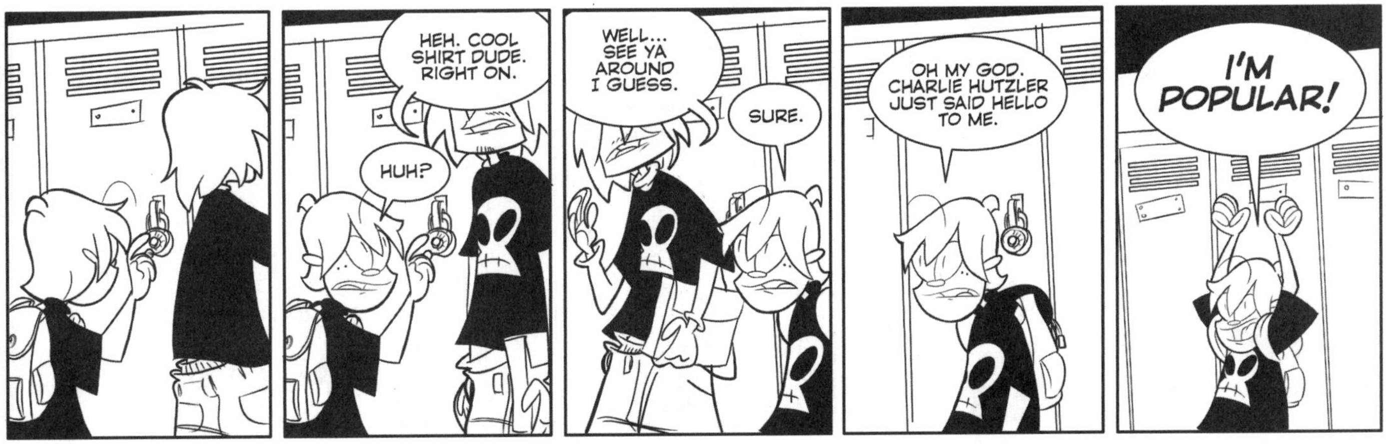
HEH. COOL SHIRT DUDE. RIGHT ON.
HUH?
WELL... SEE YA AROUND I GUESS.
SURE.
OH MY GOD. CHARLIE HUTZLER JUST SAID HELLO TO ME.
I'M POPULAR!

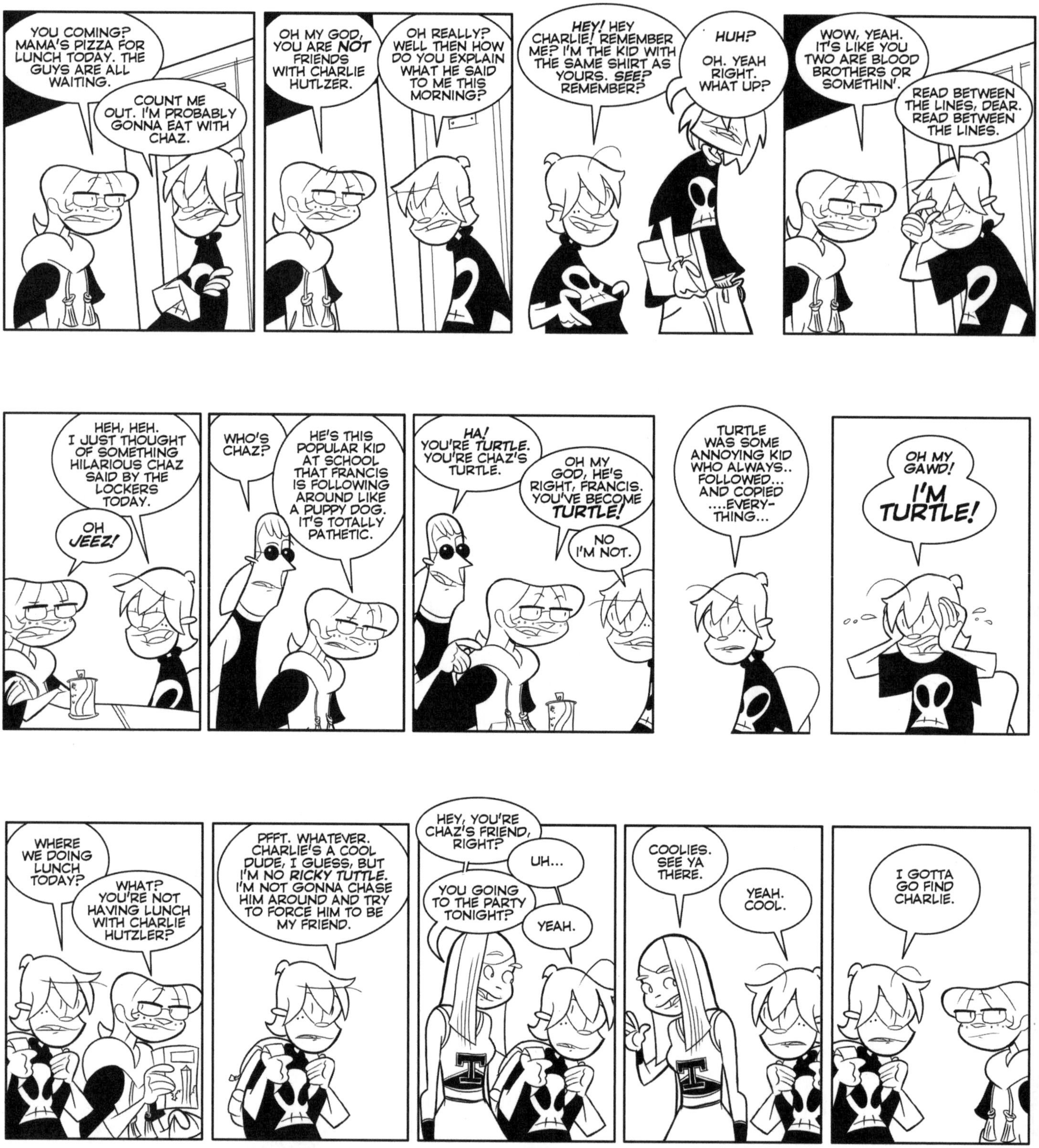

YOU COMING? MAMA'S PIZZA FOR LUNCH TODAY. THE GUYS ARE ALL WAITING.
COUNT ME OUT. I'M PROBABLY GONNA EAT WITH CHAZ.
OH MY GOD, YOU ARE NOT FRIENDS WITH CHARLIE HUTLZER.
OH REALLY? WELL THEN HOW DO YOU EXPLAIN WHAT HE SAID TO ME THIS MORNING?
HEY! HEY CHARLIE! REMEMBER ME? I'M THE KID WITH THE SAME SHIRT AS YOURS. SEE? REMEMBER?
HUH?
OH. YEAH RIGHT. WHAT UP?
WOW, YEAH. IT'S LIKE YOU TWO ARE BLOOD BROTHERS OR SOMETHIN'.
READ BETWEEN THE LINES, DEAR. READ BETWEEN THE LINES.
HEH, HEH. I JUST THOUGHT OF SOMETHING HILARIOUS CHAZ SAID BY THE LOCKERS TODAY.
OH JEEZ!
WHO'S CHAZ?
HE'S THIS POPULAR KID AT SCHOOL THAT FRANCIS IS FOLLOWING AROUND LIKE A PUPPY DOG. IT'S TOTALLY PATHETIC.
HA! YOU'RE TURTLE. YOU'RE CHAZ'S TURTLE.
OH MY GOD, HE'S RIGHT, FRANCIS. YOU'VE BECOME TURTLE!
NO I'M NOT.
TURTLE WAS SOME ANNOYING KID WHO ALWAYS.. FOLLOWED... AND COPIED ....EVERY-THING...
OH MY GAWD! I'M TURTLE!
WHERE WE DOING LUNCH TODAY?
WHAT? YOU'RE NOT HAVING LUNCH WITH CHARLIE HUTZLER?
PFFT. WHATEVER. CHARLIE'S A COOL DUDE, I GUESS, BUT I'M NO RICKY TUTTLE. I'M NOT GONNA CHASE HIM AROUND AND TRY TO FORCE HIM TO BE MY FRIEND.
HEY, YOU'RE CHAZ'S FRIEND, RIGHT?
UH...
YOU GOING TO THE PARTY TONIGHT?
YEAH.
COOLIES. SEE YA THERE.
YEAH. COOL.
I GOTTA GO FIND CHARLIE.

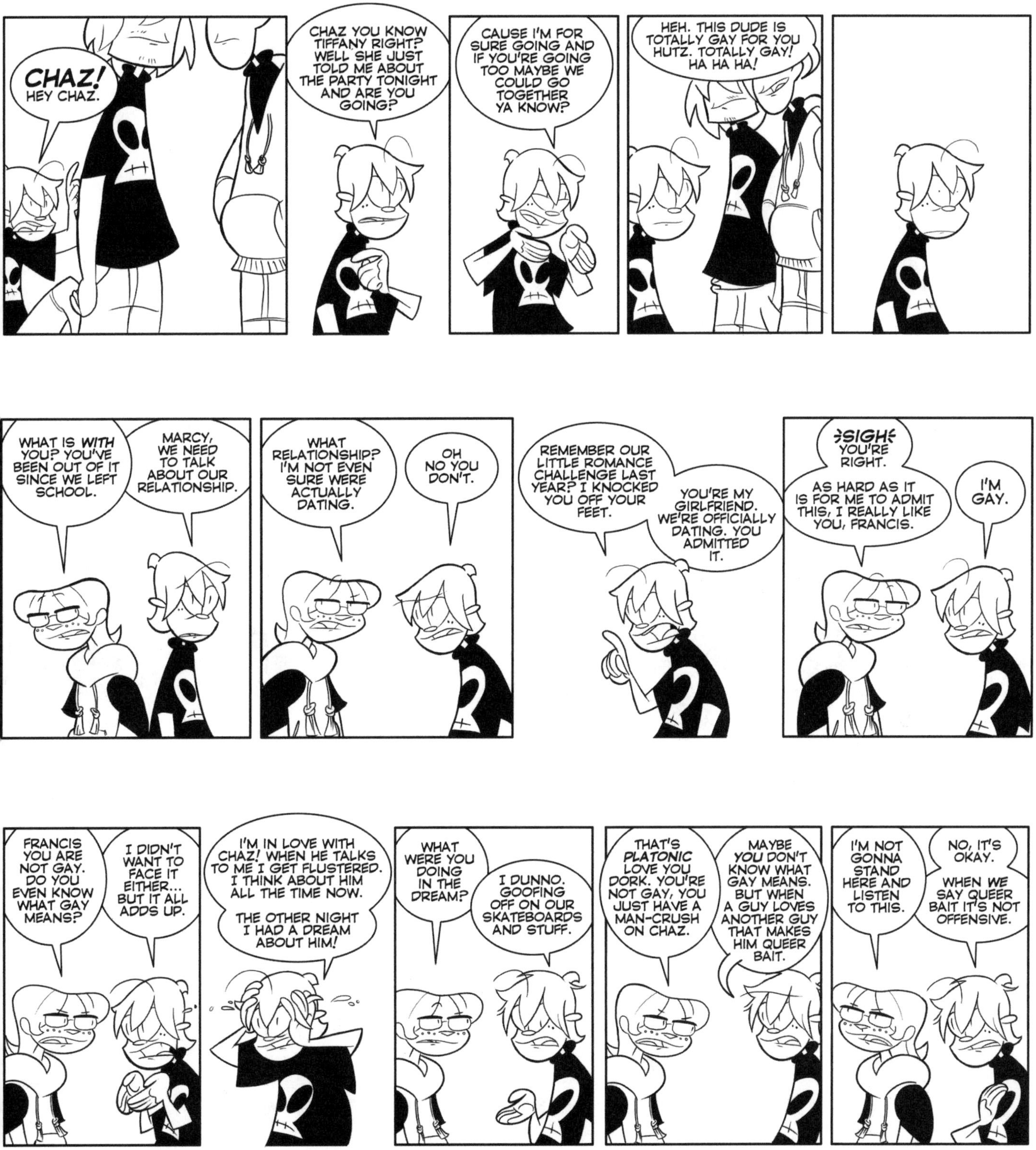
CHAZ! HEY CHAZ.
CHAZ YOU KNOW TIFFANY RIGHT? WELL SHE JUST TOLD ME ABOUT THE PARTY TONIGHT AND ARE YOU GOING?
CAUSE I'M FOR SURE GOING AND IF YOU'RE GOING TOO MAYBE WE COULD GO TOGETHER YA KNOW?
HEH. THIS DUDE IS TOTALLY GAY FOR YOU HUTZ. TOTALLY GAY! HA HA HA!
WHAT IS WITH YOU? YOU'VE BEEN OUT OF IT SINCE WE LEFT SCHOOL.
MARCY, WE NEED TO TALK ABOUT OUR RELATIONSHIP.
WHAT RELATIONSHIP? I'M NOT EVEN SURE WERE ACTUALLY DATING.
OH NO YOU DON'T.
REMEMBER OUR LITTLE ROMANCE CHALLENGE LAST YEAR? I KNOCKED YOU OFF YOUR FEET.
YOU'RE MY GIRLFRIEND. WE'RE OFFICIALLY DATING. YOU ADMITTED IT.
SIGH YOU'RE RIGHT.
AS HARD AS IT IS FOR ME TO ADMIT THIS, I REALLY LIKE YOU, FRANCIS.
I'M GAY.
FRANCIS YOU ARE NOT GAY. DO YOU EVEN KNOW WHAT GAY MEANS?
I DIDN'T WANT TO FACE IT EITHER... BUT IT ALL ADDS UP.
I'M IN LOVE WITH CHAZ! WHEN HE TALKS TO ME I GET FLUSTERED. I THINK ABOUT HIM ALL THE TIME NOW.
THE OTHER NIGHT I HAD A DREAM ABOUT HIM!
WHAT WERE YOU DOING IN THE DREAM?
I DUNNO. GOOFING OFF ON OUR SKATEBOARDS AND STUFF.
THAT'S PLATONIC LOVE YOU DORK. YOU'RE NOT GAY, YOU JUST HAVE A MAN-CRUSH ON CHAZ.
MAYBE YOU DON'T KNOW WHAT GAY MEANS. BUT WHEN A GUY LOVES ANOTHER GUY THAT MAKES HIM QUEER BAIT.
I'M NOT GONNA STAND HERE AND LISTEN TO THIS.
NO, IT'S OKAY.
WHEN WE SAY QUEER BAIT IT'S NOT OFFENSIVE.

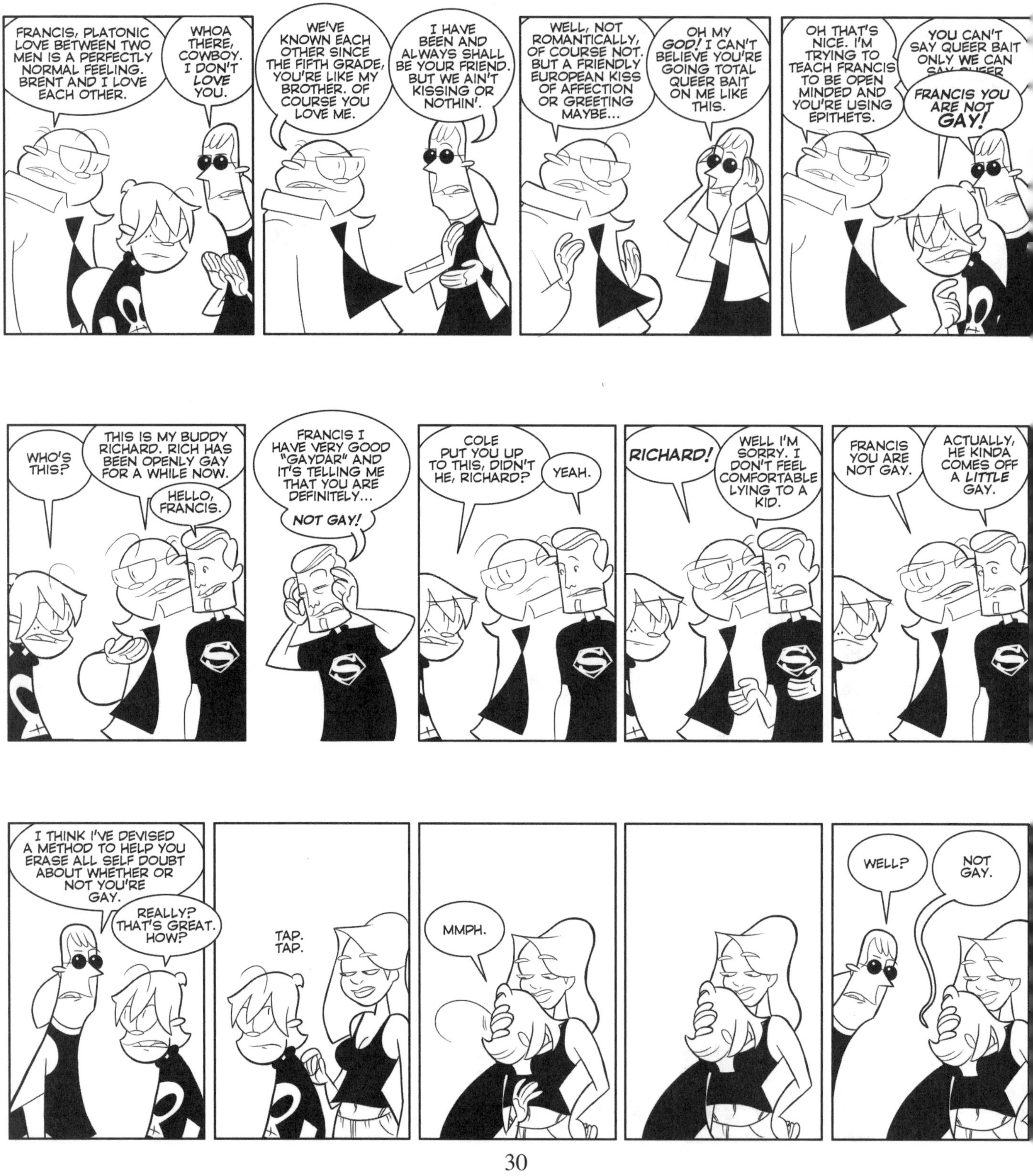
FRANCIS, PLATONIC LOVE BETWEEN TWO MEN IS A PERFECTLY NORMAL FEELING. BRENT AND I LOVE EACH OTHER.
WHOA THERE, COWBOY. I DON'T *LOVE* YOU.
WE'VE KNOWN EACH OTHER SINCE THE FIFTH GRADE, YOU'RE LIKE MY BROTHER. OF COURSE YOU LOVE ME.
I HAVE BEEN AND ALWAYS SHALL BE YOUR FRIEND. BUT WE AIN'T KISSING OR NOTHIN'.
WELL, NOT ROMANTICALLY, OF COURSE NOT. BUT A FRIENDLY EUROPEAN KISS OF AFFECTION OR GREETING MAYBE...
OH MY *GOD!* I CAN'T BELIEVE YOU'RE GOING TOTAL QUEER BAIT ON ME LIKE THIS.
OH THAT'S NICE. I'M TRYING TO TEACH FRANCIS TO BE OPEN MINDED AND YOU'RE USING EPITHETS.
YOU CAN'T SAY QUEER BAIT ONLY WE CAN
FRANCIS YOU ARE NOT *GAY!*
WHO'S THIS?
THIS IS MY BUDDY RICHARD. RICH HAS BEEN OPENLY GAY FOR A WHILE NOW.
HELLO, FRANCIS.
FRANCIS I HAVE VERY GOOD "GAYDAR" AND IT'S TELLING ME THAT YOU ARE DEFINITELY...
NOT GAY!
COLE PUT YOU UP TO THIS, DIDN'T HE, RICHARD?
YEAH.
RICHARD!
WELL I'M SORRY. I DON'T FEEL COMFORTABLE LYING TO A KID.
FRANCIS YOU ARE NOT GAY.
ACTUALLY, HE KINDA COMES OFF A *LITTLE* GAY.
I THINK I'VE DEVISED A METHOD TO HELP YOU ERASE ALL SELF DOUBT ABOUT WHETHER OR NOT YOU'RE GAY.
REALLY? THAT'S GREAT. HOW?
TAP. TAP.
MMPH.
WELL?
NOT GAY.

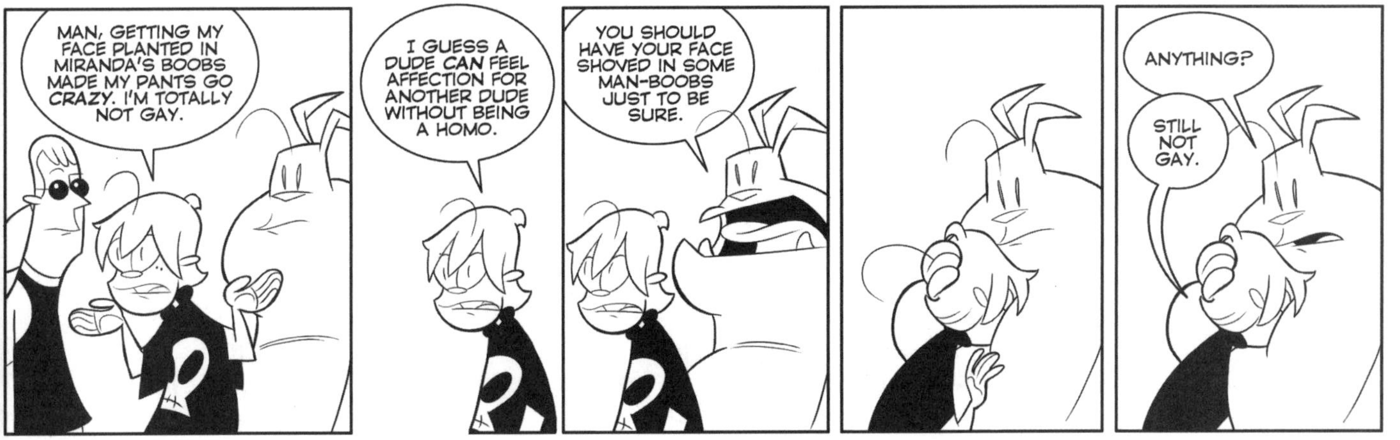
MAN, GETTING MY FACE PLANTED IN MIRANDA'S BOOBS MADE MY PANTS GO CRAZY. I'M TOTALLY NOT GAY.
I GUESS A DUDE CAN FEEL AFFECTION FOR ANOTHER DUDE WITHOUT BEING A HOMO.
YOU SHOULD HAVE YOUR FACE SHOVED IN SOME MAN-BOOBS JUST TO BE SURE.
ANYTHING?
STILL NOT GAY.

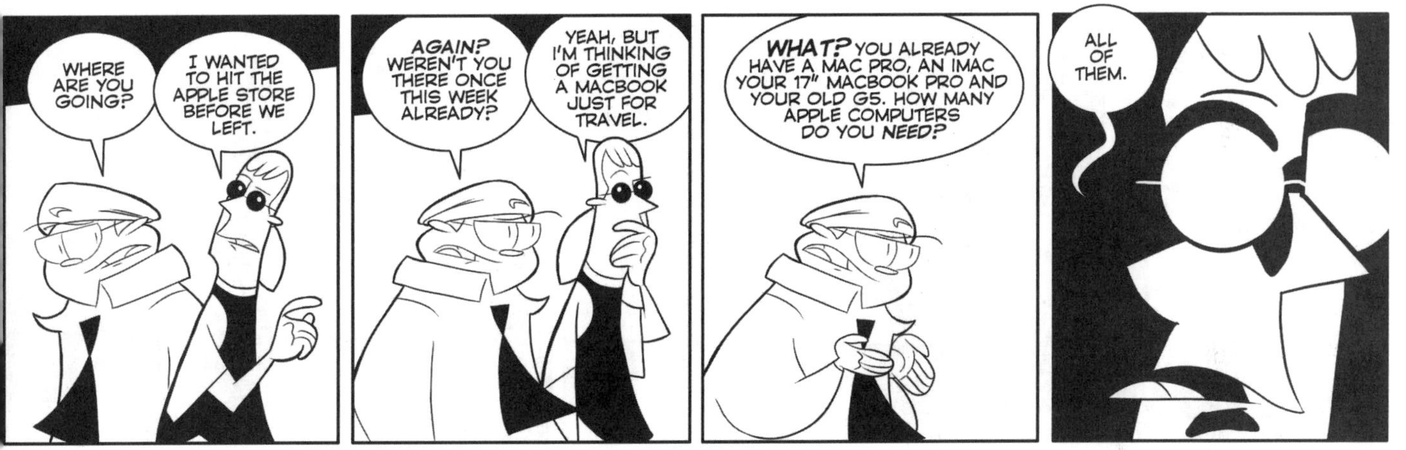
WHERE ARE YOU GOING?
I WANTED TO HIT THE APPLE STORE BEFORE WE LEFT.
AGAIN? WEREN'T YOU THERE ONCE THIS WEEK ALREADY?
YEAH, BUT I'M THINKING OF GETTING A MACBOOK JUST FOR TRAVEL.
WHAT? YOU ALREADY HAVE A MAC PRO, AN IMAC YOUR 17" MACBOOK PRO AND YOUR OLD G5. HOW MANY APPLE COMPUTERS DO YOU NEED?
ALL OF THEM.

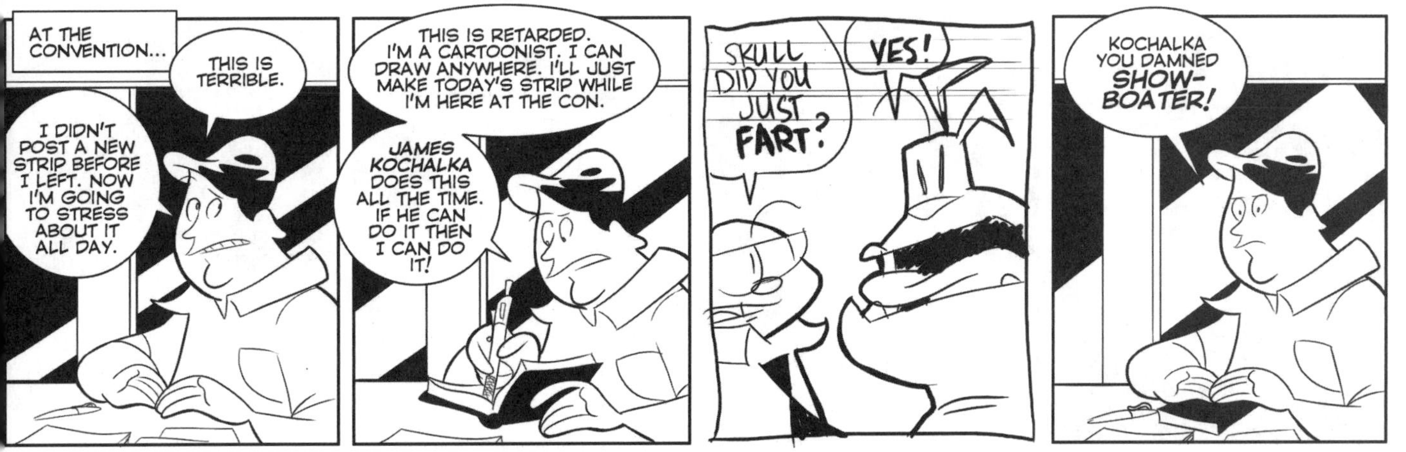
AT THE CONVENTION...
THIS IS TERRIBLE.
I DIDN'T POST A NEW STRIP BEFORE I LEFT. NOW I'M GOING TO STRESS ABOUT IT ALL DAY.
THIS IS RETARDED. I'M A CARTOONIST. I CAN DRAW ANYWHERE. I'LL JUST MAKE TODAY'S STRIP WHILE I'M HERE AT THE CON.
JAMES KOCHALKA DOES THIS ALL THE TIME. IF HE CAN DO IT THEN I CAN DO IT!
SKULL DID YOU JUST FART?
YES!
KOCHALKA YOU DAMNED SHOW-BOATER!

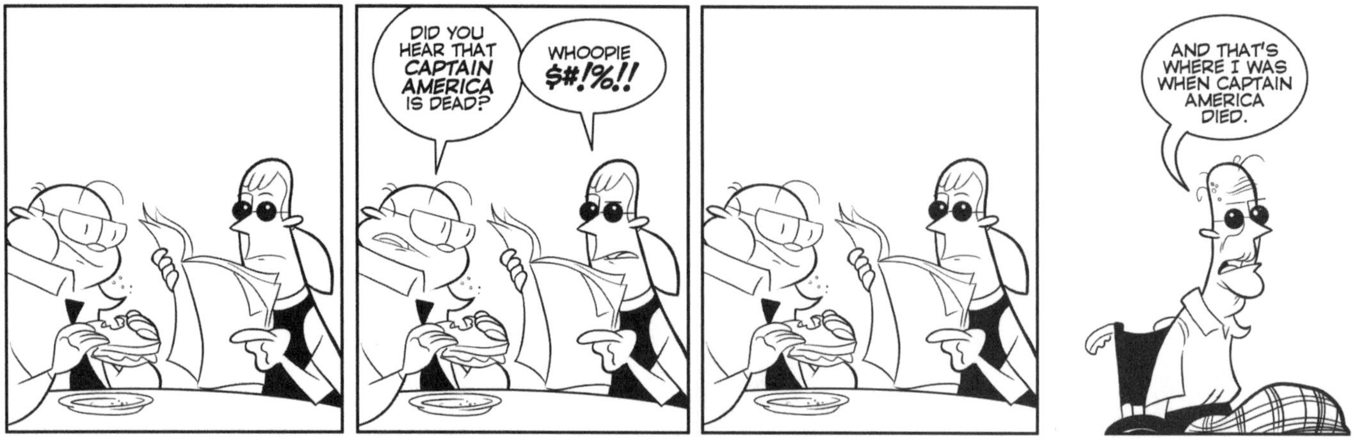
DID YOU HEAR THAT CAPTAIN AMERICA IS DEAD?
WHOOPIE $#!%!!
AND THAT'S WHERE I WAS WHEN CAPTAIN AMERICA DIED.

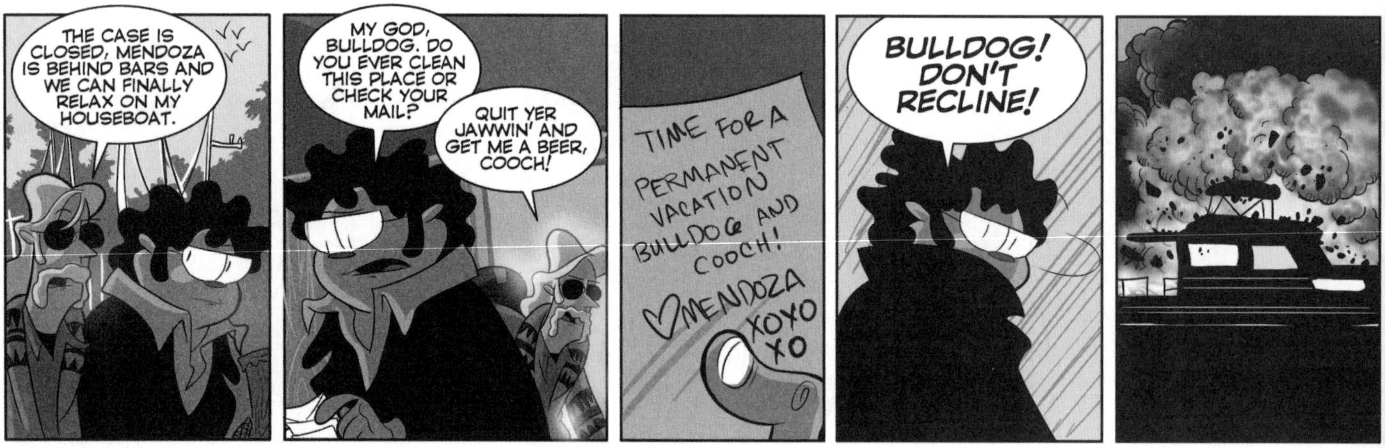
THE CASE IS CLOSED, MENDOZA IS BEHIND BARS AND WE CAN FINALLY RELAX ON MY HOUSEBOAT.
MY GOD, BULLDOG. DO YOU EVER CLEAN THIS PLACE OR CHECK YOUR MAIL?
QUIT YER JAWWIN' AND GET ME A BEER, COOCH!
TIME FOR A PERMANENT VACATION BULLDOG AND COOCH!
♥MENDOZA XOXO XO
BULLDOG! DON'T RECLINE!

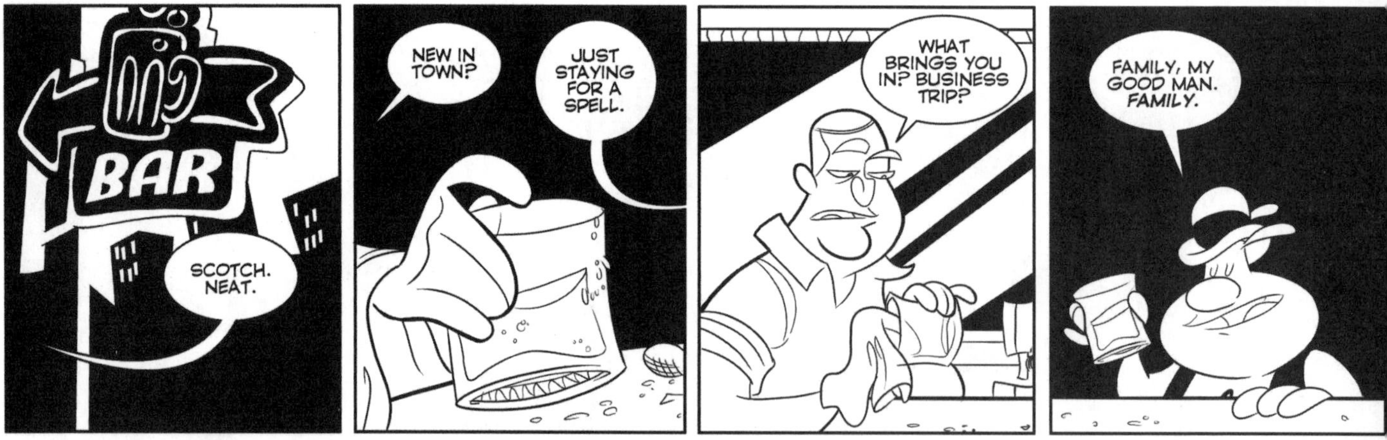
BAR
SCOTCH. NEAT.
NEW IN TOWN?
JUST STAYING FOR A SPELL.
WHAT BRINGS YOU IN? BUSINESS TRIP?
FAMILY, MY GOOD MAN. FAMILY.

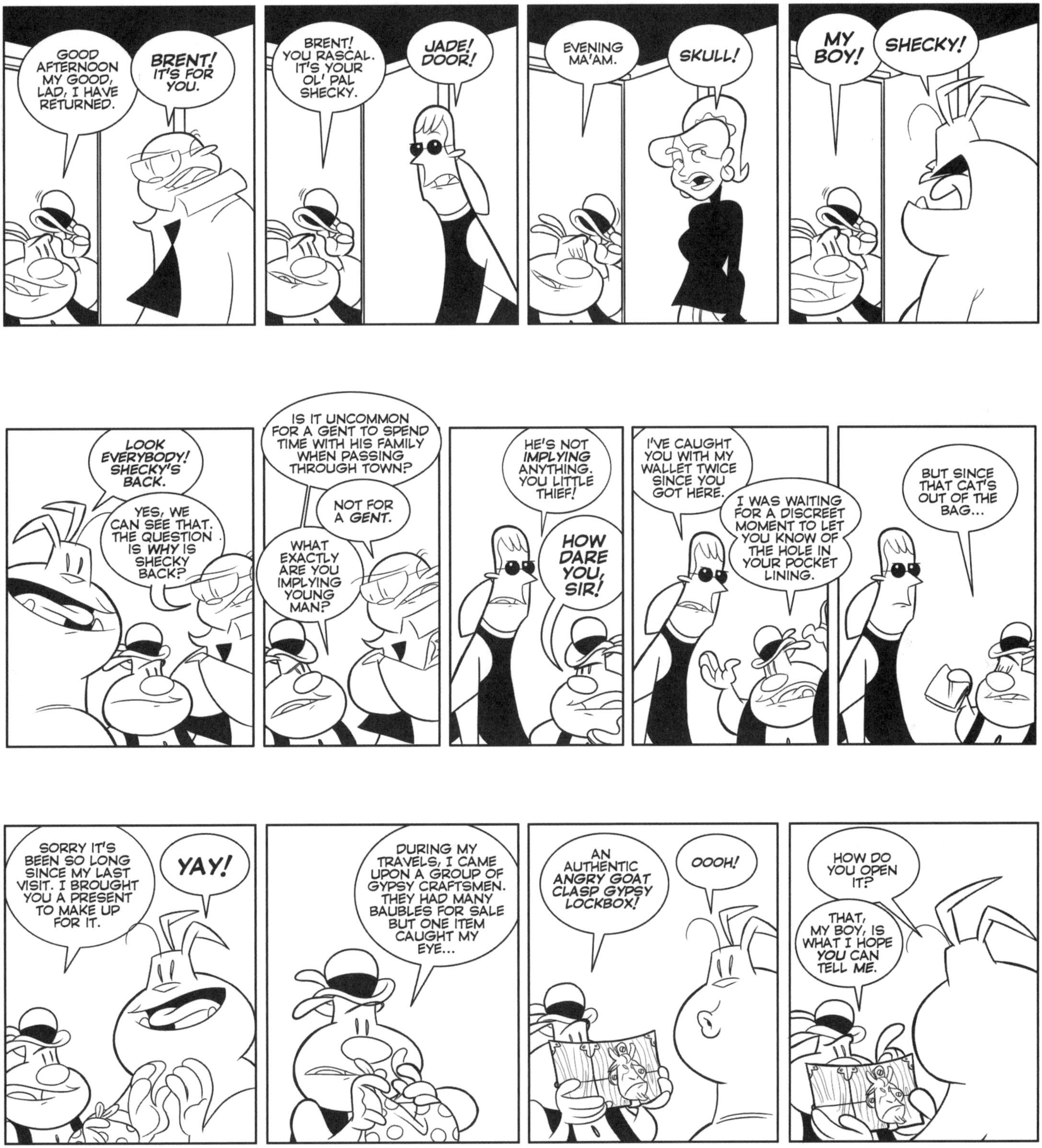
GOOD AFTERNOON MY GOOD, LAD, I HAVE RETURNED.
BRENT! IT'S FOR YOU.
BRENT! YOU RASCAL. IT'S YOUR OL' PAL SHECKY.
JADE! DOOR!
EVENING MA'AM.
SKULL!
MY BOY!
SHECKY!
LOOK EVERYBODY! SHECKY'S BACK.
YES, WE CAN SEE THAT. THE QUESTION IS WHY IS SHECKY BACK?
IS IT UNCOMMON FOR A GENT TO SPEND TIME WITH HIS FAMILY WHEN PASSING THROUGH TOWN?
NOT FOR A GENT.
WHAT EXACTLY ARE YOU IMPLYING YOUNG MAN?
HE'S NOT IMPLYING ANYTHING. YOU LITTLE THIEF!
HOW DARE YOU, SIR!
I'VE CAUGHT YOU WITH MY WALLET TWICE SINCE YOU GOT HERE.
I WAS WAITING FOR A DISCREET MOMENT TO LET YOU KNOW OF THE HOLE IN YOUR POCKET LINING.
BUT SINCE THAT CAT'S OUT OF THE BAG...
SORRY IT'S BEEN SO LONG SINCE MY LAST VISIT. I BROUGHT YOU A PRESENT TO MAKE UP FOR IT.
YAY!
DURING MY TRAVELS, I CAME UPON A GROUP OF GYPSY CRAFTSMEN. THEY HAD MANY BAUBLES FOR SALE BUT ONE ITEM CAUGHT MY EYE...
AN AUTHENTIC ANGRY GOAT CLASP GYPSY LOCKBOX!
OOOH!
HOW DO YOU OPEN IT?
THAT, MY BOY, IS WHAT I HOPE YOU CAN TELL ME.

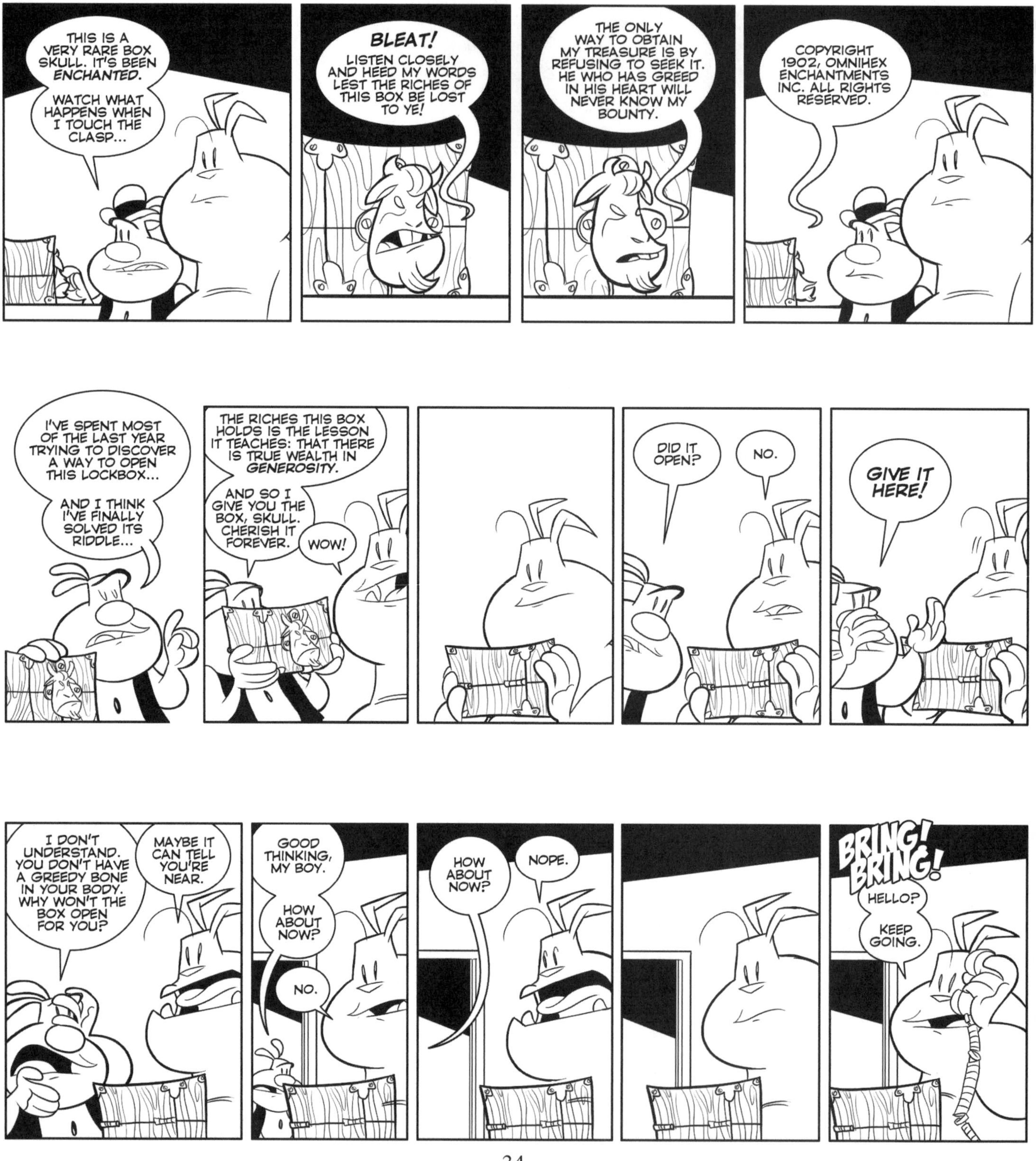
THIS IS A VERY RARE BOX SKULL. IT'S BEEN *ENCHANTED*.
WATCH WHAT HAPPENS WHEN I TOUCH THE CLASP...
BLEAT!
LISTEN CLOSELY AND HEED MY WORDS LEST THE RICHES OF THIS BOX BE LOST TO YE!
THE ONLY WAY TO OBTAIN MY TREASURE IS BY REFUSING TO SEEK IT. HE WHO HAS GREED IN HIS HEART WILL NEVER KNOW MY BOUNTY.
COPYRIGHT 1902, OMNIHEX ENCHANTMENTS INC. ALL RIGHTS RESERVED.
I'VE SPENT MOST OF THE LAST YEAR TRYING TO DISCOVER A WAY TO OPEN THIS LOCKBOX...
AND I THINK I'VE FINALLY SOLVED ITS RIDDLE...
THE RICHES THIS BOX HOLDS IS THE LESSON IT TEACHES: THAT THERE IS TRUE WEALTH IN *GENEROSITY*.
AND SO I GIVE YOU THE BOX, SKULL. CHERISH IT FOREVER.
WOW!
DID IT OPEN?
NO.
GIVE IT HERE!
I DON'T UNDERSTAND. YOU DON'T HAVE A GREEDY BONE IN YOUR BODY. WHY WON'T THE BOX OPEN FOR YOU?
MAYBE IT CAN TELL YOU'RE NEAR.
GOOD THINKING, MY BOY.
HOW ABOUT NOW?
NO.
HOW ABOUT NOW?
NOPE.
BRING! BRING!
HELLO?
KEEP GOING.

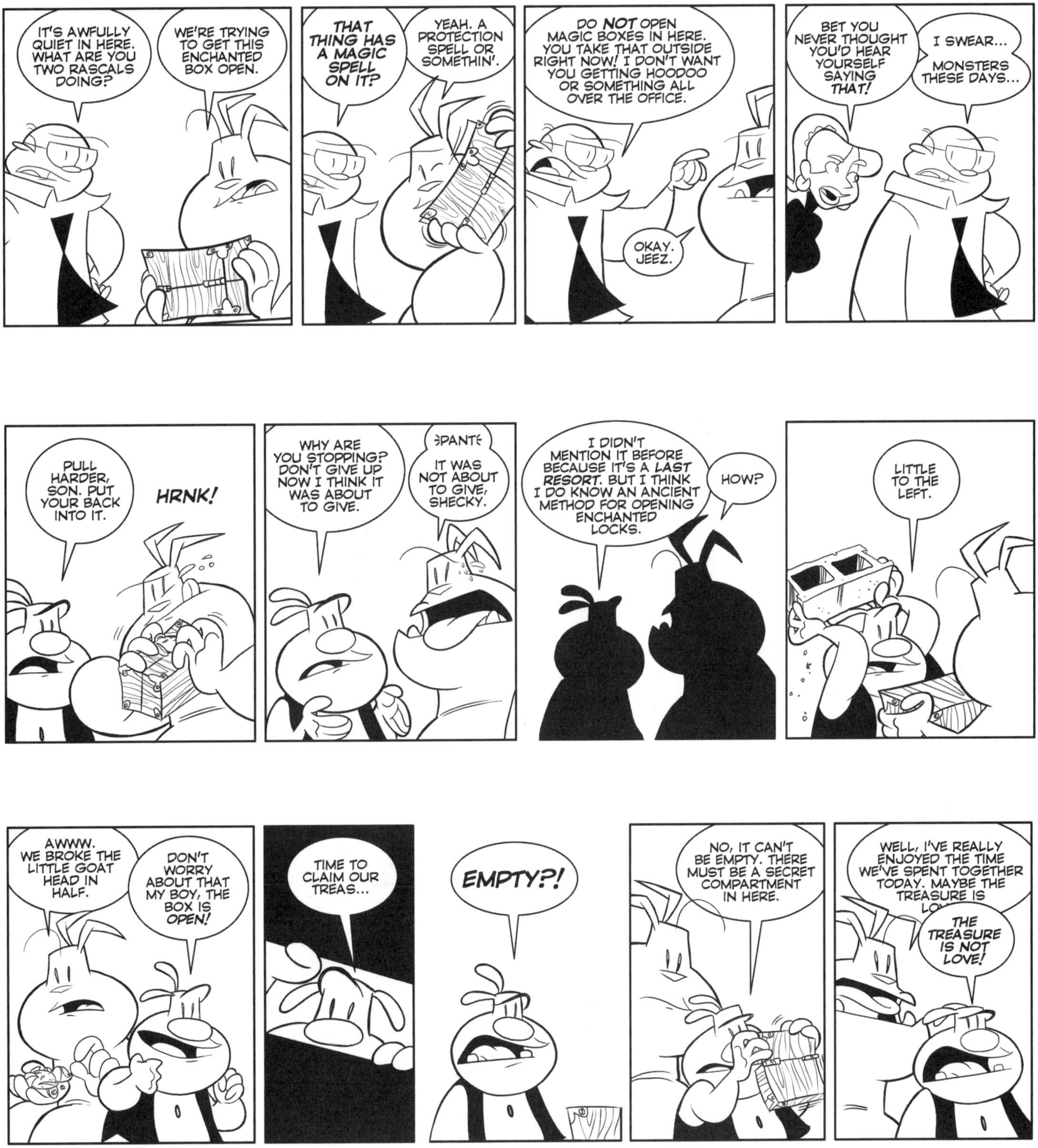

IT'S AWFULLY QUIET IN HERE. WHAT ARE YOU TWO RASCALS DOING?
WE'RE TRYING TO GET THIS ENCHANTED BOX OPEN.
THAT THING HAS A MAGIC SPELL ON IT?
YEAH. A PROTECTION SPELL OR SOMETHIN'.
DO NOT OPEN MAGIC BOXES IN HERE. YOU TAKE THAT OUTSIDE RIGHT NOW! I DON'T WANT YOU GETTING HOODOO OR SOMETHING ALL OVER THE OFFICE.
OKAY. JEEZ.
BET YOU NEVER THOUGHT YOU'D HEAR YOURSELF SAYING THAT!
I SWEAR... MONSTERS THESE DAYS...
PULL HARDER, SON. PUT YOUR BACK INTO IT.
HRNK!
WHY ARE YOU STOPPING? DON'T GIVE UP NOW I THINK IT WAS ABOUT TO GIVE.
PANT
IT WAS NOT ABOUT TO GIVE, SHECKY.
I DIDN'T MENTION IT BEFORE BECAUSE IT'S A LAST RESORT. BUT I THINK I DO KNOW AN ANCIENT METHOD FOR OPENING ENCHANTED LOCKS.
HOW?
LITTLE TO THE LEFT.
AWWW. WE BROKE THE LITTLE GOAT HEAD IN HALF.
DON'T WORRY ABOUT THAT MY BOY, THE BOX IS OPEN!
TIME TO CLAIM OUR TREAS...
EMPTY?!
NO, IT CAN'T BE EMPTY. THERE MUST BE A SECRET COMPARTMENT IN HERE.
WELL, I'VE REALLY ENJOYED THE TIME WE'VE SPENT TOGETHER TODAY. MAYBE THE TREASURE IS
THE TREASURE IS NOT LOVE!

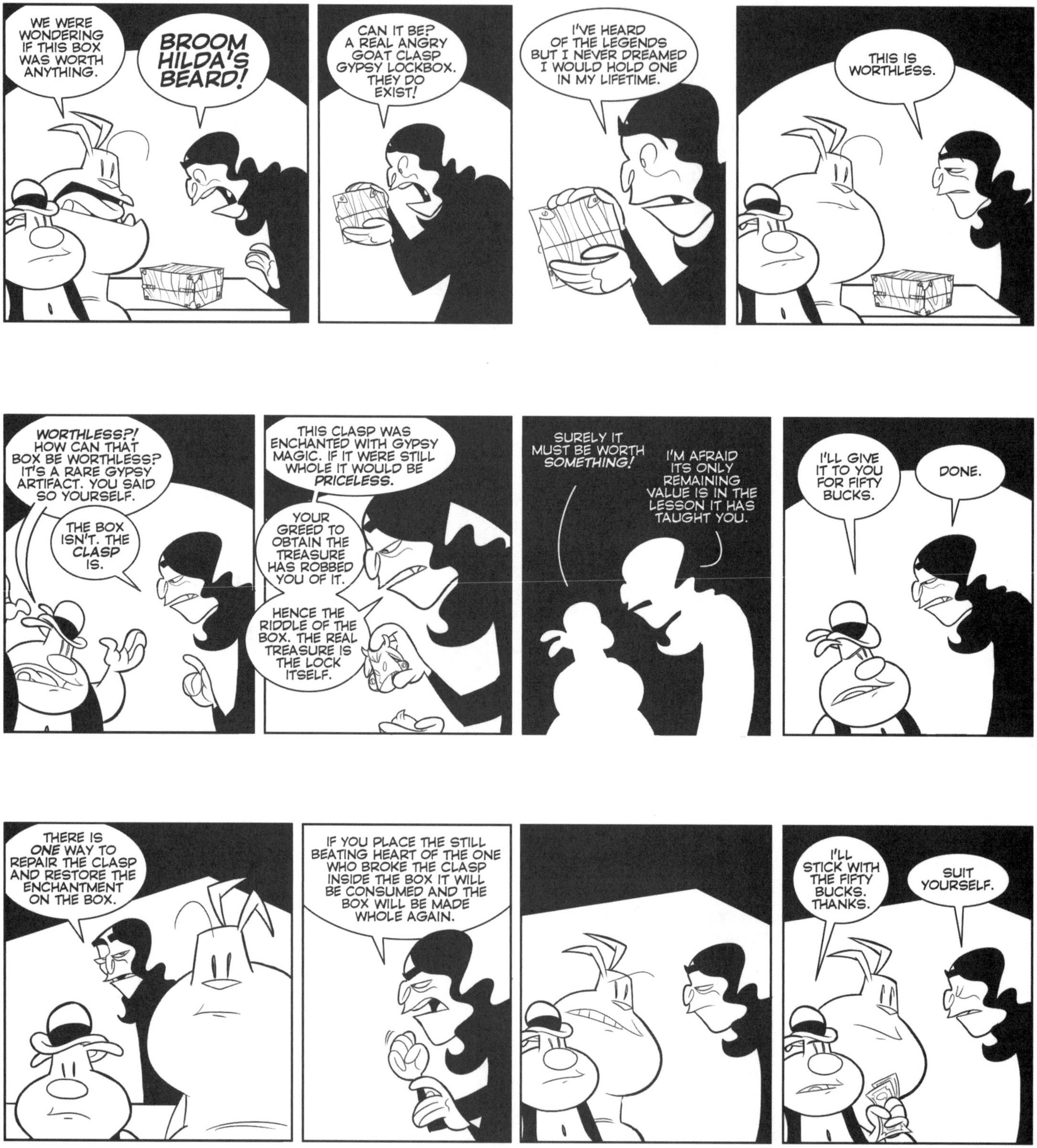
WE WERE WONDERING IF THIS BOX WAS WORTH ANYTHING.
BROOM HILDA'S BEARD!
CAN IT BE? A REAL ANGRY GOAT CLASP GYPSY LOCKBOX. THEY DO EXIST!
I'VE HEARD OF THE LEGENDS BUT I NEVER DREAMED I WOULD HOLD ONE IN MY LIFETIME.
THIS IS WORTHLESS.
WORTHLESS?! HOW CAN THAT BOX BE WORTHLESS? IT'S A RARE GYPSY ARTIFACT. YOU SAID SO YOURSELF.
THE BOX ISN'T. THE CLASP IS.
THIS CLASP WAS ENCHANTED WITH GYPSY MAGIC. IF IT WERE STILL WHOLE IT WOULD BE PRICELESS.
YOUR GREED TO OBTAIN THE TREASURE HAS ROBBED YOU OF IT.
HENCE THE RIDDLE OF THE BOX. THE REAL TREASURE IS THE LOCK ITSELF.
SURELY IT MUST BE WORTH SOMETHING!
I'M AFRAID ITS ONLY REMAINING VALUE IS IN THE LESSON IT HAS TAUGHT YOU.
I'LL GIVE IT TO YOU FOR FIFTY BUCKS.
DONE.
THERE IS ONE WAY TO REPAIR THE CLASP AND RESTORE THE ENCHANTMENT ON THE BOX.
IF YOU PLACE THE STILL BEATING HEART OF THE ONE WHO BROKE THE CLASP INSIDE THE BOX IT WILL BE CONSUMED AND THE BOX WILL BE MADE WHOLE AGAIN.
I'LL STICK WITH THE FIFTY BUCKS. THANKS.
SUIT YOURSELF.

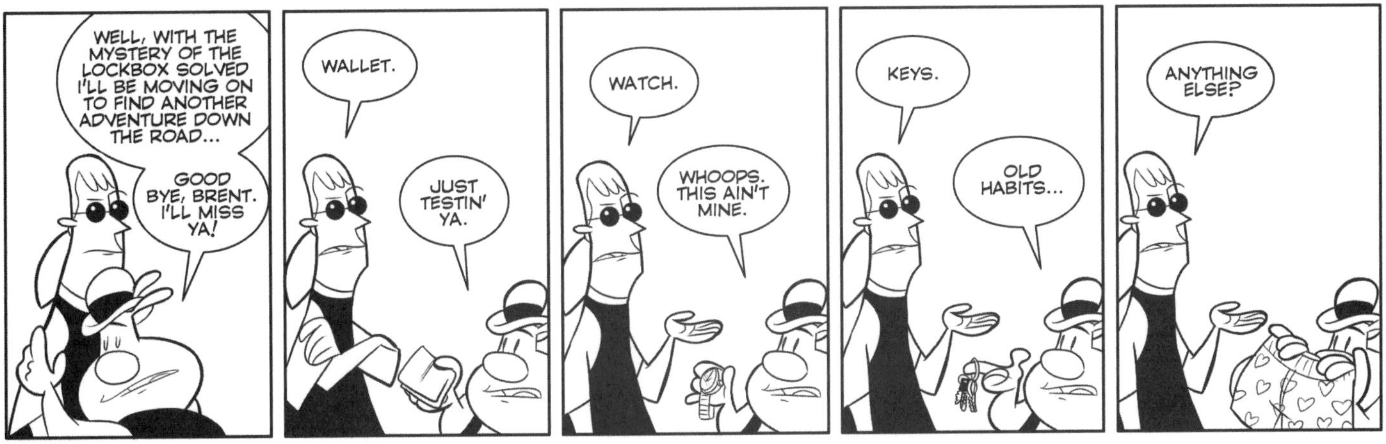
WELL, WITH THE MYSTERY OF THE LOCKBOX SOLVED I'LL BE MOVING ON TO FIND ANOTHER ADVENTURE DOWN THE ROAD...
GOOD BYE, BRENT. I'LL MISS YA!
WALLET.
JUST TESTIN' YA.
WATCH.
WHOOPS. THIS AIN'T MINE.
KEYS.
OLD HABITS...
ANYTHING ELSE?

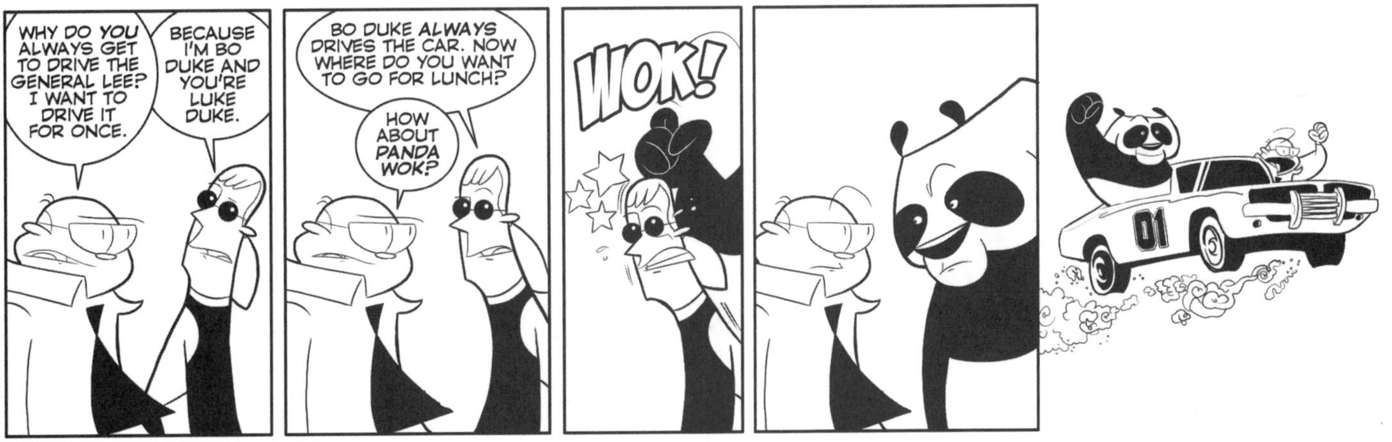
WHY DO YOU ALWAYS GET TO DRIVE THE GENERAL LEE? I WANT TO DRIVE IT FOR ONCE.
BECAUSE I'M BO DUKE AND YOU'RE LUKE DUKE.
BO DUKE ALWAYS DRIVES THE CAR. NOW WHERE DO YOU WANT TO GO FOR LUNCH?
HOW ABOUT PANDA WOK?
WOK!
01

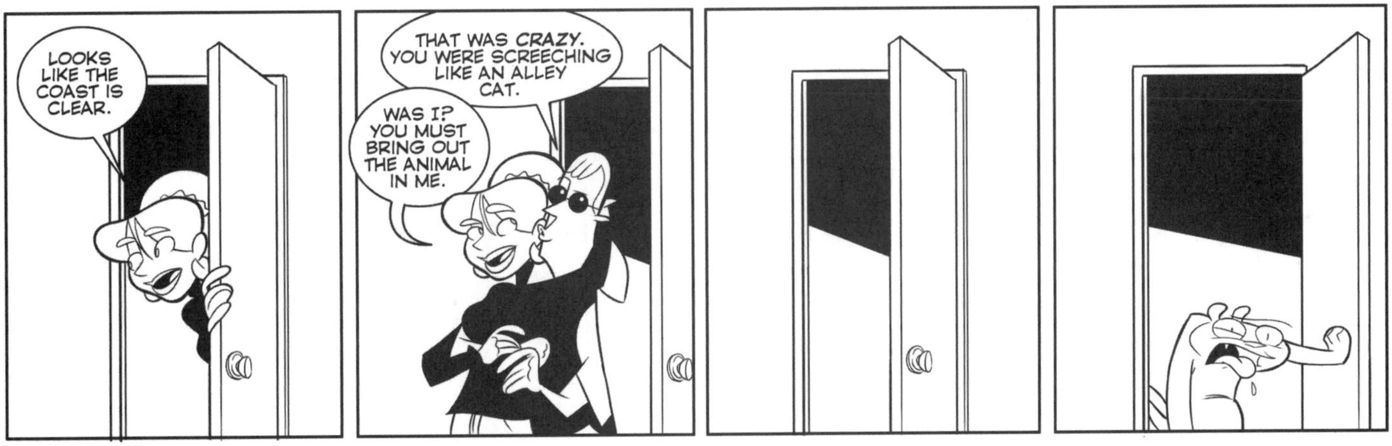
LOOKS LIKE THE COAST IS CLEAR.
THAT WAS CRAZY. YOU WERE SCREECHING LIKE AN ALLEY CAT.
WAS I? YOU MUST BRING OUT THE ANIMAL IN ME.

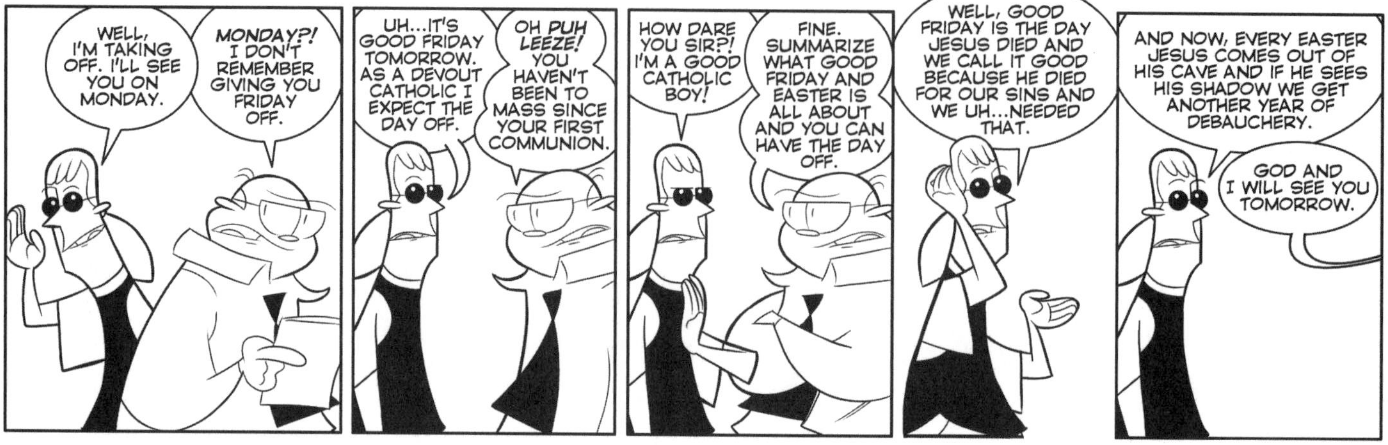
WELL, I'M TAKING OFF. I'LL SEE YOU ON MONDAY.
MONDAY?! I DON'T REMEMBER GIVING YOU FRIDAY OFF.
UH...IT'S GOOD FRIDAY TOMORROW. AS A DEVOUT CATHOLIC I EXPECT THE DAY OFF.
OH PUH LEEZE! YOU HAVEN'T BEEN TO MASS SINCE YOUR FIRST COMMUNION.
HOW DARE YOU SIR?! I'M A GOOD CATHOLIC BOY!
FINE. SUMMARIZE WHAT GOOD FRIDAY AND EASTER IS ALL ABOUT AND YOU CAN HAVE THE DAY OFF.
WELL, GOOD FRIDAY IS THE DAY JESUS DIED AND WE CALL IT GOOD BECAUSE HE DIED FOR OUR SINS AND WE UH...NEEDED THAT.
AND NOW, EVERY EASTER JESUS COMES OUT OF HIS CAVE AND IF HE SEES HIS SHADOW WE GET ANOTHER YEAR OF DEBAUCHERY.
GOD AND I WILL SEE YOU TOMORROW.

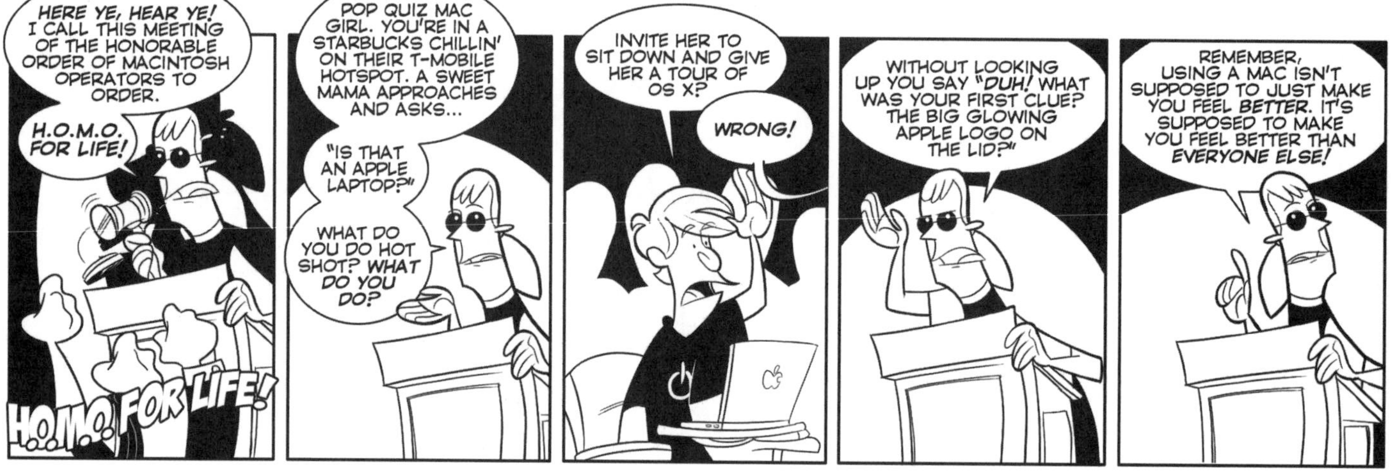
HERE YE, HEAR YE! I CALL THIS MEETING OF THE HONORABLE ORDER OF MACINTOSH OPERATORS TO ORDER.
H.O.M.O. FOR LIFE!
H.O.M.O. FOR LIFE!
POP QUIZ MAC GIRL. YOU'RE IN A STARBUCKS CHILLIN' ON THEIR T-MOBILE HOTSPOT. A SWEET MAMA APPROACHES AND ASKS...
"IS THAT AN APPLE LAPTOP?"
WHAT DO YOU DO HOT SHOT? WHAT DO YOU DO?
INVITE HER TO SIT DOWN AND GIVE HER A TOUR OF OS X?
WRONG!
WITHOUT LOOKING UP YOU SAY "DUH! WHAT WAS YOUR FIRST CLUE? THE BIG GLOWING APPLE LOGO ON THE LID?"
REMEMBER, USING A MAC ISN'T SUPPOSED TO JUST MAKE YOU FEEL BETTER. IT'S SUPPOSED TO MAKE YOU FEEL BETTER THAN EVERYONE ELSE!

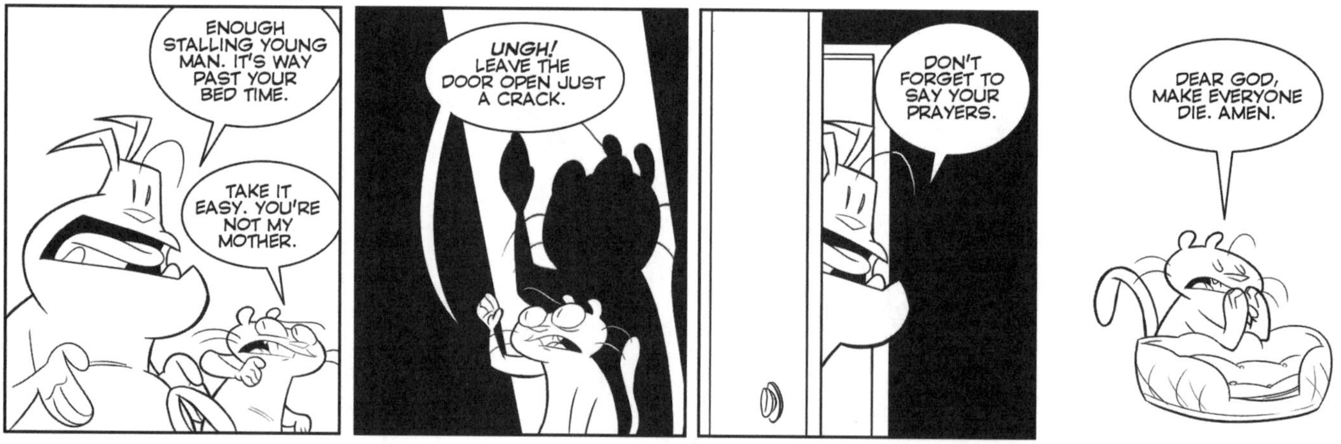
ENOUGH STALLING YOUNG MAN. IT'S WAY PAST YOUR BED TIME.
TAKE IT EASY. YOU'RE NOT MY MOTHER.
UNGH! LEAVE THE DOOR OPEN JUST A CRACK.
DON'T FORGET TO SAY YOUR PRAYERS.
DEAR GOD, MAKE EVERYONE DIE. AMEN.

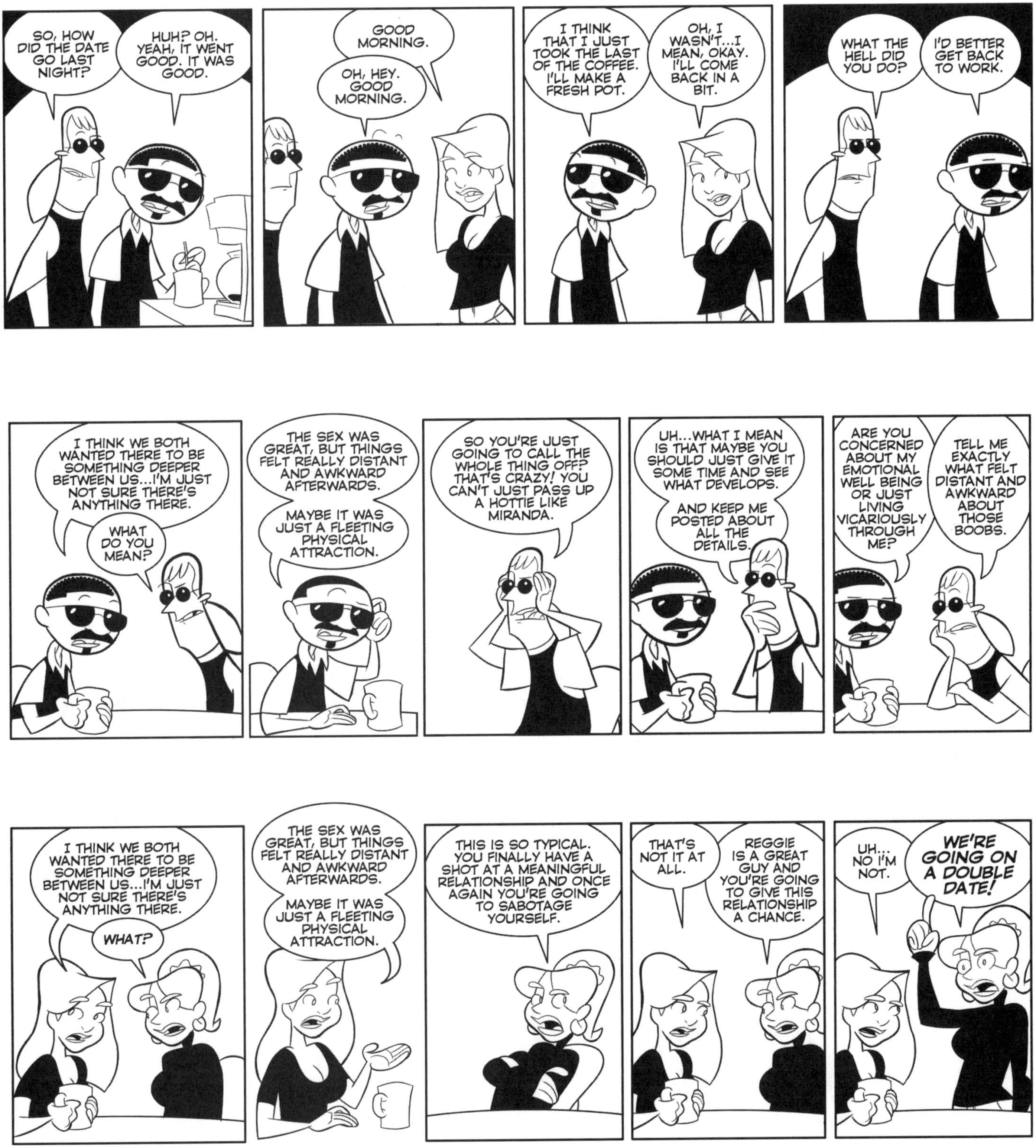
SO, HOW DID THE DATE GO LAST NIGHT?
HUH? OH. YEAH, IT WENT GOOD. IT WAS GOOD.
GOOD MORNING.
OH, HEY. GOOD MORNING.
I THINK THAT I JUST TOOK THE LAST OF THE COFFEE. I'LL MAKE A FRESH POT.
OH, I WASN'T...I MEAN, OKAY. I'LL COME BACK IN A BIT.
WHAT THE HELL DID YOU DO?
I'D BETTER GET BACK TO WORK.
I THINK WE BOTH WANTED THERE TO BE SOMETHING DEEPER BETWEEN US...I'M JUST NOT SURE THERE'S ANYTHING THERE.
WHAT DO YOU MEAN?
THE SEX WAS GREAT, BUT THINGS FELT REALLY DISTANT AND AWKWARD AFTERWARDS.
MAYBE IT WAS JUST A FLEETING PHYSICAL ATTRACTION.
SO YOU'RE JUST GOING TO CALL THE WHOLE THING OFF? THAT'S CRAZY! YOU CAN'T JUST PASS UP A HOTTIE LIKE MIRANDA.
UH...WHAT I MEAN IS THAT MAYBE YOU SHOULD JUST GIVE IT SOME TIME AND SEE WHAT DEVELOPS.
AND KEEP ME POSTED ABOUT ALL THE DETAILS.
ARE YOU CONCERNED ABOUT MY EMOTIONAL WELL BEING OR JUST LIVING VICARIOUSLY THROUGH ME?
TELL ME EXACTLY WHAT FELT DISTANT AND AWKWARD ABOUT THOSE BOOBS.
I THINK WE BOTH WANTED THERE TO BE SOMETHING DEEPER BETWEEN US...I'M JUST NOT SURE THERE'S ANYTHING THERE.
WHAT?
THE SEX WAS GREAT, BUT THINGS FELT REALLY DISTANT AND AWKWARD AFTERWARDS.
MAYBE IT WAS JUST A FLEETING PHYSICAL ATTRACTION.
THIS IS SO TYPICAL. YOU FINALLY HAVE A SHOT AT A MEANINGFUL RELATIONSHIP AND ONCE AGAIN YOU'RE GOING TO SABOTAGE YOURSELF.
THAT'S NOT IT AT ALL.
REGGIE IS A GREAT GUY AND YOU'RE GOING TO GIVE THIS RELATIONSHIP A CHANCE.
UH... NO I'M NOT.
WE'RE GOING ON A DOUBLE DATE!

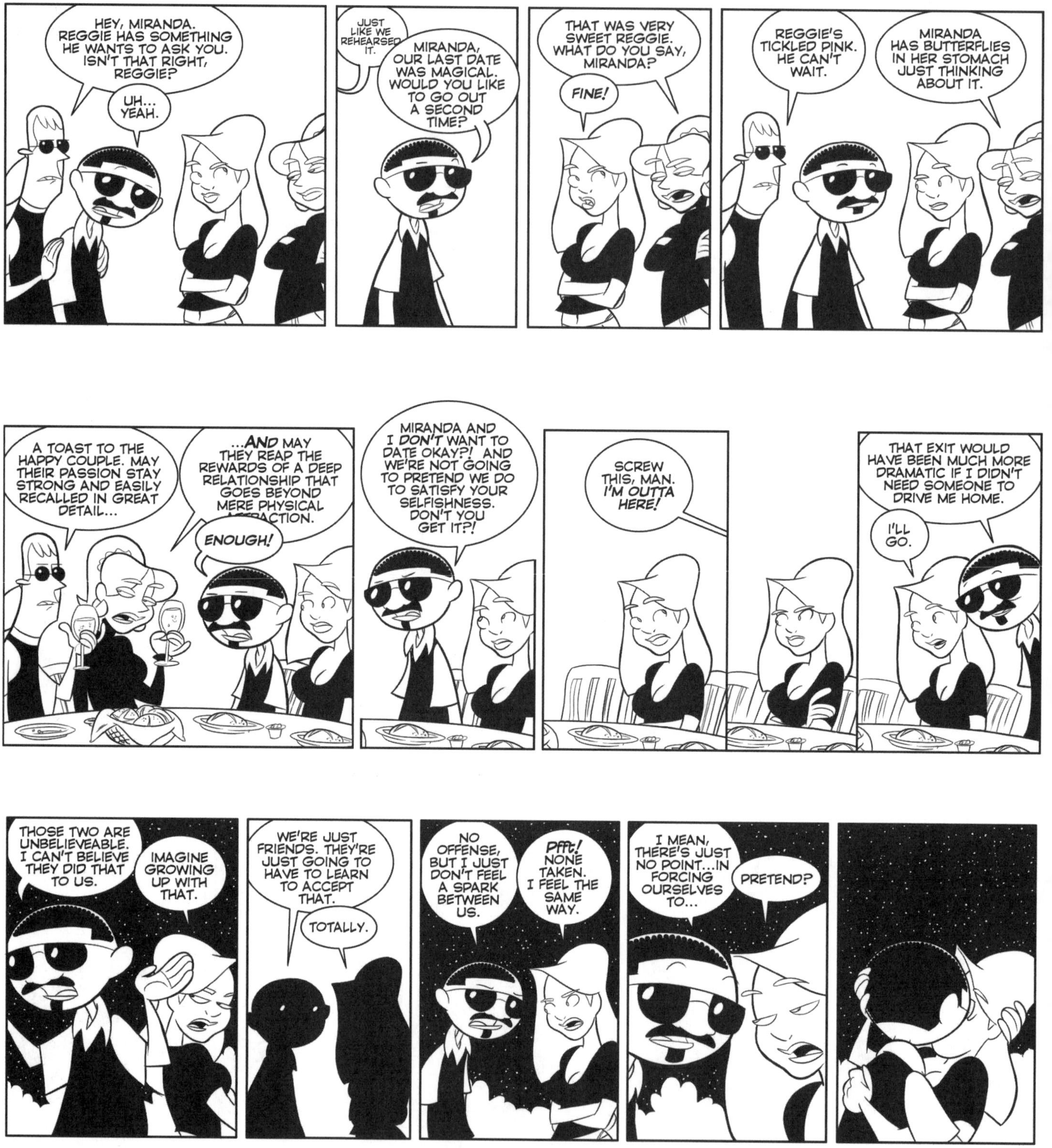
HEY, MIRANDA. REGGIE HAS SOMETHING HE WANTS TO ASK YOU. ISN'T THAT RIGHT, REGGIE?
UH... YEAH.
JUST LIKE WE REHEARSED IT.
MIRANDA, OUR LAST DATE WAS MAGICAL. WOULD YOU LIKE TO GO OUT A SECOND TIME?
THAT WAS VERY SWEET REGGIE. WHAT DO YOU SAY, MIRANDA?
FINE!
REGGIE'S TICKLED PINK. HE CAN'T WAIT.
MIRANDA HAS BUTTERFLIES IN HER STOMACH JUST THINKING ABOUT IT.
A TOAST TO THE HAPPY COUPLE. MAY THEIR PASSION STAY STRONG AND EASILY RECALLED IN GREAT DETAIL...
...AND MAY THEY REAP THE REWARDS OF A DEEP RELATIONSHIP THAT GOES BEYOND MERE PHYSICAL ACTION.
ENOUGH!
MIRANDA AND I DON'T WANT TO DATE OKAY?! AND WE'RE NOT GOING TO PRETEND WE DO TO SATISFY YOUR SELFISHNESS. DON'T YOU GET IT?!
SCREW THIS, MAN. I'M OUTTA HERE!
THAT EXIT WOULD HAVE BEEN MUCH MORE DRAMATIC IF I DIDN'T NEED SOMEONE TO DRIVE ME HOME.
I'LL GO.
THOSE TWO ARE UNBELIEVEABLE. I CAN'T BELIEVE THEY DID THAT TO US.
IMAGINE GROWING UP WITH THAT.
WE'RE JUST FRIENDS. THEY'RE JUST GOING TO HAVE TO LEARN TO ACCEPT THAT.
TOTALLY.
NO OFFENSE, BUT I JUST DON'T FEEL A SPARK BETWEEN US.
Pfft! NONE TAKEN. I FEEL THE SAME WAY.
I MEAN, THERE'S JUST NO POINT...IN FORCING OURSELVES TO...
PRETEND?

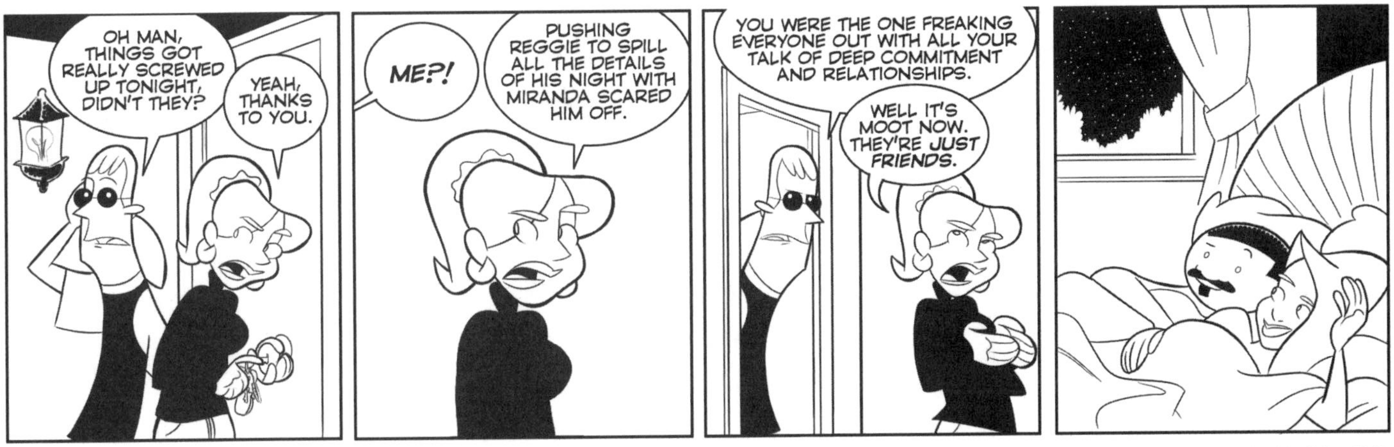
OH MAN, THINGS GOT REALLY SCREWED UP TONIGHT, DIDN'T THEY?
YEAH, THANKS TO YOU.
ME?!
PUSHING REGGIE TO SPILL ALL THE DETAILS OF HIS NIGHT WITH MIRANDA SCARED HIM OFF.
YOU WERE THE ONE FREAKING EVERYONE OUT WITH ALL YOUR TALK OF DEEP COMMITMENT AND RELATIONSHIPS.
WELL IT'S MOOT NOW. THEY'RE *JUST FRIENDS*.

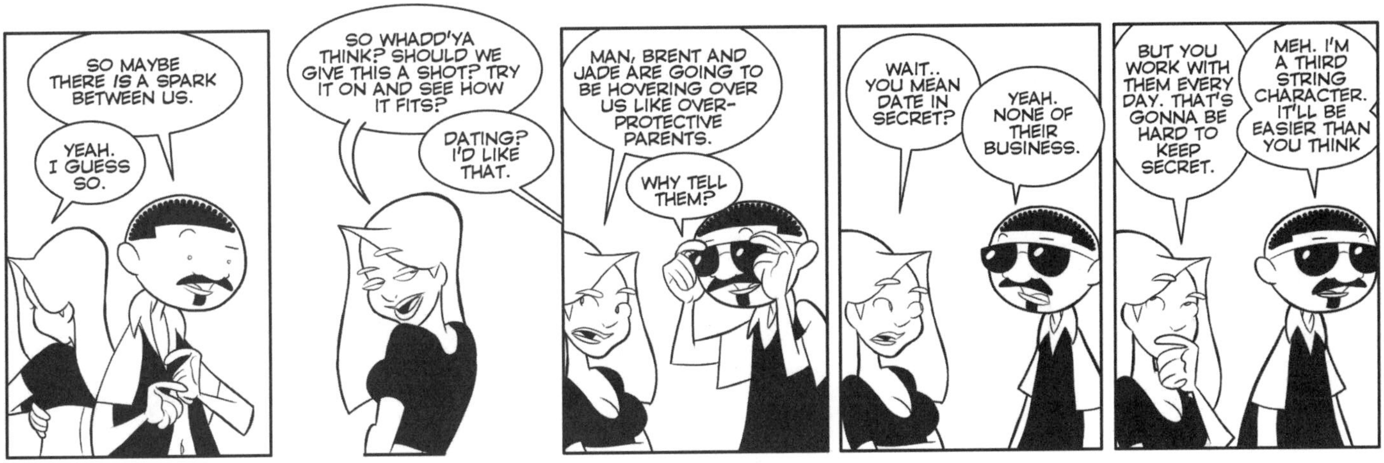
SO MAYBE THERE *IS* A SPARK BETWEEN US.
YEAH. I GUESS SO.
SO WHADD'YA THINK? SHOULD WE GIVE THIS A SHOT? TRY IT ON AND SEE HOW IT FITS?
DATING? I'D LIKE THAT.
MAN, BRENT AND JADE ARE GOING TO BE HOVERING OVER US LIKE OVER-PROTECTIVE PARENTS.
WHY TELL THEM?
WAIT.. YOU MEAN DATE IN SECRET?
YEAH. NONE OF THEIR BUSINESS.
BUT YOU WORK WITH THEM EVERY DAY. THAT'S GONNA BE HARD TO KEEP SECRET.
MEH. I'M A THIRD STRING CHARACTER. IT'LL BE EASIER THAN YOU THINK

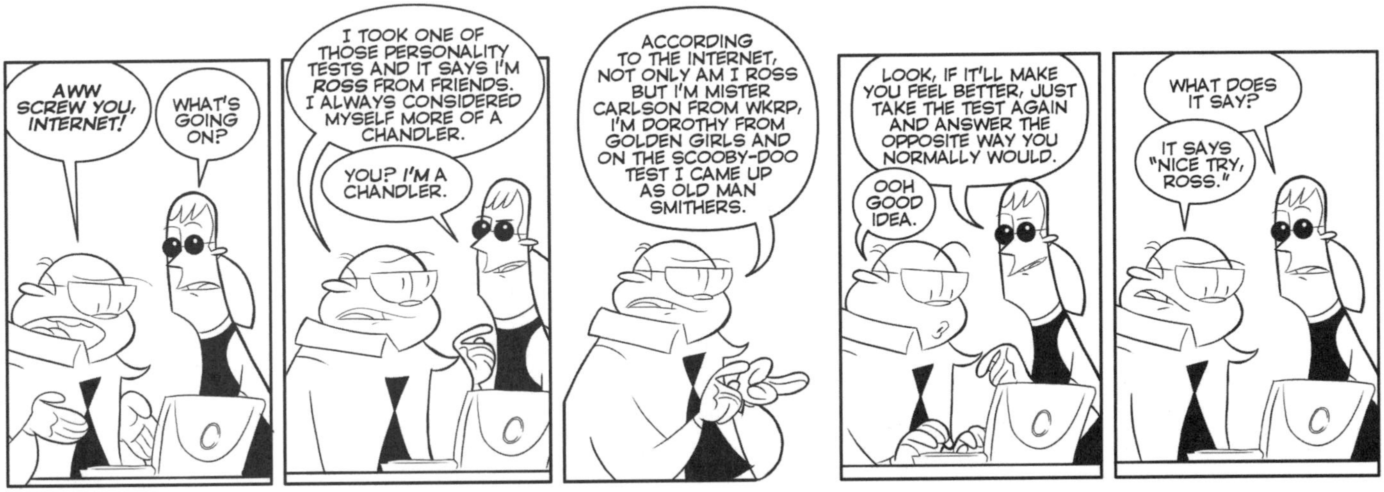
AWW SCREW YOU, INTERNET!
WHAT'S GOING ON?
I TOOK ONE OF THOSE PERSONALITY TESTS AND IT SAYS I'M *ROSS* FROM FRIENDS. I ALWAYS CONSIDERED MYSELF MORE OF A CHANDLER.
YOU? *I'M* A CHANDLER.
ACCORDING TO THE INTERNET, NOT ONLY AM I ROSS BUT I'M MISTER CARLSON FROM WKRP, I'M DOROTHY FROM GOLDEN GIRLS AND ON THE SCOOBY-DOO TEST I CAME UP AS OLD MAN SMITHERS.
LOOK, IF IT'LL MAKE YOU FEEL BETTER, JUST TAKE THE TEST AGAIN AND ANSWER THE OPPOSITE WAY YOU NORMALLY WOULD.
OOH GOOD IDEA.
WHAT DOES IT SAY?
IT SAYS "NICE TRY, ROSS."

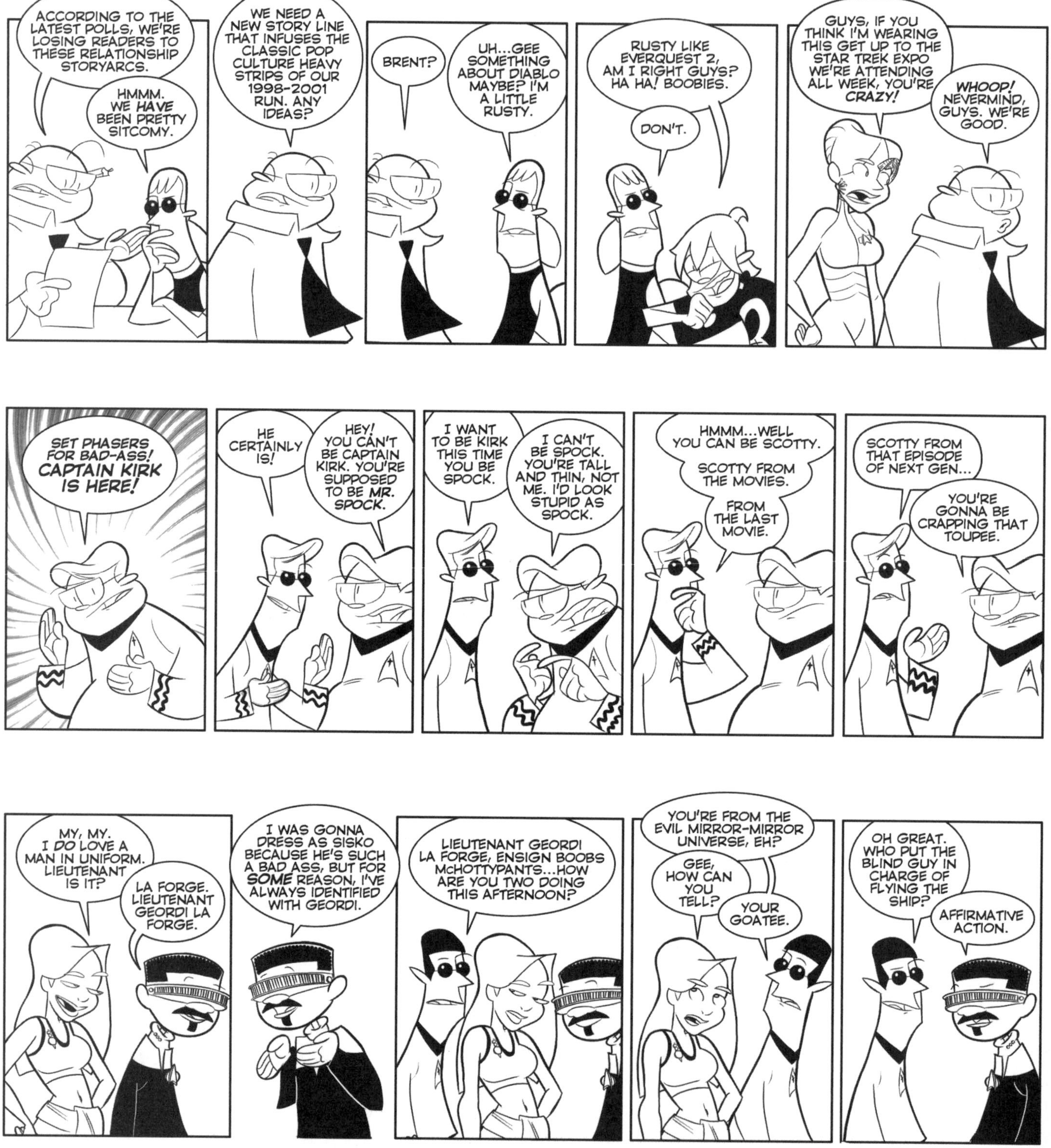
ACCORDING TO THE LATEST POLLS, WE'RE LOSING READERS TO THESE RELATIONSHIP STORYARCS.
HMMM. WE *HAVE* BEEN PRETTY SITCOMY.
WE NEED A NEW STORY LINE THAT INFUSES THE CLASSIC POP CULTURE HEAVY STRIPS OF OUR 1998-2001 RUN. ANY IDEAS?
BRENT?
UH...GEE SOMETHING ABOUT DIABLO MAYBE? I'M A LITTLE RUSTY.
RUSTY LIKE EVERQUEST 2, AM I RIGHT GUYS? HA HA! BOOBIES.
DON'T.
GUYS, IF YOU THINK I'M WEARING THIS GET UP TO THE STAR TREK EXPO WE'RE ATTENDING ALL WEEK, YOU'RE *CRAZY!*
WHOOP! NEVERMIND, GUYS. WE'RE GOOD.
SET PHASERS FOR BAD-ASS! **CAPTAIN KIRK IS HERE!**
HE CERTAINLY IS!
HEY! YOU CAN'T BE CAPTAIN KIRK. YOU'RE SUPPOSED TO BE **MR. SPOCK.**
I WANT TO BE KIRK THIS TIME YOU BE SPOCK.
I CAN'T BE SPOCK. YOU'RE TALL AND THIN, NOT ME. I'D LOOK STUPID AS SPOCK.
HMMM...WELL YOU CAN BE SCOTTY.
SCOTTY FROM THE MOVIES.
FROM THE LAST MOVIE.
SCOTTY FROM THAT EPISODE OF NEXT GEN...
YOU'RE GONNA BE CRAPPING THAT TOUPEE.
MY, MY. I *DO* LOVE A MAN IN UNIFORM. LIEUTENANT IS IT?
LA FORGE. LIEUTENANT GEORDI LA FORGE.
I WAS GONNA DRESS AS SISKO BECAUSE HE'S SUCH A BAD ASS, BUT FOR **SOME** REASON, I'VE ALWAYS IDENTIFIED WITH GEORDI.
LIEUTENANT GEORDI LA FORGE, ENSIGN BOOBS McHOTTYPANTS...HOW ARE YOU TWO DOING THIS AFTERNOON?
YOU'RE FROM THE EVIL MIRROR-MIRROR UNIVERSE, EH?
GEE, HOW CAN YOU TELL?
YOUR GOATEE.
OH GREAT. WHO PUT THE BLIND GUY IN CHARGE OF FLYING THE SHIP?
AFFIRMATIVE ACTION.

Panel 1:
AW, COOL BORG COSTUME, FRANCIS.

OH, THANKS.

Panel 2:
I MADE IT MYSELF. IT TOOK ME FOREVER, BUT I GOT ALL THE... FROM LOCAL... AND I'D

YEEAARGH! MY EYE!

Panel 3:
OH CRAP! SORRY ABOUT THAT.

WHAT IN THE NAME OF T'PRING IS GOING ON IN HERE?

Panel 4:
I THINK I ACCIDENTALLY BLINDED COLE WITH...

YEEAARGH!

Panel 5:
GUYS...WAIT UNTIL YOU SEE WHAT SKULL IS DRESSING UP WITH. YOU'RE GONNA LOVE IT. WAIT HERE.

Panel 6:
GEE, LET ME GUESS. SKULL AS A KLINGON. *AGAIN!* WHOOPIE POOPIE.

Panel 7:
SUDDENLY...

THIS IS CETI-ALPHA FIIIVEE!

KHAAAAN!

Panel 8:
THESE TREK STRIPS ARE DOING THE TRICK! READERS ARE HAPPY, WE'RE PROVIDING GOOD FAN-SERVICE AND THERE ISN'T A SAPPY STORYARC IN SIGHT.

MAY THE GOOD TIMES LIVE LONG AND PROSPER!

Panel 9:
FRANCIS, WHERE'S YOUR BORG COSTUME? WE'RE ABOUT TO LEAVE FOR THE TREK EXPO.

≶SIGH≶ I'M NOT GOING. I'M FEELING A LITTLE SAD AND CONFUSED RIGHT NOW.

YOU SEE, I MET THIS GIRL.

Panel 10:
SHE WAS WORKING AT THE COSTUME SHOP. SHE REALLY LIKES STAR TREK TOO. I...I THINK I'M IN *LOVE.*

BUT WHAT ABOUT *MARCY?*

Panel 11:
GET HIM *OUTTA HEEEERE!*

GNRK!

43

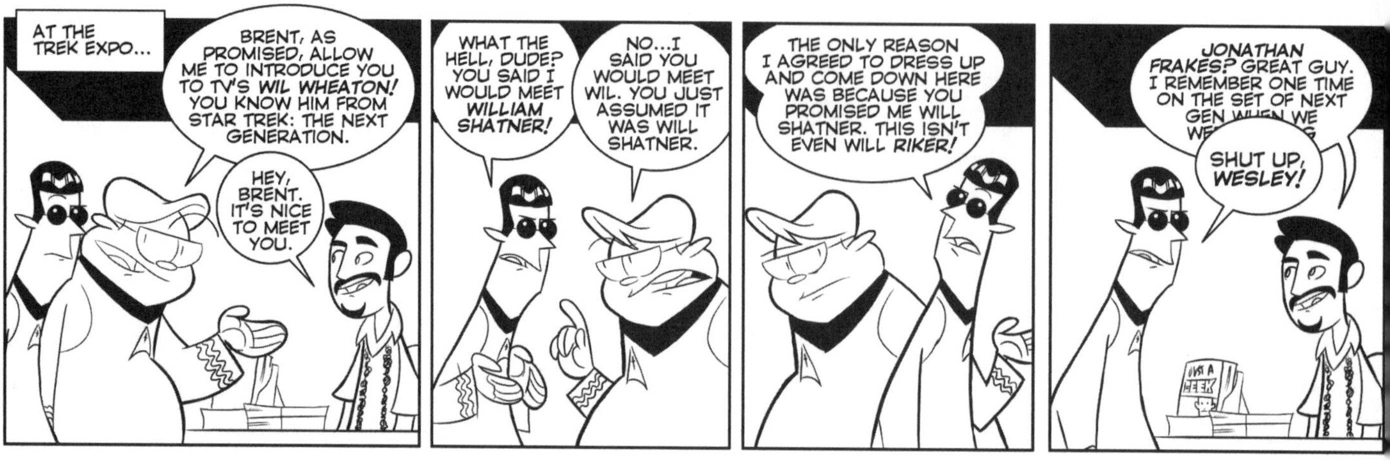
AT THE TREK EXPO...
BRENT, AS PROMISED, ALLOW ME TO INTRODUCE YOU TO TV'S **WIL WHEATON!** YOU KNOW HIM FROM STAR TREK: THE NEXT GENERATION.
HEY, BRENT. IT'S NICE TO MEET YOU.
WHAT THE HELL, DUDE? YOU SAID I WOULD MEET **WILLIAM SHATNER!**
NO...I SAID YOU WOULD MEET WIL. YOU JUST ASSUMED IT WAS WILL SHATNER.
THE ONLY REASON I AGREED TO DRESS UP AND COME DOWN HERE WAS BECAUSE YOU PROMISED ME WILL SHATNER. THIS ISN'T EVEN WILL *RIKER!*
JONATHAN FRAKES? GREAT GUY. I REMEMBER ONE TIME ON THE SET OF NEXT GEN WHEN WE
SHUT UP, **WESLEY!**

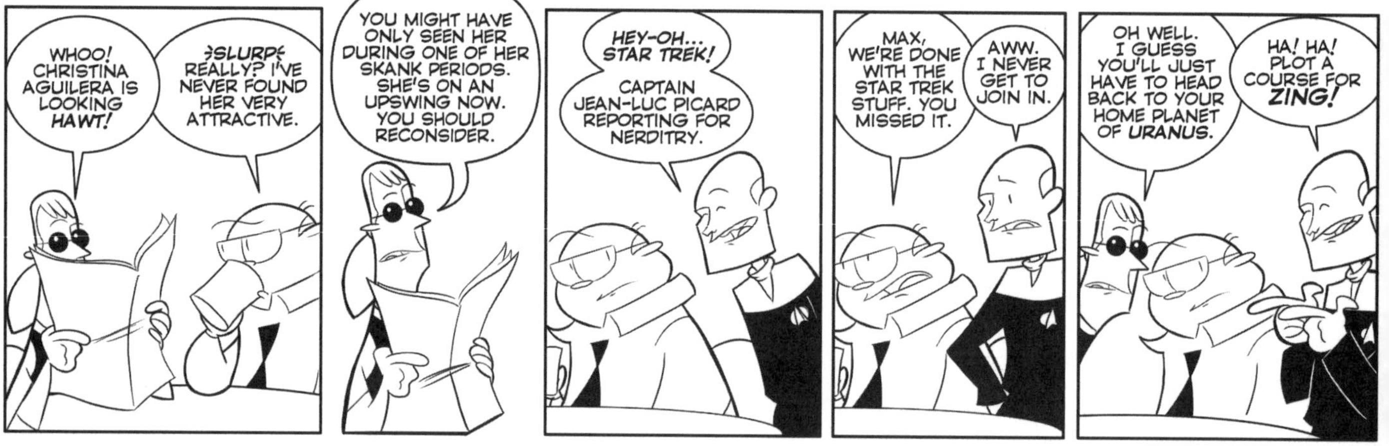
WHOO! CHRISTINA AGUILERA IS LOOKING *HAWT!*
≯SLURP≮ REALLY? I'VE NEVER FOUND HER VERY ATTRACTIVE.
YOU MIGHT HAVE ONLY SEEN HER DURING ONE OF HER SKANK PERIODS. SHE'S ON AN UPSWING NOW. YOU SHOULD RECONSIDER.
HEY-OH... STAR TREK!
CAPTAIN JEAN-LUC PICARD REPORTING FOR NERDITRY.
MAX, WE'RE DONE WITH THE STAR TREK STUFF. YOU MISSED IT.
AWW. I NEVER GET TO JOIN IN.
OH WELL. I GUESS YOU'LL JUST HAVE TO HEAD BACK TO YOUR HOME PLANET OF **URANUS.**
HA! HA! PLOT A COURSE FOR ***ZING!***

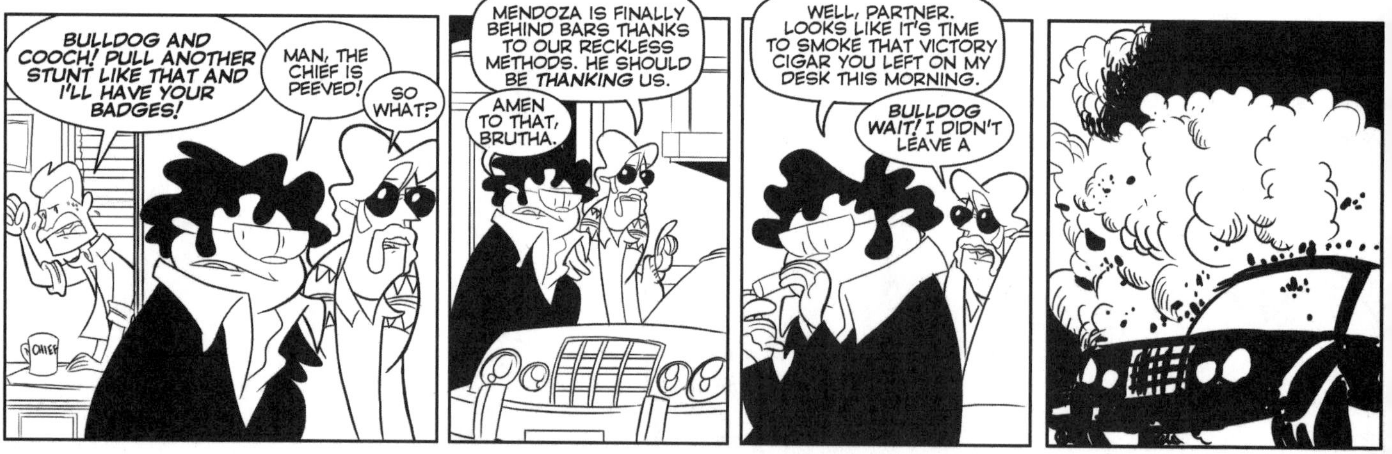
BULLDOG AND COOCH! PULL ANOTHER STUNT LIKE THAT AND I'LL HAVE YOUR BADGES!
MAN, THE CHIEF IS PEEVED!
SO WHAT?
CHIEF
MENDOZA IS FINALLY BEHIND BARS THANKS TO OUR RECKLESS METHODS. HE SHOULD BE ***THANKING*** US.
AMEN TO THAT, BRUTHA.
WELL, PARTNER. LOOKS LIKE IT'S TIME TO SMOKE THAT VICTORY CIGAR YOU LEFT ON MY DESK THIS MORNING.
BULLDOG WAIT! I DIDN'T LEAVE A

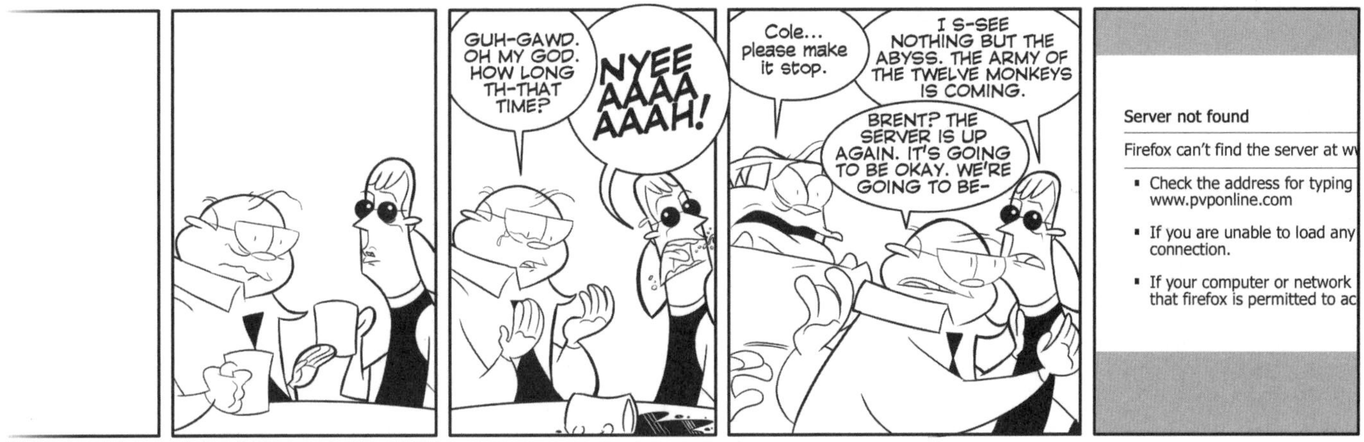
GUH-GAWD. OH MY GOD. HOW LONG TH-THAT TIME?
NYEE AAAA AAAH!
Cole... please make it stop.
I S-SEE NOTHING BUT THE ABYSS. THE ARMY OF THE TWELVE MONKEYS IS COMING.
BRENT? THE SERVER IS UP AGAIN. IT'S GOING TO BE OKAY. WE'RE GOING TO BE-
Server not found
Firefox can't find the server at w
Check the address for typing
www.pvponline.com
If you are unable to load any
connection.
If your computer or network
that firefox is permitted to ac

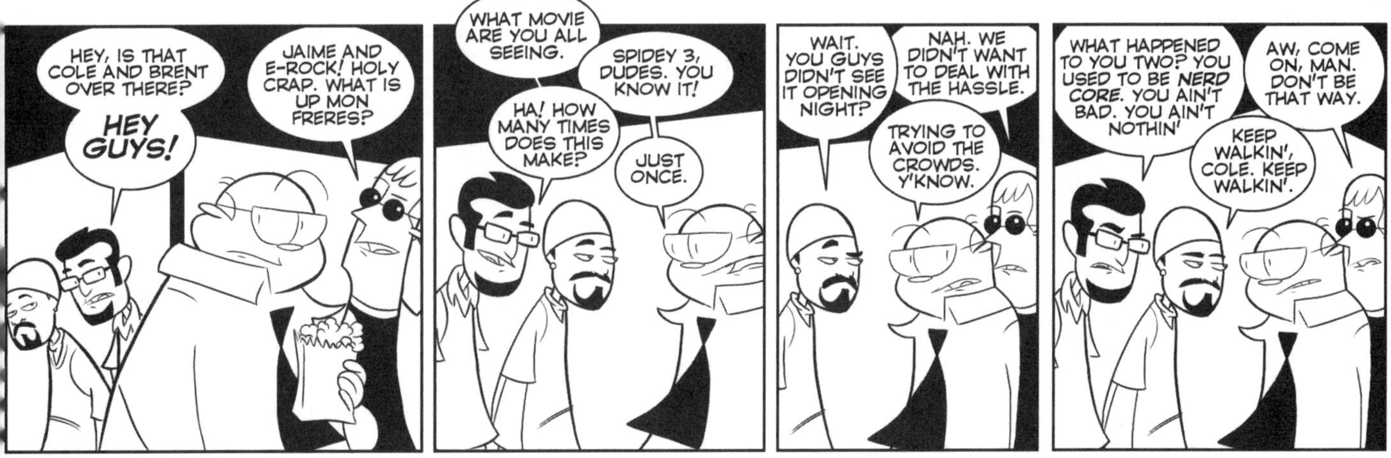
HEY, IS THAT COLE AND BRENT OVER THERE?
HEY GUYS!
JAIME AND E-ROCK! HOLY CRAP. WHAT IS UP MON FRERES?
WHAT MOVIE ARE YOU ALL SEEING.
SPIDEY 3, DUDES. YOU KNOW IT!
HA! HOW MANY TIMES DOES THIS MAKE?
JUST ONCE.
WAIT. YOU GUYS DIDN'T SEE IT OPENING NIGHT?
NAH. WE DIDN'T WANT TO DEAL WITH THE HASSLE.
TRYING TO AVOID THE CROWDS. Y'KNOW.
WHAT HAPPENED TO YOU TWO? YOU USED TO BE NERD CORE. YOU AIN'T BAD. YOU AIN'T NOTHIN'
AW, COME ON, MAN. DON'T BE THAT WAY.
KEEP WALKIN', COLE. KEEP WALKIN'.

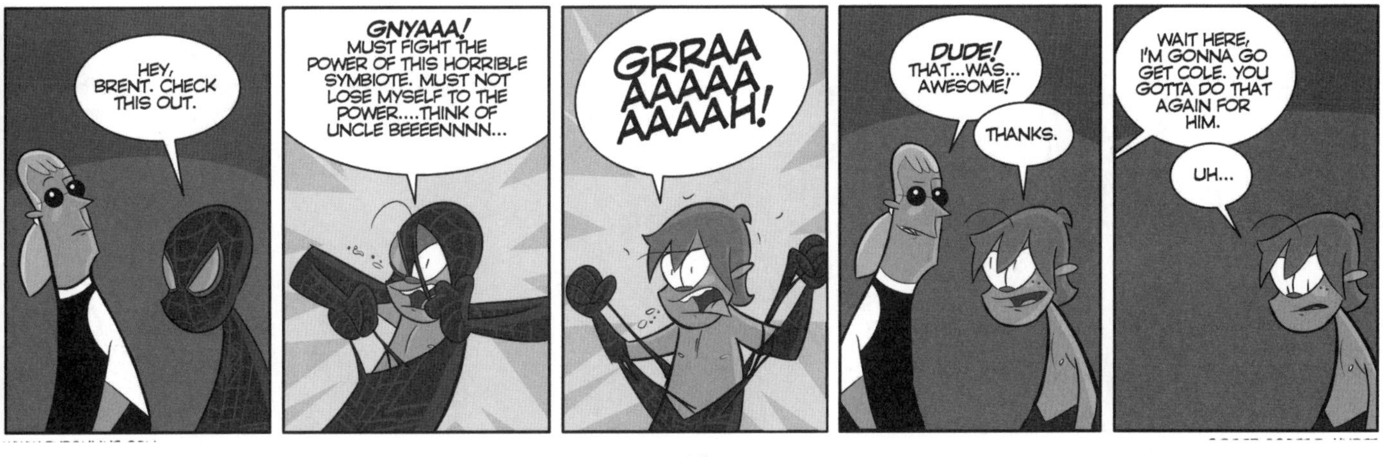
HEY, BRENT. CHECK THIS OUT.
GNYAAA! MUST FIGHT THE POWER OF THIS HORRIBLE SYMBIOTE. MUST NOT LOSE MYSELF TO THE POWER....THINK OF UNCLE BEEEENNNN...
GRRAA AAAAA AAAAH!
DUDE! THAT...WAS... AWESOME!
THANKS.
WAIT HERE, I'M GONNA GO GET COLE. YOU GOTTA DO THAT AGAIN FOR HIM.
UH...

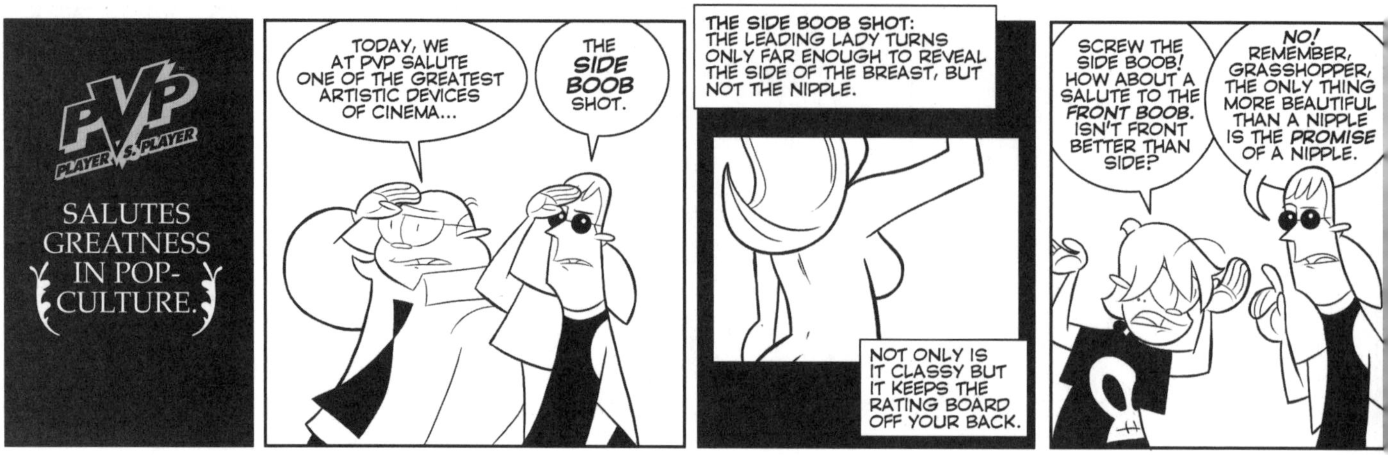
PVP PLAYER VS. PLAYER
SALUTES GREATNESS IN POP-CULTURE.
TODAY, WE AT PVP SALUTE ONE OF THE GREATEST ARTISTIC DEVICES OF CINEMA...
THE SIDE BOOB SHOT.
THE SIDE BOOB SHOT: THE LEADING LADY TURNS ONLY FAR ENOUGH TO REVEAL THE SIDE OF THE BREAST, BUT NOT THE NIPPLE.
NOT ONLY IS IT CLASSY BUT IT KEEPS THE RATING BOARD OFF YOUR BACK.
SCREW THE SIDE BOOB! HOW ABOUT A SALUTE TO THE FRONT BOOB. ISN'T FRONT BETTER THAN SIDE?
NO! REMEMBER, GRASSHOPPER, THE ONLY THING MORE BEAUTIFUL THAN A NIPPLE IS THE PROMISE OF A NIPPLE.

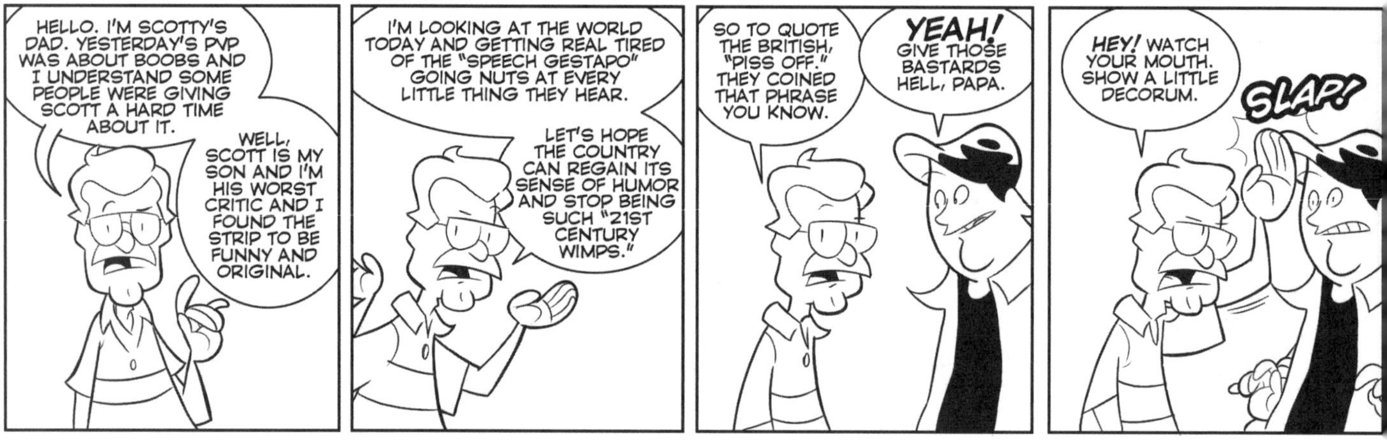
HELLO. I'M SCOTTY'S DAD. YESTERDAY'S PVP WAS ABOUT BOOBS AND I UNDERSTAND SOME PEOPLE WERE GIVING SCOTT A HARD TIME ABOUT IT.
WELL, SCOTT IS MY SON AND I'M HIS WORST CRITIC AND I FOUND THE STRIP TO BE FUNNY AND ORIGINAL.
I'M LOOKING AT THE WORLD TODAY AND GETTING REAL TIRED OF THE "SPEECH GESTAPO" GOING NUTS AT EVERY LITTLE THING THEY HEAR.
LET'S HOPE THE COUNTRY CAN REGAIN ITS SENSE OF HUMOR AND STOP BEING SUCH "21ST CENTURY WIMPS."
SO TO QUOTE THE BRITISH, "PISS OFF." THEY COINED THAT PHRASE YOU KNOW.
YEAH! GIVE THOSE BASTARDS HELL, PAPA.
HEY! WATCH YOUR MOUTH. SHOW A LITTLE DECORUM.
SLAP!

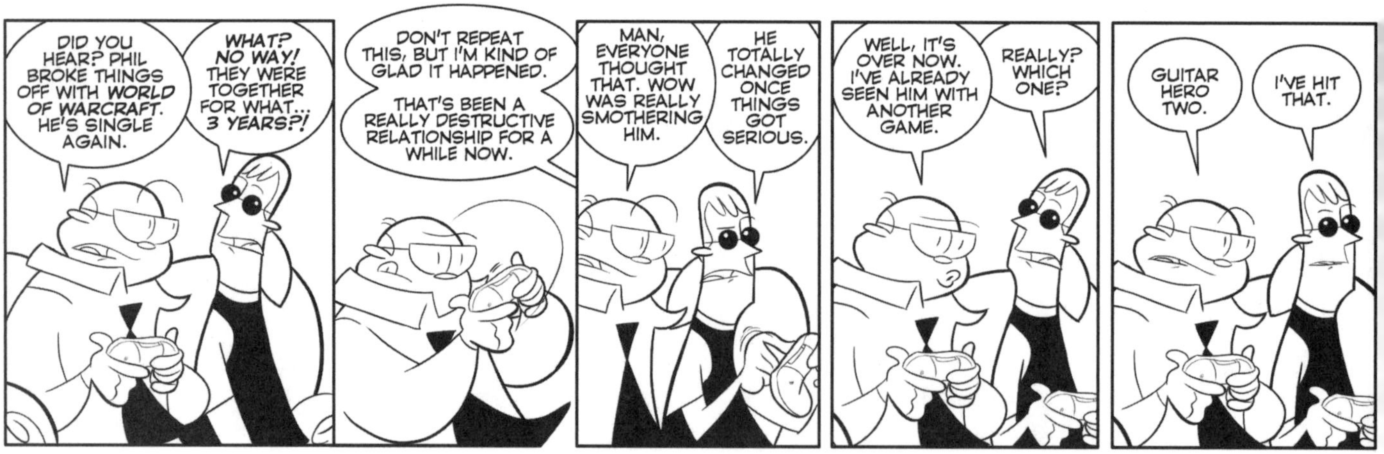
DID YOU HEAR? PHIL BROKE THINGS OFF WITH WORLD OF WARCRAFT. HE'S SINGLE AGAIN.
WHAT? NO WAY! THEY WERE TOGETHER FOR WHAT... 3 YEARS?!
DON'T REPEAT THIS, BUT I'M KIND OF GLAD IT HAPPENED.
THAT'S BEEN A REALLY DESTRUCTIVE RELATIONSHIP FOR A WHILE NOW.
MAN, EVERYONE THOUGHT THAT. WOW WAS REALLY SMOTHERING HIM.
HE TOTALLY CHANGED ONCE THINGS GOT SERIOUS.
WELL, IT'S OVER NOW. I'VE ALREADY SEEN HIM WITH ANOTHER GAME.
REALLY? WHICH ONE?
GUITAR HERO TWO.
I'VE HIT THAT.

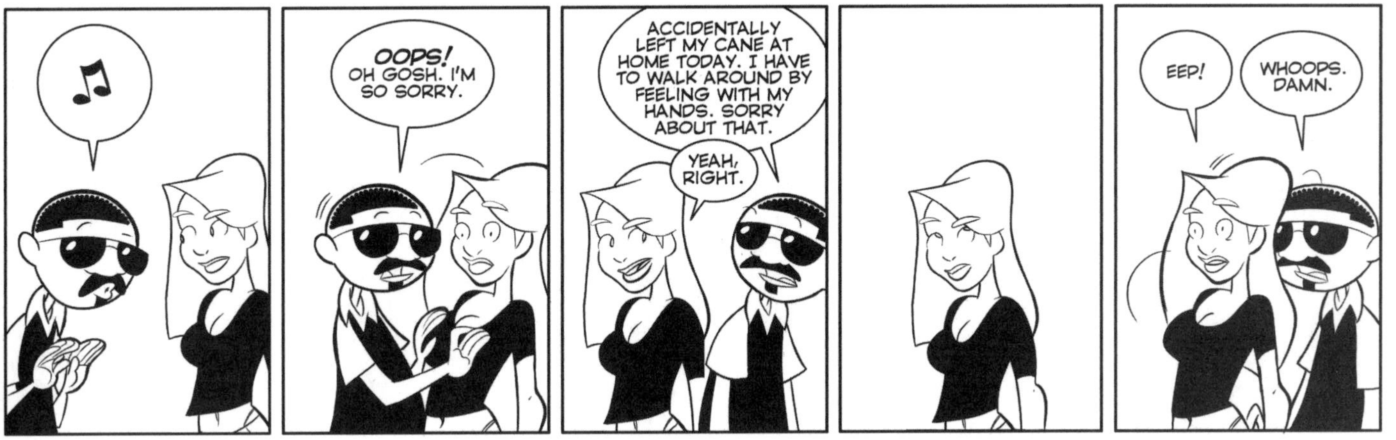
♫
OOPS! OH GOSH. I'M SO SORRY.
ACCIDENTALLY LEFT MY CANE AT HOME TODAY. I HAVE TO WALK AROUND BY FEELING WITH MY HANDS. SORRY ABOUT THAT.
YEAH, RIGHT.
EEP!
WHOOPS. DAMN.

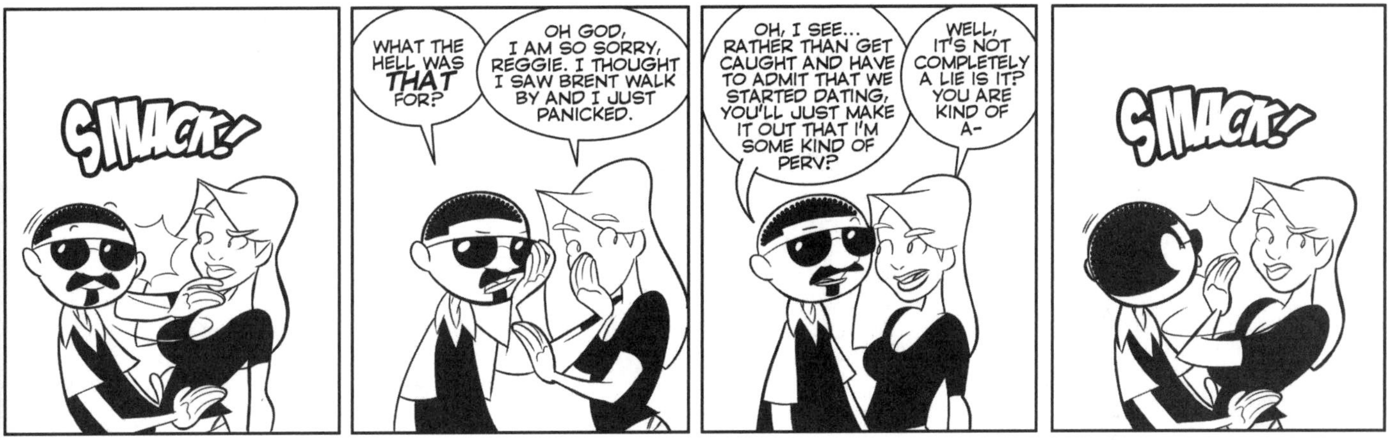
SMACK!
WHAT THE HELL WAS THAT FOR?
OH GOD, I AM SO SORRY, REGGIE. I THOUGHT I SAW BRENT WALK BY AND I JUST PANICKED.
OH, I SEE... RATHER THAN GET CAUGHT AND HAVE TO ADMIT THAT WE STARTED DATING, YOU'LL JUST MAKE IT OUT THAT I'M SOME KIND OF PERV?
WELL, IT'S NOT COMPLETELY A LIE IS IT? YOU ARE KIND OF A-
SMACK!

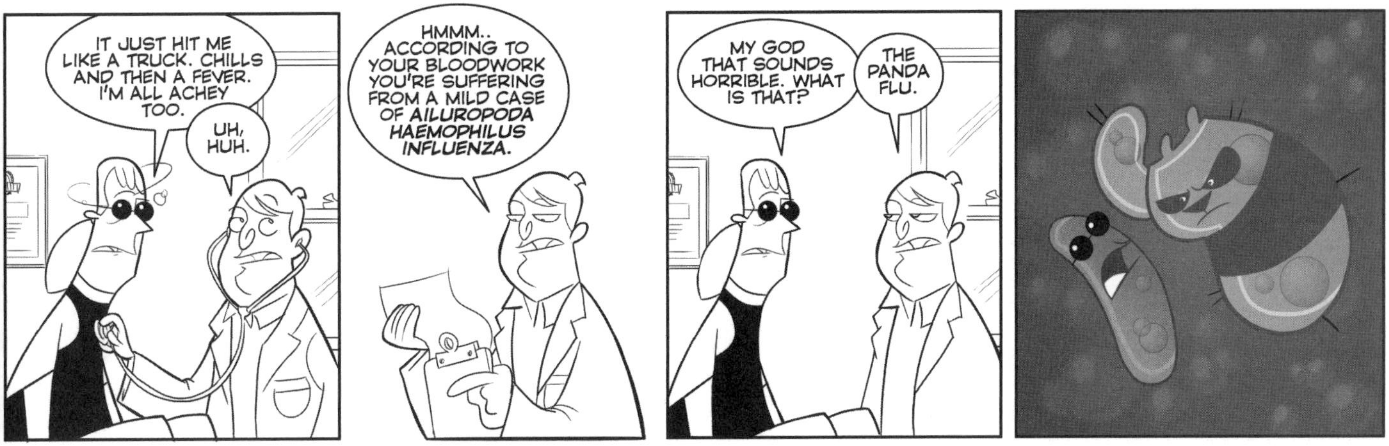
IT JUST HIT ME LIKE A TRUCK. CHILLS AND THEN A FEVER. I'M ALL ACHEY TOO.
UH, HUH.
HMMM.. ACCORDING TO YOUR BLOODWORK YOU'RE SUFFERING FROM A MILD CASE OF AILUROPODA HAEMOPHILUS INFLUENZA.
MY GOD THAT SOUNDS HORRIBLE. WHAT IS THAT?
THE PANDA FLU.

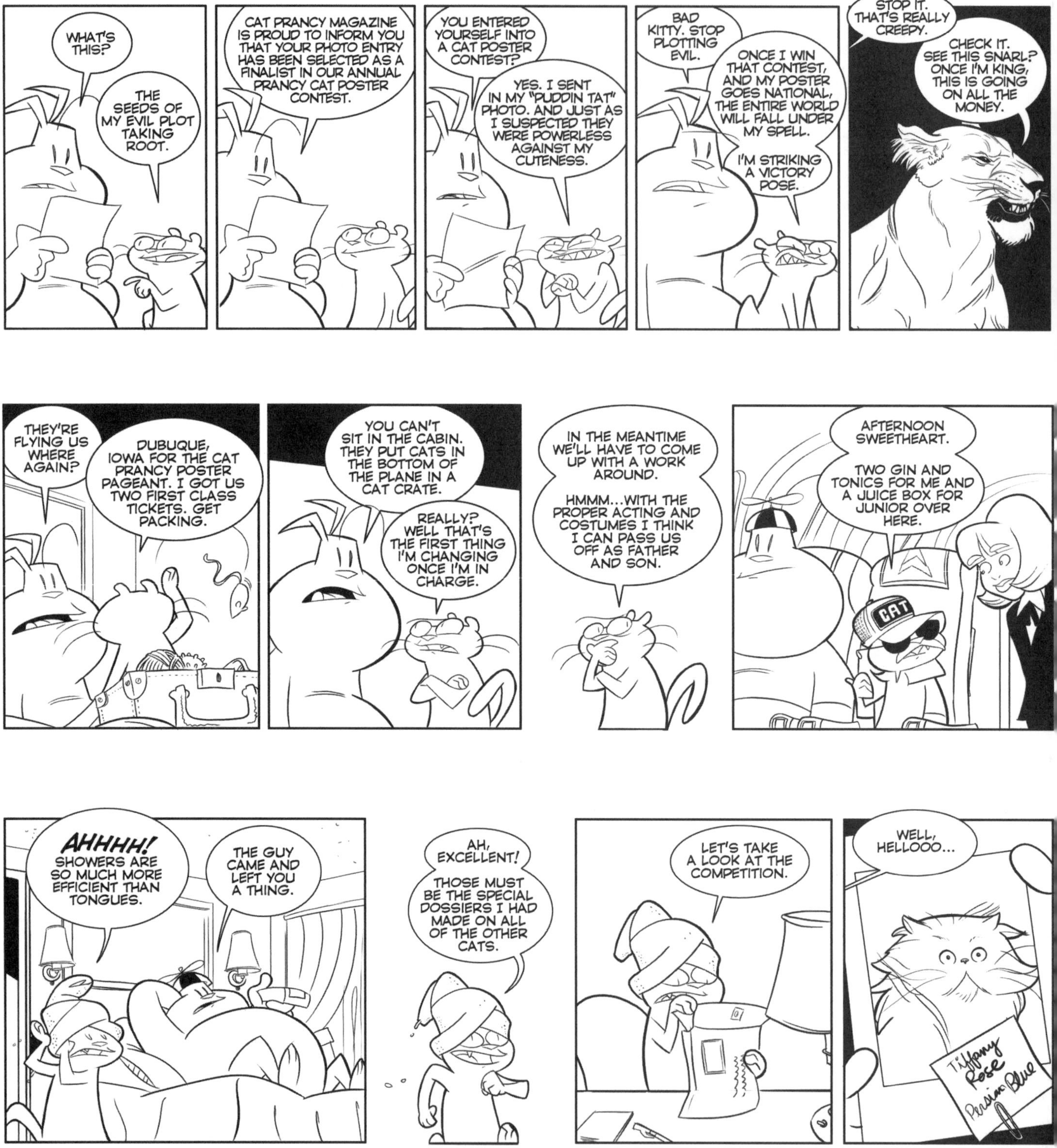
WHAT'S THIS?
THE SEEDS OF MY EVIL PLOT TAKING ROOT.
CAT PRANCY MAGAZINE IS PROUD TO INFORM YOU THAT YOUR PHOTO ENTRY HAS BEEN SELECTED AS A FINALIST IN OUR ANNUAL PRANCY CAT POSTER CONTEST.
YOU ENTERED YOURSELF INTO A CAT POSTER CONTEST?
YES. I SENT IN MY "PUDDIN TAT" PHOTO. AND JUST AS I SUSPECTED THEY WERE POWERLESS AGAINST MY CUTENESS.
BAD KITTY. STOP PLOTTING EVIL.
ONCE I WIN THAT CONTEST, AND MY POSTER GOES NATIONAL, THE ENTIRE WORLD WILL FALL UNDER MY SPELL.
I'M STRIKING A VICTORY POSE.
STOP IT. THAT'S REALLY CREEPY.
CHECK IT. SEE THIS SNARL? ONCE I'M KING, THIS IS GOING ON ALL THE MONEY.
THEY'RE FLYING US WHERE AGAIN?
DUBUQUE, IOWA FOR THE CAT PRANCY POSTER PAGEANT. I GOT US TWO FIRST CLASS TICKETS. GET PACKING.
YOU CAN'T SIT IN THE CABIN. THEY PUT CATS IN THE BOTTOM OF THE PLANE IN A CAT CRATE.
REALLY? WELL THAT'S THE FIRST THING I'M CHANGING ONCE I'M IN CHARGE.
IN THE MEANTIME WE'LL HAVE TO COME UP WITH A WORK AROUND.
HMMM...WITH THE PROPER ACTING AND COSTUMES I THINK I CAN PASS US OFF AS FATHER AND SON.
AFTERNOON SWEETHEART.
TWO GIN AND TONICS FOR ME AND A JUICE BOX FOR JUNIOR OVER HERE.
CAT
AHHHH! SHOWERS ARE SO MUCH MORE EFFICIENT THAN TONGUES.
THE GUY CAME AND LEFT YOU A THING.
AH, EXCELLENT!
THOSE MUST BE THE SPECIAL DOSSIERS I HAD MADE ON ALL OF THE OTHER CATS.
LET'S TAKE A LOOK AT THE COMPETITION.
WELL, HELLOOO...
Tiffany Rose
Persian Blue

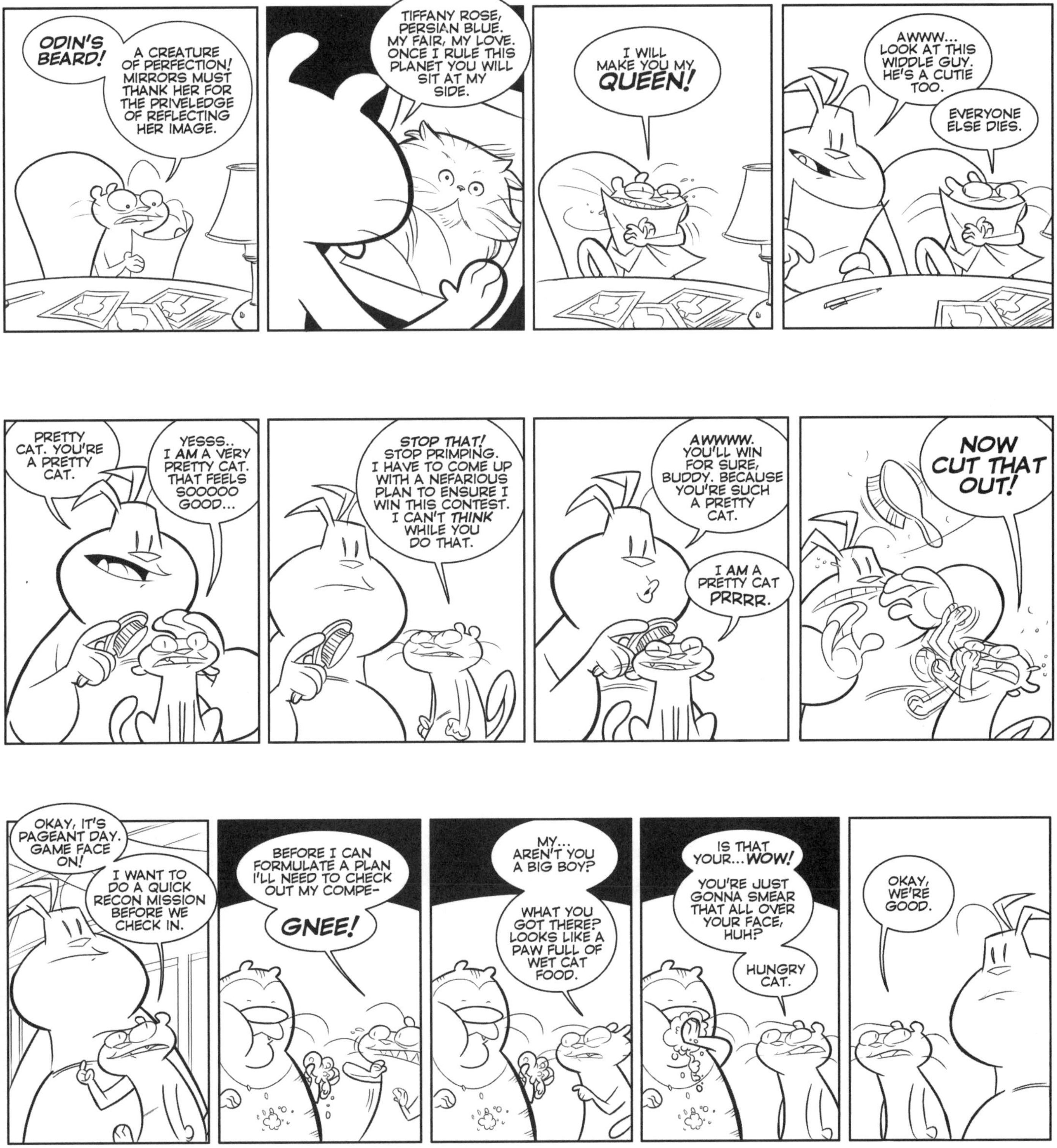
ODIN'S BEARD!
A CREATURE OF PERFECTION! MIRRORS MUST THANK HER FOR THE PRIVELEDGE OF REFLECTING HER IMAGE.
TIFFANY ROSE, PERSIAN BLUE. MY FAIR, MY LOVE. ONCE I RULE THIS PLANET YOU WILL SIT AT MY SIDE.
I WILL MAKE YOU MY QUEEN!
AWWW... LOOK AT THIS WIDDLE GUY. HE'S A CUTIE TOO.
EVERYONE ELSE DIES.
PRETTY CAT. YOU'RE A PRETTY CAT.
YESSS.. I AM A VERY PRETTY CAT. THAT FEELS SOOOOO GOOD...
STOP THAT! STOP PRIMPING. I HAVE TO COME UP WITH A NEFARIOUS PLAN TO ENSURE I WIN THIS CONTEST. I CAN'T THINK WHILE YOU DO THAT.
AWWWW. YOU'LL WIN FOR SURE, BUDDY. BECAUSE YOU'RE SUCH A PRETTY CAT.
I AM A PRETTY CAT PRRRR.
NOW CUT THAT OUT!
OKAY, IT'S PAGEANT DAY. GAME FACE ON!
I WANT TO DO A QUICK RECON MISSION BEFORE WE CHECK IN.
BEFORE I CAN FORMULATE A PLAN I'LL NEED TO CHECK OUT MY COMPE-
GNEE!
MY... AREN'T YOU A BIG BOY?
WHAT YOU GOT THERE? LOOKS LIKE A PAW FULL OF WET CAT FOOD.
IS THAT YOUR... WOW!
YOU'RE JUST GONNA SMEAR THAT ALL OVER YOUR FACE, HUH?
HUNGRY CAT.
OKAY, WE'RE GOOD.

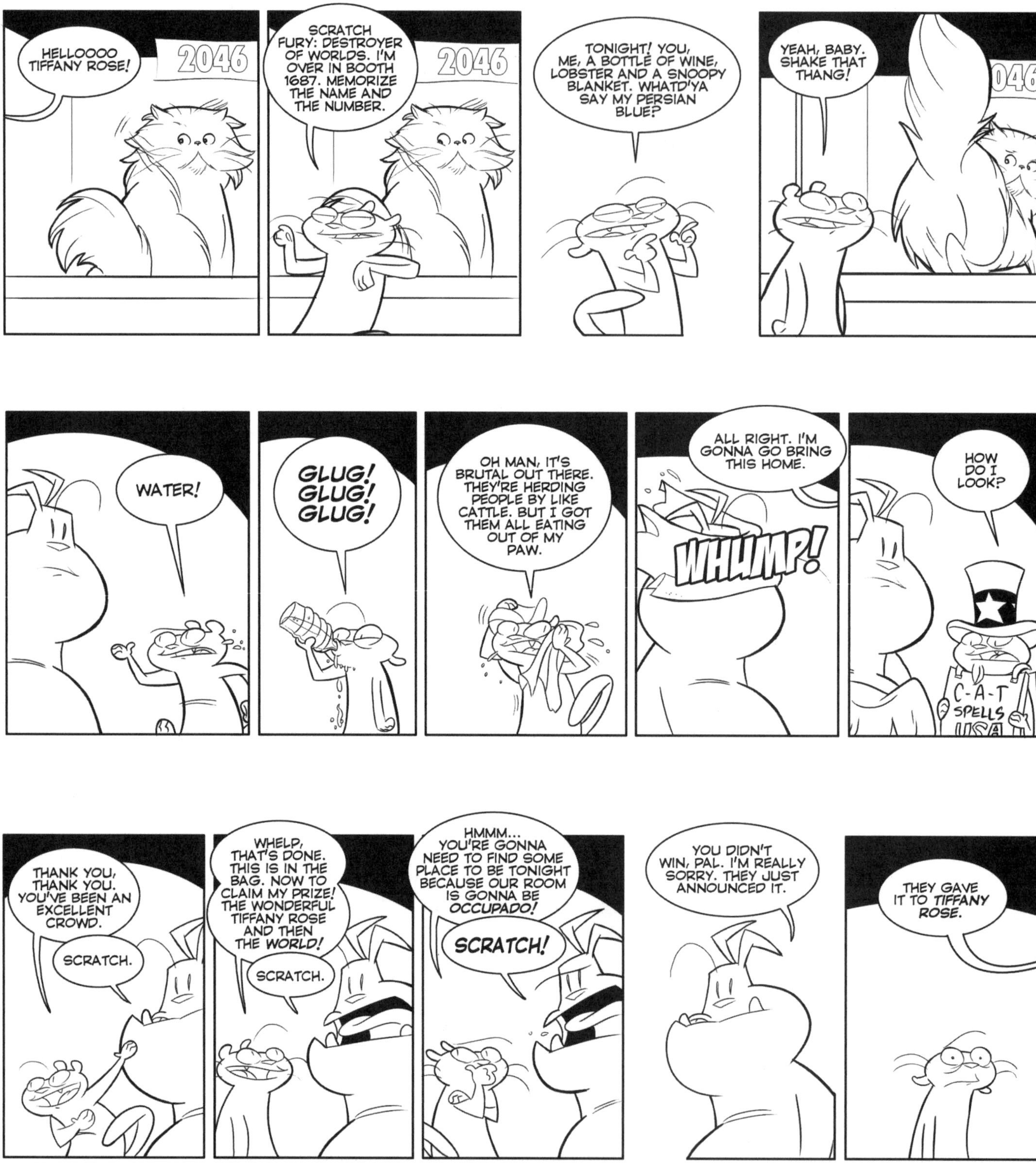
HELLOOOO TIFFANY ROSE!
2046
SCRATCH FURY: DESTROYER OF WORLDS. I'M OVER IN BOOTH 1687. MEMORIZE THE NAME AND THE NUMBER.
TONIGHT! YOU, ME, A BOTTLE OF WINE, LOBSTER AND A SNOOPY BLANKET. WHATD'YA SAY MY PERSIAN BLUE?
YEAH, BABY. SHAKE THAT THANG!
WATER!
GLUG! GLUG! GLUG!
OH MAN, IT'S BRUTAL OUT THERE. THEY'RE HERDING PEOPLE BY LIKE CATTLE. BUT I GOT THEM ALL EATING OUT OF MY PAW.
ALL RIGHT. I'M GONNA GO BRING THIS HOME.
WHUMP!
HOW DO I LOOK?
C-A-T SPELLS
THANK YOU, THANK YOU. YOU'VE BEEN AN EXCELLENT CROWD.
SCRATCH.
WHELP, THAT'S DONE. THIS IS IN THE BAG. NOW TO CLAIM MY PRIZE! THE WONDERFUL TIFFANY ROSE AND THEN THE WORLD!
SCRATCH.
HMMM... YOU'RE GONNA NEED TO FIND SOME PLACE TO BE TONIGHT BECAUSE OUR ROOM IS GONNA BE OCCUPADO!
SCRATCH!
YOU DIDN'T WIN, PAL. I'M REALLY SORRY. THEY JUST ANNOUNCED IT.
THEY GAVE IT TO TIFFANY ROSE.

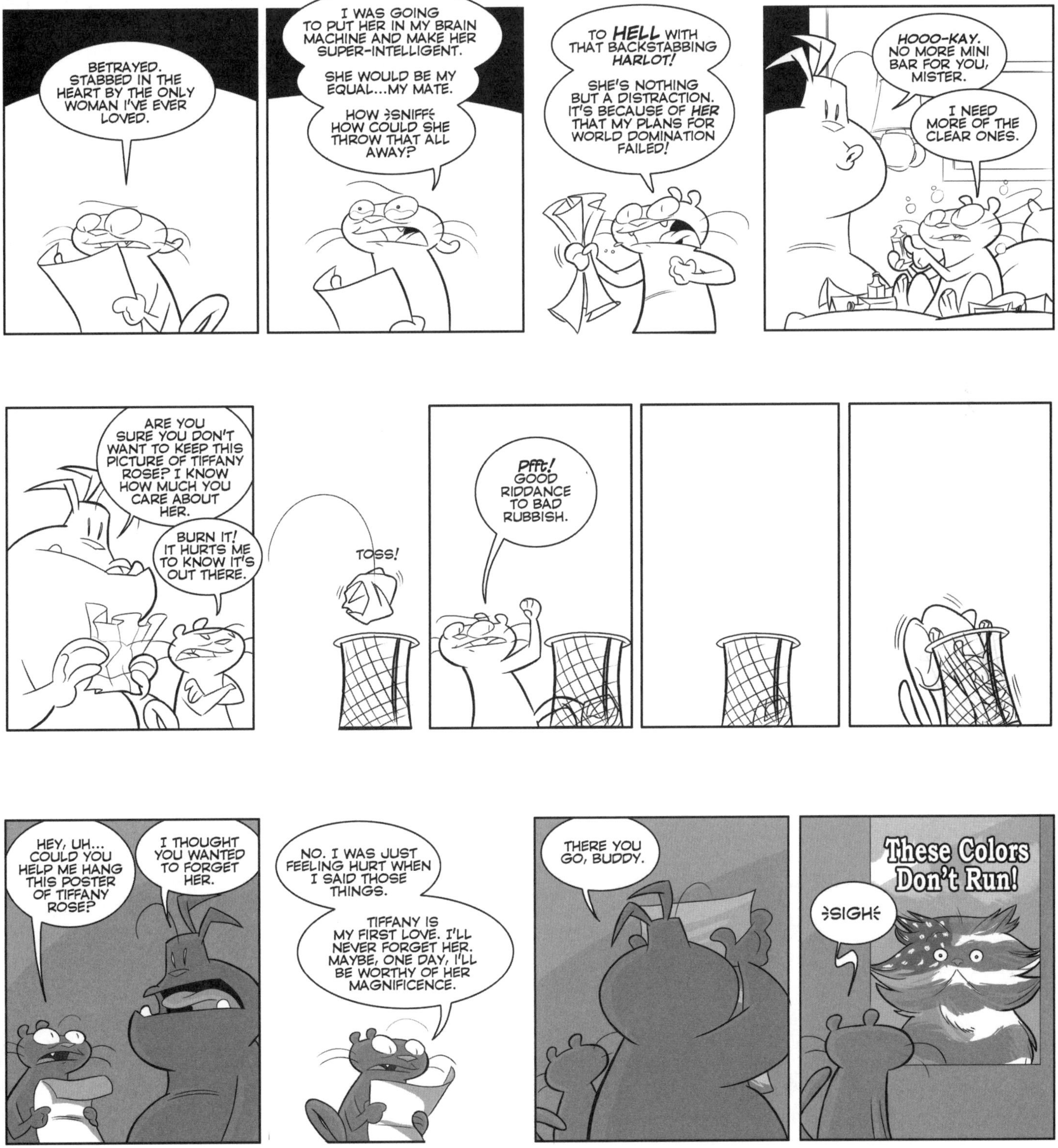
BETRAYED. STABBED IN THE HEART BY THE ONLY WOMAN I'VE EVER LOVED.
I WAS GOING TO PUT HER IN MY BRAIN MACHINE AND MAKE HER SUPER-INTELLIGENT.
SHE WOULD BE MY EQUAL...MY MATE.
HOW ⋟SNIFF⋞ HOW COULD SHE THROW THAT ALL AWAY?
TO HELL WITH THAT BACKSTABBING HARLOT!
SHE'S NOTHING BUT A DISTRACTION. IT'S BECAUSE OF HER THAT MY PLANS FOR WORLD DOMINATION FAILED!
HOOO-KAY. NO MORE MINI BAR FOR YOU, MISTER.
I NEED MORE OF THE CLEAR ONES.
ARE YOU SURE YOU DON'T WANT TO KEEP THIS PICTURE OF TIFFANY ROSE? I KNOW HOW MUCH YOU CARE ABOUT HER.
BURN IT! IT HURTS ME TO KNOW IT'S OUT THERE.
TOSS!
Pfft! GOOD RIDDANCE TO BAD RUBBISH.
HEY, UH... COULD YOU HELP ME HANG THIS POSTER OF TIFFANY ROSE?
I THOUGHT YOU WANTED TO FORGET HER.
NO. I WAS JUST FEELING HURT WHEN I SAID THOSE THINGS.
TIFFANY IS MY FIRST LOVE. I'LL NEVER FORGET HER. MAYBE, ONE DAY, I'LL BE WORTHY OF HER MAGNIFICENCE.
THERE YOU GO, BUDDY.
These Colors Don't Run!
⋟SIGH⋞

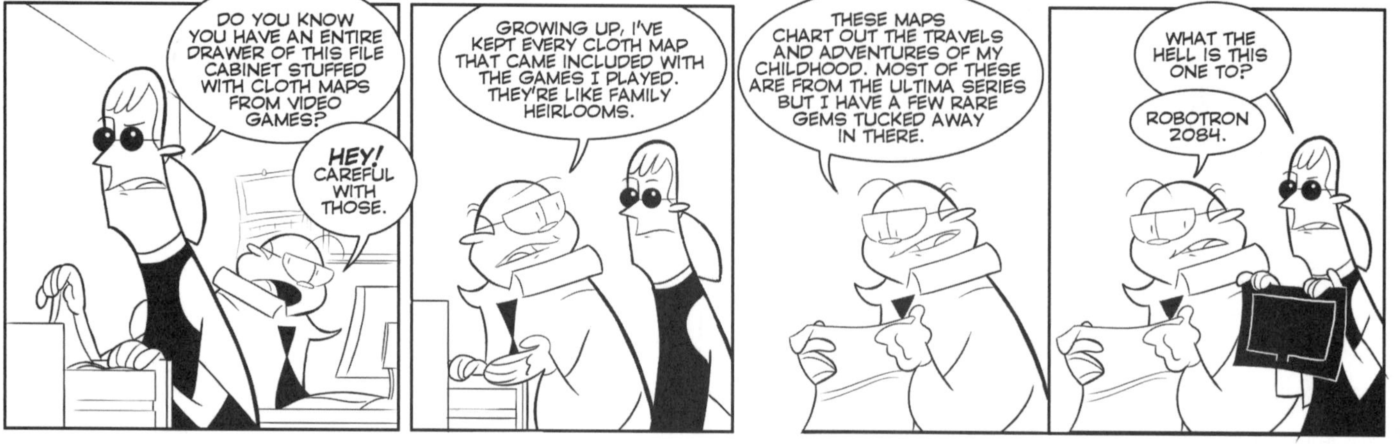
DO YOU KNOW YOU HAVE AN ENTIRE DRAWER OF THIS FILE CABINET STUFFED WITH CLOTH MAPS FROM VIDEO GAMES?
HEY! CAREFUL WITH THOSE.
GROWING UP, I'VE KEPT EVERY CLOTH MAP THAT CAME INCLUDED WITH THE GAMES I PLAYED. THEY'RE LIKE FAMILY HEIRLOOMS.
THESE MAPS CHART OUT THE TRAVELS AND ADVENTURES OF MY CHILDHOOD. MOST OF THESE ARE FROM THE ULTIMA SERIES BUT I HAVE A FEW RARE GEMS TUCKED AWAY IN THERE.
WHAT THE HELL IS THIS ONE TO?
ROBOTRON 2084.

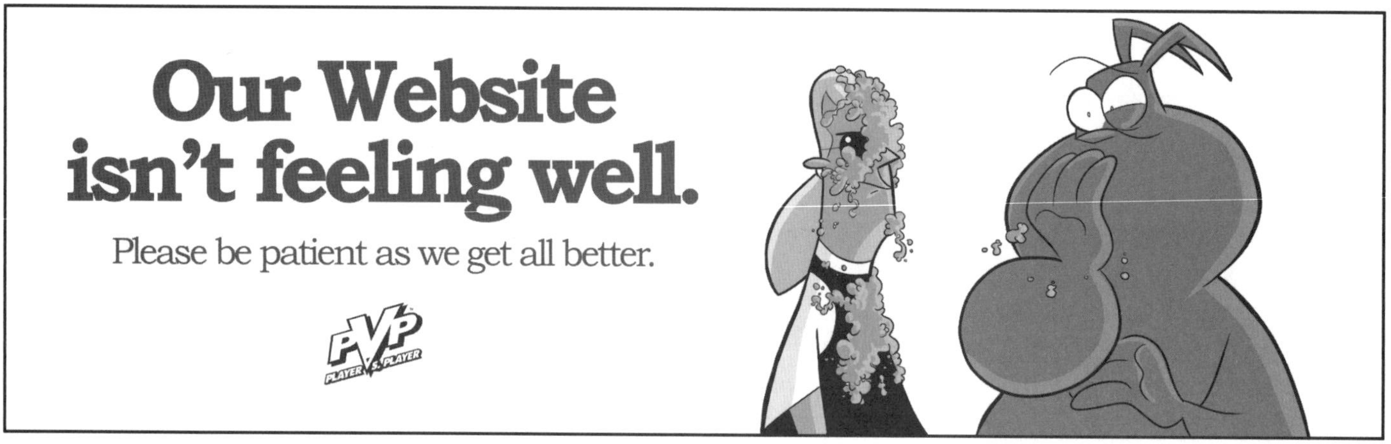
Our Website isn't feeling well.
Please be patient as we get all better.
PVP PLAYER VS. PLAYER

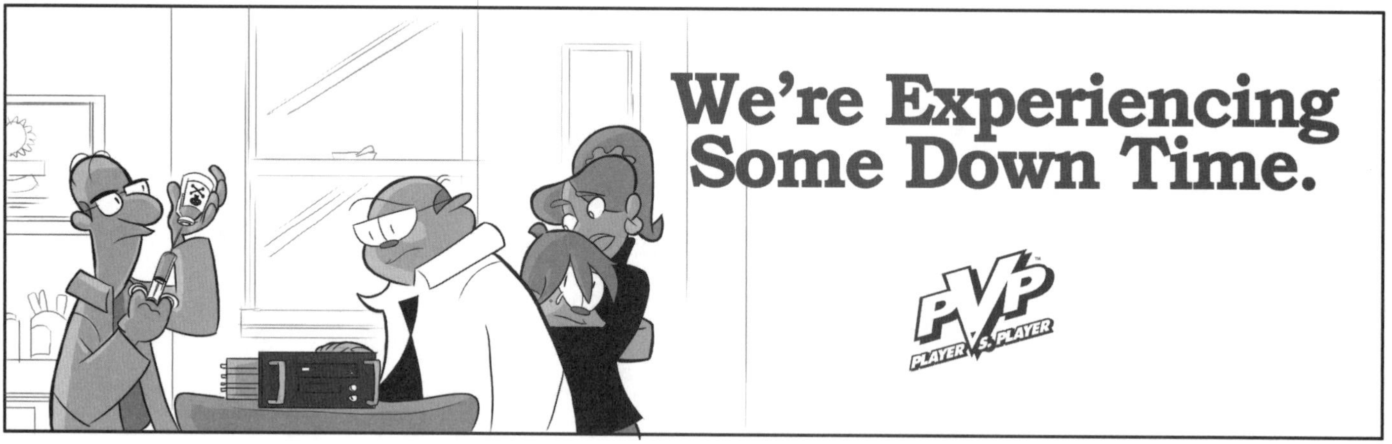
We're Experiencing Some Down Time.
PVP PLAYER VS. PLAYER

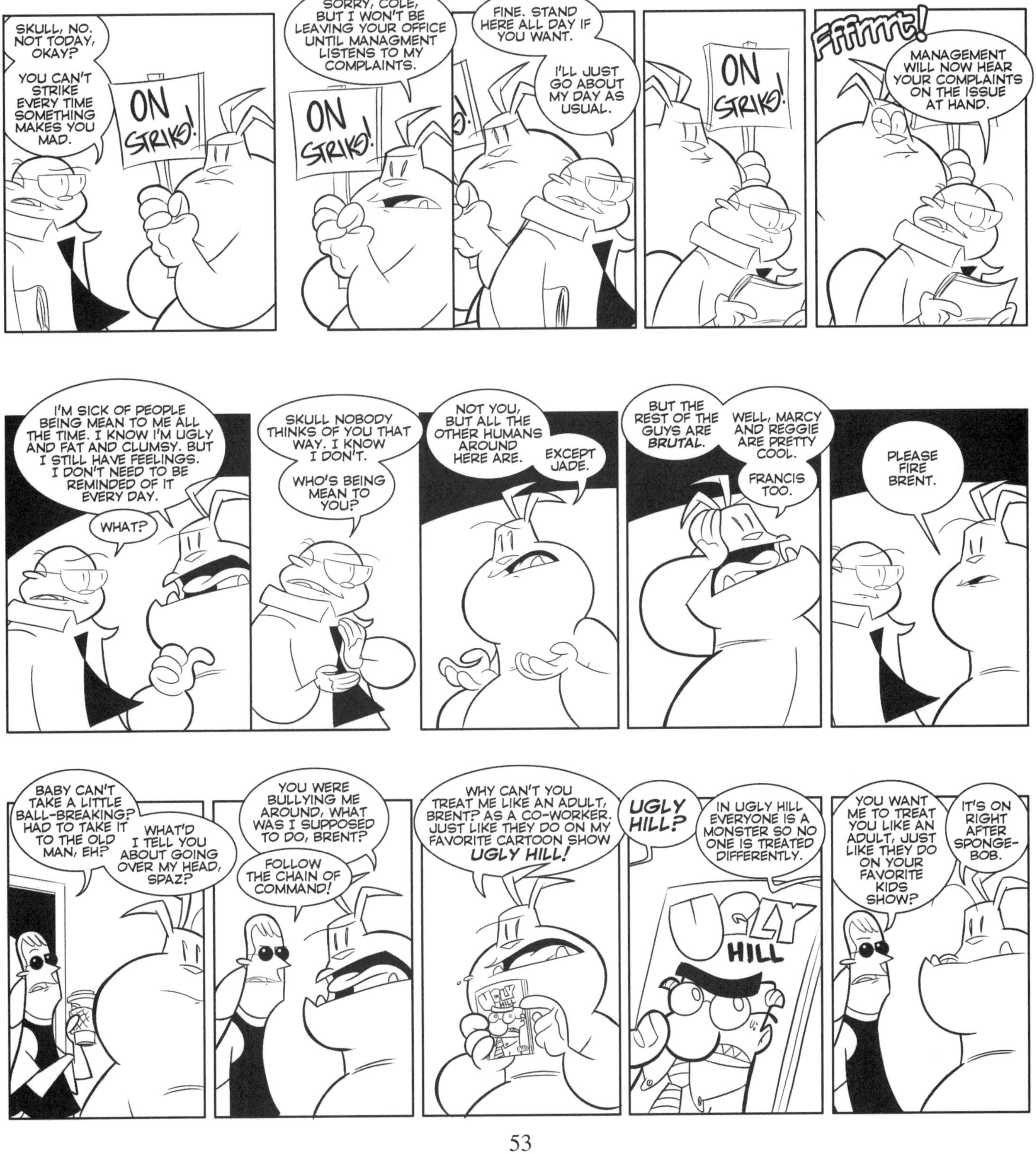
SKULL, NO. NOT TODAY, OKAY?
YOU CAN'T STRIKE EVERY TIME SOMETHING MAKES YOU MAD.
ON STRIKE!
SORRY, COLE, BUT I WON'T BE LEAVING YOUR OFFICE UNTIL MANAGMENT LISTENS TO MY COMPLAINTS.
ON STRIKE!
FINE. STAND HERE ALL DAY IF YOU WANT.
I'LL JUST GO ABOUT MY DAY AS USUAL.
ON STRIKE!
Fffrrrrt!
MANAGEMENT WILL NOW HEAR YOUR COMPLAINTS ON THE ISSUE AT HAND.
I'M SICK OF PEOPLE BEING MEAN TO ME ALL THE TIME. I KNOW I'M UGLY AND FAT AND CLUMSY. BUT I STILL HAVE FEELINGS. I DON'T NEED TO BE REMINDED OF IT EVERY DAY.
WHAT?
SKULL NOBODY THINKS OF YOU THAT WAY. I KNOW I DON'T.
WHO'S BEING MEAN TO YOU?
NOT YOU, BUT ALL THE OTHER HUMANS AROUND HERE ARE.
EXCEPT JADE.
BUT THE REST OF THE GUYS ARE BRUTAL.
WELL, MARCY AND REGGIE ARE PRETTY COOL.
FRANCIS TOO.
PLEASE FIRE BRENT.
BABY CAN'T TAKE A LITTLE BALL-BREAKING? HAD TO TAKE IT TO THE OLD MAN, EH?
WHAT'D I TELL YOU ABOUT GOING OVER MY HEAD, SPAZ?
YOU WERE BULLYING ME AROUND, WHAT WAS I SUPPOSED TO DO, BRENT?
FOLLOW THE CHAIN OF COMMAND!
WHY CAN'T YOU TREAT ME LIKE AN ADULT, BRENT? AS A CO-WORKER. JUST LIKE THEY DO ON MY FAVORITE CARTOON SHOW UGLY HILL!
UGLY HILL?
IN UGLY HILL EVERYONE IS A MONSTER SO NO ONE IS TREATED DIFFERENTLY.
UGLY HILL
YOU WANT ME TO TREAT YOU LIKE AN ADULT, JUST LIKE THEY DO ON YOUR FAVORITE KIDS SHOW?
IT'S ON RIGHT AFTER SPONGE-BOB.

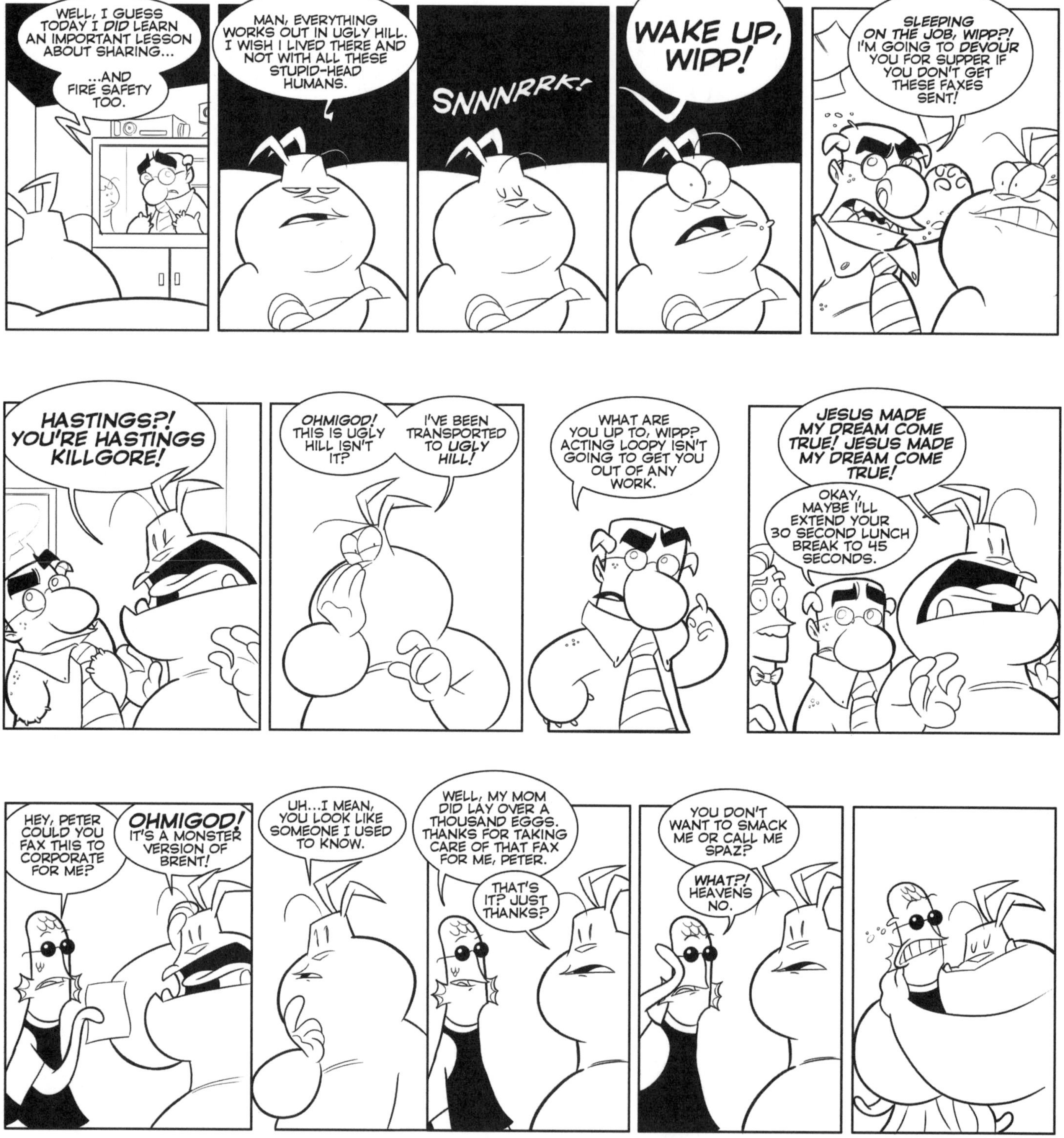

WELL, I GUESS TODAY I DID LEARN AN IMPORTANT LESSON ABOUT SHARING...
...AND FIRE SAFETY TOO.
MAN, EVERYTHING WORKS OUT IN UGLY HILL. I WISH I LIVED THERE AND NOT WITH ALL THESE STUPID-HEAD HUMANS.
SNNNRRK!
WAKE UP, WIPP!
SLEEPING ON THE JOB, WIPP?! I'M GOING TO DEVOUR YOU FOR SUPPER IF YOU DON'T GET THESE FAXES SENT!
HASTINGS?! YOU'RE HASTINGS KILLGORE!
OHMIGOD! THIS IS UGLY HILL ISN'T IT?
I'VE BEEN TRANSPORTED TO UGLY HILL!
WHAT ARE YOU UP TO, WIPP? ACTING LOOPY ISN'T GOING TO GET YOU OUT OF ANY WORK.
JESUS MADE MY DREAM COME TRUE! JESUS MADE MY DREAM COME TRUE!
OKAY, MAYBE I'LL EXTEND YOUR 30 SECOND LUNCH BREAK TO 45 SECONDS.
HEY, PETER COULD YOU FAX THIS TO CORPORATE FOR ME?
OHMIGOD! IT'S A MONSTER VERSION OF BRENT!
UH...I MEAN, YOU LOOK LIKE SOMEONE I USED TO KNOW.
WELL, MY MOM DID LAY OVER A THOUSAND EGGS. THANKS FOR TAKING CARE OF THAT FAX FOR ME, PETER.
THAT'S IT? JUST THANKS?
YOU DON'T WANT TO SMACK ME OR CALL ME SPAZ?
WHAT?! HEAVEN'S NO.

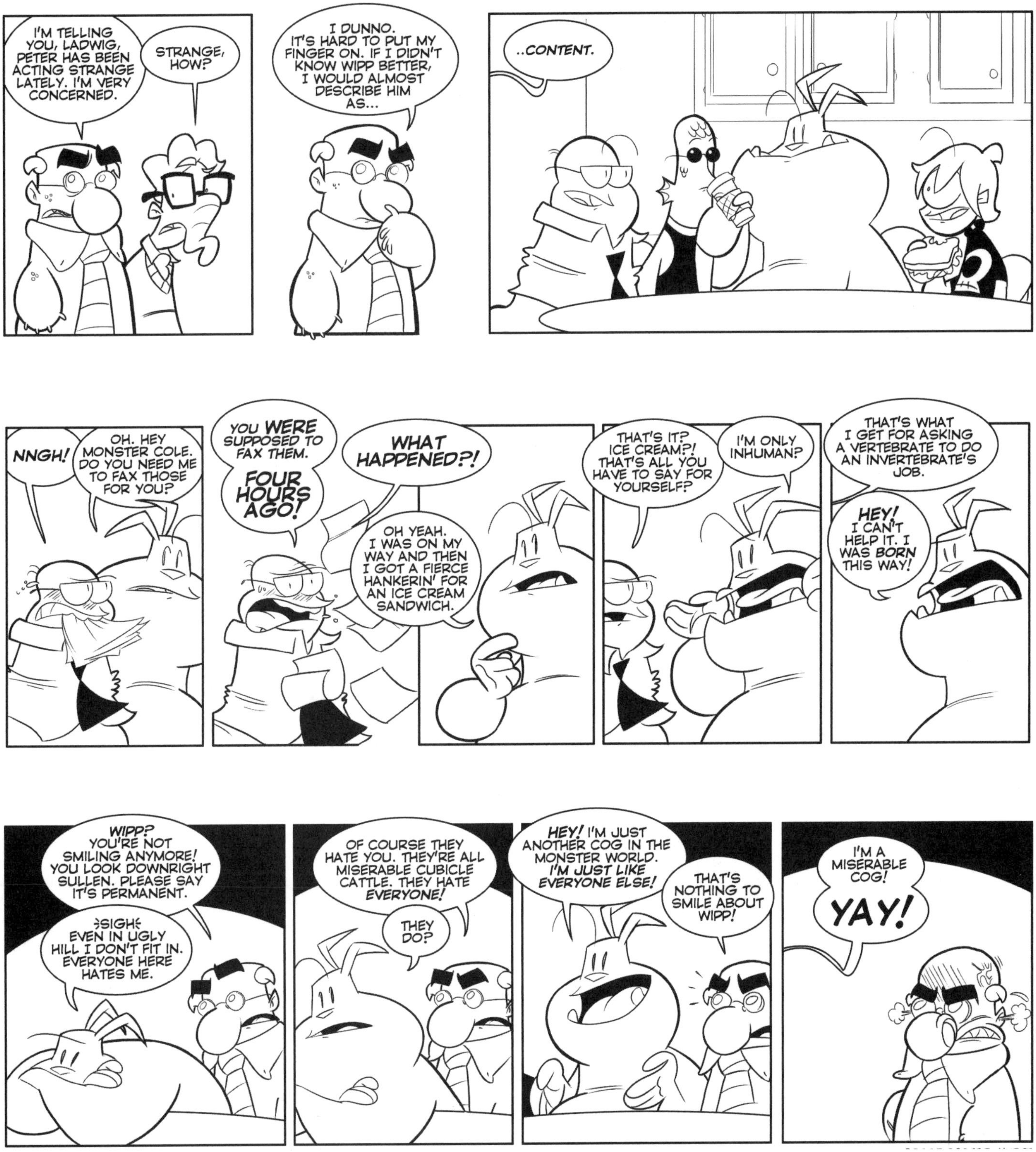
I'M TELLING YOU, LADWIG, PETER HAS BEEN ACTING STRANGE LATELY. I'M VERY CONCERNED.
STRANGE, HOW?
I DUNNO. IT'S HARD TO PUT MY FINGER ON. IF I DIDN'T KNOW WIPP BETTER, I WOULD ALMOST DESCRIBE HIM AS...
..CONTENT.
NNGH!
OH. HEY MONSTER COLE. DO YOU NEED ME TO FAX THOSE FOR YOU?
YOU WERE SUPPOSED TO FAX THEM.
FOUR HOURS AGO!
WHAT HAPPENED?!
OH YEAH. I WAS ON MY WAY AND THEN I GOT A FIERCE HANKERIN' FOR AN ICE CREAM SANDWICH.
THAT'S IT? ICE CREAM?! THAT'S ALL YOU HAVE TO SAY FOR YOURSELF?
I'M ONLY INHUMAN?
THAT'S WHAT I GET FOR ASKING A VERTEBRATE TO DO AN INVERTEBRATE'S JOB.
HEY! I CAN'T HELP IT. I WAS BORN THIS WAY!
WIPP? YOU'RE NOT SMILING ANYMORE! YOU LOOK DOWNRIGHT SULLEN. PLEASE SAY IT'S PERMANENT.
SIGH EVEN IN UGLY HILL I DON'T FIT IN. EVERYONE HERE HATES ME.
OF COURSE THEY HATE YOU. THEY'RE ALL MISERABLE CUBICLE CATTLE. THEY HATE EVERYONE!
THEY DO?
HEY! I'M JUST ANOTHER COG IN THE MONSTER WORLD. I'M JUST LIKE EVERYONE ELSE!
THAT'S NOTHING TO SMILE ABOUT WIPP!
I'M A MISERABLE COG!
YAY!

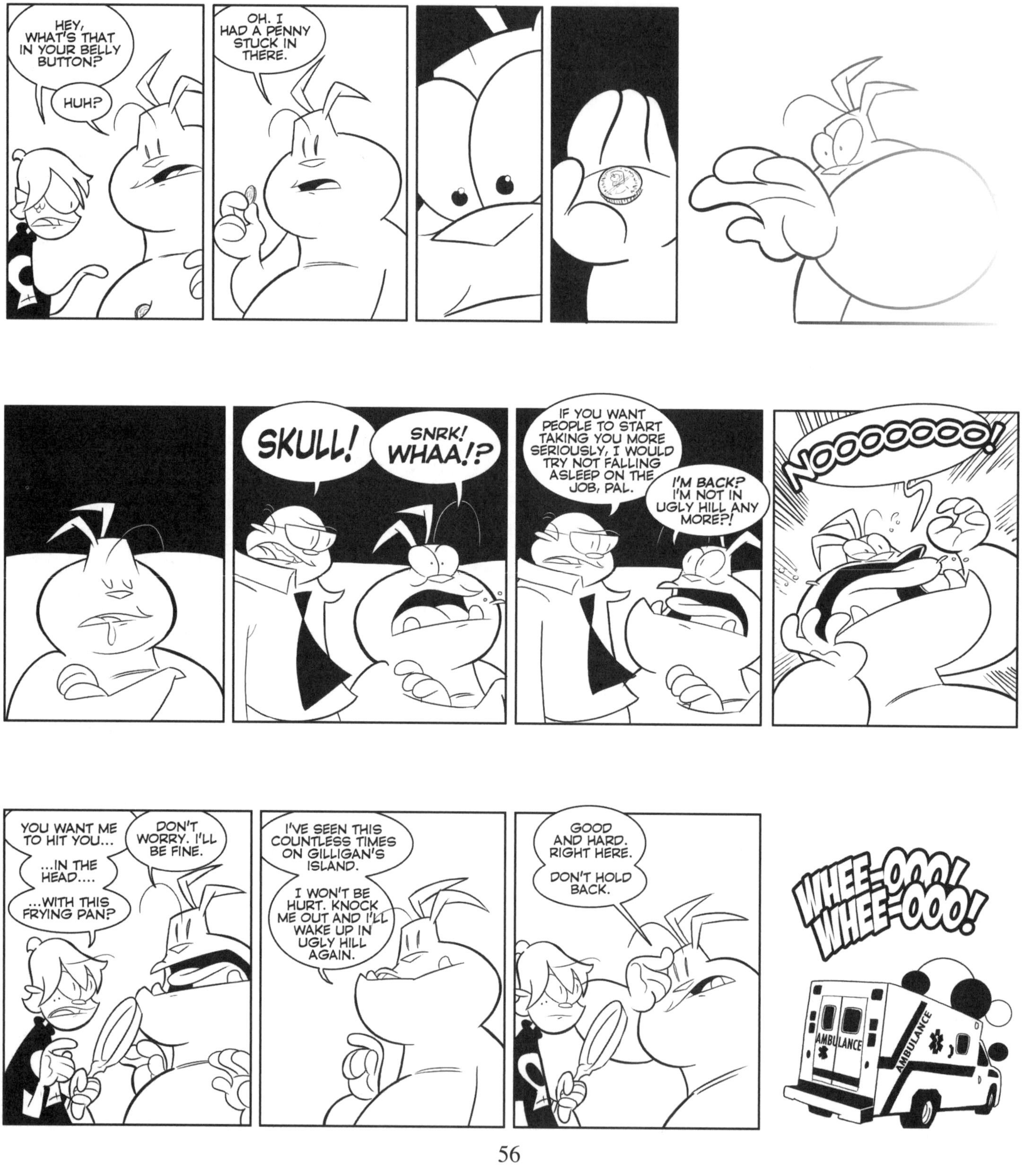
HEY, WHAT'S THAT IN YOUR BELLY BUTTON?
HUH?
OH. I HAD A PENNY STUCK IN THERE.
SKULL!
SNRK! WHAA!?
IF YOU WANT PEOPLE TO START TAKING YOU MORE SERIOUSLY, I WOULD TRY NOT FALLING ASLEEP ON THE JOB, PAL.
I'M BACK? I'M NOT IN UGLY HILL ANY MORE?!
NOOOOOOOO!
YOU WANT ME TO HIT YOU...
...IN THE HEAD....
...WITH THIS FRYING PAN?
DON'T WORRY. I'LL BE FINE.
I'VE SEEN THIS COUNTLESS TIMES ON GILLIGAN'S ISLAND.
I WON'T BE HURT. KNOCK ME OUT AND I'LL WAKE UP IN UGLY HILL AGAIN.
GOOD AND HARD. RIGHT HERE.
DON'T HOLD BACK.
WHEE-OOO! WHEE-OOO!
AMBULANCE
AMBULANCE

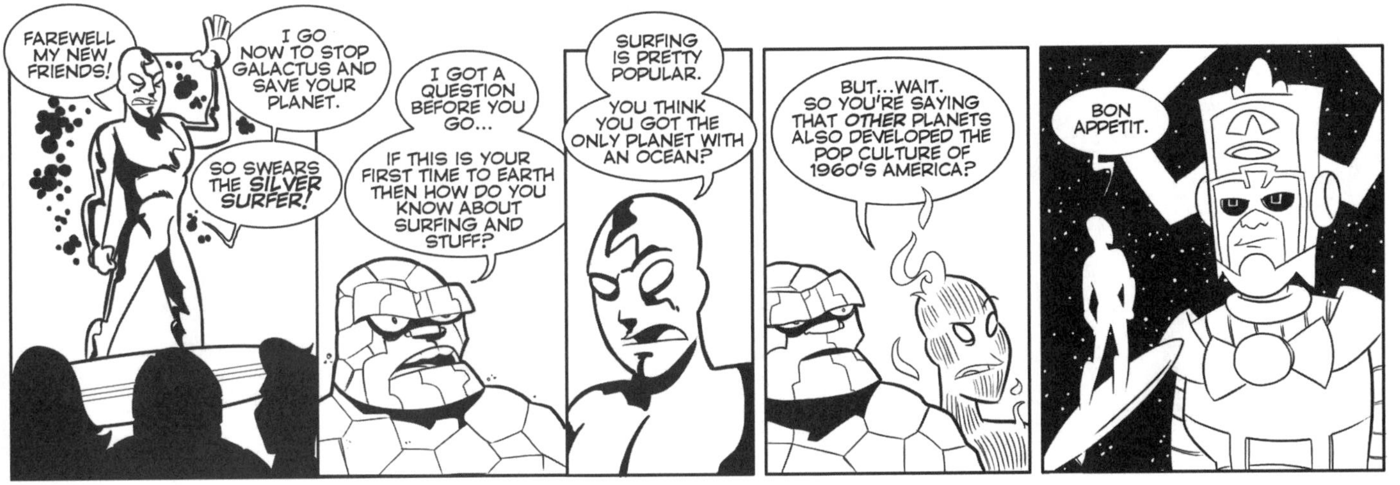
FAREWELL MY NEW FRIENDS!
I GO NOW TO STOP GALACTUS AND SAVE YOUR PLANET.
SO SWEARS THE SILVER SURFER!
I GOT A QUESTION BEFORE YOU GO...
IF THIS IS YOUR FIRST TIME TO EARTH THEN HOW DO YOU KNOW ABOUT SURFING AND STUFF?
SURFING IS PRETTY POPULAR.
YOU THINK YOU GOT THE ONLY PLANET WITH AN OCEAN?
BUT...WAIT. SO YOU'RE SAYING THAT OTHER PLANETS ALSO DEVELOPED THE POP CULTURE OF 1960'S AMERICA?
BON APPETIT.

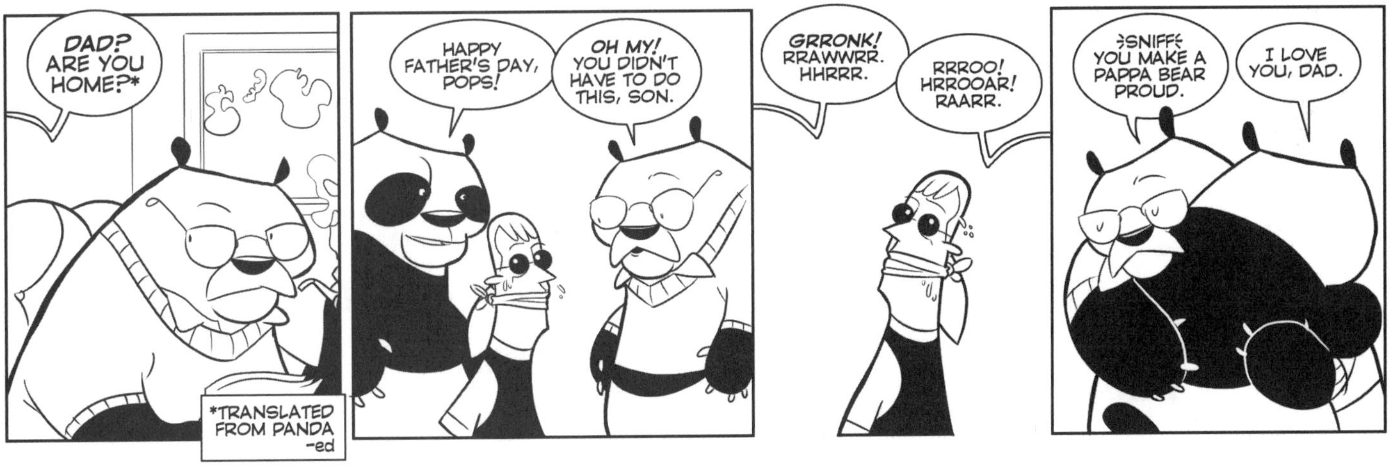
DAD? ARE YOU HOME?*
*TRANSLATED FROM PANDA -ed
HAPPY FATHER'S DAY, POPS!
OH MY! YOU DIDN'T HAVE TO DO THIS, SON.
GRRONK! RRAWWRR. HHRRR.
RRROO! HRROOAR! RAARR.
SNIFF YOU MAKE A PAPPA BEAR PROUD.
I LOVE YOU, DAD.

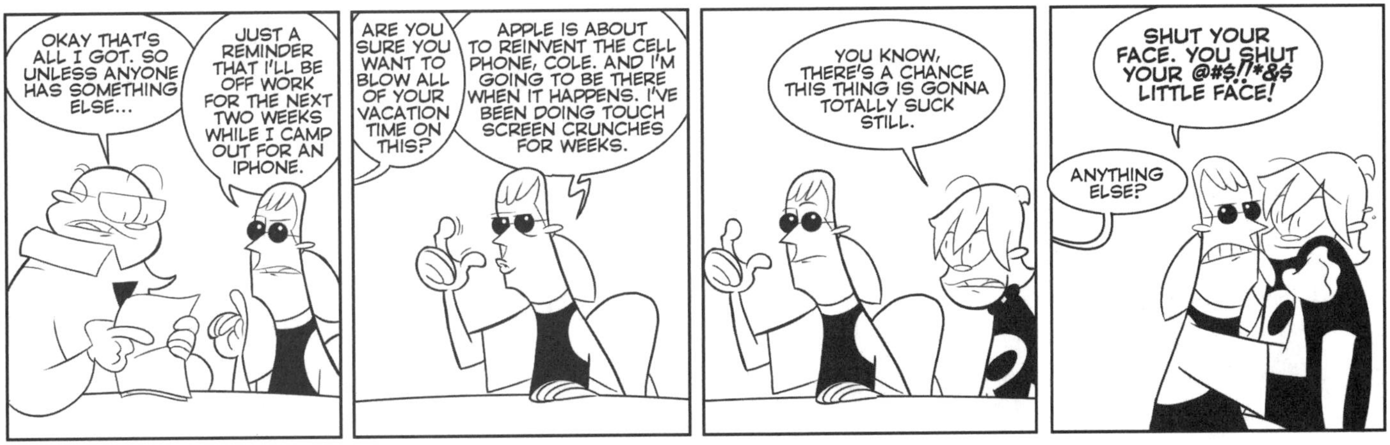
OKAY THAT'S ALL I GOT. SO UNLESS ANYONE HAS SOMETHING ELSE...
JUST A REMINDER THAT I'LL BE OFF WORK FOR THE NEXT TWO WEEKS WHILE I CAMP OUT FOR AN IPHONE.
ARE YOU SURE YOU WANT TO BLOW ALL OF YOUR VACATION TIME ON THIS?
APPLE IS ABOUT TO REINVENT THE CELL PHONE, COLE. AND I'M GOING TO BE THERE WHEN IT HAPPENS. I'VE BEEN DOING TOUCH SCREEN CRUNCHES FOR WEEKS.
YOU KNOW, THERE'S A CHANCE THIS THING IS GONNA TOTALLY SUCK STILL.
SHUT YOUR FACE. YOU SHUT YOUR @#$!!*&$ LITTLE FACE!
ANYTHING ELSE?

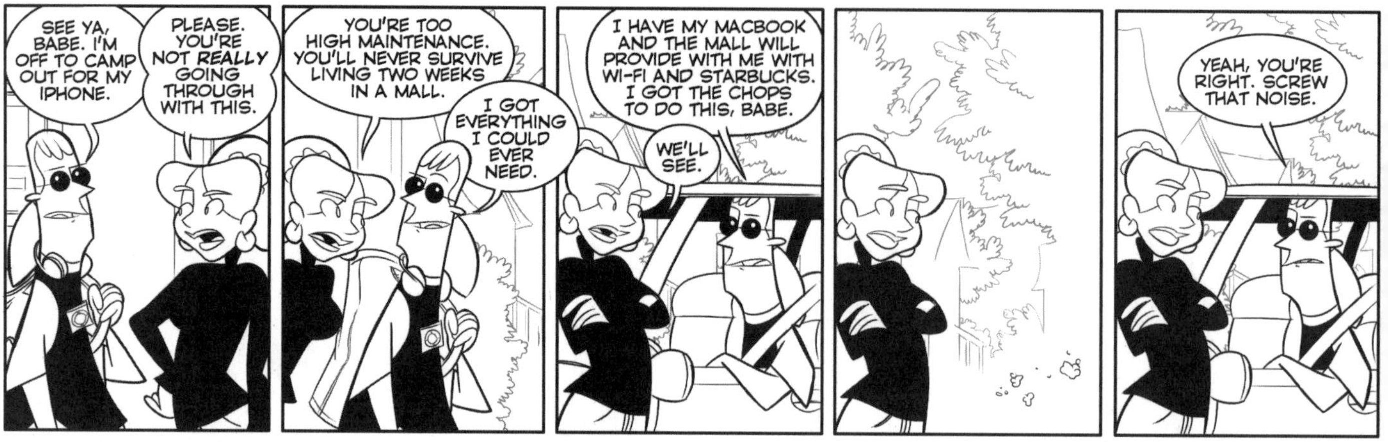

SEE YA, BABE. I'M OFF TO CAMP OUT FOR MY IPHONE.
PLEASE. YOU'RE NOT **REALLY** GOING THROUGH WITH THIS.
YOU'RE TOO HIGH MAINTENANCE. YOU'LL NEVER SURVIVE LIVING TWO WEEKS IN A MALL.
I GOT EVERYTHING I COULD EVER NEED.
I HAVE MY MACBOOK AND THE MALL WILL PROVIDE WITH ME WITH WI-FI AND STARBUCKS. I GOT THE CHOPS TO DO THIS, BABE.
WE'LL SEE.
YEAH, YOU'RE RIGHT. SCREW THAT NOISE.

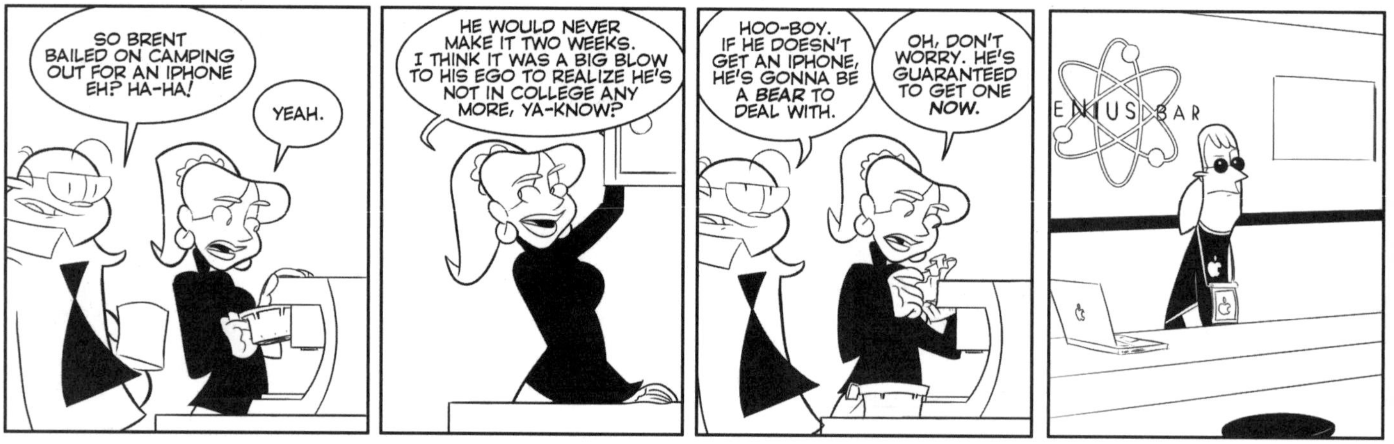

SO BRENT BAILED ON CAMPING OUT FOR AN IPHONE EH? HA-HA!
YEAH.
HE WOULD NEVER MAKE IT TWO WEEKS. I THINK IT WAS A BIG BLOW TO HIS EGO TO REALIZE HE'S NOT IN COLLEGE ANY MORE, YA-KNOW?
HOO-BOY. IF HE DOESN'T GET AN IPHONE, HE'S GONNA BE A **BEAR** TO DEAL WITH.
OH, DON'T WORRY. HE'S GUARANTEED TO GET ONE **NOW**.
ENIUS BAR

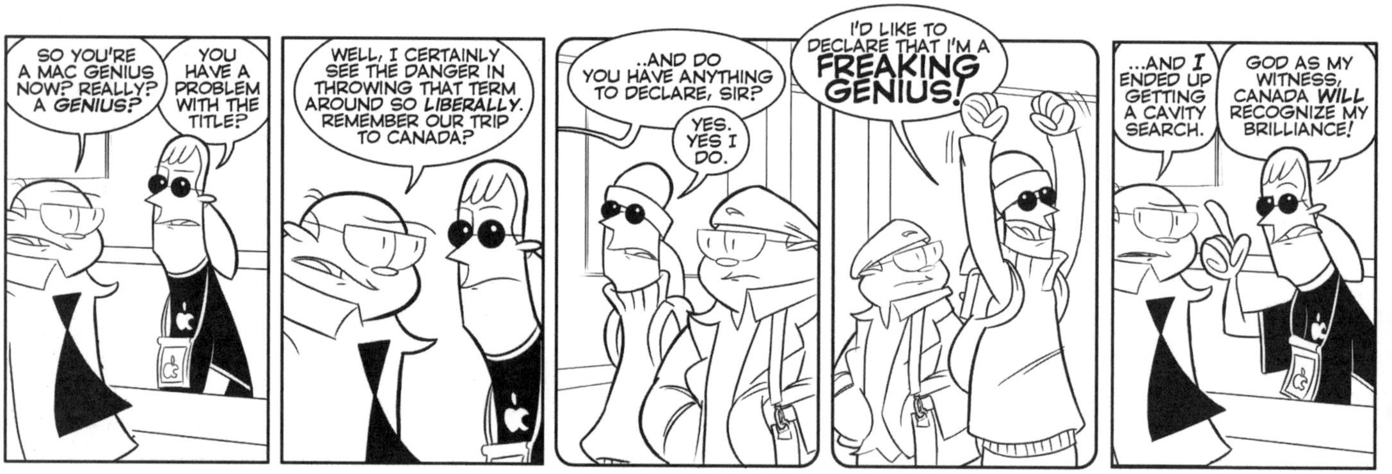

SO YOU'RE A MAC GENIUS NOW? REALLY? A ***GENIUS?***
YOU HAVE A PROBLEM WITH THE TITLE?
WELL, I CERTAINLY SEE THE DANGER IN THROWING THAT TERM AROUND SO ***LIBERALLY***. REMEMBER OUR TRIP TO CANADA?
..AND DO YOU HAVE ANYTHING TO DECLARE, SIR?
YES. YES I DO.
I'D LIKE TO DECLARE THAT I'M A **FREAKING GENIUS!**
...AND ***I*** ENDED UP GETTING A CAVITY SEARCH.
GOD AS MY WITNESS, CANADA ***WILL*** RECOGNIZE MY BRILLIANCE!

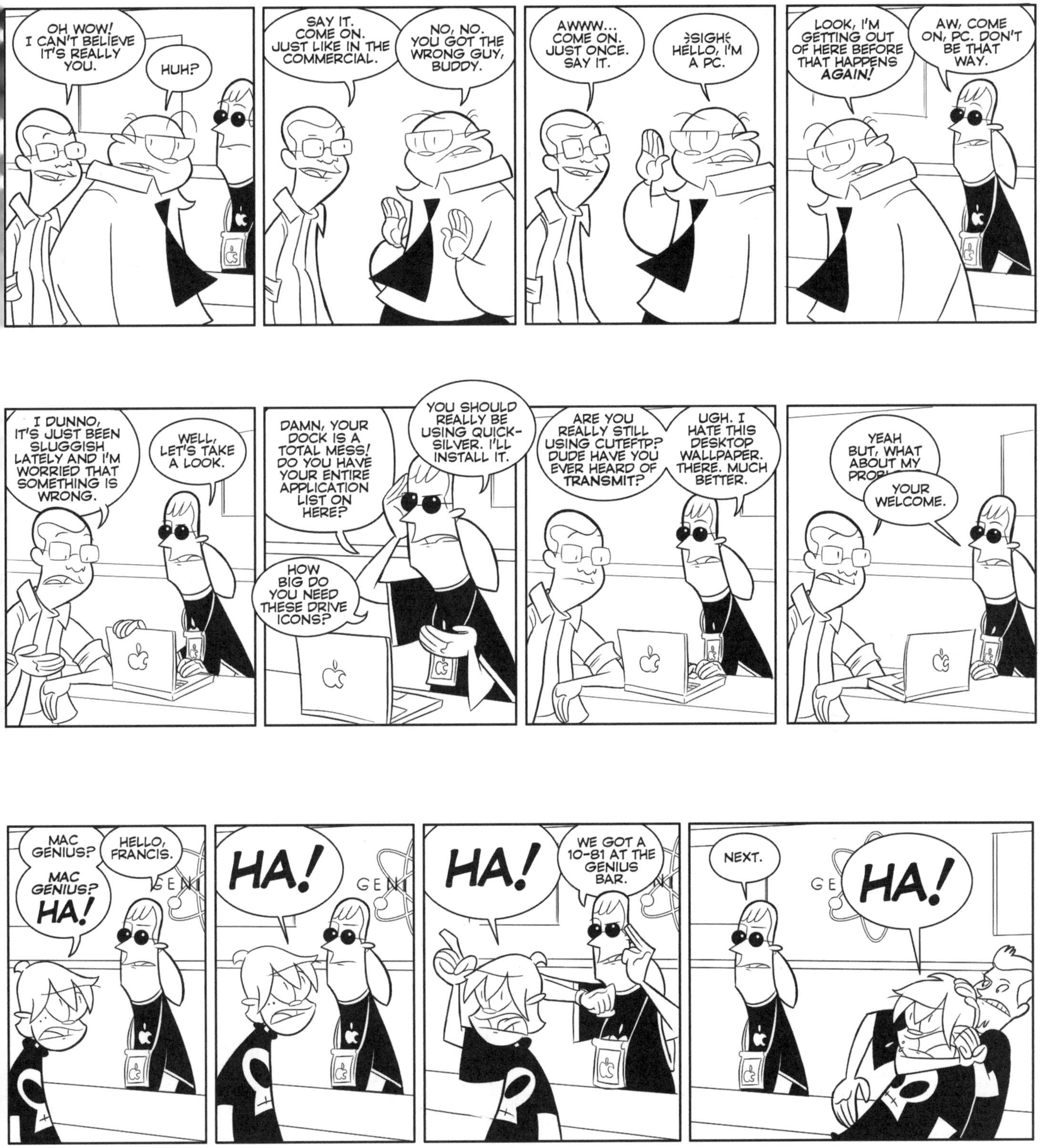
OH WOW! I CAN'T BELIEVE IT'S REALLY YOU.
HUH?
SAY IT. COME ON. JUST LIKE IN THE COMMERCIAL.
NO, NO. YOU GOT THE WRONG GUY, BUDDY.
AWWW... COME ON. JUST ONCE. SAY IT.
SIGH HELLO, I'M A PC.
LOOK, I'M GETTING OUT OF HERE BEFORE THAT HAPPENS AGAIN!
AW, COME ON, PC. DON'T BE THAT WAY.
I DUNNO, IT'S JUST BEEN SLUGGISH LATELY AND I'M WORRIED THAT SOMETHING IS WRONG.
WELL, LET'S TAKE A LOOK.
DAMN, YOUR DOCK IS A TOTAL MESS! DO YOU HAVE YOUR ENTIRE APPLICATION LIST ON HERE?
YOU SHOULD REALLY BE USING QUICK-SILVER. I'LL INSTALL IT.
HOW BIG DO YOU NEED THESE DRIVE ICONS?
ARE YOU REALLY STILL USING CUTEFTP? DUDE HAVE YOU EVER HEARD OF TRANSMIT?
UGH. I HATE THIS DESKTOP WALLPAPER. THERE. MUCH BETTER.
YEAH BUT, WHAT ABOUT MY
YOUR WELCOME.
MAC GENIUS?
MAC GENIUS? HA!
HELLO, FRANCIS.
HA!
HA!
WE GOT A 10-81 AT THE GENIUS BAR.
NEXT.
HA!

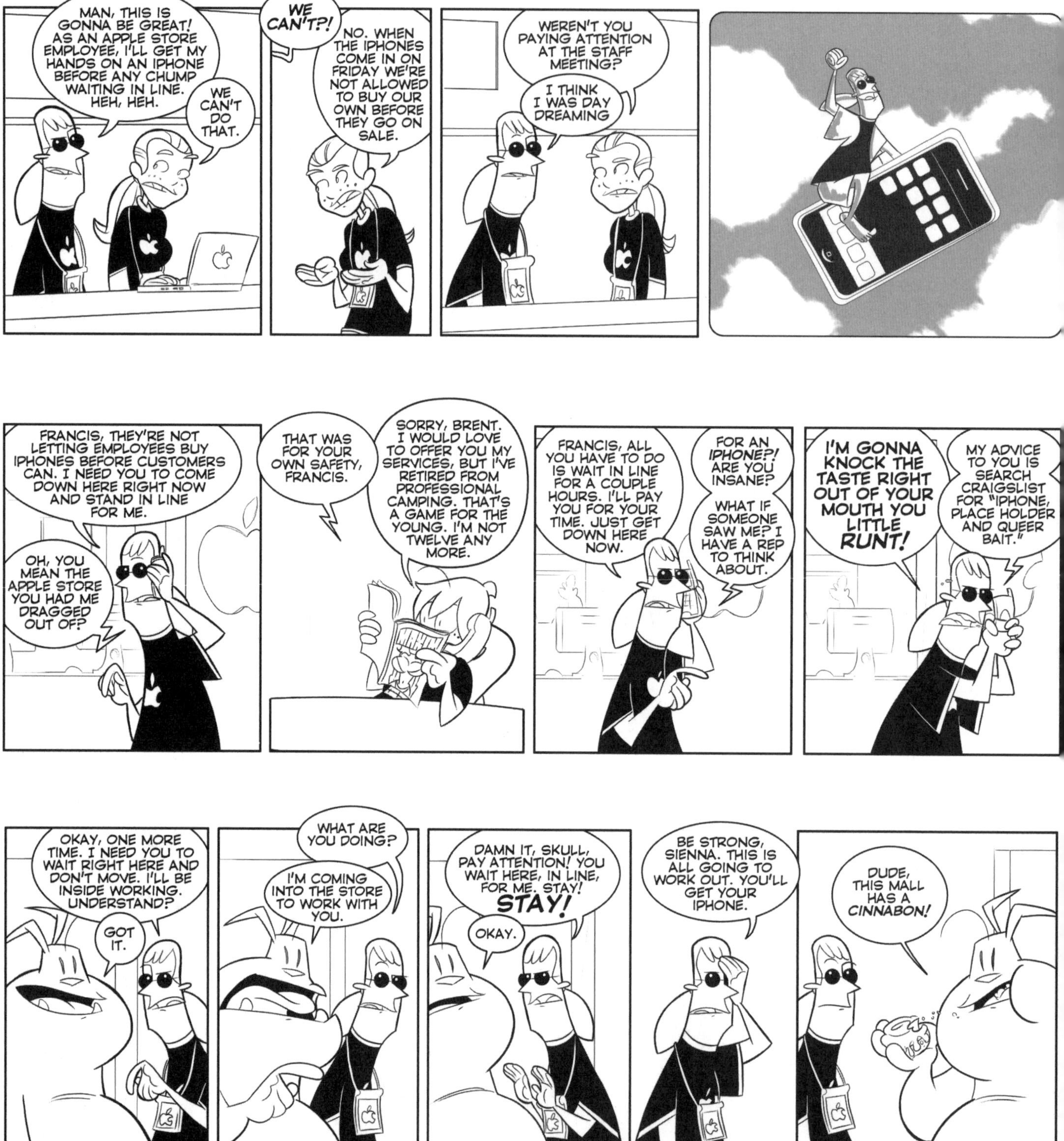
MAN, THIS IS GONNA BE GREAT! AS AN APPLE STORE EMPLOYEE, I'LL GET MY HANDS ON AN IPHONE BEFORE ANY CHUMP WAITING IN LINE. HEH, HEH.
WE CAN'T DO THAT.
WE CAN'T?!
NO. WHEN THE IPHONES COME IN ON FRIDAY WE'RE NOT ALLOWED TO BUY OUR OWN BEFORE THEY GO ON SALE.
WEREN'T YOU PAYING ATTENTION AT THE STAFF MEETING?
I THINK I WAS DAY DREAMING
FRANCIS, THEY'RE NOT LETTING EMPLOYEES BUY IPHONES BEFORE CUSTOMERS CAN. I NEED YOU TO COME DOWN HERE RIGHT NOW AND STAND IN LINE FOR ME.
OH, YOU MEAN THE APPLE STORE YOU HAD ME DRAGGED OUT OF?
THAT WAS FOR YOUR OWN SAFETY, FRANCIS.
SORRY, BRENT. I WOULD LOVE TO OFFER YOU MY SERVICES, BUT I'VE RETIRED FROM PROFESSIONAL CAMPING. THAT'S A GAME FOR THE YOUNG. I'M NOT TWELVE ANY MORE.
FRANCIS, ALL YOU HAVE TO DO IS WAIT IN LINE FOR A COUPLE HOURS. I'LL PAY YOU FOR YOUR TIME. JUST GET DOWN HERE NOW.
FOR AN IPHONE?! ARE YOU INSANE?
WHAT IF SOMEONE SAW ME? I HAVE A REP TO THINK ABOUT.
I'M GONNA KNOCK THE TASTE RIGHT OUT OF YOUR MOUTH YOU LITTLE RUNT!
MY ADVICE TO YOU IS SEARCH CRAIGSLIST FOR "IPHONE, PLACE HOLDER AND QUEER BAIT."
OKAY, ONE MORE TIME. I NEED YOU TO WAIT RIGHT HERE AND DON'T MOVE. I'LL BE INSIDE WORKING. UNDERSTAND?
GOT IT.
WHAT ARE YOU DOING?
I'M COMING INTO THE STORE TO WORK WITH YOU.
DAMN IT, SKULL, PAY ATTENTION! YOU WAIT HERE, IN LINE, FOR ME. STAY! STAY!
OKAY.
BE STRONG, SIENNA. THIS IS ALL GOING TO WORK OUT. YOU'LL GET YOUR IPHONE.
DUDE, THIS MALL HAS A CINNABON!

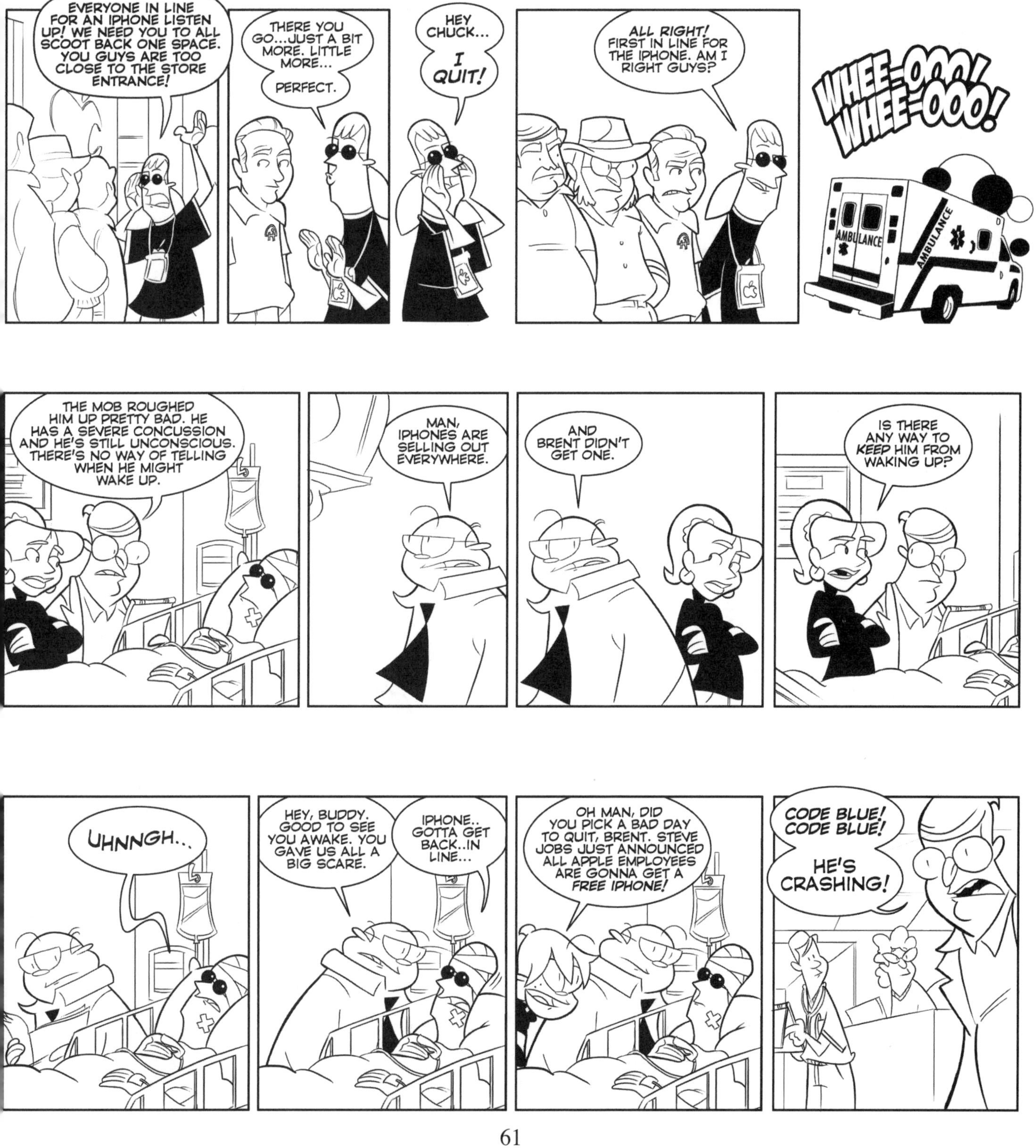
EVERYONE IN LINE FOR AN IPHONE LISTEN UP! WE NEED YOU TO ALL SCOOT BACK ONE SPACE. YOU GUYS ARE TOO CLOSE TO THE STORE ENTRANCE!
THERE YOU GO...JUST A BIT MORE. LITTLE MORE...
PERFECT.
HEY CHUCK...
I QUIT!
ALL RIGHT! FIRST IN LINE FOR THE IPHONE. AM I RIGHT GUYS?
WHEE-OOO! WHEE-OOO!
AMBULANCE
AMBULANCE
THE MOB ROUGHED HIM UP PRETTY BAD. HE HAS A SEVERE CONCUSSION AND HE'S STILL UNCONSCIOUS. THERE'S NO WAY OF TELLING WHEN HE MIGHT WAKE UP.
MAN, IPHONES ARE SELLING OUT EVERYWHERE.
AND BRENT DIDN'T GET ONE.
IS THERE ANY WAY TO KEEP HIM FROM WAKING UP?
UHNNGH...
HEY, BUDDY. GOOD TO SEE YOU AWAKE. YOU GAVE US ALL A BIG SCARE.
IPHONE.. GOTTA GET BACK..IN LINE...
OH MAN, DID YOU PICK A BAD DAY TO QUIT, BRENT. STEVE JOBS JUST ANNOUNCED ALL APPLE EMPLOYEES ARE GONNA GET A FREE IPHONE!
CODE BLUE! CODE BLUE!
HE'S CRASHING!

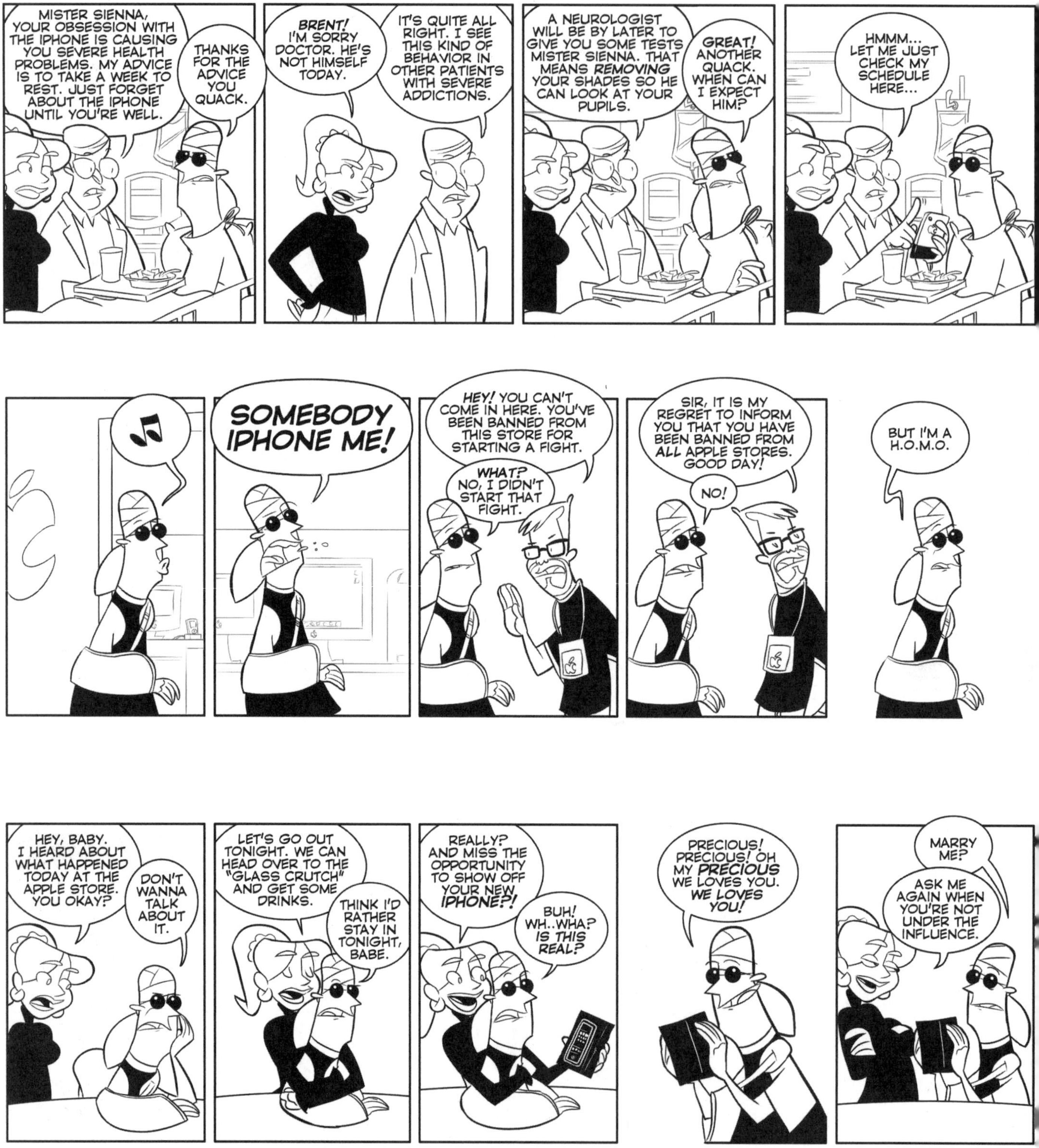
MISTER SIENNA, YOUR OBSESSION WITH THE IPHONE IS CAUSING YOU SEVERE HEALTH PROBLEMS. MY ADVICE IS TO TAKE A WEEK TO REST. JUST FORGET ABOUT THE IPHONE UNTIL YOU'RE WELL.
THANKS FOR THE ADVICE YOU QUACK.
BRENT! I'M SORRY DOCTOR. HE'S NOT HIMSELF TODAY.
IT'S QUITE ALL RIGHT. I SEE THIS KIND OF BEHAVIOR IN OTHER PATIENTS WITH SEVERE ADDICTIONS.
A NEUROLOGIST WILL BE BY LATER TO GIVE YOU SOME TESTS MISTER SIENNA. THAT MEANS REMOVING YOUR SHADES SO HE CAN LOOK AT YOUR PUPILS.
GREAT! ANOTHER QUACK. WHEN CAN I EXPECT HIM?
HMMM... LET ME JUST CHECK MY SCHEDULE HERE...
SOMEBODY IPHONE ME!
HEY! YOU CAN'T COME IN HERE. YOU'VE BEEN BANNED FROM THIS STORE FOR STARTING A FIGHT.
WHAT? NO, I DIDN'T START THAT FIGHT.
SIR, IT IS MY REGRET TO INFORM YOU THAT YOU HAVE BEEN BANNED FROM ALL APPLE STORES. GOOD DAY!
NO!
BUT I'M A H.O.M.O.
HEY, BABY. I HEARD ABOUT WHAT HAPPENED TODAY AT THE APPLE STORE. YOU OKAY?
DON'T WANNA TALK ABOUT IT.
LET'S GO OUT TONIGHT. WE CAN HEAD OVER TO THE "GLASS CRUTCH" AND GET SOME DRINKS.
THINK I'D RATHER STAY IN TONIGHT, BABE.
REALLY? AND MISS THE OPPORTUNITY TO SHOW OFF YOUR NEW IPHONE?!
BUH! WH..WHA? IS THIS REAL?
PRECIOUS! PRECIOUS! OH MY PRECIOUS WE LOVES YOU. WE LOVES YOU!
MARRY ME?
ASK ME AGAIN WHEN YOU'RE NOT UNDER THE INFLUENCE.

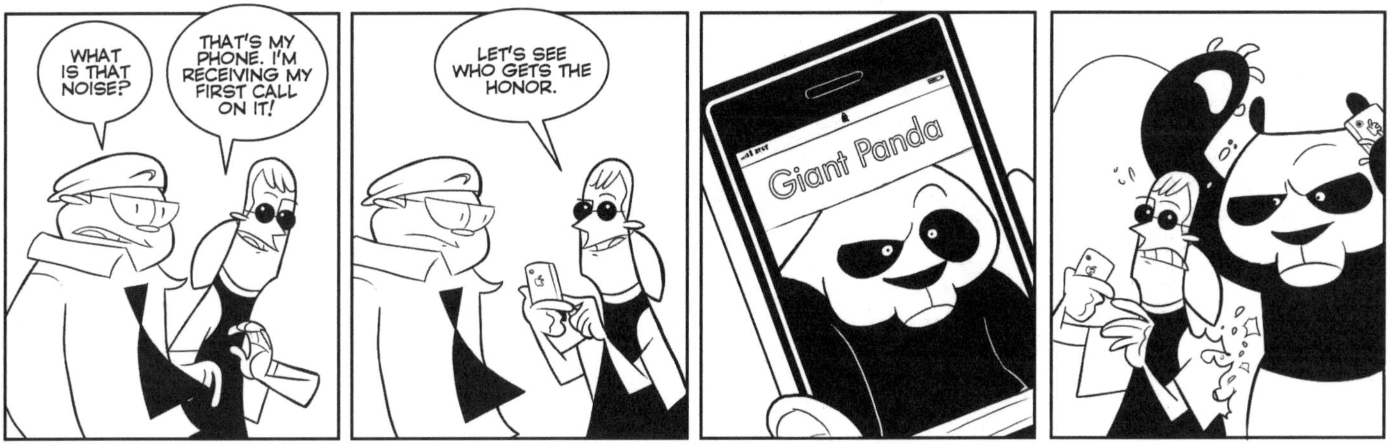
WHAT IS THAT NOISE?
THAT'S MY PHONE. I'M RECEIVING MY FIRST CALL ON IT!
LET'S SEE WHO GETS THE HONOR.
Giant Panda

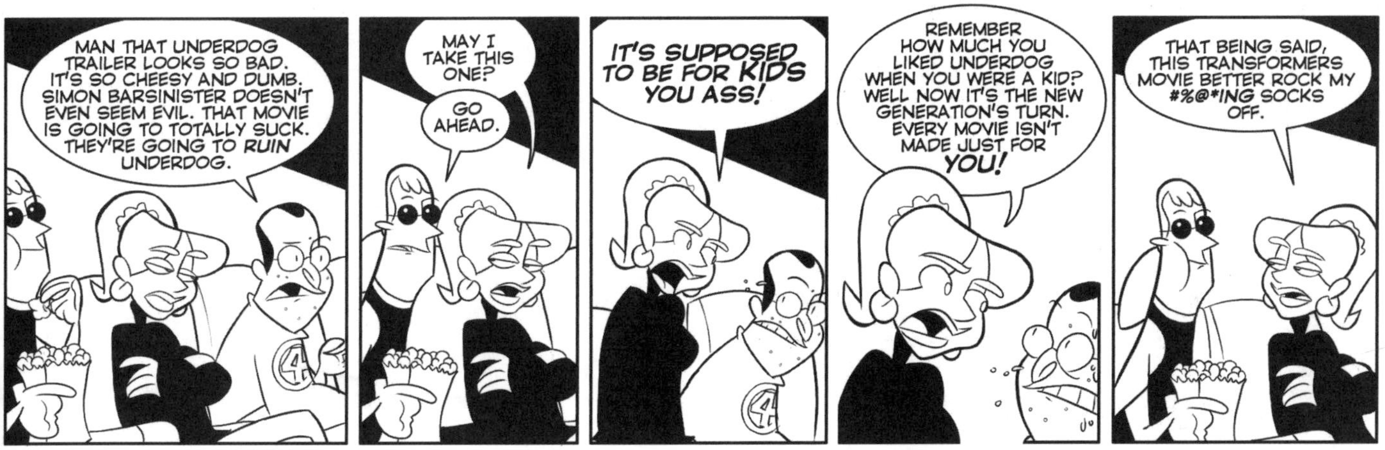
MAN THAT UNDERDOG TRAILER LOOKS SO BAD. IT'S SO CHEESY AND DUMB. SIMON BARSINISTER DOESN'T EVEN SEEM EVIL. THAT MOVIE IS GOING TO TOTALLY SUCK. THEY'RE GOING TO RUIN UNDERDOG.
MAY I TAKE THIS ONE?
GO AHEAD.
IT'S SUPPOSED TO BE FOR KIDS YOU ASS!
REMEMBER HOW MUCH YOU LIKED UNDERDOG WHEN YOU WERE A KID? WELL NOW IT'S THE NEW GENERATION'S TURN. EVERY MOVIE ISN'T MADE JUST FOR YOU!
THAT BEING SAID, THIS TRANSFORMERS MOVIE BETTER ROCK MY #%@*ING SOCKS OFF.

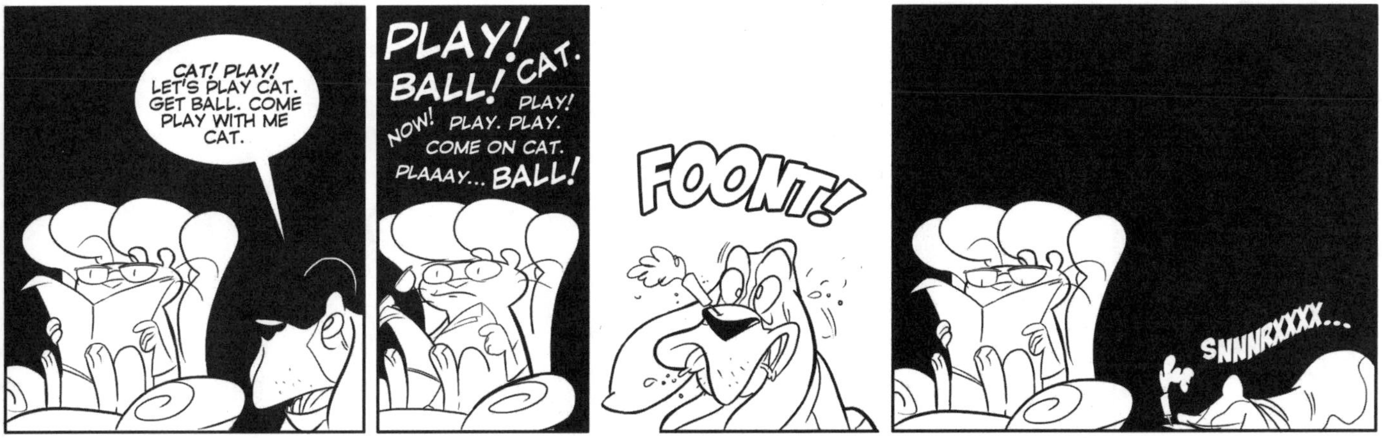
CAT! PLAY! LET'S PLAY CAT. GET BALL. COME PLAY WITH ME CAT.
PLAY! BALL! CAT. PLAY! NOW! PLAY. PLAY. COME ON CAT. PLAAAY... BALL!
FOONT!
SNNNRXXXX...

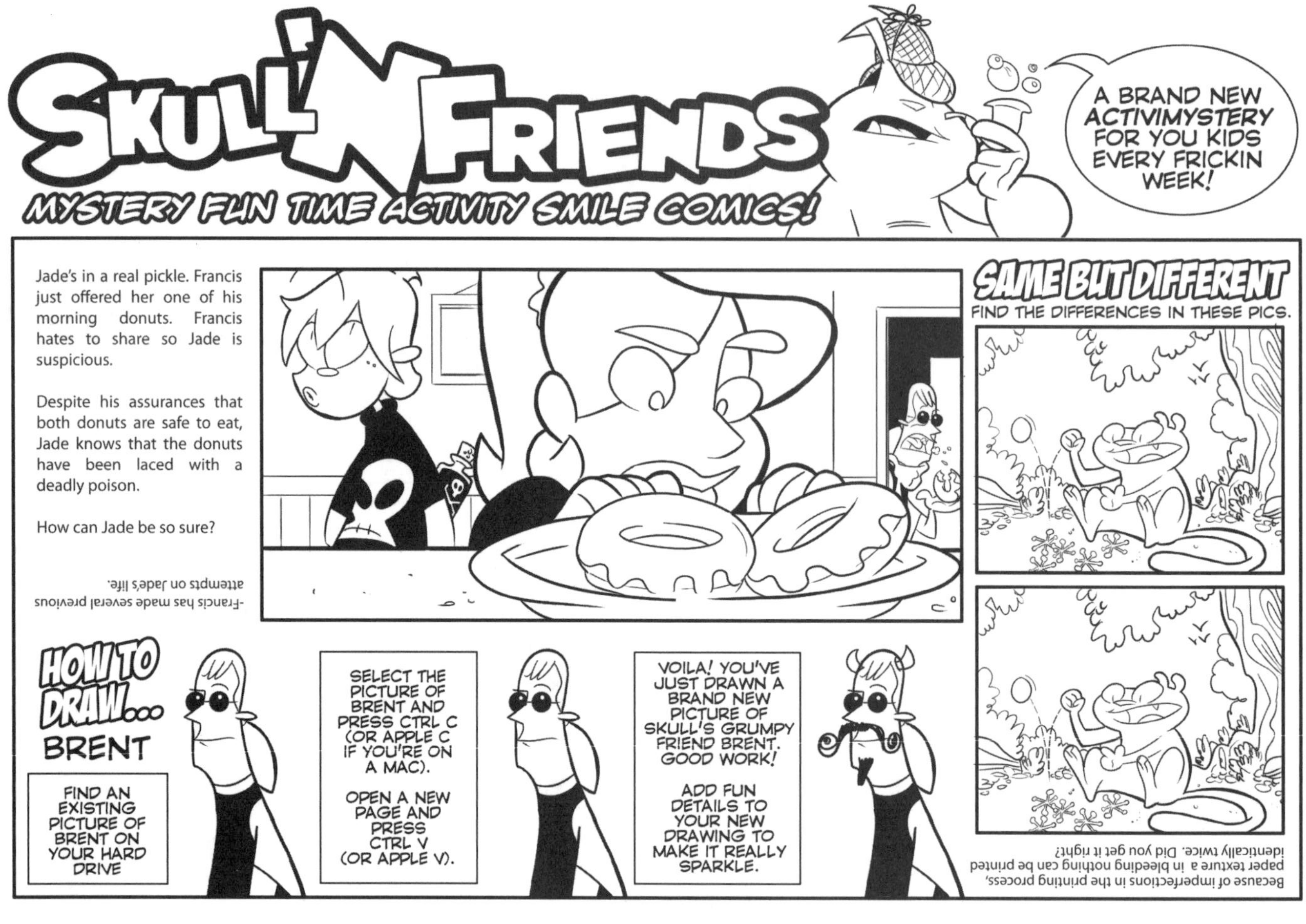
SKULL 'N FRIENDS
MYSTERY FUN TIME ACTIVITY SMILE COMICS!
A BRAND NEW ACTIVIMYSTERY FOR YOU KIDS EVERY FRICKIN WEEK!
Jade's in a real pickle. Francis just offered her one of his morning donuts. Francis hates to share so Jade is suspicious.
Despite his assurances that both donuts are safe to eat, Jade knows that the donuts have been laced with a deadly poison.
How can Jade be so sure?
-Francis has made several previous attempts on Jade's life.
SAME BUT DIFFERENT
FIND THE DIFFERENCES IN THESE PICS.
Because of imperfections in the printing process, paper texture a in bleeding nothing can be printed identically twice. Did you get it right?
HOW TO DRAW... BRENT
FIND AN EXISTING PICTURE OF BRENT ON YOUR HARD DRIVE
SELECT THE PICTURE OF BRENT AND PRESS CTRL C (OR APPLE C IF YOU'RE ON A MAC).
OPEN A NEW PAGE AND PRESS CTRL V (OR APPLE V).
VOILA! YOU'VE JUST DRAWN A BRAND NEW PICTURE OF SKULL'S GRUMPY FRIEND BRENT. GOOD WORK!
ADD FUN DETAILS TO YOUR NEW DRAWING TO MAKE IT REALLY SPARKLE.

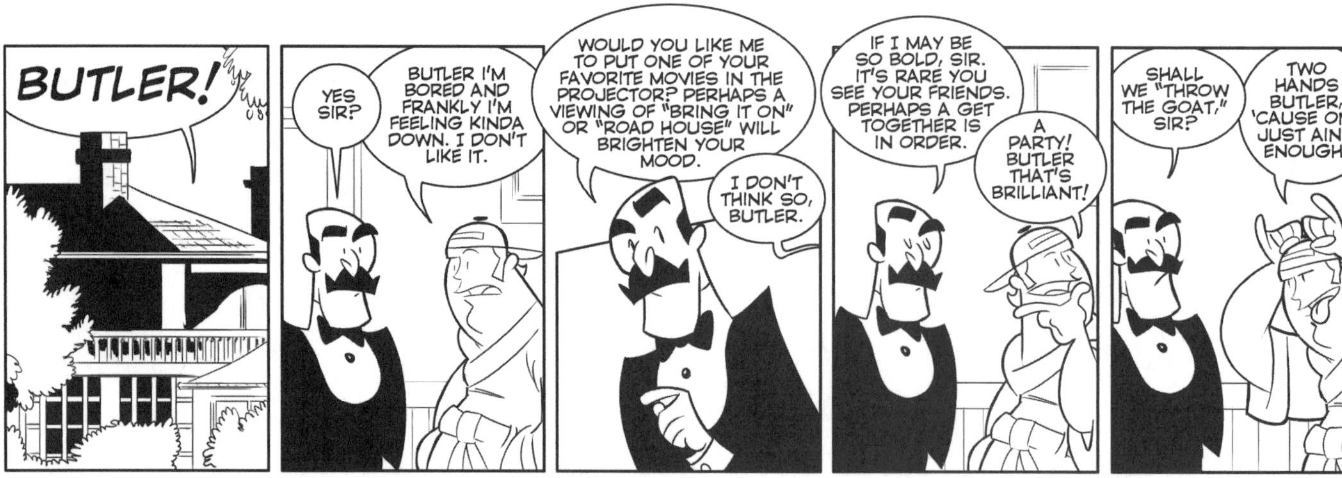
BUTLER!
YES SIR?
BUTLER I'M BORED AND FRANKLY I'M FEELING KINDA DOWN. I DON'T LIKE IT.
WOULD YOU LIKE ME TO PUT ONE OF YOUR FAVORITE MOVIES IN THE PROJECTOR? PERHAPS A VIEWING OF "BRING IT ON" OR "ROAD HOUSE" WILL BRIGHTEN YOUR MOOD.
I DON'T THINK SO, BUTLER.
IF I MAY BE SO BOLD, SIR. IT'S RARE YOU SEE YOUR FRIENDS. PERHAPS A GET TOGETHER IS IN ORDER.
A PARTY! BUTLER THAT'S BRILLIANT!
SHALL WE "THROW THE GOAT," SIR?
TWO HANDS BUTLER, 'CAUSE ONE JUST AIN'T ENOUGH.

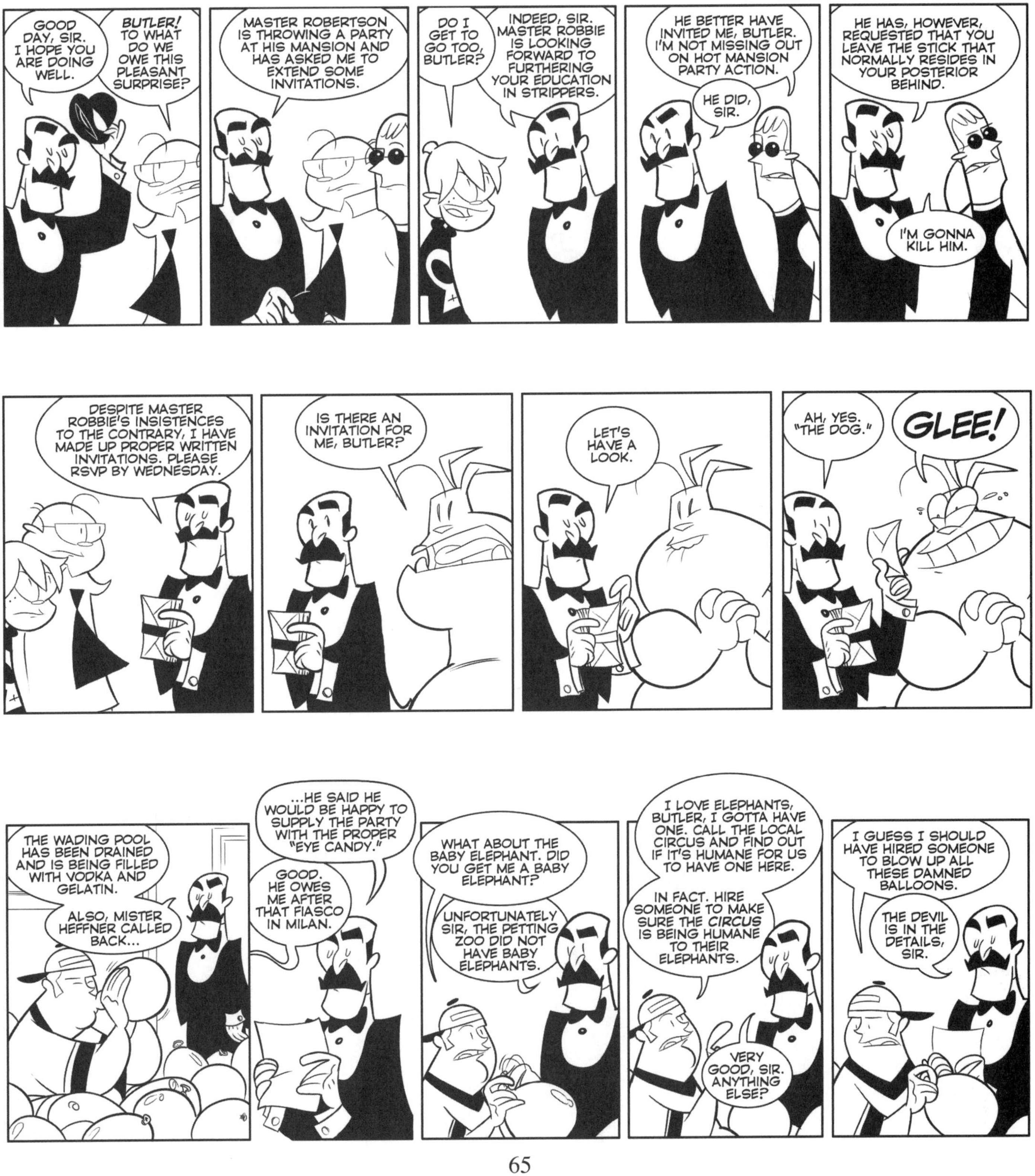
GOOD DAY, SIR. I HOPE YOU ARE DOING WELL.
BUTLER! TO WHAT DO WE OWE THIS PLEASANT SURPRISE?
MASTER ROBERTSON IS THROWING A PARTY AT HIS MANSION AND HAS ASKED ME TO EXTEND SOME INVITATIONS.
DO I GET TO GO TOO, BUTLER?
INDEED, SIR. MASTER ROBBIE IS LOOKING FORWARD TO FURTHERING YOUR EDUCATION IN STRIPPERS.
HE BETTER HAVE INVITED ME, BUTLER. I'M NOT MISSING OUT ON HOT MANSION PARTY ACTION.
HE DID, SIR.
HE HAS, HOWEVER, REQUESTED THAT YOU LEAVE THE STICK THAT NORMALLY RESIDES IN YOUR POSTERIOR BEHIND.
I'M GONNA KILL HIM.
DESPITE MASTER ROBBIE'S INSISTENCES TO THE CONTRARY, I HAVE MADE UP PROPER WRITTEN INVITATIONS. PLEASE RSVP BY WEDNESDAY.
IS THERE AN INVITATION FOR ME, BUTLER?
LET'S HAVE A LOOK.
AH, YES. "THE DOG."
GLEE!
THE WADING POOL HAS BEEN DRAINED AND IS BEING FILLED WITH VODKA AND GELATIN.
ALSO, MISTER HEFFNER CALLED BACK...
...HE SAID HE WOULD BE HAPPY TO SUPPLY THE PARTY WITH THE PROPER "EYE CANDY."
GOOD. HE OWES ME AFTER THAT FIASCO IN MILAN.
WHAT ABOUT THE BABY ELEPHANT. DID YOU GET ME A BABY ELEPHANT?
UNFORTUNATELY SIR, THE PETTING ZOO DID NOT HAVE BABY ELEPHANTS.
I LOVE ELEPHANTS, BUTLER, I GOTTA HAVE ONE. CALL THE LOCAL CIRCUS AND FIND OUT IF IT'S HUMANE FOR US TO HAVE ONE HERE.
IN FACT. HIRE SOMEONE TO MAKE SURE THE CIRCUS IS BEING HUMANE TO THEIR ELEPHANTS.
VERY GOOD, SIR. ANYTHING ELSE?
I GUESS I SHOULD HAVE HIRED SOMEONE TO BLOW UP ALL THESE DAMNED BALLOONS.
THE DEVIL IS IN THE DETAILS, SIR.

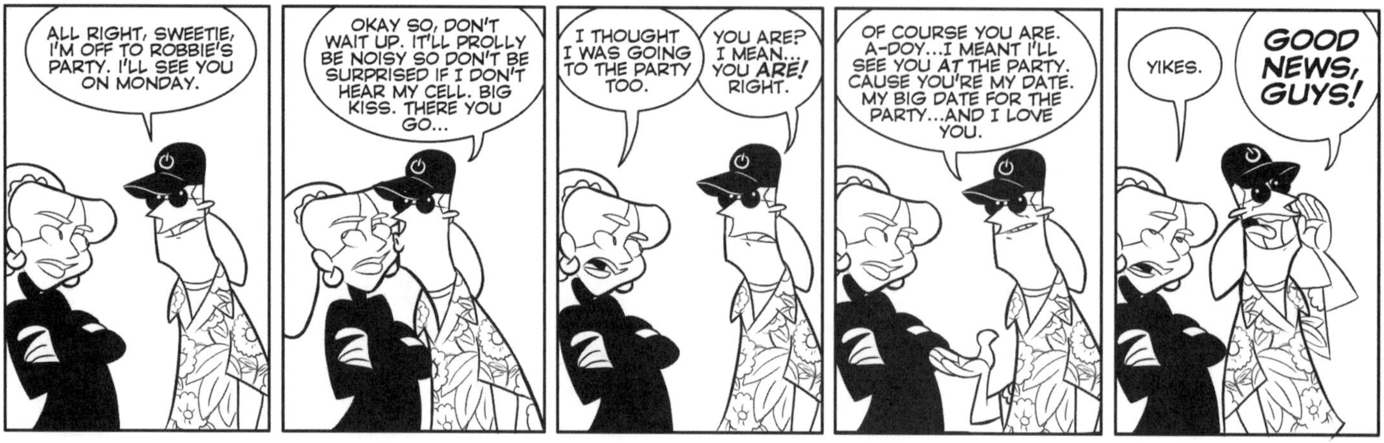
ALL RIGHT, SWEETIE, I'M OFF TO ROBBIE'S PARTY. I'LL SEE YOU ON MONDAY.
OKAY SO, DON'T WAIT UP. IT'LL PROLLY BE NOISY SO DON'T BE SURPRISED IF I DON'T HEAR MY CELL. BIG KISS. THERE YOU GO...
I THOUGHT I WAS GOING TO THE PARTY TOO.
YOU ARE? I MEAN... YOU ***ARE!*** RIGHT.
OF COURSE YOU ARE. A-DOY...I MEANT I'LL SEE YOU ***AT*** THE PARTY. CAUSE YOU'RE MY DATE. MY BIG DATE FOR THE PARTY...AND I LOVE YOU.
YIKES.
GOOD NEWS, GUYS!

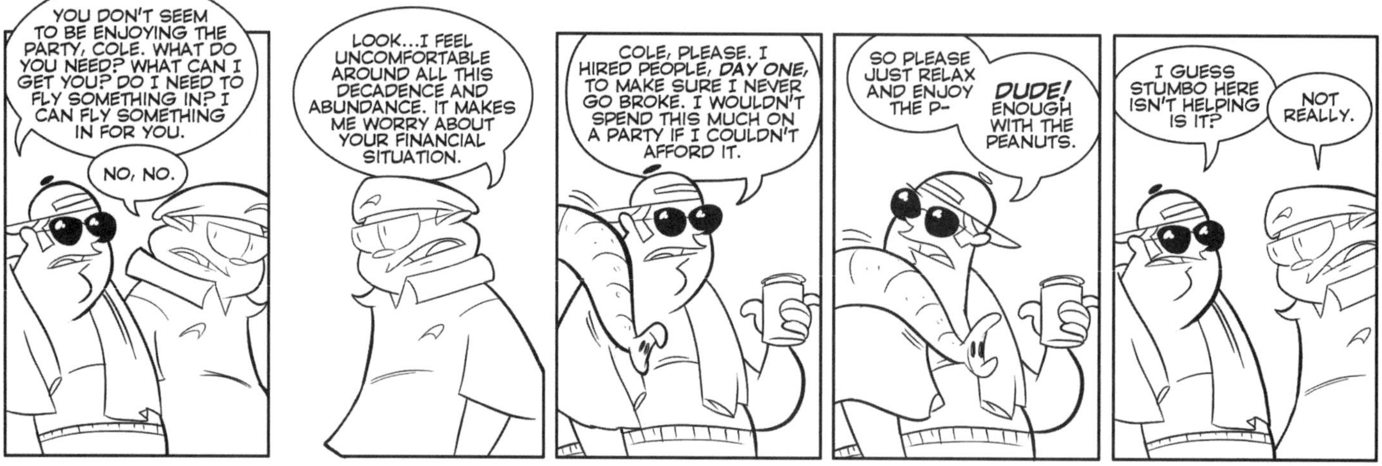
YOU DON'T SEEM TO BE ENJOYING THE PARTY, COLE. WHAT DO YOU NEED? WHAT CAN I GET YOU? DO I NEED TO FLY SOMETHING IN? I CAN FLY SOMETHING IN FOR YOU.
NO, NO.
LOOK...I FEEL UNCOMFORTABLE AROUND ALL THIS DECADENCE AND ABUNDANCE. IT MAKES ME WORRY ABOUT YOUR FINANCIAL SITUATION.
COLE, PLEASE. I HIRED PEOPLE, ***DAY ONE,*** TO MAKE SURE I NEVER GO BROKE. I WOULDN'T SPEND THIS MUCH ON A PARTY IF I COULDN'T AFFORD IT.
SO PLEASE JUST RELAX AND ENJOY THE P-
DUDE! ENOUGH WITH THE PEANUTS.
I GUESS STUMBO HERE ISN'T HELPING IS IT?
NOT REALLY.

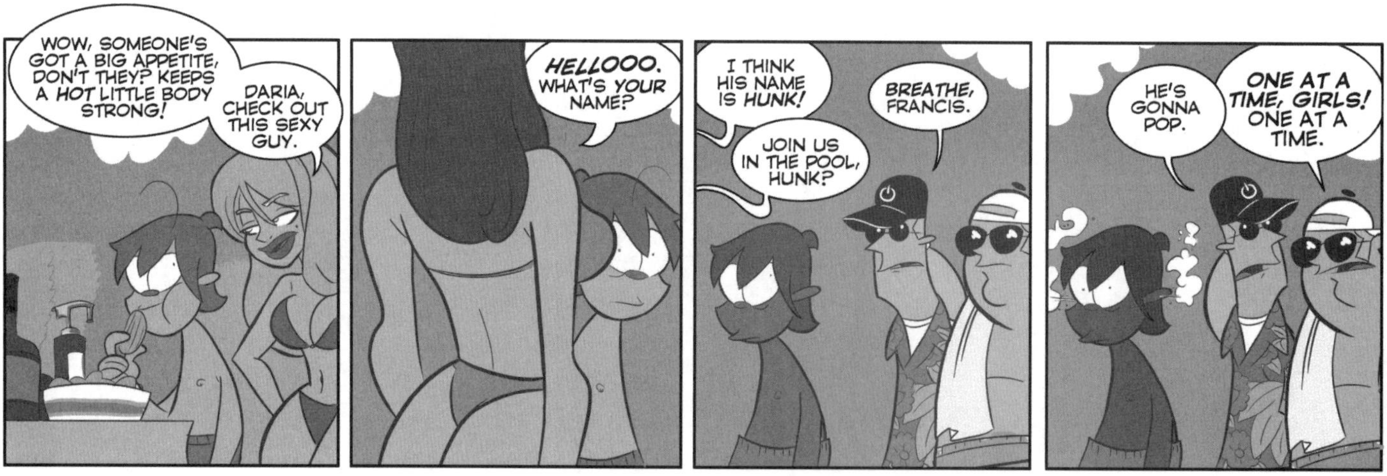
WOW, SOMEONE'S GOT A BIG APPETITE, DON'T THEY? KEEPS A ***HOT*** LITTLE BODY STRONG!
DARIA, CHECK OUT THIS SEXY GUY.
HELLOOO. WHAT'S ***YOUR*** NAME?
I THINK HIS NAME IS ***HUNK!***
JOIN US IN THE POOL, HUNK?
BREATHE, FRANCIS.
HE'S GONNA POP.
ONE AT A TIME, GIRLS! ONE AT A TIME.

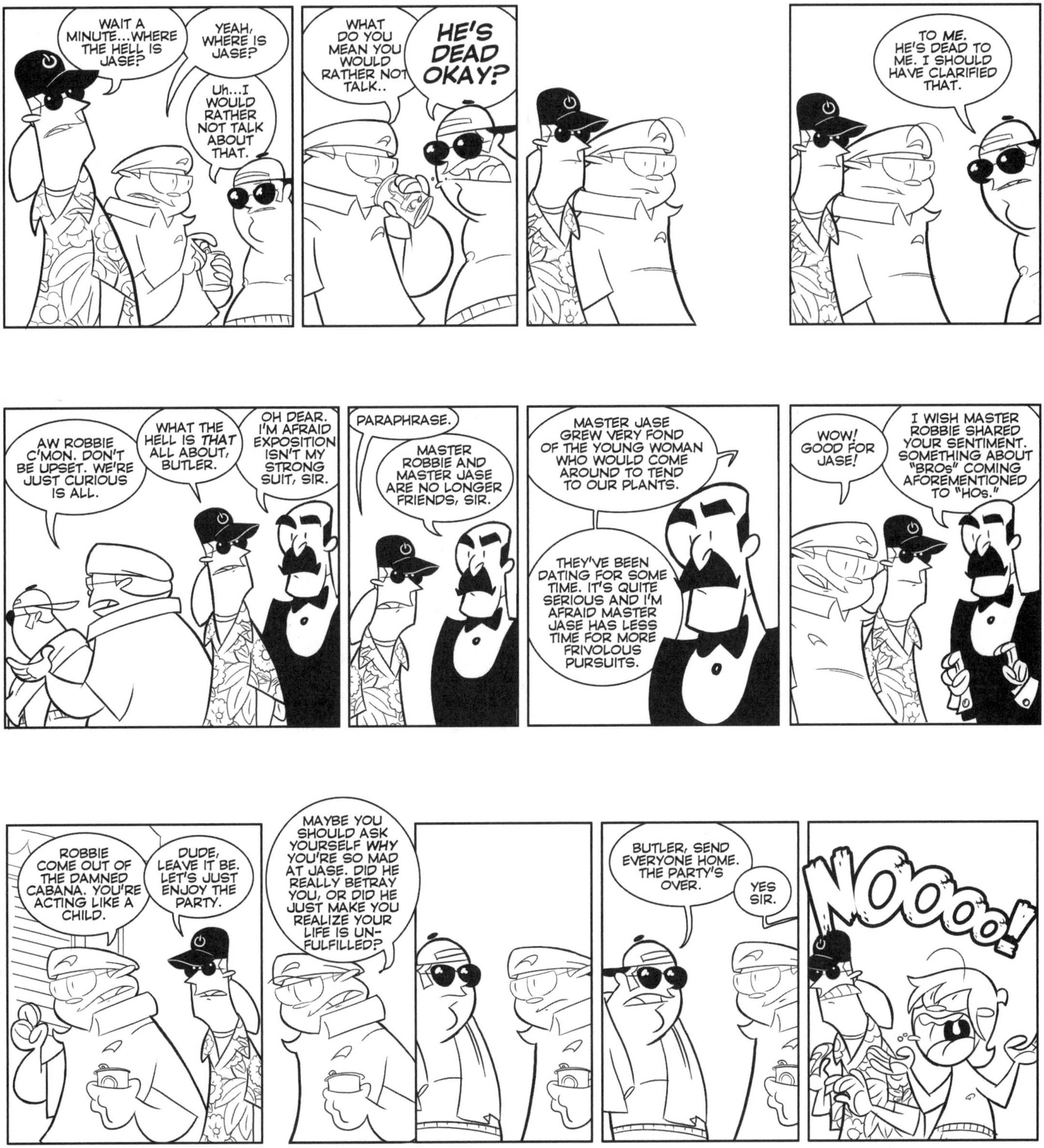
WAIT A MINUTE...WHERE THE HELL IS JASE?
YEAH, WHERE IS JASE?
Uh...I WOULD RATHER NOT TALK ABOUT THAT.
WHAT DO YOU MEAN YOU WOULD RATHER NOT TALK..
HE'S DEAD OKAY?
TO ME. HE'S DEAD TO ME. I SHOULD HAVE CLARIFIED THAT.
AW ROBBIE C'MON. DON'T BE UPSET. WE'RE JUST CURIOUS IS ALL.
WHAT THE HELL IS THAT ALL ABOUT, BUTLER.
OH DEAR. I'M AFRAID EXPOSITION ISN'T MY STRONG SUIT, SIR.
PARAPHRASE.
MASTER ROBBIE AND MASTER JASE ARE NO LONGER FRIENDS, SIR.
MASTER JASE GREW VERY FOND OF THE YOUNG WOMAN WHO WOULD COME AROUND TO TEND TO OUR PLANTS.
THEY'VE BEEN DATING FOR SOME TIME. IT'S QUITE SERIOUS AND I'M AFRAID MASTER JASE HAS LESS TIME FOR MORE FRIVOLOUS PURSUITS.
WOW! GOOD FOR JASE!
I WISH MASTER ROBBIE SHARED YOUR SENTIMENT. SOMETHING ABOUT "BROs" COMING AFOREMENTIONED TO "HOs."
ROBBIE COME OUT OF THE DAMNED CABANA. YOU'RE ACTING LIKE A CHILD.
DUDE, LEAVE IT BE. LET'S JUST ENJOY THE PARTY.
MAYBE YOU SHOULD ASK YOURSELF WHY YOU'RE SO MAD AT JASE. DID HE REALLY BETRAY YOU, OR DID HE JUST MAKE YOU REALIZE YOUR LIFE IS UN-FULFILLED?
BUTLER, SEND EVERYONE HOME. THE PARTY'S OVER.
YES SIR.
NOOOOO!

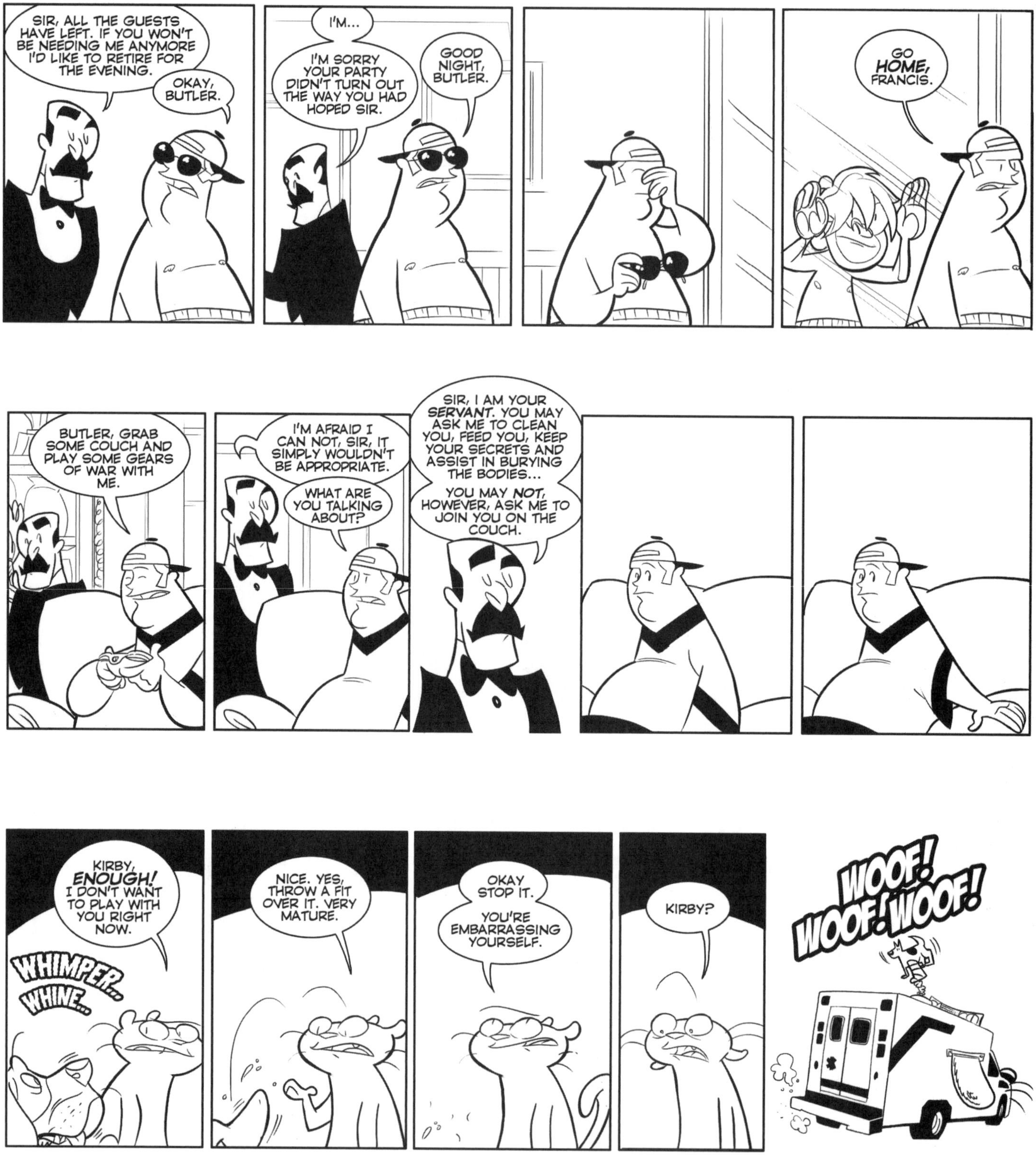
SIR, ALL THE GUESTS HAVE LEFT. IF YOU WON'T BE NEEDING ME ANYMORE I'D LIKE TO RETIRE FOR THE EVENING.
OKAY, BUTLER.
I'M...
I'M SORRY YOUR PARTY DIDN'T TURN OUT THE WAY YOU HAD HOPED SIR.
GOOD NIGHT, BUTLER.
GO HOME, FRANCIS.
BUTLER, GRAB SOME COUCH AND PLAY SOME GEARS OF WAR WITH ME.
I'M AFRAID I CAN NOT, SIR, IT SIMPLY WOULDN'T BE APPROPRIATE.
WHAT ARE YOU TALKING ABOUT?
SIR, I AM YOUR SERVANT. YOU MAY ASK ME TO CLEAN YOU, FEED YOU, KEEP YOUR SECRETS AND ASSIST IN BURYING THE BODIES...
YOU MAY NOT, HOWEVER, ASK ME TO JOIN YOU ON THE COUCH.
KIRBY, ENOUGH! I DON'T WANT TO PLAY WITH YOU RIGHT NOW.
WHIMPER... WHINE...
NICE. YES, THROW A FIT OVER IT. VERY MATURE.
OKAY STOP IT.
YOU'RE EMBARRASSING YOURSELF.
KIRBY?
WOOF! WOOF! WOOF!

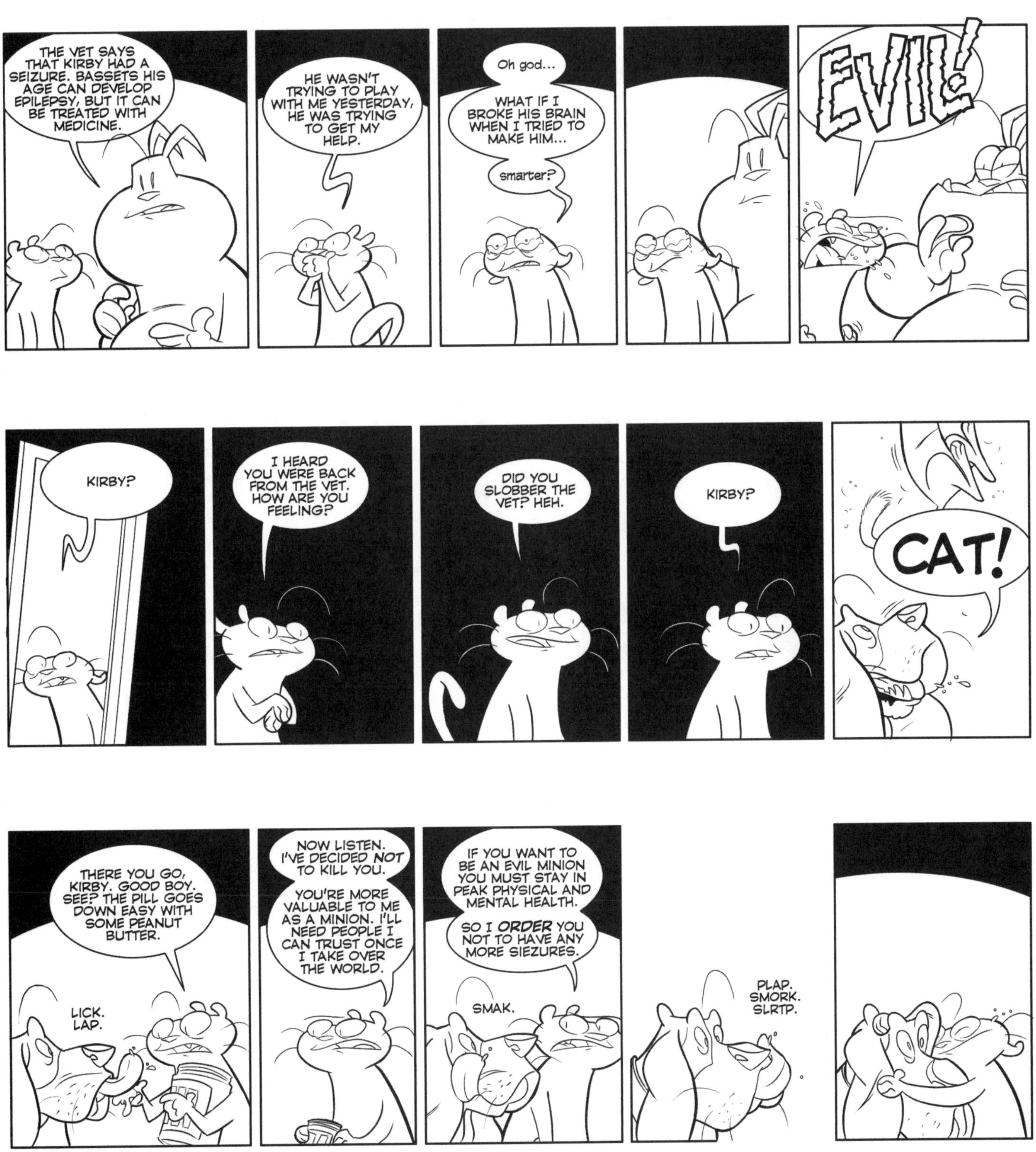
THE VET SAYS THAT KIRBY HAD A SEIZURE. BASSETS HIS AGE CAN DEVELOP EPILEPSY, BUT IT CAN BE TREATED WITH MEDICINE.
HE WASN'T TRYING TO PLAY WITH ME YESTERDAY, HE WAS TRYING TO GET MY HELP.
Oh god...
WHAT IF I BROKE HIS BRAIN WHEN I TRIED TO MAKE HIM...
smarter?
EVIL!
KIRBY?
I HEARD YOU WERE BACK FROM THE VET. HOW ARE YOU FEELING?
DID YOU SLOBBER THE VET? HEH.
KIRBY?
CAT!
THERE YOU GO, KIRBY. GOOD BOY. SEE? THE PILL GOES DOWN EASY WITH SOME PEANUT BUTTER.
LICK. LAP.
NOW LISTEN. I'VE DECIDED NOT TO KILL YOU.
YOU'RE MORE VALUABLE TO ME AS A MINION. I'LL NEED PEOPLE I CAN TRUST ONCE I TAKE OVER THE WORLD.
IF YOU WANT TO BE AN EVIL MINION YOU MUST STAY IN PEAK PHYSICAL AND MENTAL HEALTH.
SO I ORDER YOU NOT TO HAVE ANY MORE SIEZURES.
SMAK.
PLAP. SMORK. SLRTP.

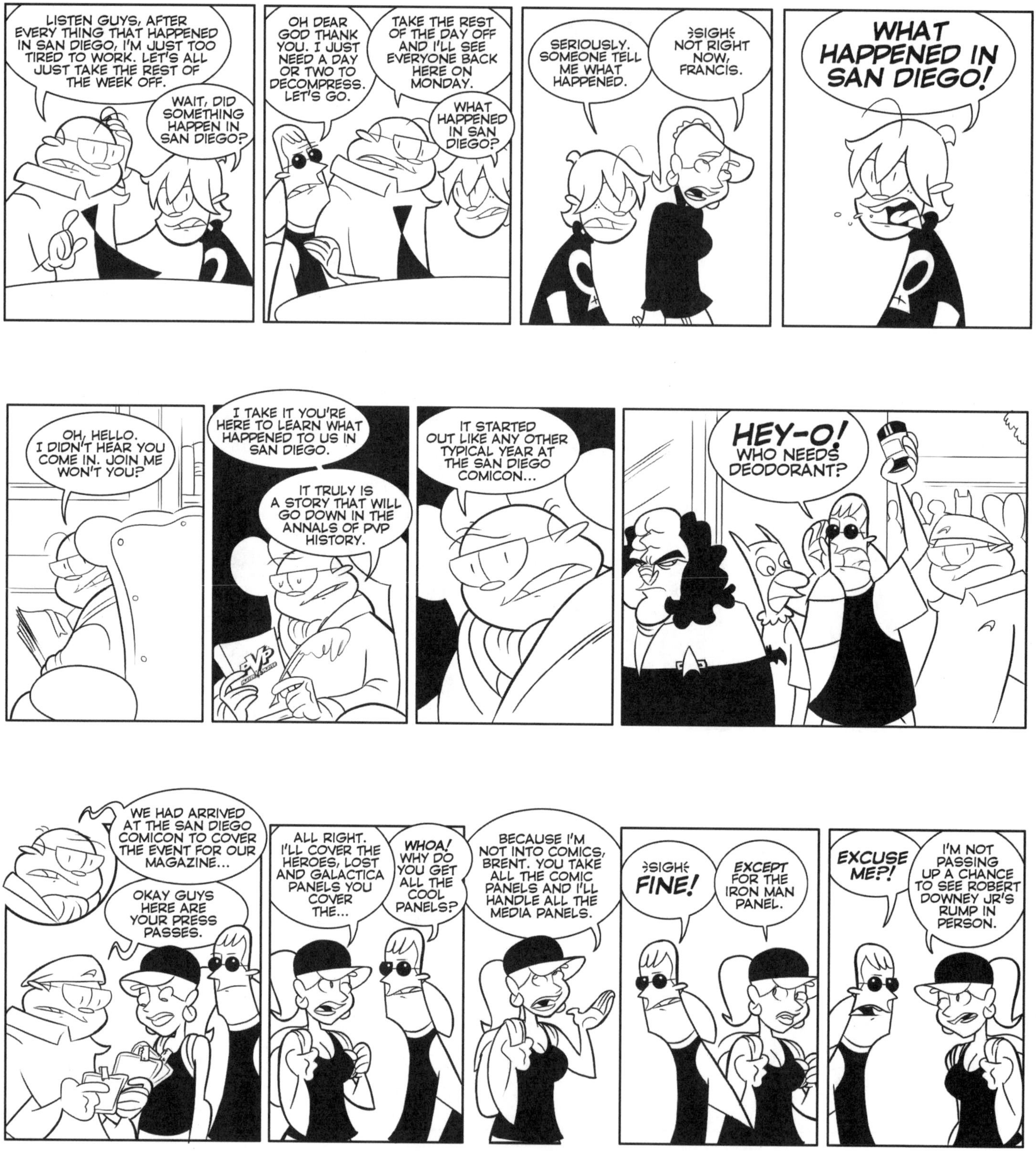
LISTEN GUYS, AFTER EVERY THING THAT HAPPENED IN SAN DIEGO, I'M JUST TOO TIRED TO WORK. LET'S ALL JUST TAKE THE REST OF THE WEEK OFF.
WAIT, DID SOMETHING HAPPEN IN SAN DIEGO?
OH DEAR GOD THANK YOU. I JUST NEED A DAY OR TWO TO DECOMPRESS. LET'S GO.
TAKE THE REST OF THE DAY OFF AND I'LL SEE EVERYONE BACK HERE ON MONDAY.
WHAT HAPPENED IN SAN DIEGO?
SERIOUSLY. SOMEONE TELL ME WHAT HAPPENED.
SIGH NOT RIGHT NOW, FRANCIS.
WHAT HAPPENED IN SAN DIEGO!
OH, HELLO. I DIDN'T HEAR YOU COME IN. JOIN ME WON'T YOU?
I TAKE IT YOU'RE HERE TO LEARN WHAT HAPPENED TO US IN SAN DIEGO.
IT TRULY IS A STORY THAT WILL GO DOWN IN THE ANNALS OF PVP HISTORY.
IT STARTED OUT LIKE ANY OTHER TYPICAL YEAR AT THE SAN DIEGO COMICON...
HEY-O! WHO NEEDS DEODORANT?
WE HAD ARRIVED AT THE SAN DIEGO COMICON TO COVER THE EVENT FOR OUR MAGAZINE...
OKAY GUYS HERE ARE YOUR PRESS PASSES.
ALL RIGHT. I'LL COVER THE HEROES, LOST AND GALACTICA PANELS YOU COVER THE...
WHOA! WHY DO YOU GET ALL THE COOL PANELS?
BECAUSE I'M NOT INTO COMICS, BRENT. YOU TAKE ALL THE COMIC PANELS AND I'LL HANDLE ALL THE MEDIA PANELS.
SIGH FINE!
EXCEPT FOR THE IRON MAN PANEL.
EXCUSE ME?!
I'M NOT PASSING UP A CHANCE TO SEE ROBERT DOWNEY JR'S RUMP IN PERSON.

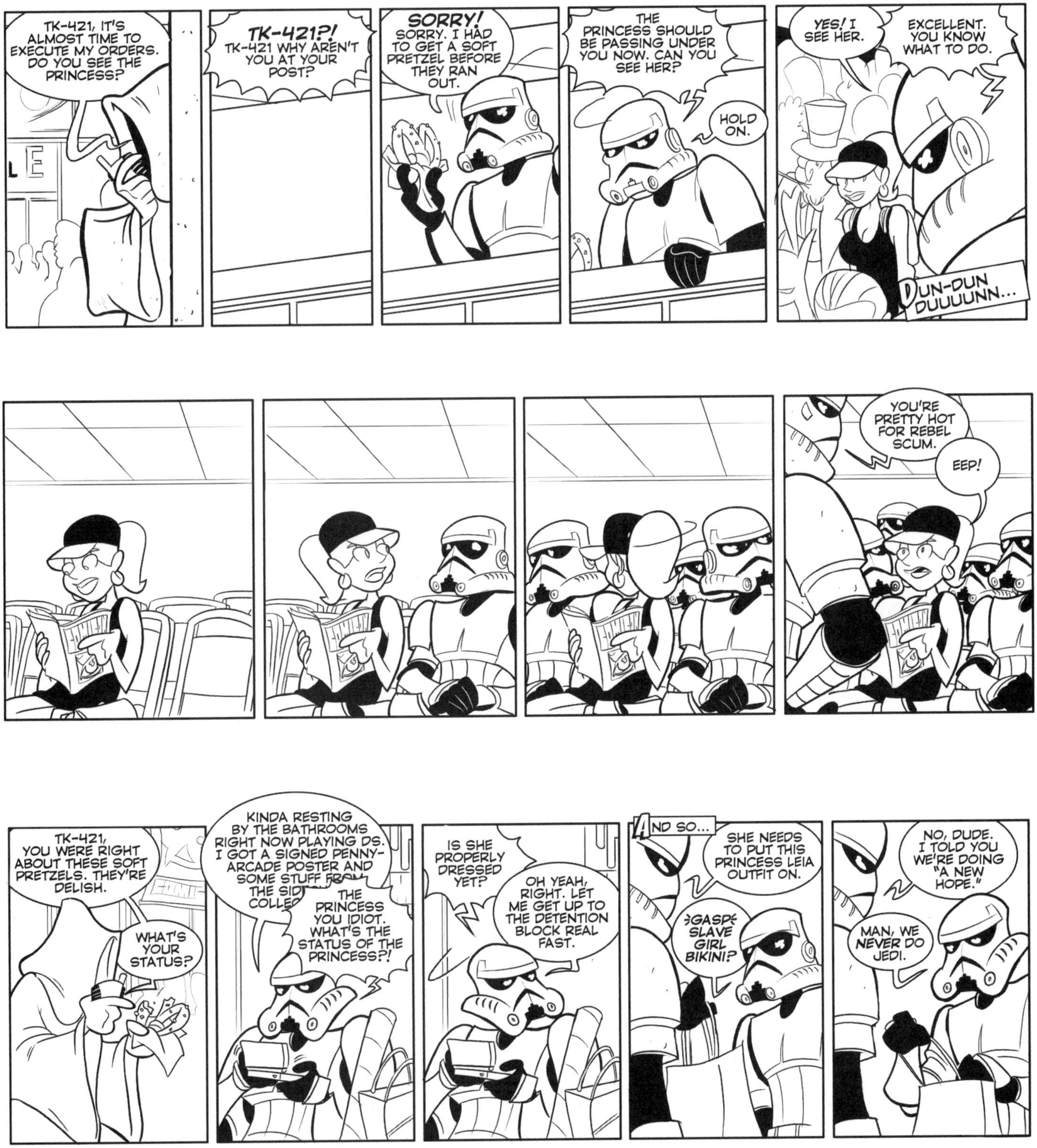
TK-421, IT'S ALMOST TIME TO EXECUTE MY ORDERS. DO YOU SEE THE PRINCESS?
TK-421?! TK-421 WHY AREN'T YOU AT YOUR POST?
SORRY! SORRY. I HAD TO GET A SOFT PRETZEL BEFORE THEY RAN OUT.
THE PRINCESS SHOULD BE PASSING UNDER YOU NOW. CAN YOU SEE HER?
HOLD ON.
YES! I SEE HER.
EXCELLENT. YOU KNOW WHAT TO DO.
DUN-DUN DUUUUNN...
YOU'RE PRETTY HOT FOR REBEL SCUM.
EEP!
TK-421, YOU WERE RIGHT ABOUT THESE SOFT PRETZELS. THEY'RE DELISH.
WHAT'S YOUR STATUS?
KINDA RESTING BY THE BATHROOMS RIGHT NOW PLAYING DS. I GOT A SIGNED PENNY-ARCADE POSTER AND SOME STUFF
THE PRINCESS YOU IDIOT. WHAT'S THE STATUS OF THE PRINCESS?!
IS SHE PROPERLY DRESSED YET?
OH YEAH, RIGHT. LET ME GET UP TO THE DETENTION BLOCK REAL FAST.
AND SO...
SHE NEEDS TO PUT THIS PRINCESS LEIA OUTFIT ON.
GASP SLAVE GIRL BIKINI?
NO, DUDE. I TOLD YOU WE'RE DOING "A NEW HOPE."
MAN, WE NEVER DO JEDI.

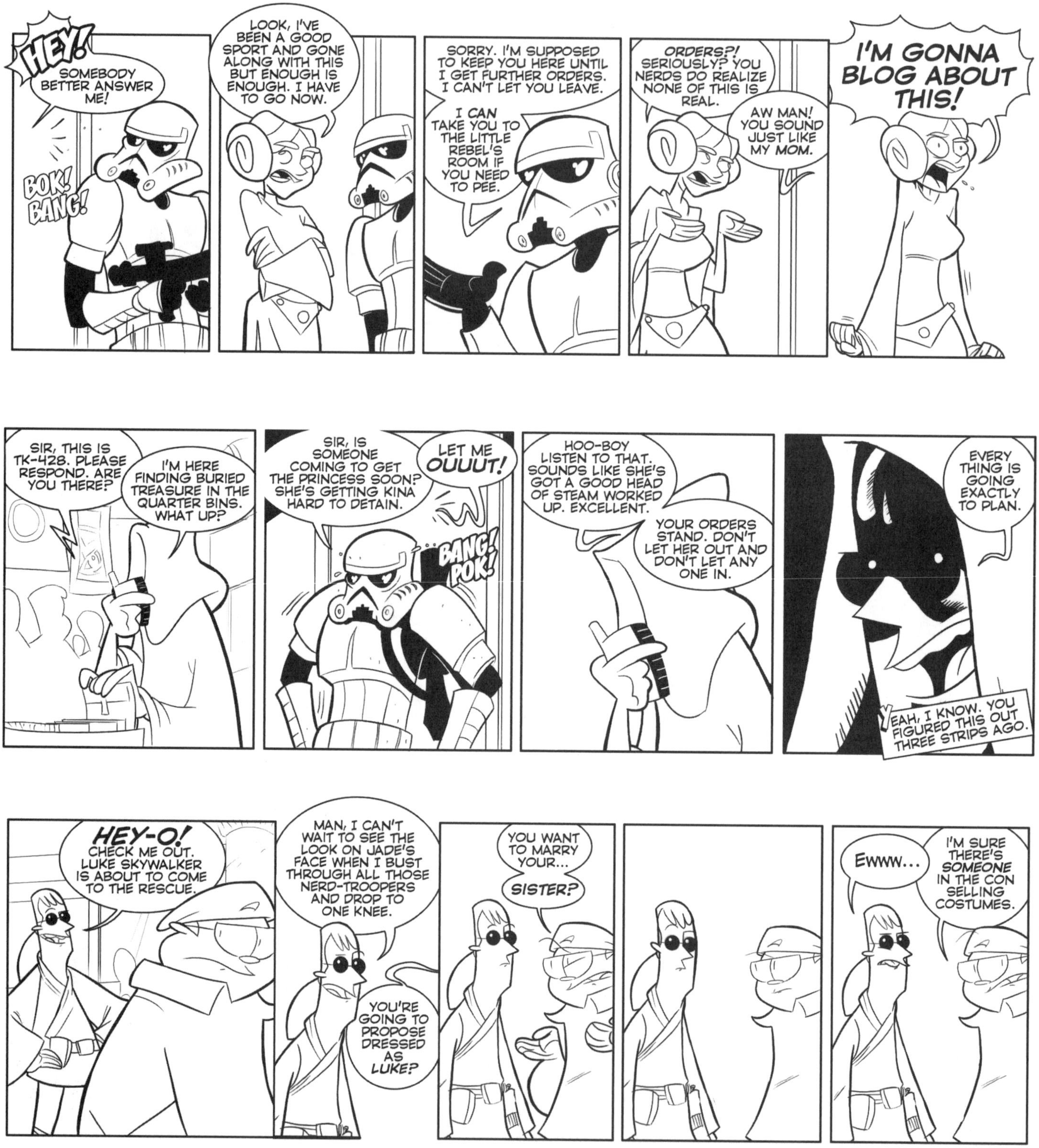
HEY!
SOMEBODY BETTER ANSWER ME!
BOK! BANG!
LOOK, I'VE BEEN A GOOD SPORT AND GONE ALONG WITH THIS BUT ENOUGH IS ENOUGH. I HAVE TO GO NOW.
SORRY. I'M SUPPOSED TO KEEP YOU HERE UNTIL I GET FURTHER ORDERS. I CAN'T LET YOU LEAVE.
I CAN TAKE YOU TO THE LITTLE REBEL'S ROOM IF YOU NEED TO PEE.
ORDERS?! SERIOUSLY? YOU NERDS DO REALIZE NONE OF THIS IS REAL.
AW MAN! YOU SOUND JUST LIKE MY MOM.
I'M GONNA BLOG ABOUT THIS!
SIR, THIS IS TK-428. PLEASE RESPOND. ARE YOU THERE?
I'M HERE FINDING BURIED TREASURE IN THE QUARTER BINS. WHAT UP?
SIR, IS SOMEONE COMING TO GET THE PRINCESS SOON? SHE'S GETTING KINA HARD TO DETAIN.
LET ME OUUUT!
BANG! POK!
HOO-BOY LISTEN TO THAT. SOUNDS LIKE SHE'S GOT A GOOD HEAD OF STEAM WORKED UP. EXCELLENT.
YOUR ORDERS STAND. DON'T LET HER OUT AND DON'T LET ANY ONE IN.
EVERY THING IS GOING EXACTLY TO PLAN.
YEAH, I KNOW. YOU FIGURED THIS OUT THREE STRIPS AGO.
HEY-O! CHECK ME OUT. LUKE SKYWALKER IS ABOUT TO COME TO THE RESCUE.
MAN, I CAN'T WAIT TO SEE THE LOOK ON JADE'S FACE WHEN I BUST THROUGH ALL THOSE NERD-TROOPERS AND DROP TO ONE KNEE.
YOU'RE GOING TO PROPOSE DRESSED AS LUKE?
YOU WANT TO MARRY YOUR... SISTER?
EWWW...
I'M SURE THERE'S SOMEONE IN THE CON SELLING COSTUMES.

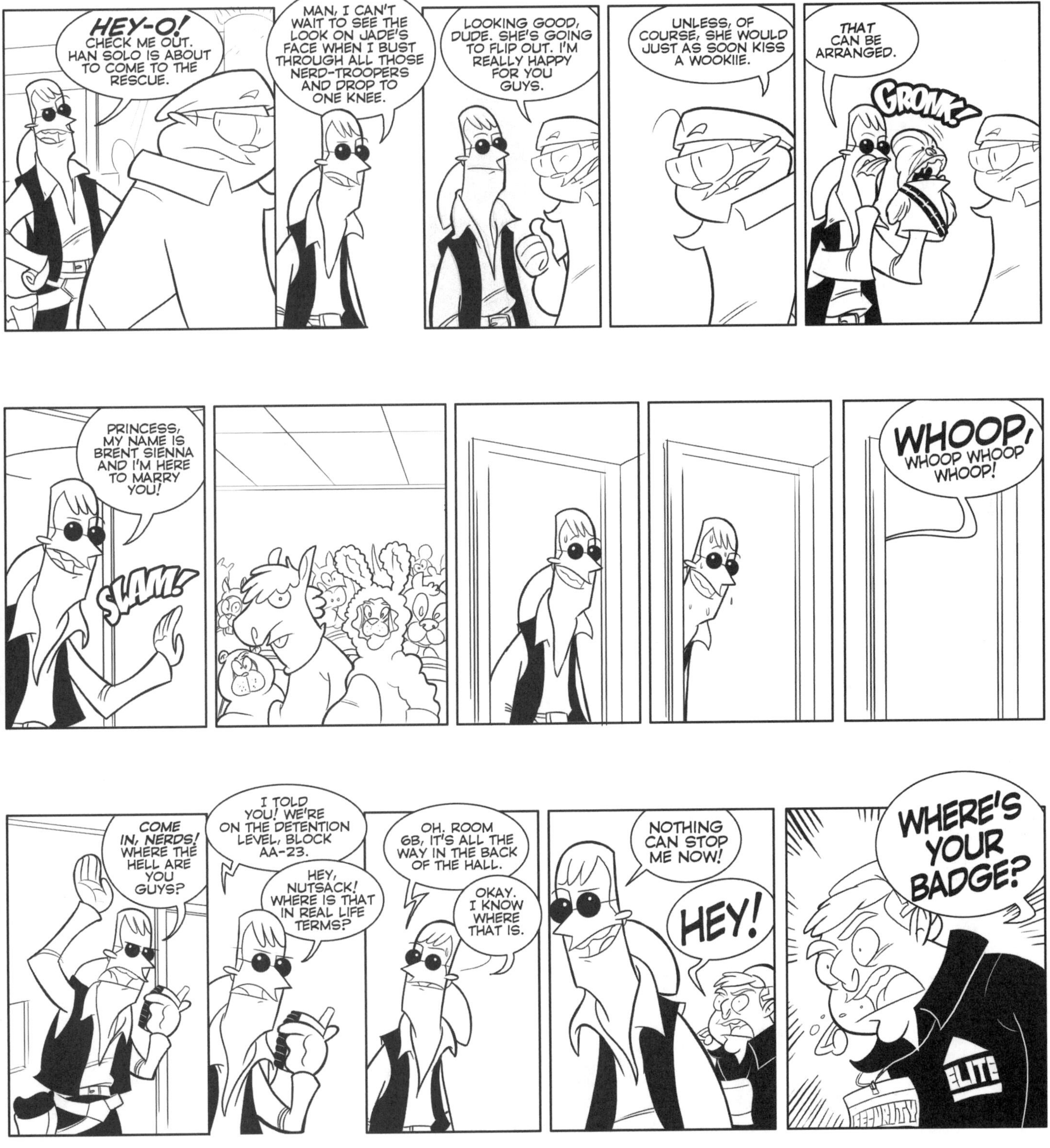
HEY-O! CHECK ME OUT. HAN SOLO IS ABOUT TO COME TO THE RESCUE.
MAN, I CAN'T WAIT TO SEE THE LOOK ON JADE'S FACE WHEN I BUST THROUGH ALL THOSE NERD-TROOPERS AND DROP TO ONE KNEE.
LOOKING GOOD, DUDE. SHE'S GOING TO FLIP OUT. I'M REALLY HAPPY FOR YOU GUYS.
UNLESS, OF COURSE, SHE WOULD JUST AS SOON KISS A WOOKIIE.
THAT CAN BE ARRANGED.
GRONK!
PRINCESS, MY NAME IS BRENT SIENNA AND I'M HERE TO MARRY YOU!
SLAM!
WHOOP! WHOOP WHOOP WHOOP!
COME IN, NERDS! WHERE THE HELL ARE YOU GUYS?
I TOLD YOU! WE'RE ON THE DETENTION LEVEL, BLOCK AA-23.
HEY, NUTSACK! WHERE IS THAT IN REAL LIFE TERMS?
OH. ROOM 6B, IT'S ALL THE WAY IN THE BACK OF THE HALL.
OKAY. I KNOW WHERE THAT IS.
NOTHING CAN STOP ME NOW!
HEY!
WHERE'S YOUR BADGE?
ELITE

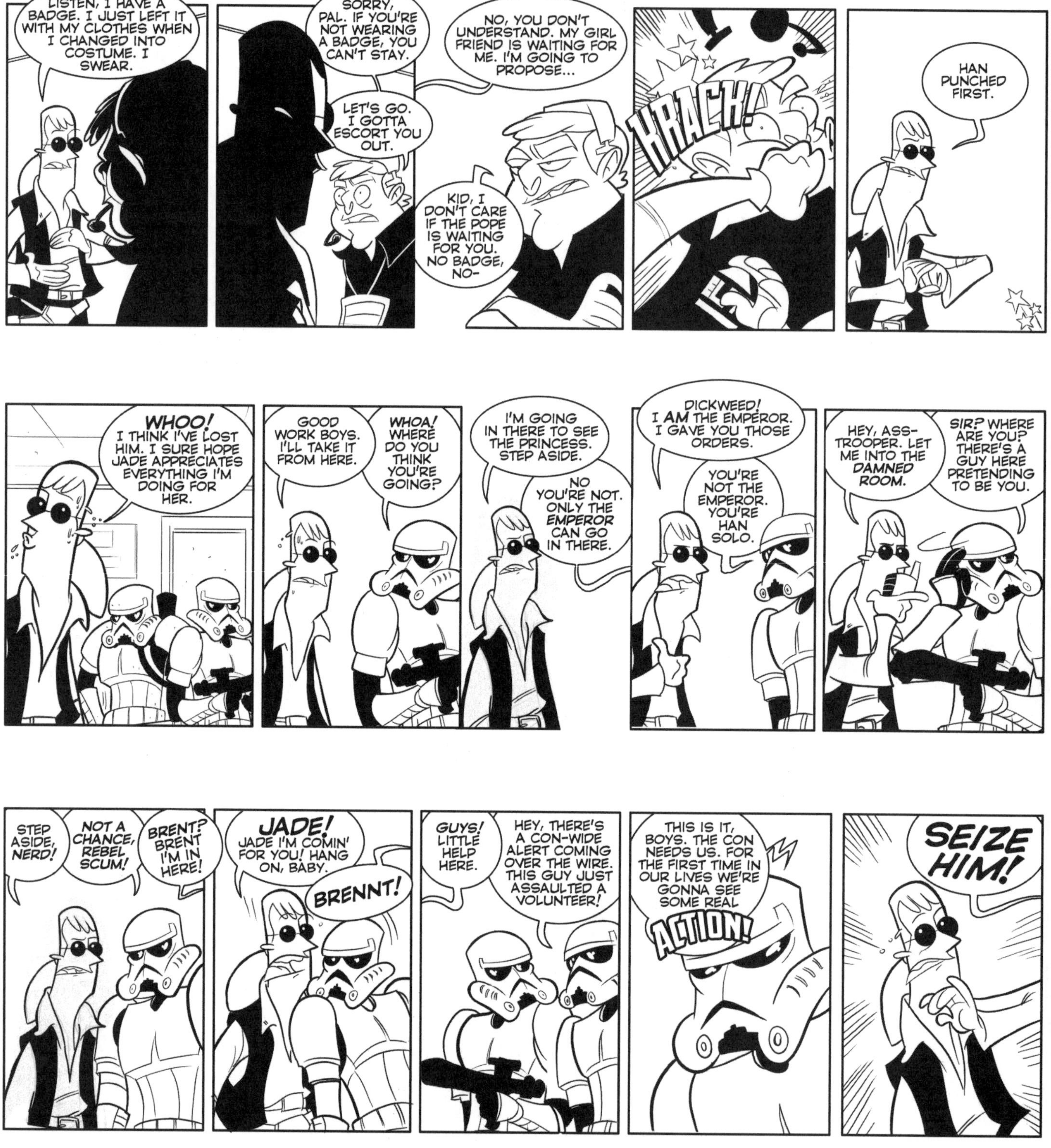
LISTEN, I HAVE A BADGE. I JUST LEFT IT WITH MY CLOTHES WHEN I CHANGED INTO COSTUME. I SWEAR.
SORRY, PAL. IF YOU'RE NOT WEARING A BADGE, YOU CAN'T STAY.
LET'S GO. I GOTTA ESCORT YOU OUT.
NO, YOU DON'T UNDERSTAND. MY GIRL FRIEND IS WAITING FOR ME. I'M GOING TO PROPOSE...
KID, I DON'T CARE IF THE POPE IS WAITING FOR YOU. NO BADGE, NO-
HRACK!
HAN PUNCHED FIRST.
WHOO! I THINK I'VE LOST HIM. I SURE HOPE JADE APPRECIATES EVERYTHING I'M DOING FOR HER.
GOOD WORK BOYS. I'LL TAKE IT FROM HERE.
WHOA! WHERE DO YOU THINK YOU'RE GOING?
I'M GOING IN THERE TO SEE THE PRINCESS. STEP ASIDE.
NO YOU'RE NOT. ONLY THE EMPEROR CAN GO IN THERE.
DICKWEED! I AM THE EMPEROR. I GAVE YOU THOSE ORDERS.
YOU'RE NOT THE EMPEROR. YOU'RE HAN SOLO.
HEY, ASS-TROOPER. LET ME INTO THE DAMNED ROOM.
SIR? WHERE ARE YOU? THERE'S A GUY HERE PRETENDING TO BE YOU.
STEP ASIDE, NERD!
NOT A CHANCE, REBEL SCUM!
BRENT? BRENT I'M IN HERE!
JADE! JADE I'M COMIN' FOR YOU! HANG ON, BABY.
BRENNT!
GUYS! LITTLE HELP HERE.
HEY, THERE'S A CON-WIDE ALERT COMING OVER THE WIRE. THIS GUY JUST ASSAULTED A VOLUNTEER!
THIS IS IT, BOYS. THE CON NEEDS US. FOR THE FIRST TIME IN OUR LIVES WE'RE GONNA SEE SOME REAL
ACTION!
SEIZE HIM!

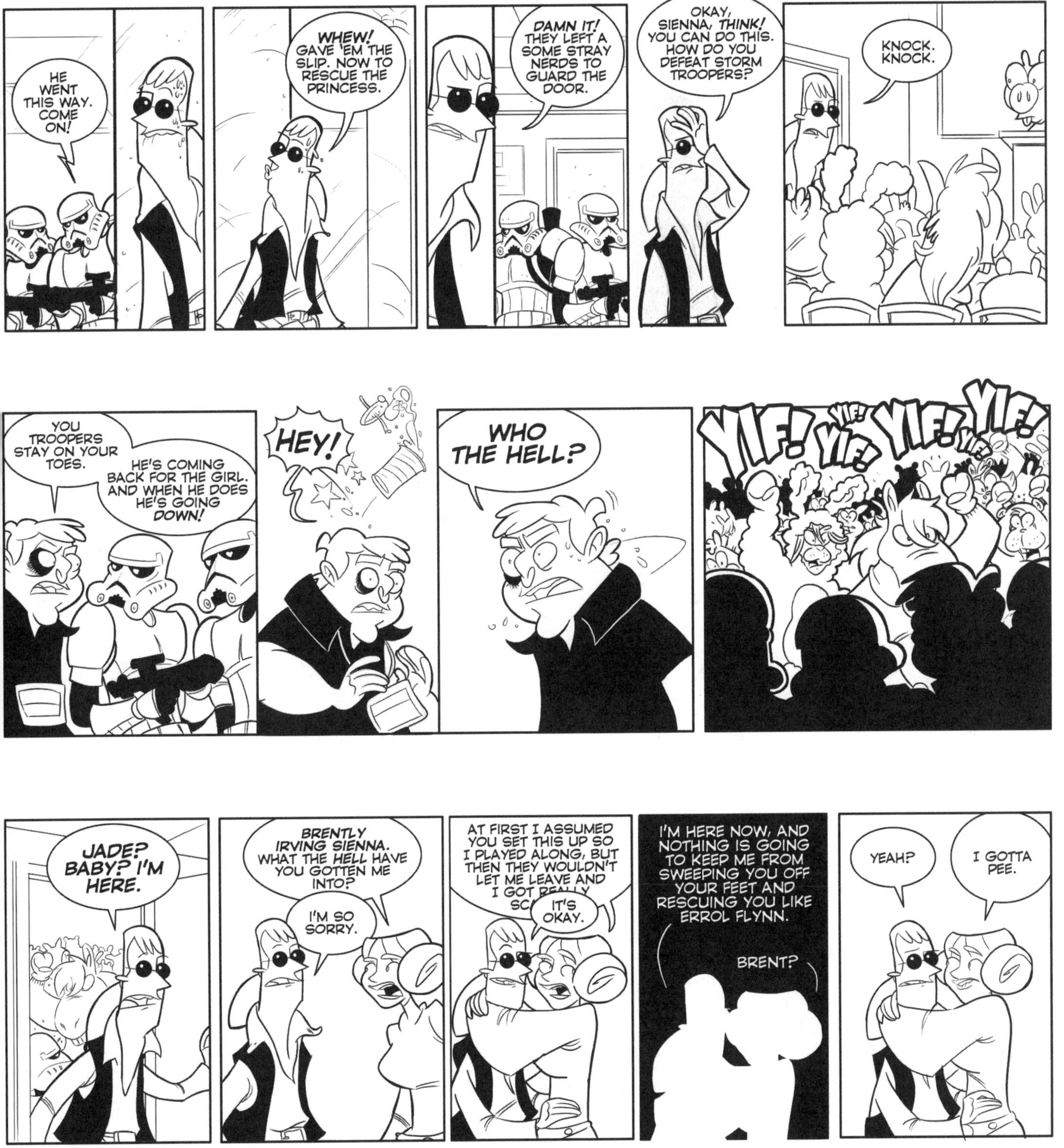
HE WENT THIS WAY. COME ON!
WHEW! GAVE 'EM THE SLIP. NOW TO RESCUE THE PRINCESS.
DAMN IT! THEY LEFT A SOME STRAY NERDS TO GUARD THE DOOR.
OKAY, SIENNA, THINK! YOU CAN DO THIS. HOW DO YOU DEFEAT STORM TROOPERS?
KNOCK. KNOCK.
YOU TROOPERS STAY ON YOUR TOES.
HE'S COMING BACK FOR THE GIRL. AND WHEN HE DOES HE'S GOING DOWN!
HEY!
WHO THE HELL?
YIF! YIF! YIF! YIF! YIF! YIF!
JADE? BABY? I'M HERE.
BRENTLY IRVING SIENNA. WHAT THE HELL HAVE YOU GOTTEN ME INTO?
I'M SO SORRY.
AT FIRST I ASSUMED YOU SET THIS UP SO I PLAYED ALONG, BUT THEN THEY WOULDN'T LET ME LEAVE AND I GOT
IT'S OKAY.
I'M HERE NOW, AND NOTHING IS GOING TO KEEP ME FROM SWEEPING YOU OFF YOUR FEET AND RESCUING YOU LIKE ERROL FLYNN.
BRENT?
YEAH?
I GOTTA PEE.

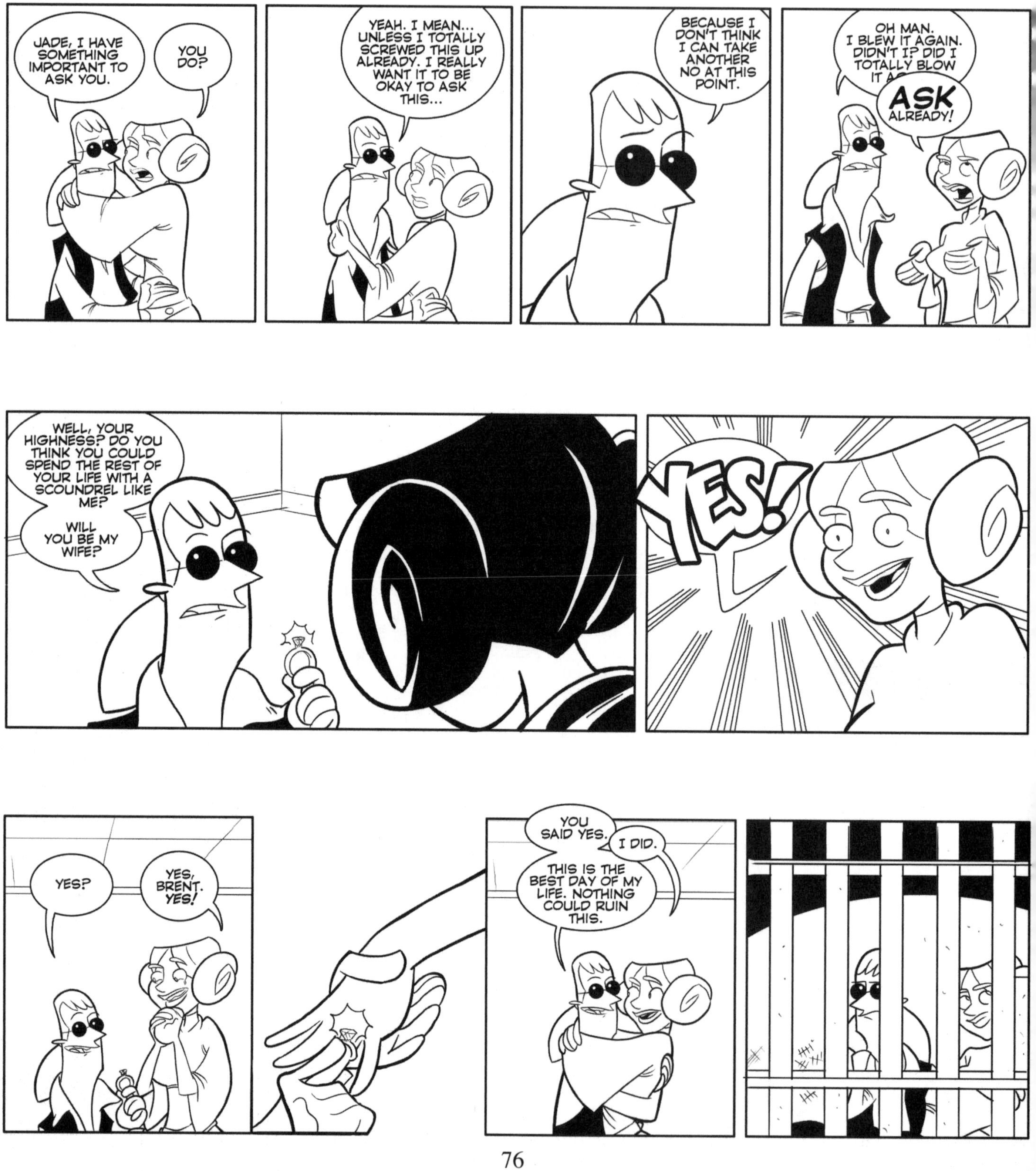
JADE, I HAVE SOMETHING IMPORTANT TO ASK YOU.
YOU DO?
YEAH. I MEAN... UNLESS I TOTALLY SCREWED THIS UP ALREADY. I REALLY WANT IT TO BE OKAY TO ASK THIS...
BECAUSE I DON'T THINK I CAN TAKE ANOTHER NO AT THIS POINT.
OH MAN. I BLEW IT AGAIN. DIDN'T I? DID I TOTALLY BLOW IT A
ASK ALREADY!
WELL, YOUR HIGHNESS? DO YOU THINK YOU COULD SPEND THE REST OF YOUR LIFE WITH A SCOUNDREL LIKE ME?
WILL YOU BE MY WIFE?
YES!
YES?
YES, BRENT. YES!
YOU SAID YES.
I DID.
THIS IS THE BEST DAY OF MY LIFE. NOTHING COULD RUIN THIS.

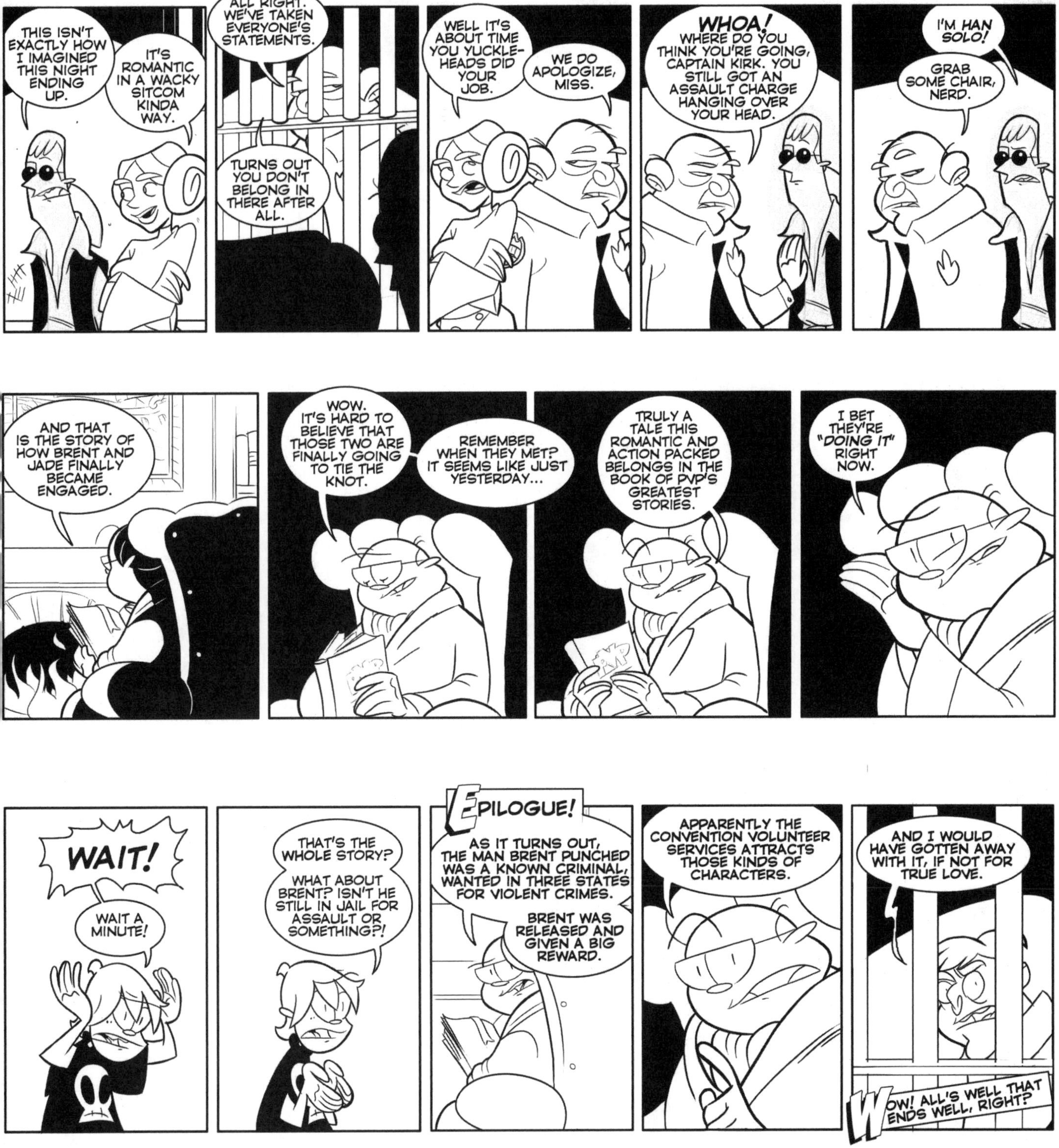
THIS ISN'T EXACTLY HOW I IMAGINED THIS NIGHT ENDING UP.
IT'S ROMANTIC IN A WACKY SITCOM KINDA WAY.
ALL RIGHT. WE'VE TAKEN EVERYONE'S STATEMENTS.
TURNS OUT YOU DON'T BELONG IN THERE AFTER ALL.
WELL IT'S ABOUT TIME YOU YUCKLE-HEADS DID YOUR JOB.
WE DO APOLOGIZE, MISS.
WHOA! WHERE DO YOU THINK YOU'RE GOING, CAPTAIN KIRK. YOU STILL GOT AN ASSAULT CHARGE HANGING OVER YOUR HEAD.
I'M HAN SOLO!
GRAB SOME CHAIR, NERD.
AND THAT IS THE STORY OF HOW BRENT AND JADE FINALLY BECAME ENGAGED.
WOW. IT'S HARD TO BELIEVE THAT THOSE TWO ARE FINALLY GOING TO TIE THE KNOT.
REMEMBER WHEN THEY MET? IT SEEMS LIKE JUST YESTERDAY...
TRULY A TALE THIS ROMANTIC AND ACTION PACKED BELONGS IN THE BOOK OF PVP'S GREATEST STORIES.
I BET THEY'RE "DOING IT" RIGHT NOW.
WAIT!
WAIT A MINUTE!
THAT'S THE WHOLE STORY?
WHAT ABOUT BRENT? ISN'T HE STILL IN JAIL FOR ASSAULT OR SOMETHING?!
EPILOGUE!
AS IT TURNS OUT, THE MAN BRENT PUNCHED WAS A KNOWN CRIMINAL, WANTED IN THREE STATES FOR VIOLENT CRIMES.
BRENT WAS RELEASED AND GIVEN A BIG REWARD.
APPARENTLY THE CONVENTION VOLUNTEER SERVICES ATTRACTS THOSE KINDS OF CHARACTERS.
AND I WOULD HAVE GOTTEN AWAY WITH IT, IF NOT FOR TRUE LOVE.
WOW! ALL'S WELL THAT ENDS WELL, RIGHT?

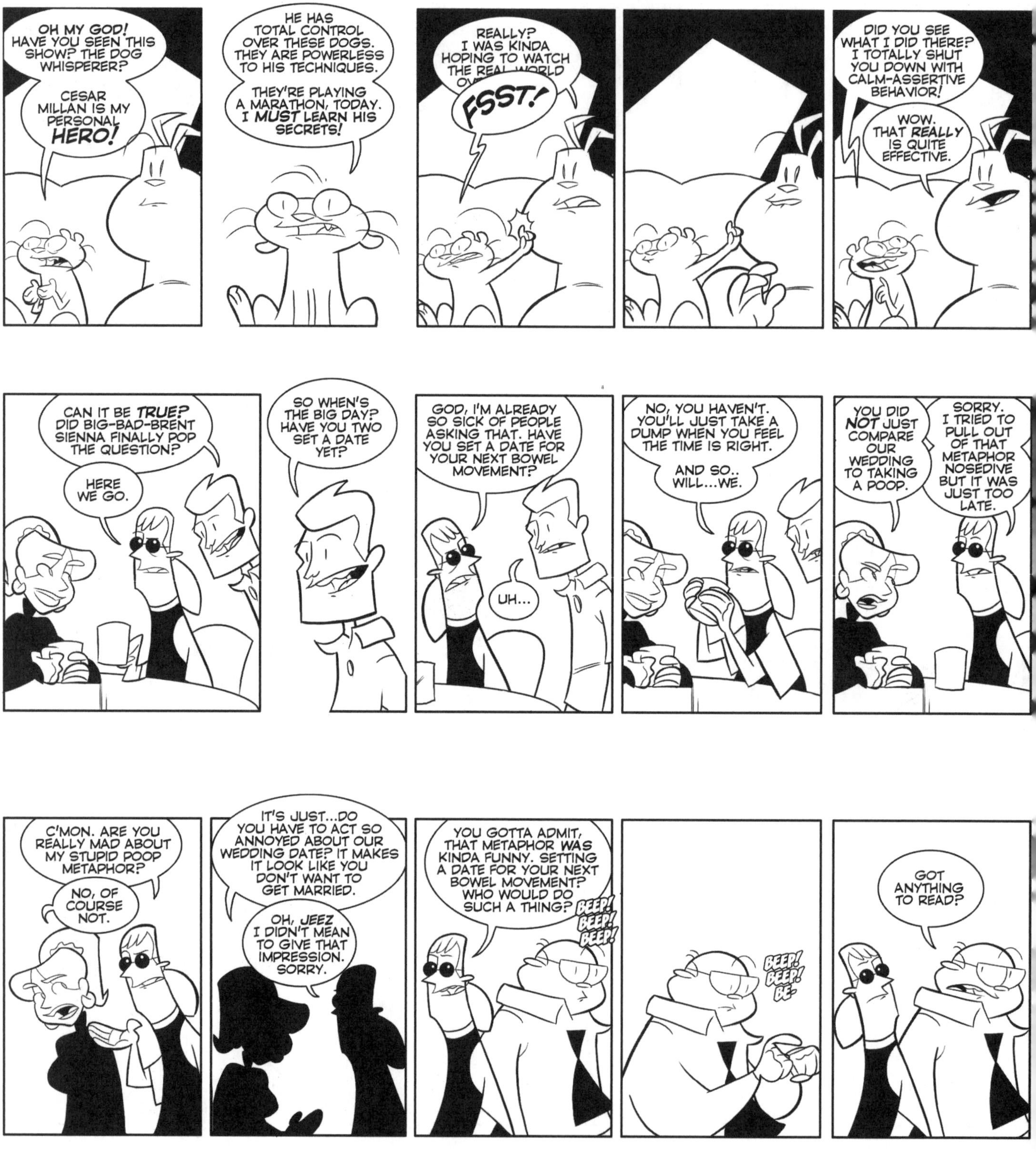
OH MY GOD! HAVE YOU SEEN THIS SHOW? THE DOG WHISPERER?
CESAR MILLAN IS MY PERSONAL HERO!
HE HAS TOTAL CONTROL OVER THESE DOGS. THEY ARE POWERLESS TO HIS TECHNIQUES.
THEY'RE PLAYING A MARATHON, TODAY. I MUST LEARN HIS SECRETS!
REALLY? I WAS KINDA HOPING TO WATCH THE REAL WORLD
FSST!
DID YOU SEE WHAT I DID THERE? I TOTALLY SHUT YOU DOWN WITH CALM-ASSERTIVE BEHAVIOR!
WOW. THAT REALLY IS QUITE EFFECTIVE.
CAN IT BE TRUE? DID BIG-BAD-BRENT SIENNA FINALLY POP THE QUESTION?
HERE WE GO.
SO WHEN'S THE BIG DAY? HAVE YOU TWO SET A DATE YET?
GOD, I'M ALREADY SO SICK OF PEOPLE ASKING THAT. HAVE YOU SET A DATE FOR YOUR NEXT BOWEL MOVEMENT?
UH...
NO, YOU HAVEN'T. YOU'LL JUST TAKE A DUMP WHEN YOU FEEL THE TIME IS RIGHT.
AND SO.. WILL...WE.
YOU DID NOT JUST COMPARE OUR WEDDING TO TAKING A POOP.
SORRY. I TRIED TO PULL OUT OF THAT METAPHOR NOSEDIVE BUT IT WAS JUST TOO LATE.
C'MON. ARE YOU REALLY MAD ABOUT MY STUPID POOP METAPHOR?
NO, OF COURSE NOT.
IT'S JUST...DO YOU HAVE TO ACT SO ANNOYED ABOUT OUR WEDDING DATE? IT MAKES IT LOOK LIKE YOU DON'T WANT TO GET MARRIED.
OH, JEEZ I DIDN'T MEAN TO GIVE THAT IMPRESSION. SORRY.
YOU GOTTA ADMIT, THAT METAPHOR WAS KINDA FUNNY. SETTING A DATE FOR YOUR NEXT BOWEL MOVEMENT? WHO WOULD DO SUCH A THING?
BEEP! BEEP! BEEP!
BEEP! BEEP! BE-
GOT ANYTHING TO READ?

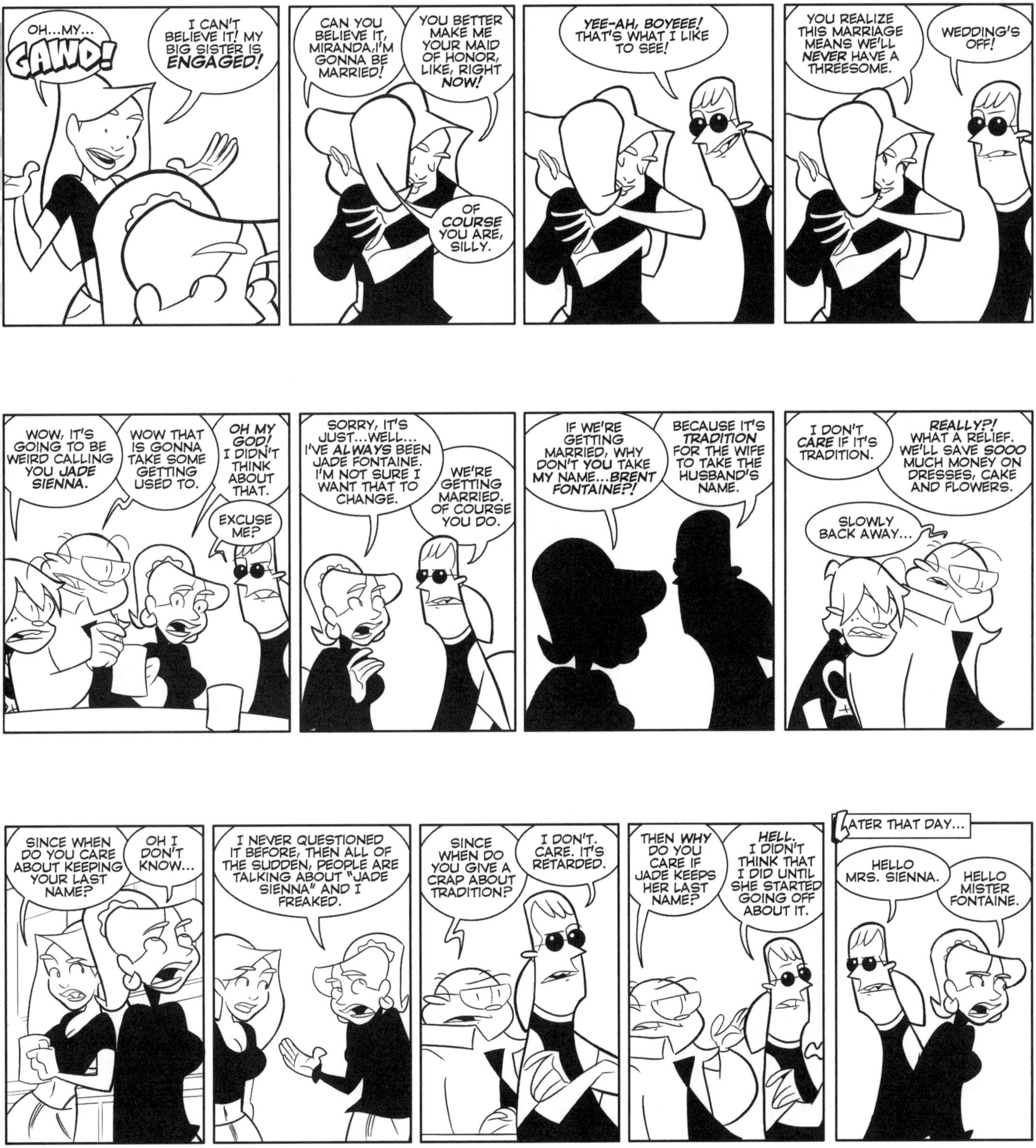
OH...MY...
GAWD!
I CAN'T BELIEVE IT! MY BIG SISTER IS ENGAGED!
CAN YOU BELIEVE IT, MIRANDA, I'M GONNA BE MARRIED!
YOU BETTER MAKE ME YOUR MAID OF HONOR, LIKE, RIGHT NOW!
OF COURSE YOU ARE, SILLY.
YEE-AH, BOYEEE! THAT'S WHAT I LIKE TO SEE!
YOU REALIZE THIS MARRIAGE MEANS WE'LL NEVER HAVE A THREESOME.
WEDDING'S OFF!
WOW, IT'S GOING TO BE WEIRD CALLING YOU JADE SIENNA.
WOW THAT IS GONNA TAKE SOME GETTING USED TO.
OH MY GOD! I DIDN'T THINK ABOUT THAT.
EXCUSE ME?
SORRY, IT'S JUST...WELL... I'VE ALWAYS BEEN JADE FONTAINE. I'M NOT SURE I WANT THAT TO CHANGE.
WE'RE GETTING MARRIED. OF COURSE YOU DO.
IF WE'RE GETTING MARRIED, WHY DON'T YOU TAKE MY NAME...BRENT FONTAINE?!
BECAUSE IT'S TRADITION FOR THE WIFE TO TAKE THE HUSBAND'S NAME.
I DON'T CARE IF IT'S TRADITION.
REALLY?! WHAT A RELIEF. WE'LL SAVE SOOO MUCH MONEY ON DRESSES, CAKE AND FLOWERS.
SLOWLY BACK AWAY...
SINCE WHEN DO YOU CARE ABOUT KEEPING YOUR LAST NAME?
OH I DON'T KNOW...
I NEVER QUESTIONED IT BEFORE, THEN ALL OF THE SUDDEN, PEOPLE ARE TALKING ABOUT "JADE SIENNA" AND I FREAKED.
SINCE WHEN DO YOU GIVE A CRAP ABOUT TRADITION?
I DON'T. CARE. IT'S RETARDED.
THEN WHY DO YOU CARE IF JADE KEEPS HER LAST NAME?
HELL. I DIDN'T THINK THAT I DID UNTIL SHE STARTED GOING OFF ABOUT IT.
LATER THAT DAY...
HELLO MRS. SIENNA.
HELLO MISTER FONTAINE.

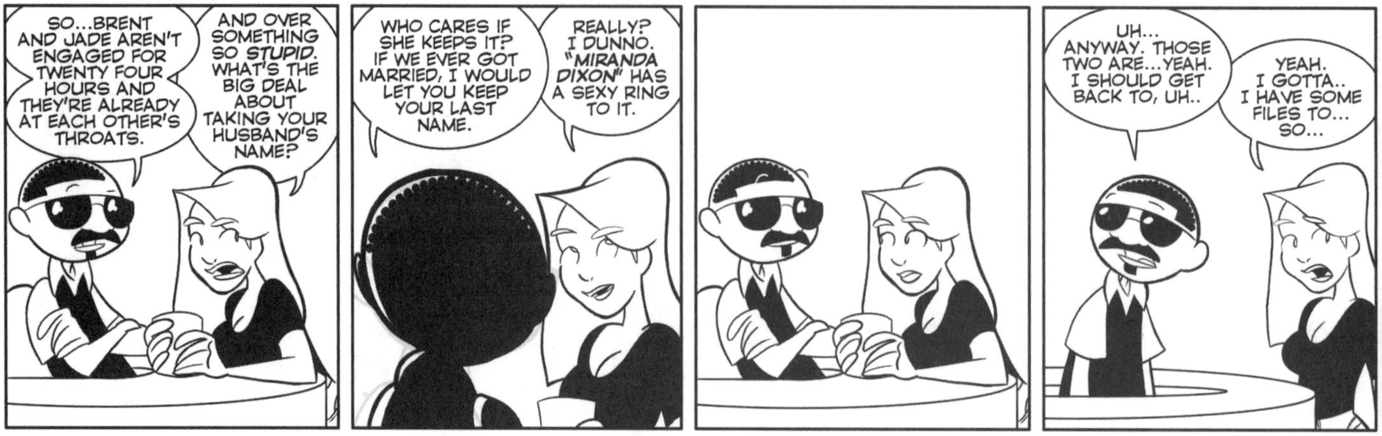
SO...BRENT AND JADE AREN'T ENGAGED FOR TWENTY FOUR HOURS AND THEY'RE ALREADY AT EACH OTHER'S THROATS.
AND OVER SOMETHING SO STUPID. WHAT'S THE BIG DEAL ABOUT TAKING YOUR HUSBAND'S NAME?
WHO CARES IF SHE KEEPS IT? IF WE EVER GOT MARRIED, I WOULD LET YOU KEEP YOUR LAST NAME.
REALLY? I DUNNO. "MIRANDA DIXON" HAS A SEXY RING TO IT.
UH... ANYWAY. THOSE TWO ARE...YEAH. I SHOULD GET BACK TO, UH..
YEAH. I GOTTA.. I HAVE SOME FILES TO... SO...

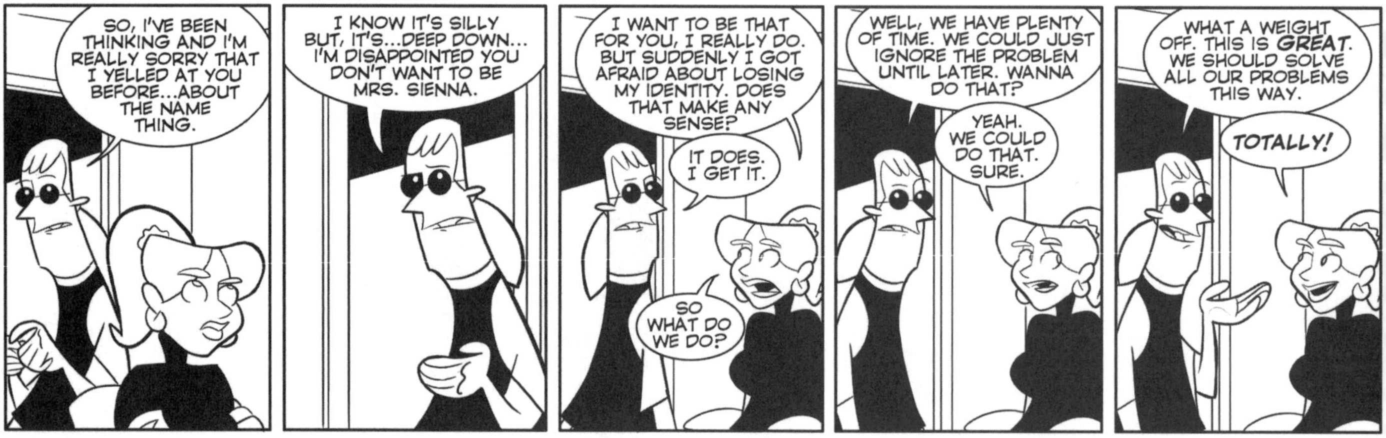
SO, I'VE BEEN THINKING AND I'M REALLY SORRY THAT I YELLED AT YOU BEFORE...ABOUT THE NAME THING.
I KNOW IT'S SILLY BUT, IT'S...DEEP DOWN... I'M DISAPPOINTED YOU DON'T WANT TO BE MRS. SIENNA.
I WANT TO BE THAT FOR YOU, I REALLY DO. BUT SUDDENLY I GOT AFRAID ABOUT LOSING MY IDENTITY. DOES THAT MAKE ANY SENSE?
IT DOES. I GET IT.
SO WHAT DO WE DO?
WELL, WE HAVE PLENTY OF TIME. WE COULD JUST IGNORE THE PROBLEM UNTIL LATER. WANNA DO THAT?
YEAH. WE COULD DO THAT. SURE.
WHAT A WEIGHT OFF. THIS IS GREAT. WE SHOULD SOLVE ALL OUR PROBLEMS THIS WAY.
TOTALLY!

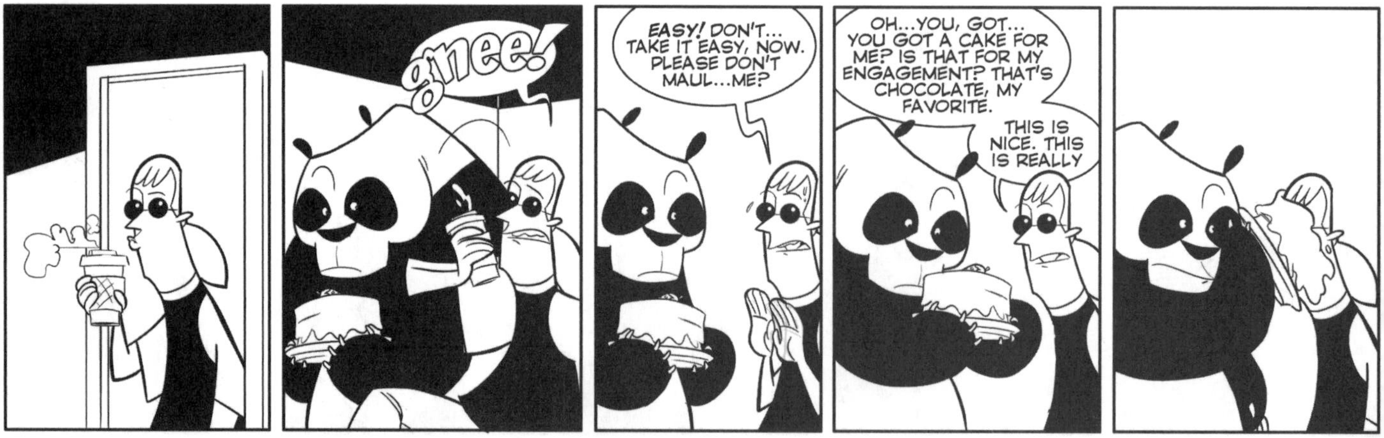
gnee!
EASY! DON'T... TAKE IT EASY, NOW. PLEASE DON'T MAUL...ME?
OH...YOU, GOT... YOU GOT A CAKE FOR ME? IS THAT FOR MY ENGAGEMENT? THAT'S CHOCOLATE, MY FAVORITE.
THIS IS NICE. THIS IS REALLY

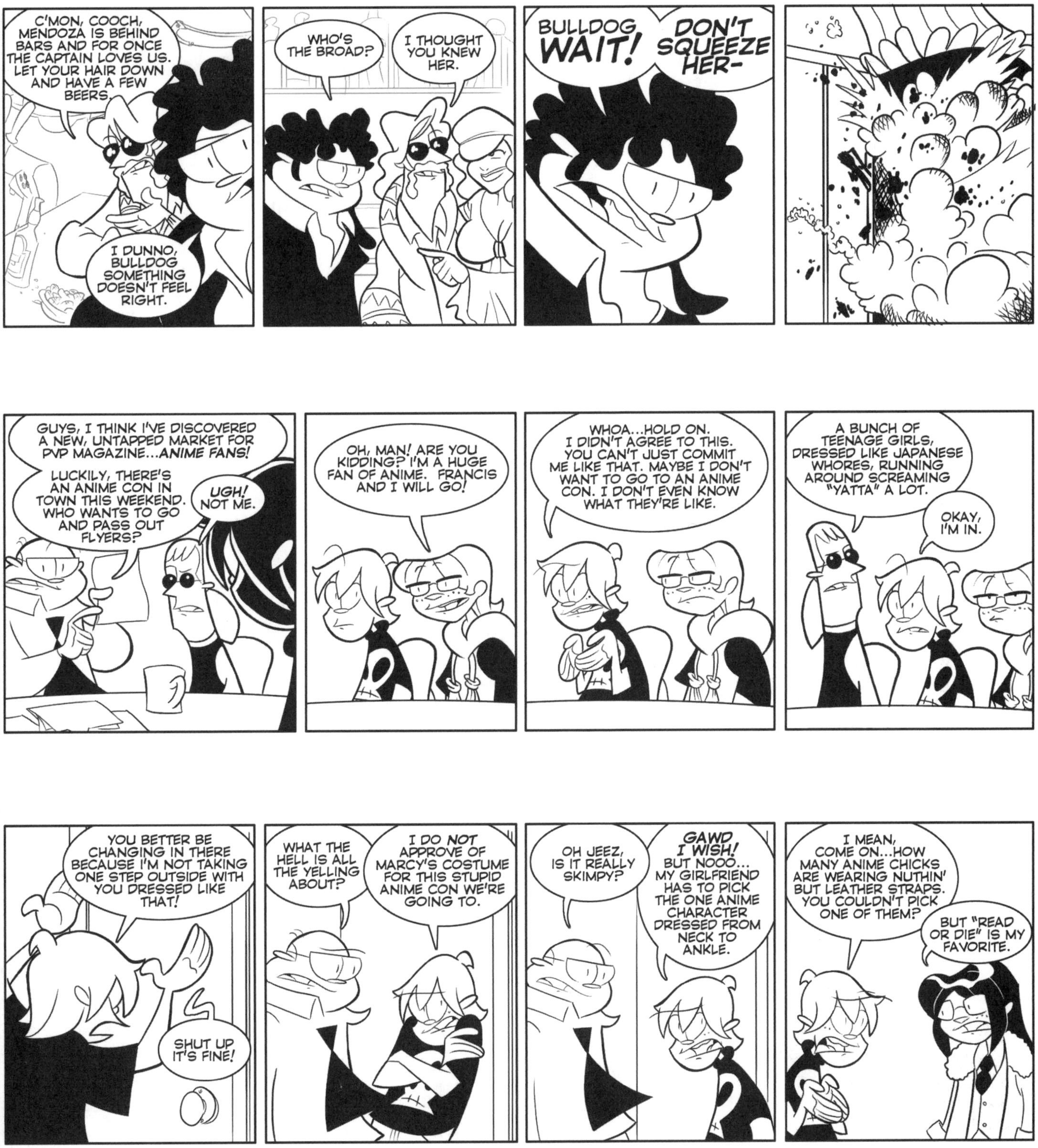
C'MON, COOCH, MENDOZA IS BEHIND BARS AND FOR ONCE THE CAPTAIN LOVES US. LET YOUR HAIR DOWN AND HAVE A FEW BEERS.
I DUNNO, BULLDOG SOMETHING DOESN'T FEEL RIGHT.
WHO'S THE BROAD?
I THOUGHT YOU KNEW HER.
BULLDOG WAIT!
DON'T SQUEEZE HER-
GUYS, I THINK I'VE DISCOVERED A NEW, UNTAPPED MARKET FOR PVP MAGAZINE...ANIME FANS!
LUCKILY, THERE'S AN ANIME CON IN TOWN THIS WEEKEND. WHO WANTS TO GO AND PASS OUT FLYERS?
UGH! NOT ME.
OH, MAN! ARE YOU KIDDING? I'M A HUGE FAN OF ANIME. FRANCIS AND I WILL GO!
WHOA...HOLD ON. I DIDN'T AGREE TO THIS. YOU CAN'T JUST COMMIT ME LIKE THAT. MAYBE I DON'T WANT TO GO TO AN ANIME CON. I DON'T EVEN KNOW WHAT THEY'RE LIKE.
A BUNCH OF TEENAGE GIRLS, DRESSED LIKE JAPANESE WHORES, RUNNING AROUND SCREAMING "YATTA" A LOT.
OKAY, I'M IN.
YOU BETTER BE CHANGING IN THERE BECAUSE I'M NOT TAKING ONE STEP OUTSIDE WITH YOU DRESSED LIKE THAT!
SHUT UP IT'S FINE!
WHAT THE HELL IS ALL THE YELLING ABOUT?
I DO NOT APPROVE OF MARCY'S COSTUME FOR THIS STUPID ANIME CON WE'RE GOING TO.
OH JEEZ, IS IT REALLY SKIMPY?
GAWD I WISH! BUT NOOO... MY GIRLFRIEND HAS TO PICK THE ONE ANIME CHARACTER DRESSED FROM NECK TO ANKLE.
I MEAN, COME ON...HOW MANY ANIME CHICKS ARE WEARING NUTHIN' BUT LEATHER STRAPS. YOU COULDN'T PICK ONE OF THEM?
BUT "READ OR DIE" IS MY FAVORITE.

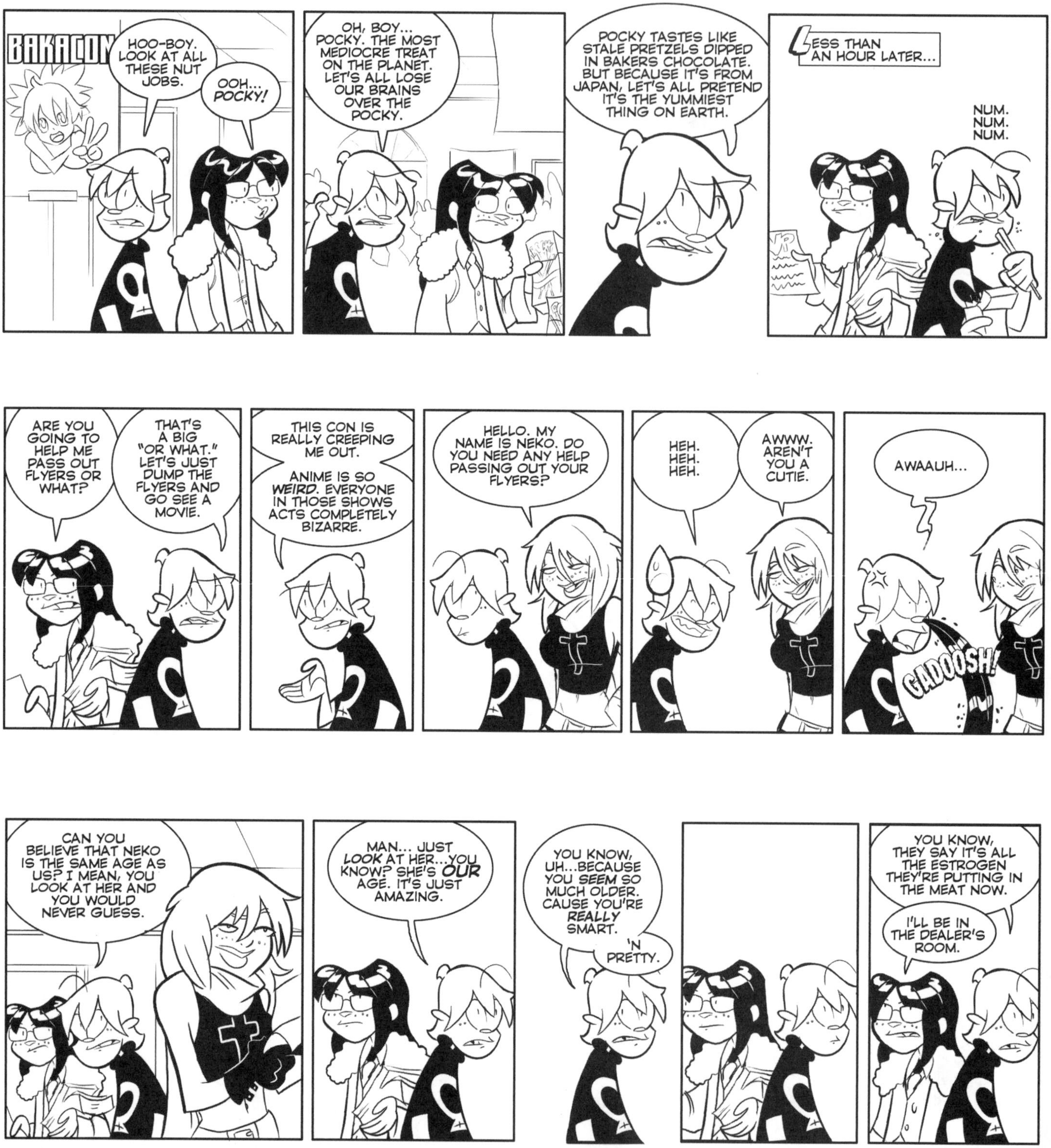
BAKACON
HOO-BOY. LOOK AT ALL THESE NUT JOBS.
OOH... POCKY!
OH, BOY... POCKY. THE MOST MEDIOCRE TREAT ON THE PLANET. LET'S ALL LOSE OUR BRAINS OVER THE POCKY.
POCKY TASTES LIKE STALE PRETZELS DIPPED IN BAKERS CHOCOLATE. BUT BECAUSE IT'S FROM JAPAN, LET'S ALL PRETEND IT'S THE YUMMIEST THING ON EARTH.
LESS THAN AN HOUR LATER...
NUM. NUM. NUM.
ARE YOU GOING TO HELP ME PASS OUT FLYERS OR WHAT?
THAT'S A BIG "OR WHAT." LET'S JUST DUMP THE FLYERS AND GO SEE A MOVIE.
THIS CON IS REALLY CREEPING ME OUT.
ANIME IS SO WEIRD. EVERYONE IN THOSE SHOWS ACTS COMPLETELY BIZARRE.
HELLO. MY NAME IS NEKO. DO YOU NEED ANY HELP PASSING OUT YOUR FLYERS?
HEH. HEH. HEH.
AWWW. AREN'T YOU A CUTIE.
AWAAUH...
GADOOSH!
CAN YOU BELIEVE THAT NEKO IS THE SAME AGE AS US? I MEAN, YOU LOOK AT HER AND YOU WOULD NEVER GUESS.
MAN... JUST LOOK AT HER... YOU KNOW? SHE'S OUR AGE. IT'S JUST AMAZING.
YOU KNOW, UH... BECAUSE YOU SEEM SO MUCH OLDER. CAUSE YOU'RE REALLY SMART.
'N PRETTY.
YOU KNOW, THEY SAY IT'S ALL THE ESTROGEN THEY'RE PUTTING IN THE MEAT NOW.
I'LL BE IN THE DEALER'S ROOM.

I'M OUT OF FLYERS. WHERE'S FRANCIS?

HE SAID HE WAS GOING TO GO PUT HIS COSPLAY STUFF ON.

HA, HAH! UH...YEAH. YOU OBVIOUSLY DON'T KNOW FRANCIS VERY WELL. HE WOULD NEVER PUT ON A COSPLAY OUTFIT IN A MILLION YEARS.

HEY. WHAT UP?

FRANCIS, WHAT THE HELL?! YOU'RE DRESSED LIKE CHUN LI?

IT WAS ALL THEY HAD. I'M A GAMER. IT'S COOL.

YOU DRESSED LIKE A GIRL? THAT'S SO TOTALLY SHWAY, FRANCIS.

TEE HEE. KONICHIWA.

RRRRR...

OHMIGOSH NEKO, ARE YOU OKAY?

GHHNN...

YOU...SHOT ME IN THE BACK? YOU SHOT ME IN THE BACK?!!

KLIK! KLAK!

WHRR!

KLIK!

KLANK!

YOU WILL PAY FOR YOUR DISHONOR!

OMNI-MECHA-BITCH FOUR THOUSAND!!!

83

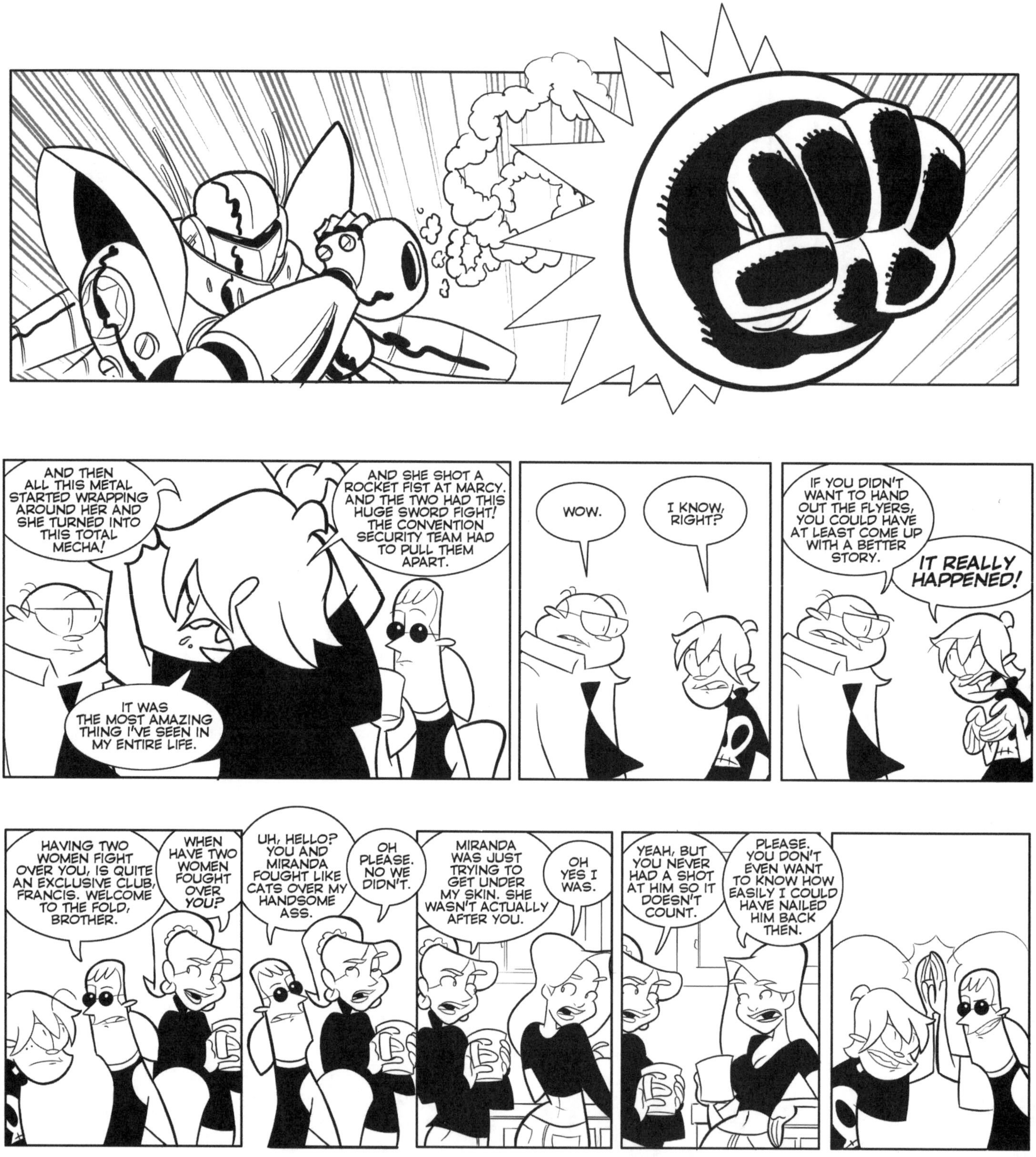
AND THEN ALL THIS METAL STARTED WRAPPING AROUND HER AND SHE TURNED INTO THIS TOTAL MECHA!
AND SHE SHOT A ROCKET FIST AT MARCY. AND THE TWO HAD THIS HUGE SWORD FIGHT! THE CONVENTION SECURITY TEAM HAD TO PULL THEM APART.
IT WAS THE MOST AMAZING THING I'VE SEEN IN MY ENTIRE LIFE.
WOW.
I KNOW, RIGHT?
IF YOU DIDN'T WANT TO HAND OUT THE FLYERS, YOU COULD HAVE AT LEAST COME UP WITH A BETTER STORY.
IT REALLY HAPPENED!
HAVING TWO WOMEN FIGHT OVER YOU, IS QUITE AN EXCLUSIVE CLUB, FRANCIS. WELCOME TO THE FOLD, BROTHER.
WHEN HAVE TWO WOMEN FOUGHT OVER YOU?
UH, HELLO? YOU AND MIRANDA FOUGHT LIKE CATS OVER MY HANDSOME ASS.
OH PLEASE. NO WE DIDN'T.
MIRANDA WAS JUST TRYING TO GET UNDER MY SKIN. SHE WASN'T ACTUALLY AFTER YOU.
OH YES I WAS.
YEAH, BUT YOU NEVER HAD A SHOT AT HIM SO IT DOESN'T COUNT.
PLEASE. YOU DON'T EVEN WANT TO KNOW HOW EASILY I COULD HAVE NAILED HIM BACK THEN.

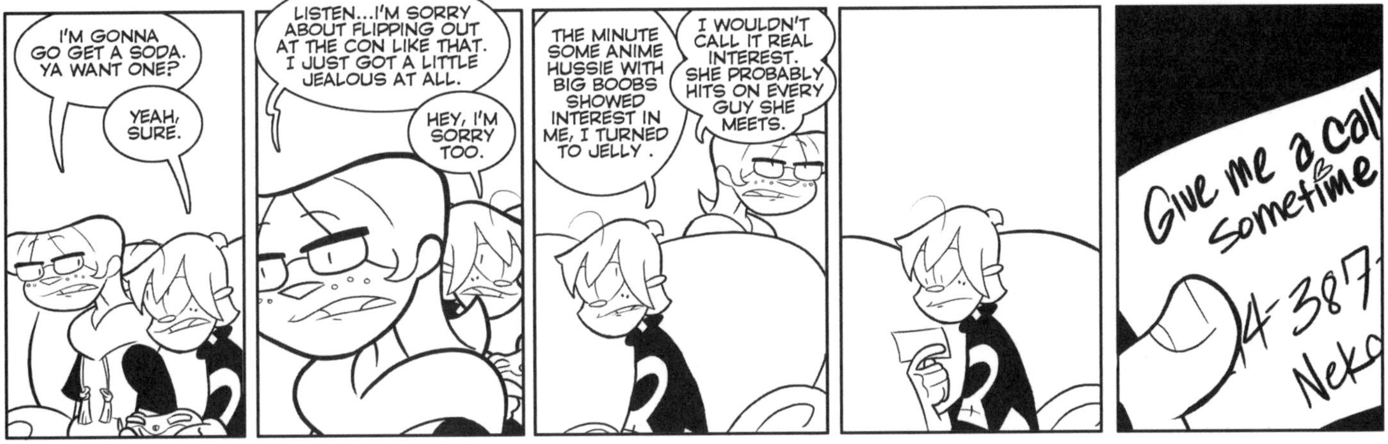
I'M GONNA GO GET A SODA. YA WANT ONE?
YEAH, SURE.
LISTEN...I'M SORRY ABOUT FLIPPING OUT AT THE CON LIKE THAT. I JUST GOT A LITTLE JEALOUS AT ALL.
HEY, I'M SORRY TOO.
THE MINUTE SOME ANIME HUSSIE WITH BIG BOOBS SHOWED INTEREST IN ME, I TURNED TO JELLY .
I WOULDN'T CALL IT REAL INTEREST. SHE PROBABLY HITS ON EVERY GUY SHE MEETS.
Give me a call
sometime
4-387
Neko

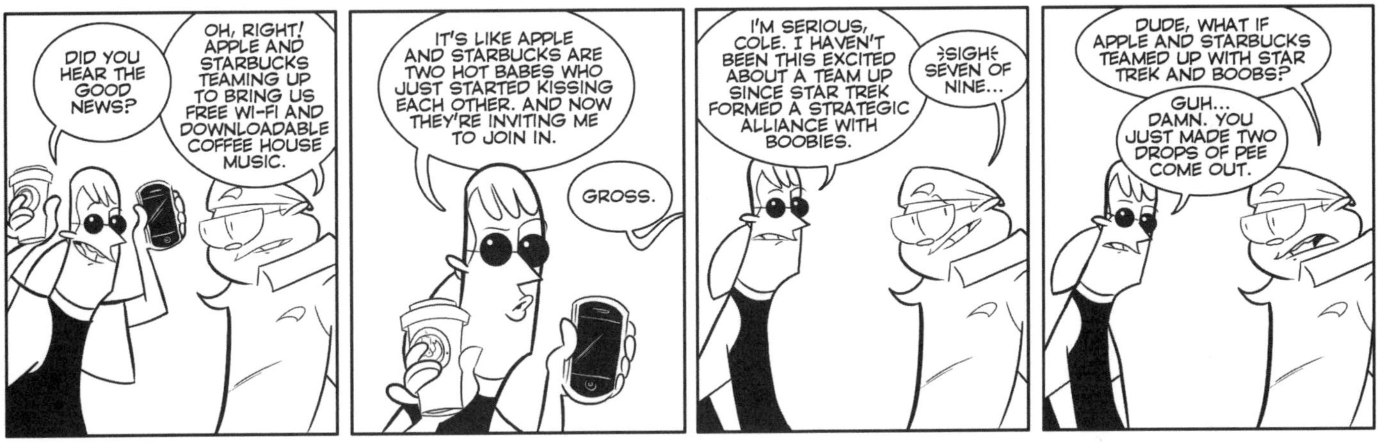
DID YOU HEAR THE GOOD NEWS?
OH, RIGHT! APPLE AND STARBUCKS TEAMING UP TO BRING US FREE WI-FI AND DOWNLOADABLE COFFEE HOUSE MUSIC.
IT'S LIKE APPLE AND STARBUCKS ARE TWO HOT BABES WHO JUST STARTED KISSING EACH OTHER. AND NOW THEY'RE INVITING ME TO JOIN IN.
GROSS.
I'M SERIOUS, COLE. I HAVEN'T BEEN THIS EXCITED ABOUT A TEAM UP SINCE STAR TREK FORMED A STRATEGIC ALLIANCE WITH BOOBIES.
SIGH SEVEN OF NINE...
DUDE, WHAT IF APPLE AND STARBUCKS TEAMED UP WITH STAR TREK AND BOOBS?
GUH... DAMN. YOU JUST MADE TWO DROPS OF PEE COME OUT.

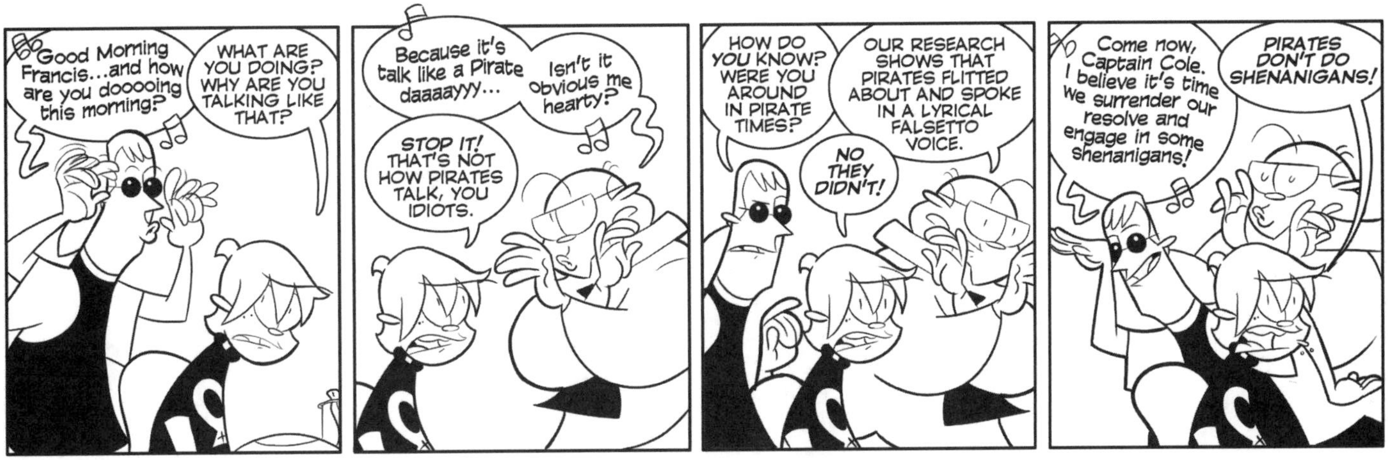
Good Morning Francis...and how are you doooooing this morning?
WHAT ARE YOU DOING? WHY ARE YOU TALKING LIKE THAT?
Because it's talk like a Pirate daaaayyy...
Isn't it obvious me hearty?
STOP IT! THAT'S NOT HOW PIRATES TALK, YOU IDIOTS.
HOW DO YOU KNOW? WERE YOU AROUND IN PIRATE TIMES?
OUR RESEARCH SHOWS THAT PIRATES FLITTED ABOUT AND SPOKE IN A LYRICAL FALSETTO VOICE.
NO THEY DIDN'T!
Come now, Captain Cole. I believe it's time we surrender our resolve and engage in some shenanigans!
PIRATES DON'T DO SHENANIGANS!

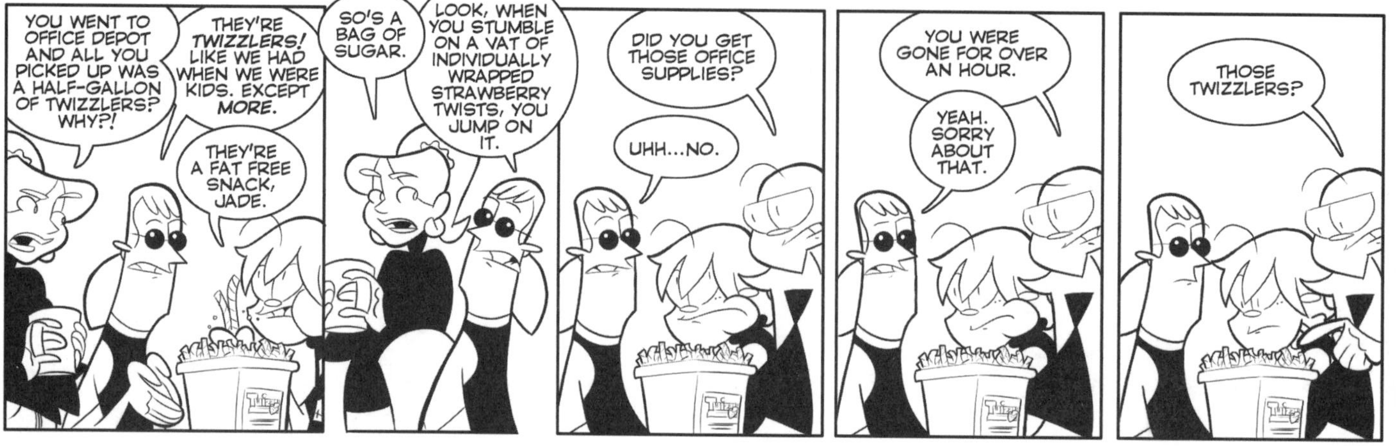
YOU WENT TO OFFICE DEPOT AND ALL YOU PICKED UP WAS A HALF-GALLON OF TWIZZLERS? WHY?!
THEY'RE TWIZZLERS! LIKE WE HAD WHEN WE WERE KIDS. EXCEPT MORE.
THEY'RE A FAT FREE SNACK, JADE.
SO'S A BAG OF SUGAR.
LOOK, WHEN YOU STUMBLE ON A VAT OF INDIVIDUALLY WRAPPED STRAWBERRY TWISTS, YOU JUMP ON IT.
DID YOU GET THOSE OFFICE SUPPLIES?
UHH...NO.
YOU WERE GONE FOR OVER AN HOUR.
YEAH. SORRY ABOUT THAT.
THOSE TWIZZLERS?

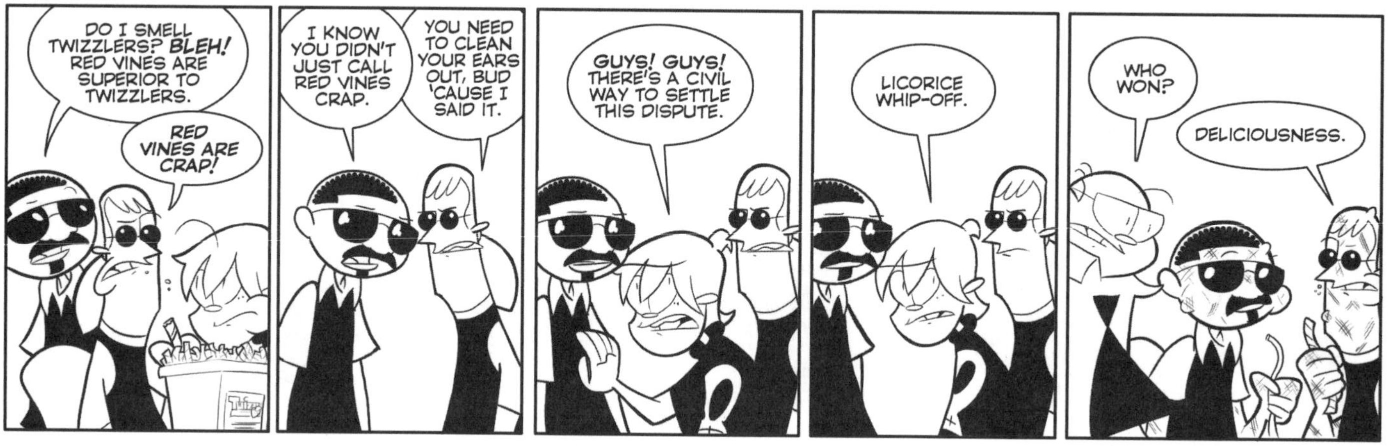
DO I SMELL TWIZZLERS? BLEH! RED VINES ARE SUPERIOR TO TWIZZLERS.
RED VINES ARE CRAP!
I KNOW YOU DIDN'T JUST CALL RED VINES CRAP.
YOU NEED TO CLEAN YOUR EARS OUT, BUD 'CAUSE I SAID IT.
GUYS! GUYS! THERE'S A CIVIL WAY TO SETTLE THIS DISPUTE.
LICORICE WHIP-OFF.
WHO WON?
DELICIOUSNESS.

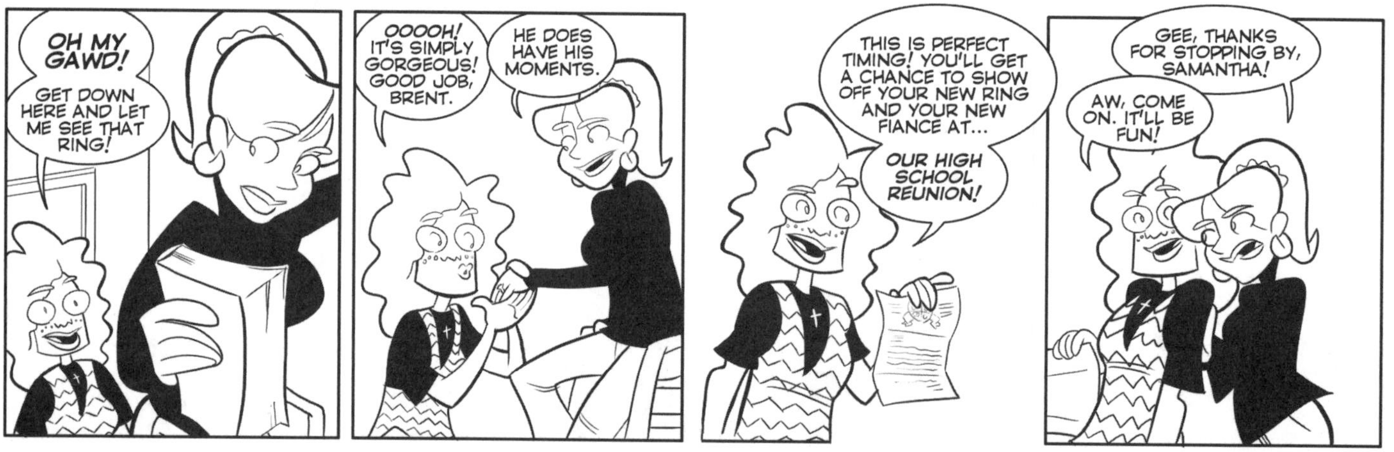
OH MY GAWD!
GET DOWN HERE AND LET ME SEE THAT RING!
OOOOH! IT'S SIMPLY GORGEOUS! GOOD JOB, BRENT.
HE DOES HAVE HIS MOMENTS.
THIS IS PERFECT TIMING! YOU'LL GET A CHANCE TO SHOW OFF YOUR NEW RING AND YOUR NEW FIANCE AT...
OUR HIGH SCHOOL REUNION!
GEE, THANKS FOR STOPPING BY, SAMANTHA!
AW, COME ON. IT'LL BE FUN!

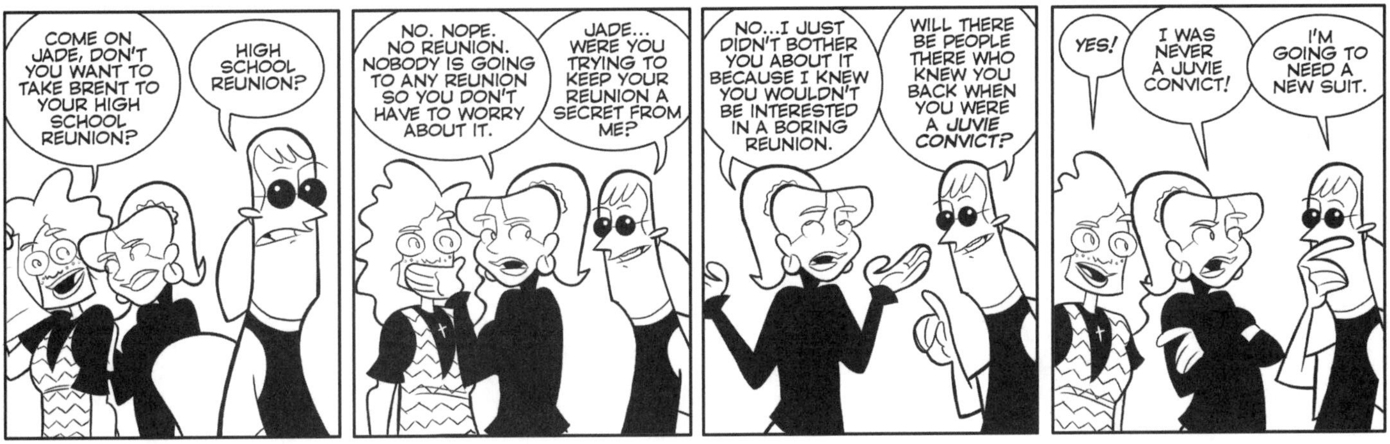
COME ON JADE, DON'T YOU WANT TO TAKE BRENT TO YOUR HIGH SCHOOL REUNION?
HIGH SCHOOL REUNION?
NO. NOPE. NO REUNION. NOBODY IS GOING TO ANY REUNION SO YOU DON'T HAVE TO WORRY ABOUT IT.
JADE... WERE YOU TRYING TO KEEP YOUR REUNION A SECRET FROM ME?
NO...I JUST DIDN'T BOTHER YOU ABOUT IT BECAUSE I KNEW YOU WOULDN'T BE INTERESTED IN A BORING REUNION.
WILL THERE BE PEOPLE THERE WHO KNEW YOU BACK WHEN YOU WERE A *JUVIE CONVICT?*
YES!
I WAS NEVER A JUVIE CONVICT!
I'M GOING TO NEED A NEW SUIT.

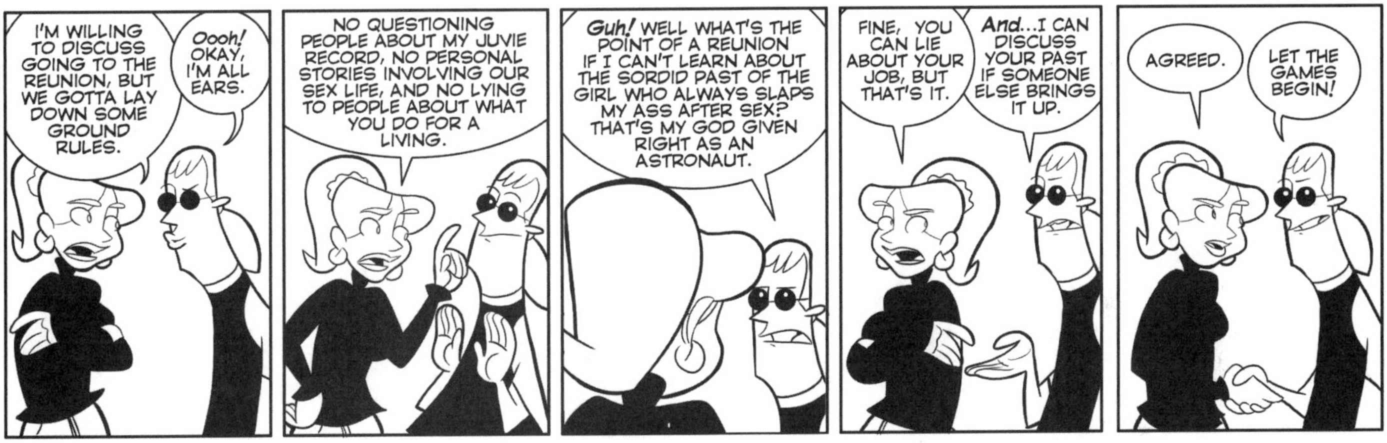
I'M WILLING TO DISCUSS GOING TO THE REUNION, BUT WE GOTTA LAY DOWN SOME GROUND RULES.
Oooh! OKAY, I'M ALL EARS.
NO QUESTIONING PEOPLE ABOUT MY JUVIE RECORD, NO PERSONAL STORIES INVOLVING OUR SEX LIFE, AND NO LYING TO PEOPLE ABOUT WHAT YOU DO FOR A LIVING.
Guh! WELL WHAT'S THE POINT OF A REUNION IF I CAN'T LEARN ABOUT THE SORDID PAST OF THE GIRL WHO ALWAYS SLAPS MY ASS AFTER SEX? THAT'S MY GOD GIVEN RIGHT AS AN ASTRONAUT.
FINE, YOU CAN LIE ABOUT YOUR JOB, BUT THAT'S IT.
And...I CAN DISCUSS YOUR PAST IF SOMEONE ELSE BRINGS IT UP.
AGREED.
LET THE GAMES BEGIN!

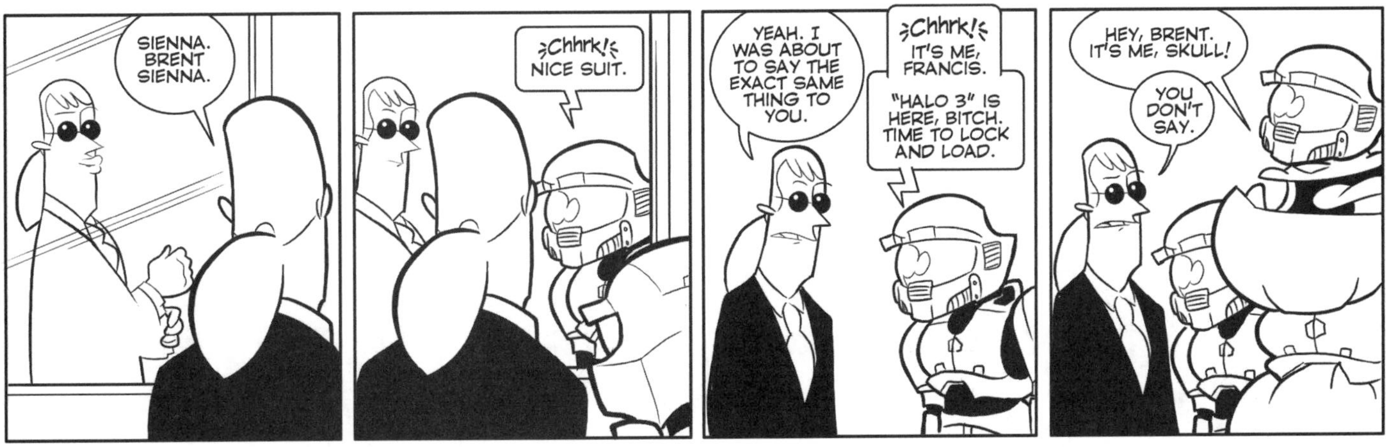
SIENNA. BRENT SIENNA.
Chhrk! NICE SUIT.
YEAH. I WAS ABOUT TO SAY THE EXACT SAME THING TO YOU.
Chhrk! IT'S ME, FRANCIS.
"HALO 3" IS HERE, BITCH. TIME TO LOCK AND LOAD.
HEY, BRENT. IT'S ME, SKULL!
YOU DON'T SAY.

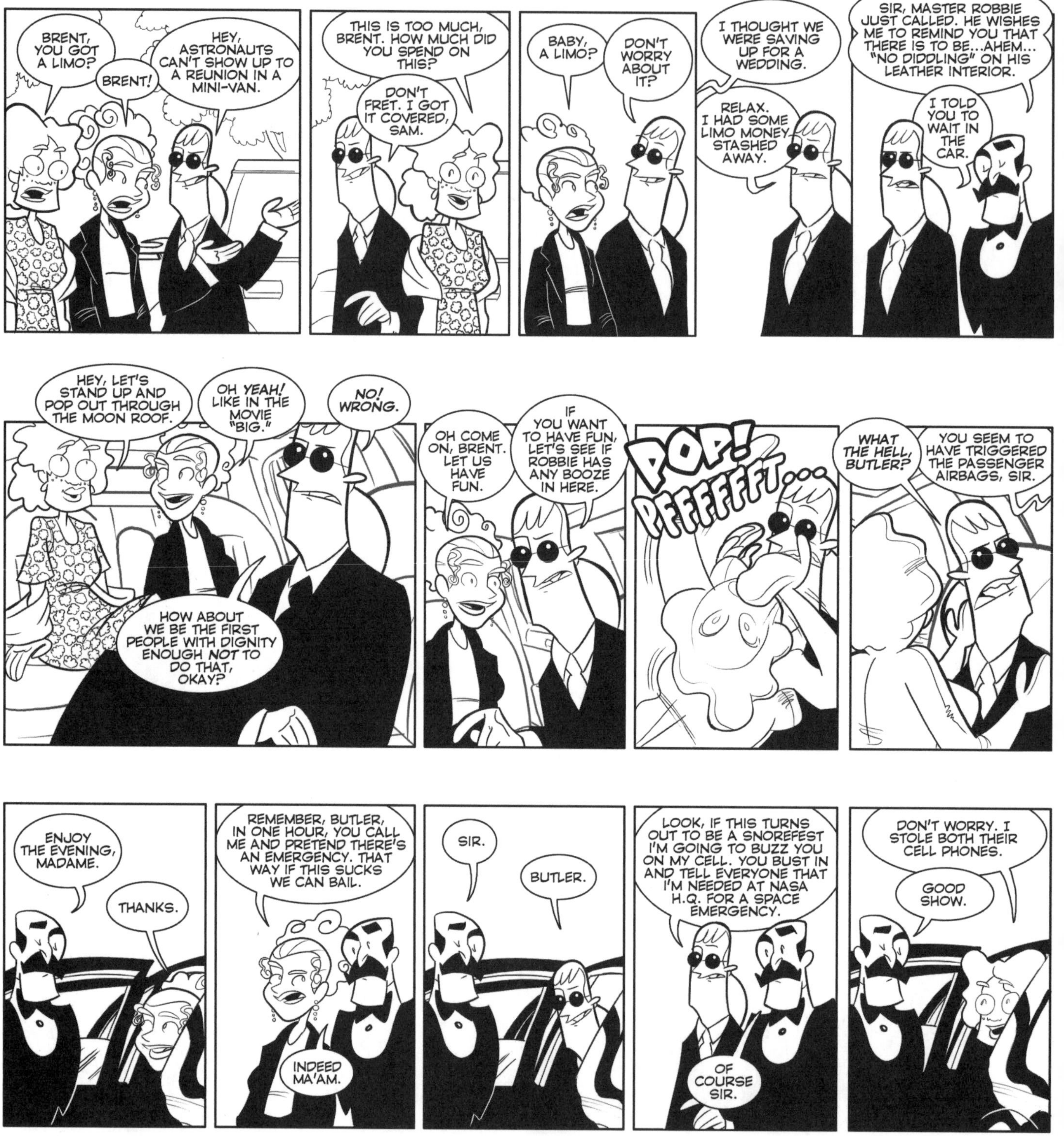
BRENT, YOU GOT A LIMO?
BRENT!
HEY, ASTRONAUTS CAN'T SHOW UP TO A REUNION IN A MINI-VAN.
THIS IS TOO MUCH, BRENT. HOW MUCH DID YOU SPEND ON THIS?
DON'T FRET. I GOT IT COVERED, SAM.
BABY, A LIMO?
DON'T WORRY ABOUT IT?
I THOUGHT WE WERE SAVING UP FOR A WEDDING.
RELAX. I HAD SOME LIMO MONEY STASHED AWAY.
SIR, MASTER ROBBIE JUST CALLED. HE WISHES ME TO REMIND YOU THAT THERE IS TO BE...AHEM... "NO DIDDLING" ON HIS LEATHER INTERIOR.
I TOLD YOU TO WAIT IN THE CAR.
HEY, LET'S STAND UP AND POP OUT THROUGH THE MOON ROOF.
OH YEAH! LIKE IN THE MOVIE "BIG."
NO! WRONG.
HOW ABOUT WE BE THE FIRST PEOPLE WITH DIGNITY ENOUGH NOT TO DO THAT, OKAY?
OH COME ON, BRENT. LET US HAVE FUN.
IF YOU WANT TO HAVE FUN, LET'S SEE IF ROBBIE HAS ANY BOOZE IN HERE.
POP! PFFFFFFT...
WHAT THE HELL, BUTLER?
YOU SEEM TO HAVE TRIGGERED THE PASSENGER AIRBAGS, SIR.
ENJOY THE EVENING, MADAME.
THANKS.
REMEMBER, BUTLER, IN ONE HOUR, YOU CALL ME AND PRETEND THERE'S AN EMERGENCY. THAT WAY IF THIS SUCKS WE CAN BAIL.
INDEED MA'AM.
SIR.
BUTLER.
LOOK, IF THIS TURNS OUT TO BE A SNOREFEST I'M GOING TO BUZZ YOU ON MY CELL. YOU BUST IN AND TELL EVERYONE THAT I'M NEEDED AT NASA H.Q. FOR A SPACE EMERGENCY.
OF COURSE SIR.
DON'T WORRY. I STOLE BOTH THEIR CELL PHONES.
GOOD SHOW.

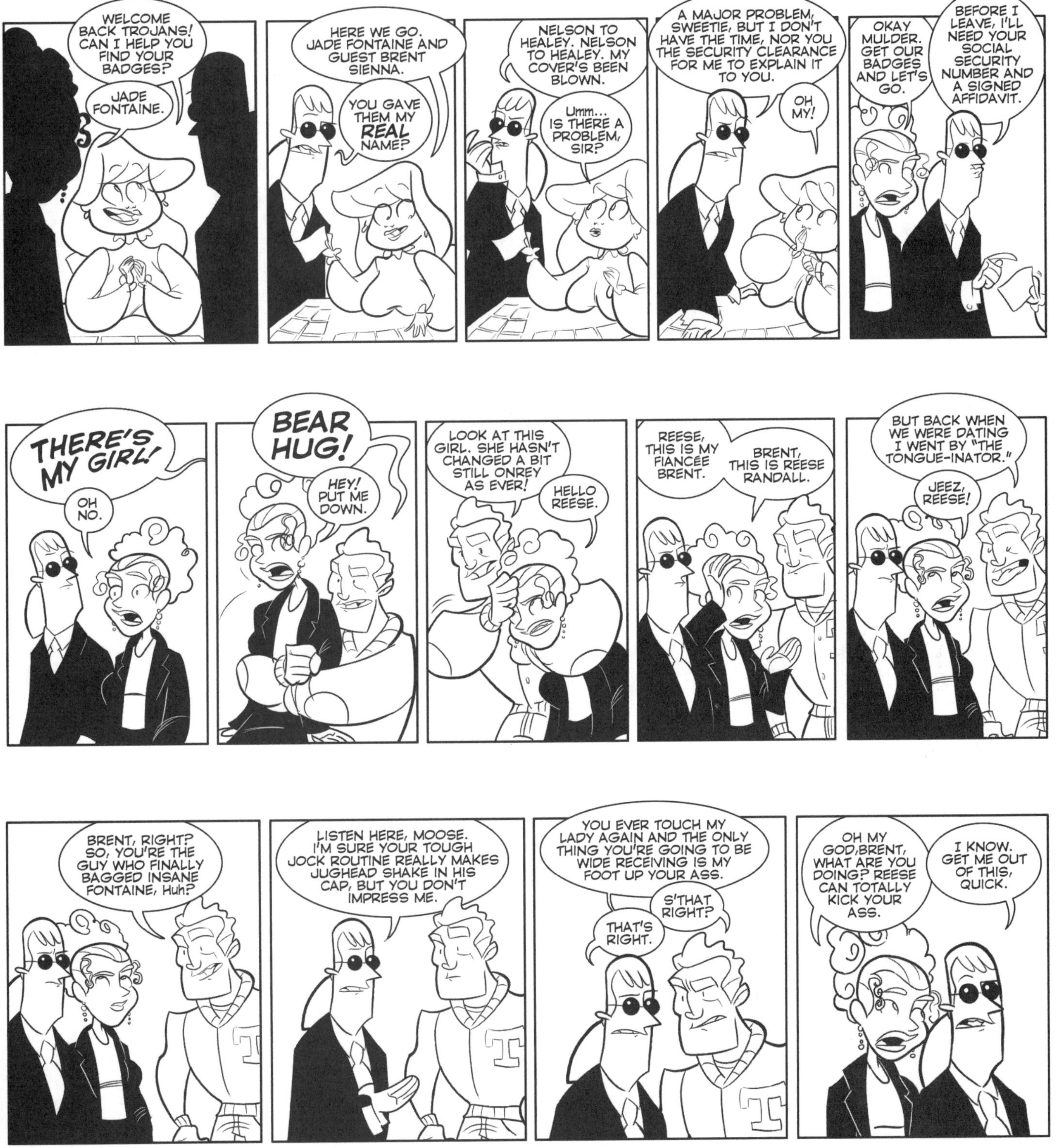
WELCOME BACK TROJANS! CAN I HELP YOU FIND YOUR BADGES?
JADE FONTAINE.
HERE WE GO. JADE FONTAINE AND GUEST BRENT SIENNA.
YOU GAVE THEM MY REAL NAME?
NELSON TO HEALEY. NELSON TO HEALEY. MY COVER'S BEEN BLOWN.
Umm... IS THERE A PROBLEM, SIR?
A MAJOR PROBLEM, SWEETIE, BUT I DON'T HAVE THE TIME, NOR YOU THE SECURITY CLEARANCE FOR ME TO EXPLAIN IT TO YOU.
OH MY!
OKAY MULDER. GET OUR BADGES AND LET'S GO.
BEFORE I LEAVE, I'LL NEED YOUR SOCIAL SECURITY NUMBER AND A SIGNED AFFIDAVIT.
THERE'S MY GIRL!
OH NO.
BEAR HUG!
HEY! PUT ME DOWN.
LOOK AT THIS GIRL. SHE HASN'T CHANGED A BIT STILL ONREY AS EVER!
HELLO REESE.
REESE, THIS IS MY FIANCÉE BRENT.
BRENT, THIS IS REESE RANDALL.
BUT BACK WHEN WE WERE DATING I WENT BY "THE TONGUE-INATOR."
JEEZ, REESE!
BRENT, RIGHT? SO, YOU'RE THE GUY WHO FINALLY BAGGED INSANE FONTAINE, Huh?
LISTEN HERE, MOOSE. I'M SURE YOUR TOUGH JOCK ROUTINE REALLY MAKES JUGHEAD SHAKE IN HIS CAP, BUT YOU DON'T IMPRESS ME.
YOU EVER TOUCH MY LADY AGAIN AND THE ONLY THING YOU'RE GOING TO BE WIDE RECEIVING IS MY FOOT UP YOUR ASS.
S'THAT RIGHT?
THAT'S RIGHT.
OH MY GOD,BRENT, WHAT ARE YOU DOING? REESE CAN TOTALLY KICK YOUR ASS.
I KNOW. GET ME OUT OF THIS, QUICK.

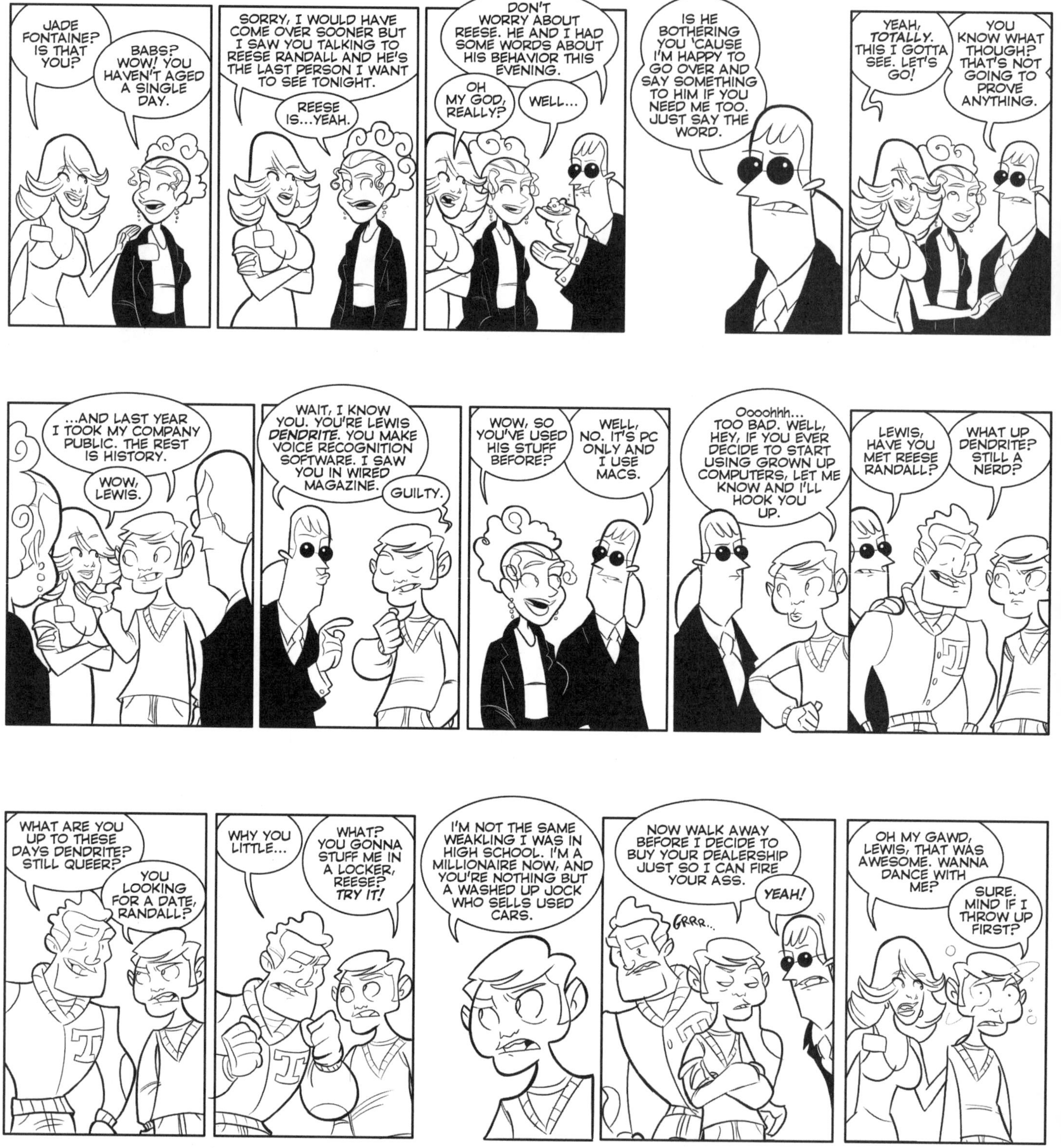
JADE FONTAINE? IS THAT YOU?
BABS? WOW! YOU HAVEN'T AGED A SINGLE DAY.
SORRY, I WOULD HAVE COME OVER SOONER BUT I SAW YOU TALKING TO REESE RANDALL AND HE'S THE LAST PERSON I WANT TO SEE TONIGHT.
REESE IS...YEAH.
DON'T WORRY ABOUT REESE. HE AND I HAD SOME WORDS ABOUT HIS BEHAVIOR THIS EVENING.
OH MY GOD, REALLY?
WELL...
IS HE BOTHERING YOU 'CAUSE I'M HAPPY TO GO OVER AND SAY SOMETHING TO HIM IF YOU NEED ME TOO. JUST SAY THE WORD.
YEAH, TOTALLY. THIS I GOTTA SEE. LET'S GO!
YOU KNOW WHAT THOUGH? THAT'S NOT GOING TO PROVE ANYTHING.
...AND LAST YEAR I TOOK MY COMPANY PUBLIC. THE REST IS HISTORY.
WOW, LEWIS.
WAIT, I KNOW YOU. YOU'RE LEWIS DENDRITE. YOU MAKE VOICE RECOGNITION SOFTWARE. I SAW YOU IN WIRED MAGAZINE.
GUILTY.
WOW, SO YOU'VE USED HIS STUFF BEFORE?
WELL, NO. IT'S PC ONLY AND I USE MACS.
Oooohhh... TOO BAD. WELL, HEY, IF YOU EVER DECIDE TO START USING GROWN UP COMPUTERS, LET ME KNOW AND I'LL HOOK YOU UP.
LEWIS, HAVE YOU MET REESE RANDALL?
WHAT UP DENDRITE? STILL A NERD?
WHAT ARE YOU UP TO THESE DAYS DENDRITE? STILL QUEER?
YOU LOOKING FOR A DATE, RANDALL?
WHY YOU LITTLE...
WHAT? YOU GONNA STUFF ME IN A LOCKER, REESE? TRY IT!
I'M NOT THE SAME WEAKLING I WAS IN HIGH SCHOOL. I'M A MILLIONAIRE NOW, AND YOU'RE NOTHING BUT A WASHED UP JOCK WHO SELLS USED CARS.
NOW WALK AWAY BEFORE I DECIDE TO BUY YOUR DEALERSHIP JUST SO I CAN FIRE YOUR ASS.
GRRR..
YEAH!
OH MY GAWD, LEWIS, THAT WAS AWESOME. WANNA DANCE WITH ME?
SURE. MIND IF I THROW UP FIRST?

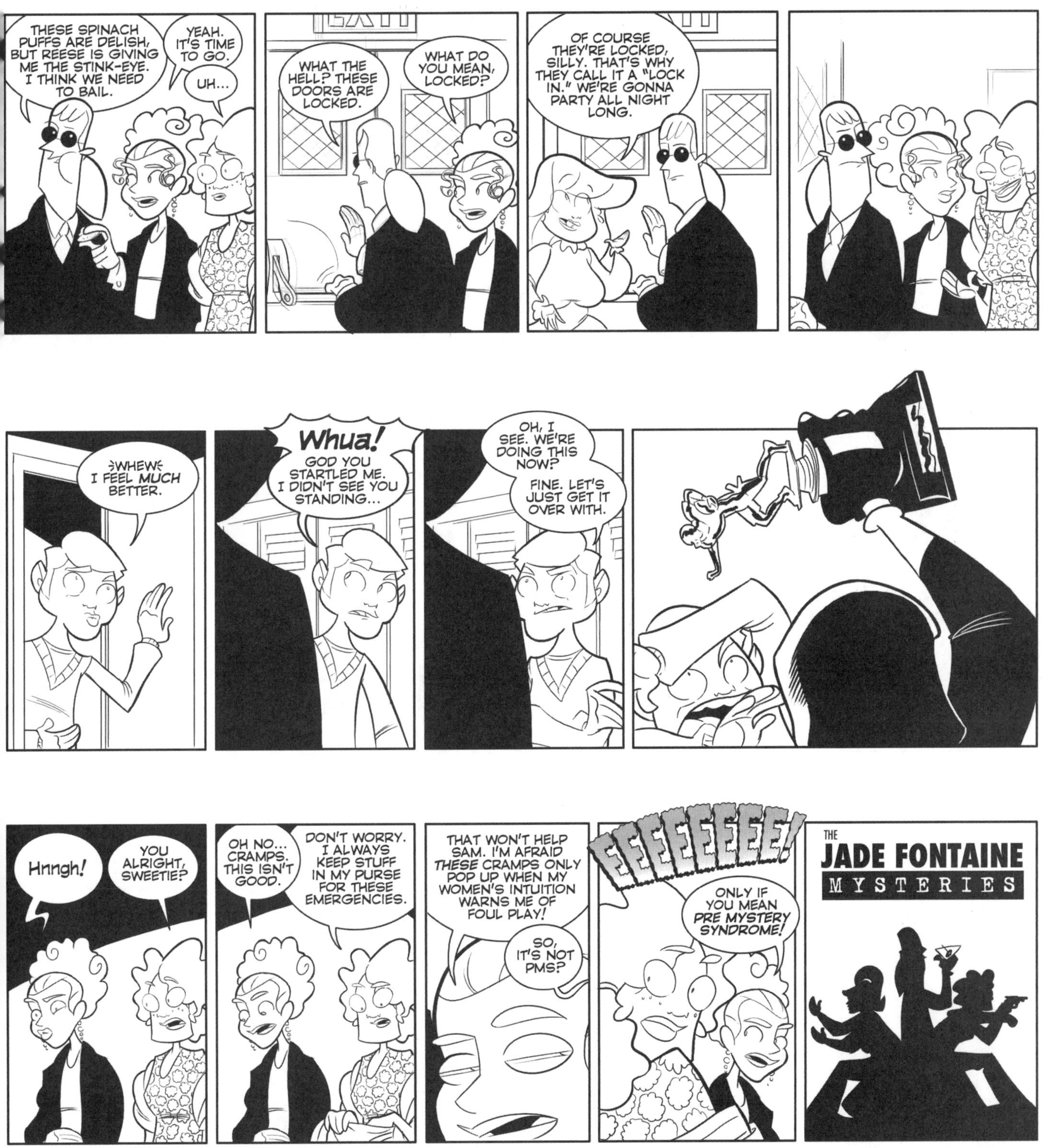
THESE SPINACH PUFFS ARE DELISH, BUT REESE IS GIVING ME THE STINK-EYE. I THINK WE NEED TO BAIL.
YEAH. IT'S TIME TO GO.
UH...
WHAT THE HELL? THESE DOORS ARE LOCKED.
WHAT DO YOU MEAN, LOCKED?
OF COURSE THEY'RE LOCKED, SILLY. THAT'S WHY THEY CALL IT A "LOCK IN." WE'RE GONNA PARTY ALL NIGHT LONG.
WHEW I FEEL MUCH BETTER.
Whua! GOD YOU STARTLED ME. I DIDN'T SEE YOU STANDING...
OH, I SEE. WE'RE DOING THIS NOW?
FINE. LET'S JUST GET IT OVER WITH.
Hnngh!
YOU ALRIGHT, SWEETIE?
OH NO... CRAMPS. THIS ISN'T GOOD.
DON'T WORRY. I ALWAYS KEEP STUFF IN MY PURSE FOR THESE EMERGENCIES.
THAT WON'T HELP SAM. I'M AFRAID THESE CRAMPS ONLY POP UP WHEN MY WOMEN'S INTUITION WARNS ME OF FOUL PLAY!
SO, IT'S NOT PMS?
EEEEEEEE!
ONLY IF YOU MEAN PRE MYSTERY SYNDROME!
THE JADE FONTAINE MYSTERIES

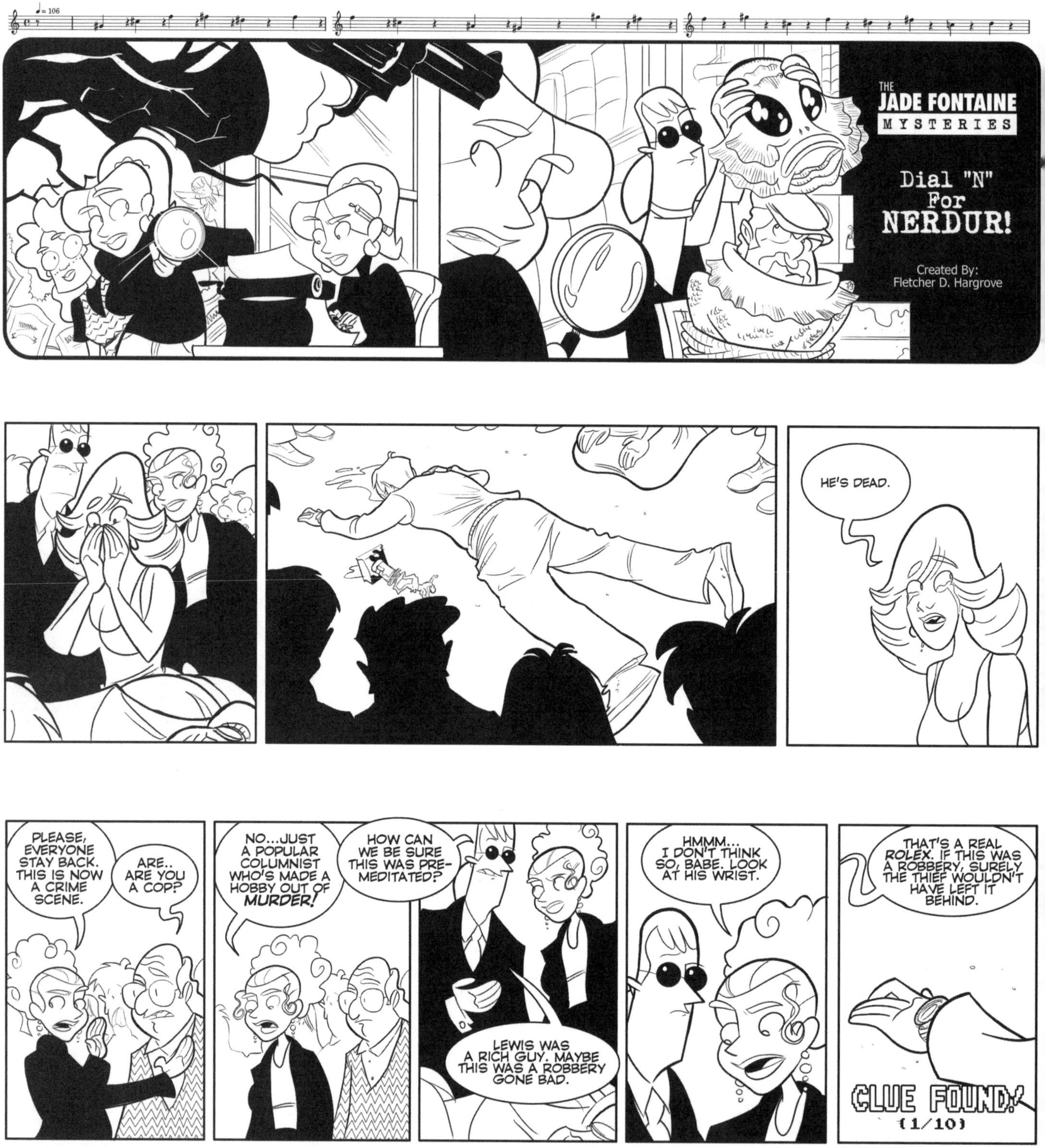
THE
JADE FONTAINE
MYSTERIES
Dial "N" For NERDUR!
Created By:
Fletcher D. Hargrove
HE'S DEAD.
PLEASE, EVERYONE STAY BACK. THIS IS NOW A CRIME SCENE.
ARE.. ARE YOU A COP?
NO...JUST A POPULAR COLUMNIST WHO'S MADE A HOBBY OUT OF MURDER!
HOW CAN WE BE SURE THIS WAS PRE-MEDITATED?
LEWIS WAS A RICH GUY. MAYBE THIS WAS A ROBBERY GONE BAD.
HMMM... I DON'T THINK SO, BABE. LOOK AT HIS WRIST.
THAT'S A REAL ROLEX. IF THIS WAS A ROBBERY, SURELY THE THIEF WOULDN'T HAVE LEFT IT BEHIND.
CLUE FOUND!
(1/10)

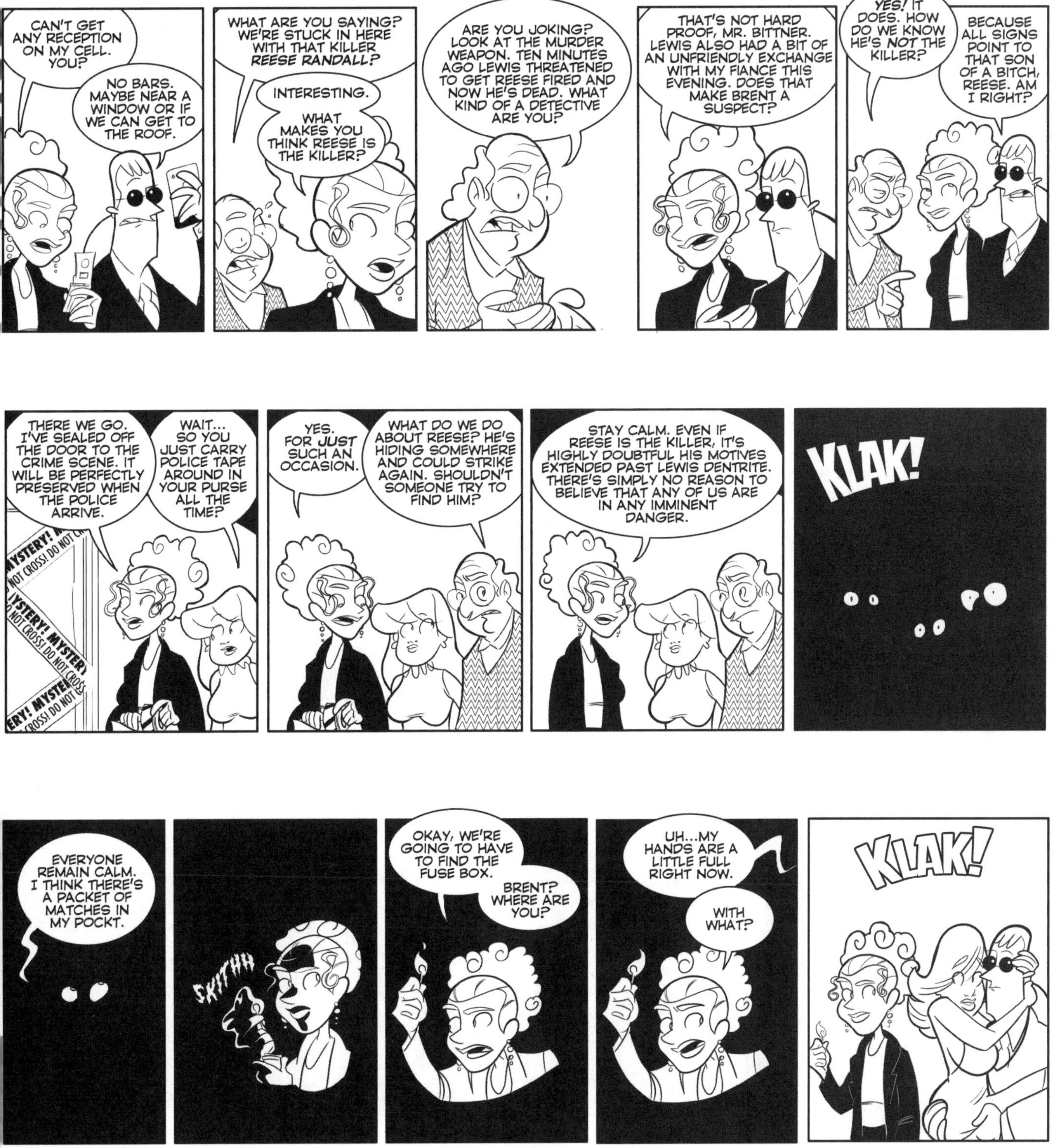
CAN'T GET ANY RECEPTION ON MY CELL. YOU?
NO BARS. MAYBE NEAR A WINDOW OR IF WE CAN GET TO THE ROOF.
WHAT ARE YOU SAYING? WE'RE STUCK IN HERE WITH THAT KILLER REESE RANDALL?
INTERESTING.
WHAT MAKES YOU THINK REESE IS THE KILLER?
ARE YOU JOKING? LOOK AT THE MURDER WEAPON. TEN MINUTES AGO LEWIS THREATENED TO GET REESE FIRED AND NOW HE'S DEAD. WHAT KIND OF A DETECTIVE ARE YOU?
THAT'S NOT HARD PROOF, MR. BITTNER. LEWIS ALSO HAD A BIT OF AN UNFRIENDLY EXCHANGE WITH MY FIANCE THIS EVENING. DOES THAT MAKE BRENT A SUSPECT?
YES! IT DOES. HOW DO WE KNOW HE'S NOT THE KILLER?
BECAUSE ALL SIGNS POINT TO THAT SON OF A BITCH, REESE. AM I RIGHT?
THERE WE GO. I'VE SEALED OFF THE DOOR TO THE CRIME SCENE. IT WILL BE PERFECTLY PRESERVED WHEN THE POLICE ARRIVE.
WAIT... SO YOU JUST CARRY POLICE TAPE AROUND IN YOUR PURSE ALL THE TIME?
YES. FOR JUST SUCH AN OCCASION.
WHAT DO WE DO ABOUT REESE? HE'S HIDING SOMEWHERE AND COULD STRIKE AGAIN. SHOULDN'T SOMEONE TRY TO FIND HIM?
STAY CALM. EVEN IF REESE IS THE KILLER, IT'S HIGHLY DOUBTFUL HIS MOTIVES EXTENDED PAST LEWIS DENTRITE. THERE'S SIMPLY NO REASON TO BELIEVE THAT ANY OF US ARE IN ANY IMMINENT DANGER.
KLAK!
EVERYONE REMAIN CALM. I THINK THERE'S A PACKET OF MATCHES IN MY POCKT.
SKITHH
OKAY, WE'RE GOING TO HAVE TO FIND THE FUSE BOX.
BRENT? WHERE ARE YOU?
UH...MY HANDS ARE A LITTLE FULL RIGHT NOW.
WITH WHAT?
KLAK!

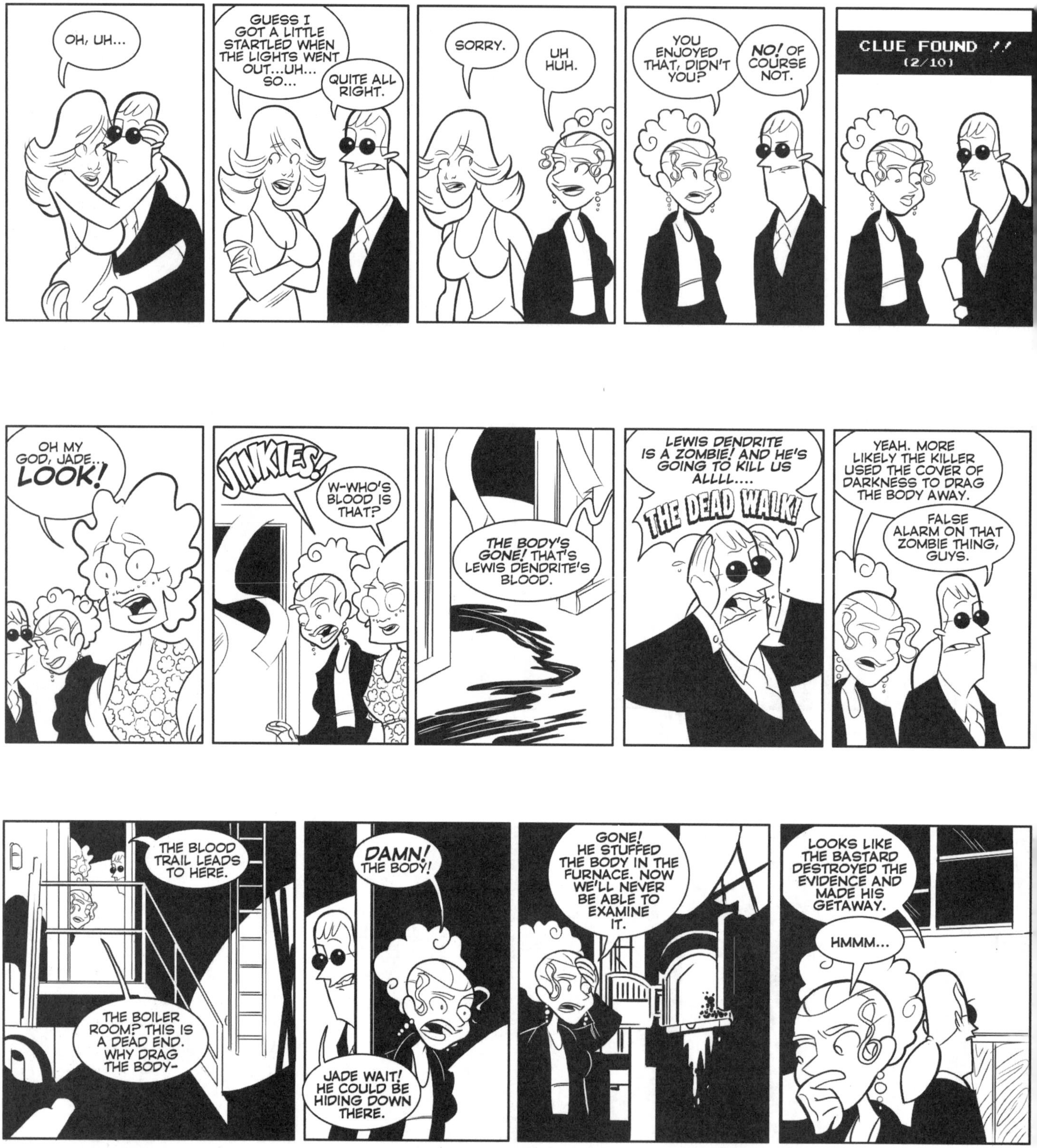
OH, UH...
GUESS I GOT A LITTLE STARTLED WHEN THE LIGHTS WENT OUT...UH... SO...
QUITE ALL RIGHT.
SORRY.
UH HUH.
YOU ENJOYED THAT, DIDN'T YOU?
NO! OF COURSE NOT.
CLUE FOUND !!
(2/10)
OH MY GOD, JADE... LOOK!
JINKIES!
W-WHO'S BLOOD IS THAT?
THE BODY'S GONE! THAT'S LEWIS DENDRITE'S BLOOD.
LEWIS DENDRITE IS A ZOMBIE! AND HE'S GOING TO KILL US ALLLL....
THE DEAD WALK!
YEAH. MORE LIKELY THE KILLER USED THE COVER OF DARKNESS TO DRAG THE BODY AWAY.
FALSE ALARM ON THAT ZOMBIE THING, GUYS.
THE BLOOD TRAIL LEADS TO HERE.
THE BOILER ROOM? THIS IS A DEAD END. WHY DRAG THE BODY-
DAMN! THE BODY!
JADE WAIT! HE COULD BE HIDING DOWN THERE.
GONE! HE STUFFED THE BODY IN THE FURNACE. NOW WE'LL NEVER BE ABLE TO EXAMINE IT.
LOOKS LIKE THE BASTARD DESTROYED THE EVIDENCE AND MADE HIS GETAWAY.
HMMM...

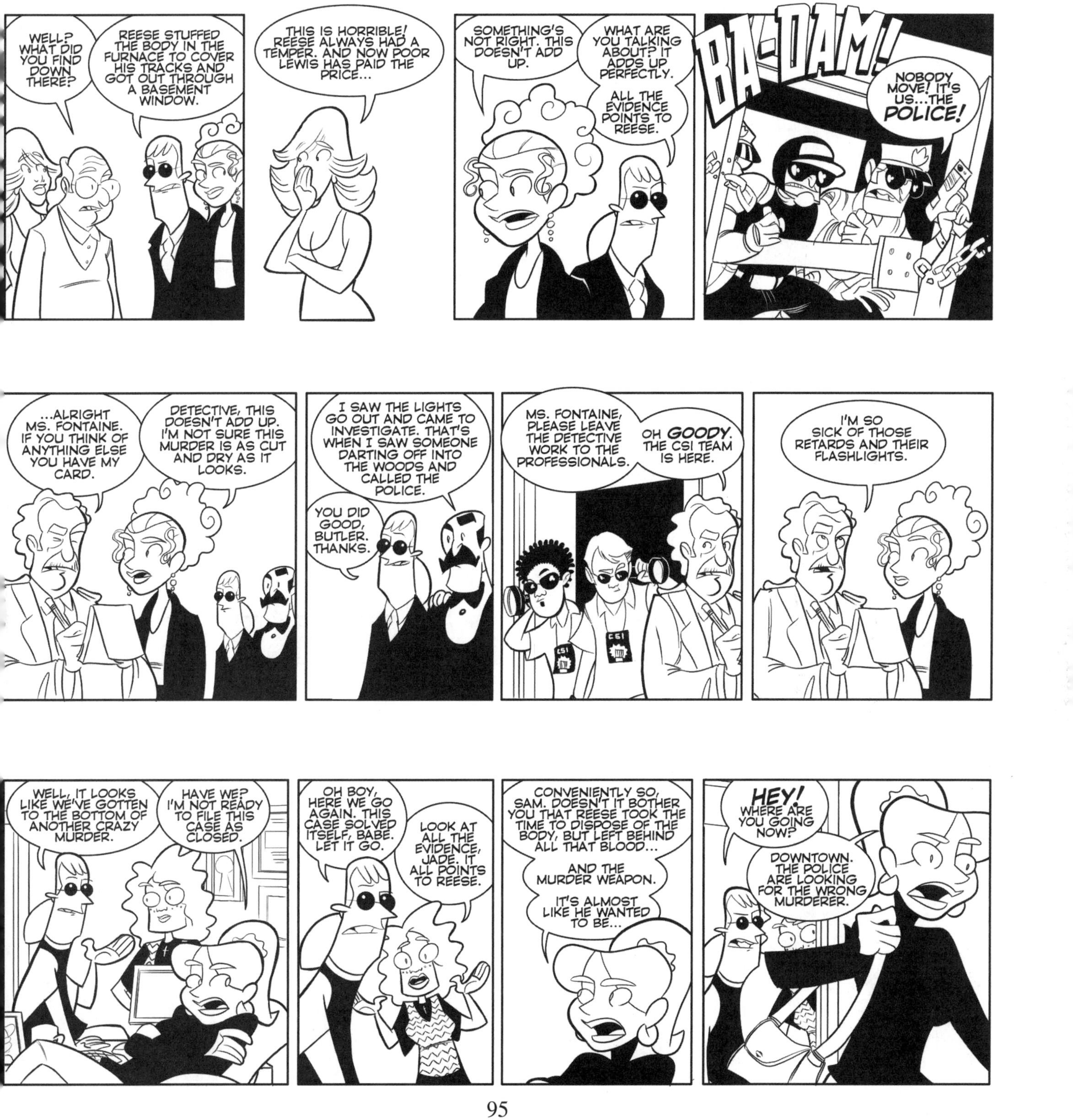

WELL? WHAT DID YOU FIND DOWN THERE?
REESE STUFFED THE BODY IN THE FURNACE TO COVER HIS TRACKS AND GOT OUT THROUGH A BASEMENT WINDOW.
THIS IS HORRIBLE! REESE ALWAYS HAD A TEMPER. AND NOW POOR LEWIS HAS PAID THE PRICE...
SOMETHING'S NOT RIGHT. THIS DOESN'T ADD UP.
WHAT ARE YOU TALKING ABOUT? IT ADDS UP PERFECTLY.
ALL THE EVIDENCE POINTS TO REESE.
BA-DAM!
NOBODY MOVE! IT'S US...THE POLICE!
...ALRIGHT MS. FONTAINE. IF YOU THINK OF ANYTHING ELSE YOU HAVE MY CARD.
DETECTIVE, THIS DOESN'T ADD UP. I'M NOT SURE THIS MURDER IS AS CUT AND DRY AS IT LOOKS.
I SAW THE LIGHTS GO OUT AND CAME TO INVESTIGATE. THAT'S WHEN I SAW SOMEONE DARTING OFF INTO THE WOODS AND CALLED THE POLICE.
YOU DID GOOD, BUTLER. THANKS.
MS. FONTAINE, PLEASE LEAVE THE DETECTIVE WORK TO THE PROFESSIONALS.
OH GOODY. THE CSI TEAM IS HERE.
CSI
CSI
I'M SO SICK OF THOSE RETARDS AND THEIR FLASHLIGHTS.
WELL, IT LOOKS LIKE WE'VE GOTTEN TO THE BOTTOM OF ANOTHER CRAZY MURDER.
HAVE WE? I'M NOT READY TO FILE THIS CASE AS CLOSED.
OH BOY, HERE WE GO AGAIN. THIS CASE SOLVED ITSELF, BABE. LET IT GO.
LOOK AT ALL THE EVIDENCE, JADE. IT ALL POINTS TO REESE.
CONVENIENTLY SO, SAM. DOESN'T IT BOTHER YOU THAT REESE TOOK THE TIME TO DISPOSE OF THE BODY, BUT LEFT BEHIND ALL THAT BLOOD...
AND THE MURDER WEAPON.
IT'S ALMOST LIKE HE WANTED TO BE...
HEY! WHERE ARE YOU GOING NOW?
DOWNTOWN. THE POLICE ARE LOOKING FOR THE WRONG MURDERER.

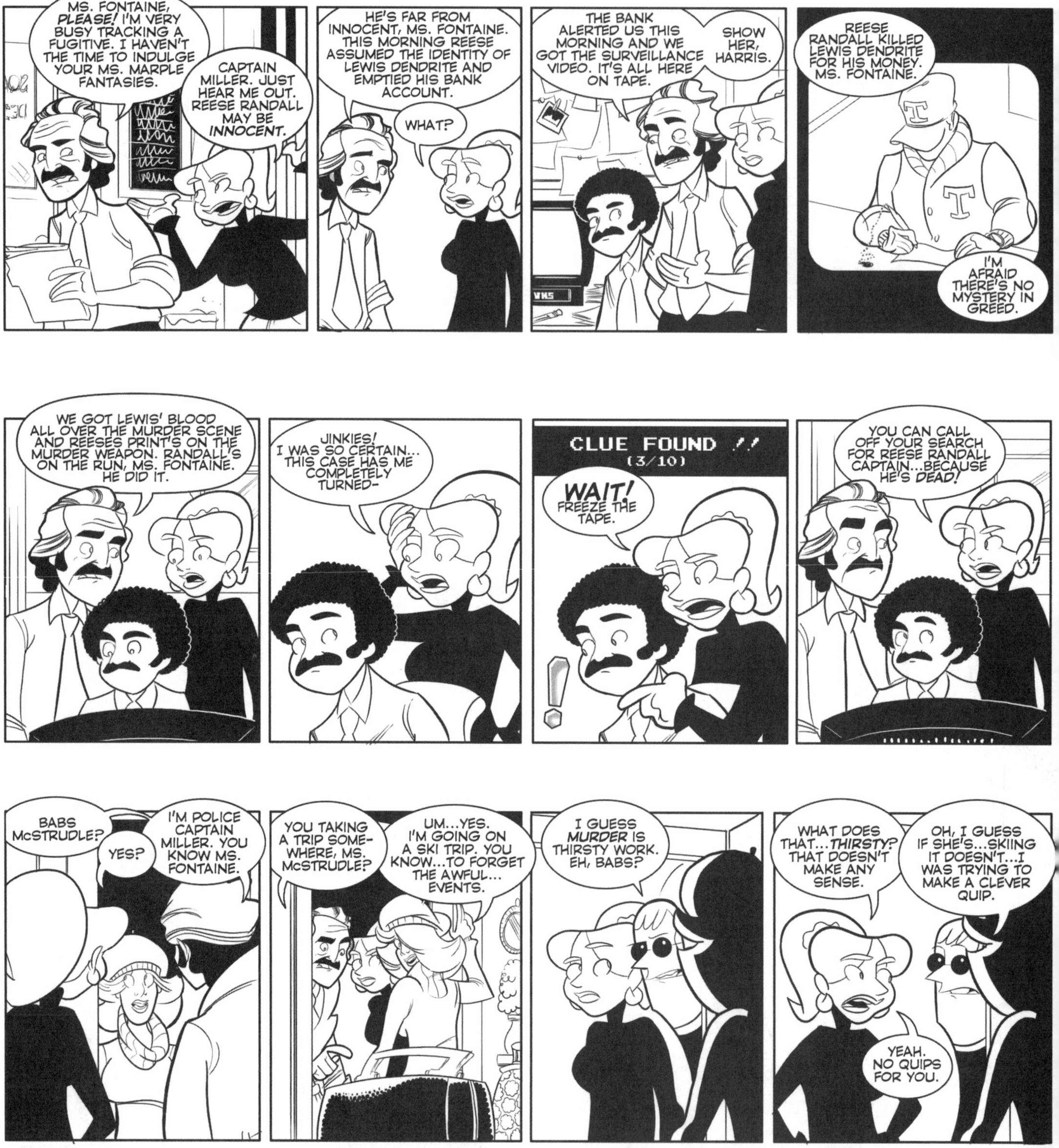
MS. FONTAINE, PLEASE! I'M VERY BUSY TRACKING A FUGITIVE. I HAVEN'T THE TIME TO INDULGE YOUR MS. MARPLE FANTASIES.
CAPTAIN MILLER. JUST HEAR ME OUT. REESE RANDALL MAY BE INNOCENT.
HE'S FAR FROM INNOCENT, MS. FONTAINE. THIS MORNING REESE ASSUMED THE IDENTITY OF LEWIS DENDRITE AND EMPTIED HIS BANK ACCOUNT.
WHAT?
THE BANK ALERTED US THIS MORNING AND WE GOT THE SURVEILLANCE VIDEO. IT'S ALL HERE ON TAPE.
SHOW HER, HARRIS.
VHS
REESE RANDALL KILLED LEWIS DENDRITE FOR HIS MONEY. MS. FONTAINE.
I'M AFRAID THERE'S NO MYSTERY IN GREED.
WE GOT LEWIS' BLOOD ALL OVER THE MURDER SCENE AND REESES PRINT'S ON THE MURDER WEAPON. RANDALL'S ON THE RUN, MS. FONTAINE. HE DID IT.
JINKIES! I WAS SO CERTAIN... THIS CASE HAS ME COMPLETELY TURNED–
CLUE FOUND !!
(3/10)
WAIT! FREEZE THE TAPE.
YOU CAN CALL OFF YOUR SEARCH FOR REESE RANDALL CAPTAIN...BECAUSE HE'S DEAD!
BABS McSTRUDLE?
YES?
I'M POLICE CAPTAIN MILLER. YOU KNOW MS. FONTAINE.
YOU TAKING A TRIP SOME-WHERE, MS. McSTRUDLE?
UM...YES. I'M GOING ON A SKI TRIP. YOU KNOW...TO FORGET THE AWFUL... EVENTS.
I GUESS MURDER IS THIRSTY WORK. EH, BABS?
WHAT DOES THAT...THIRSTY? THAT DOESN'T MAKE ANY SENSE.
OH, I GUESS IF SHE'S...SKIING IT DOESN'T...I WAS TRYING TO MAKE A CLEVER QUIP.
YEAH. NO QUIPS FOR YOU.

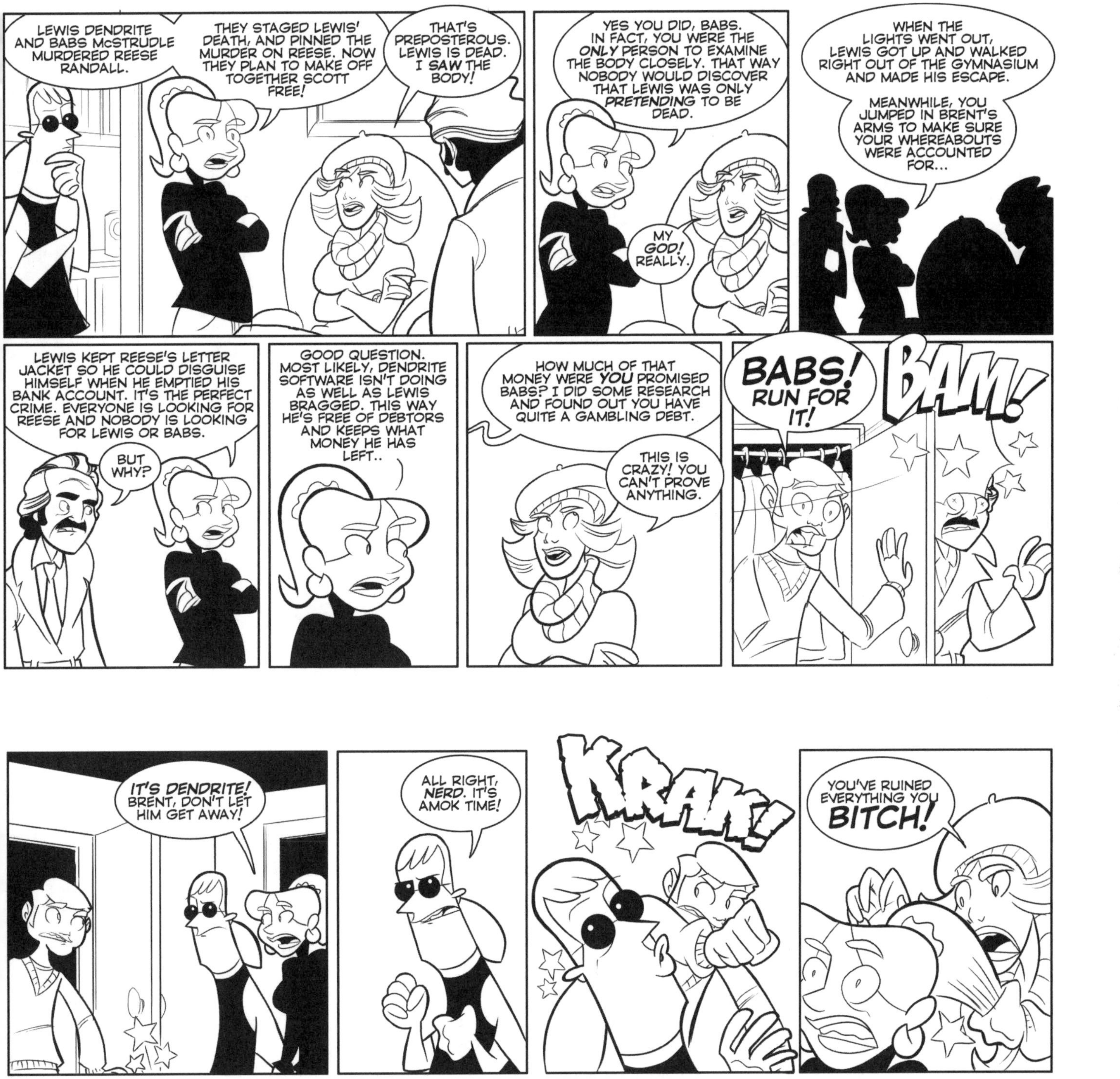
LEWIS DENDRITE AND BABS McSTRUDLE MURDERED REESE RANDALL.
THEY STAGED LEWIS' DEATH, AND PINNED THE MURDER ON REESE. NOW THEY PLAN TO MAKE OFF TOGETHER SCOTT FREE!
THAT'S PREPOSTEROUS. LEWIS IS DEAD. I SAW THE BODY!
YES YOU DID, BABS. IN FACT, YOU WERE THE ONLY PERSON TO EXAMINE THE BODY CLOSELY. THAT WAY NOBODY WOULD DISCOVER THAT LEWIS WAS ONLY PRETENDING TO BE DEAD.
MY GOD! REALLY.
WHEN THE LIGHTS WENT OUT, LEWIS GOT UP AND WALKED RIGHT OUT OF THE GYMNASIUM AND MADE HIS ESCAPE.
MEANWHILE, YOU JUMPED IN BRENT'S ARMS TO MAKE SURE YOUR WHEREABOUTS WERE ACCOUNTED FOR...
LEWIS KEPT REESE'S LETTER JACKET SO HE COULD DISGUISE HIMSELF WHEN HE EMPTIED HIS BANK ACCOUNT. IT'S THE PERFECT CRIME. EVERYONE IS LOOKING FOR REESE AND NOBODY IS LOOKING FOR LEWIS OR BABS.
BUT WHY?
GOOD QUESTION. MOST LIKELY, DENDRITE SOFTWARE ISN'T DOING AS WELL AS LEWIS BRAGGED. THIS WAY HE'S FREE OF DEBTORS AND KEEPS WHAT MONEY HE HAS LEFT..
HOW MUCH OF THAT MONEY WERE YOU PROMISED BABS? I DID SOME RESEARCH AND FOUND OUT YOU HAVE QUITE A GAMBLING DEBT.
THIS IS CRAZY! YOU CAN'T PROVE ANYTHING.
BABS! RUN FOR IT!
BAM!
IT'S DENDRITE! BRENT, DON'T LET HIM GET AWAY!
ALL RIGHT, NERD. IT'S AMOK TIME!
KRAK!
YOU'VE RUINED EVERYTHING YOU BITCH!

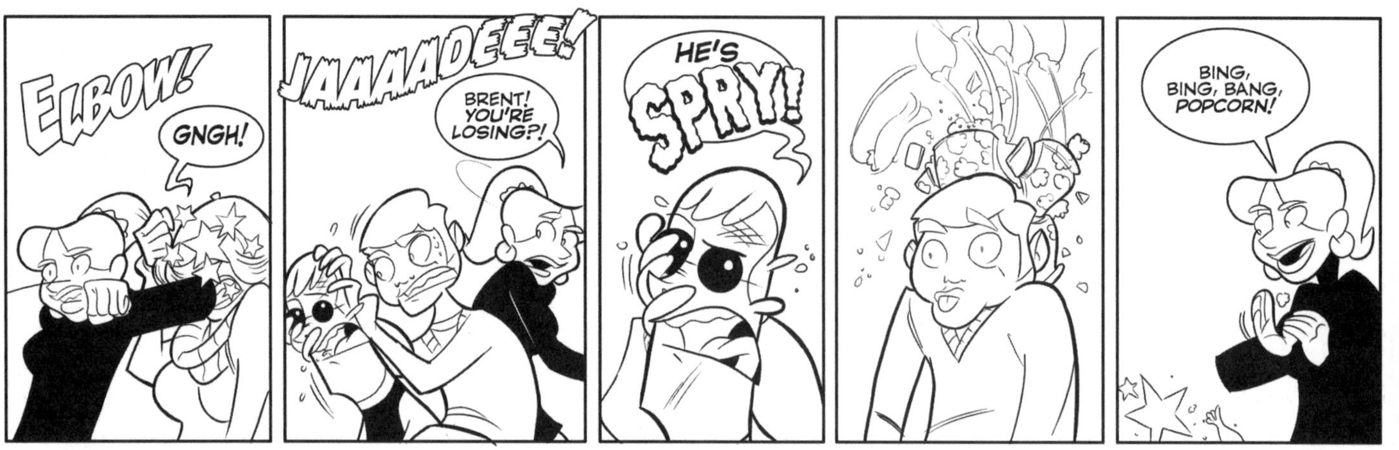
ELBOW!
GNGH!
JAAAAADEEE!
BRENT! YOU'RE LOSING?!
HE'S SPRY!
BING, BING, BANG, POPCORN!

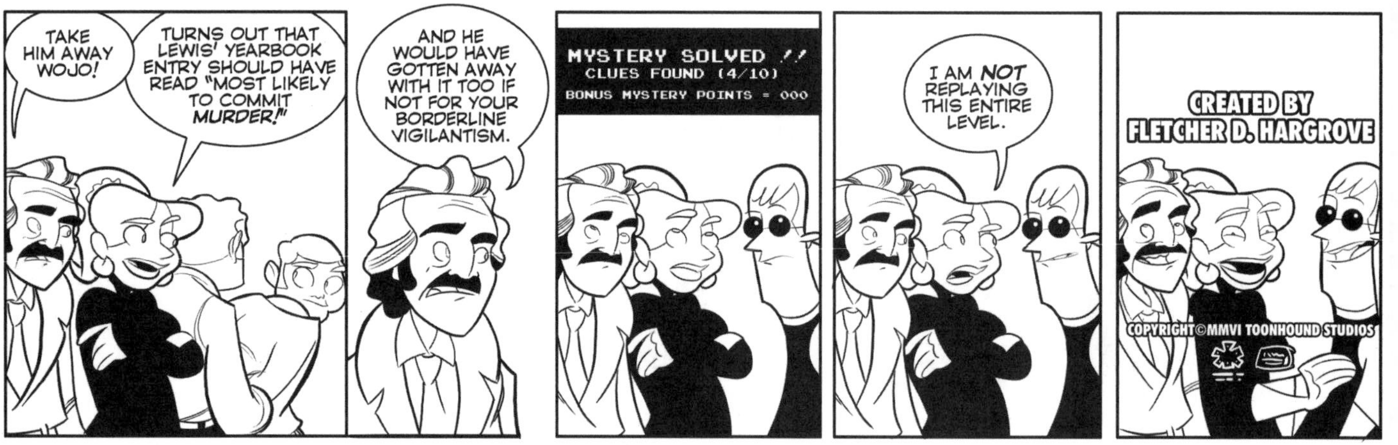
TAKE HIM AWAY WOJO!
TURNS OUT THAT LEWIS' YEARBOOK ENTRY SHOULD HAVE READ "MOST LIKELY TO COMMIT MURDER!"
AND HE WOULD HAVE GOTTEN AWAY WITH IT TOO IF NOT FOR YOUR BORDERLINE VIGILANTISM.
MYSTERY SOLVED !!
CLUES FOUND (4/10)
BONUS MYSTERY POINTS = 000
I AM NOT REPLAYING THIS ENTIRE LEVEL.
CREATED BY FLETCHER D. HARGROVE
COPYRIGHT © MMVI TOONHOUND STUDIOS

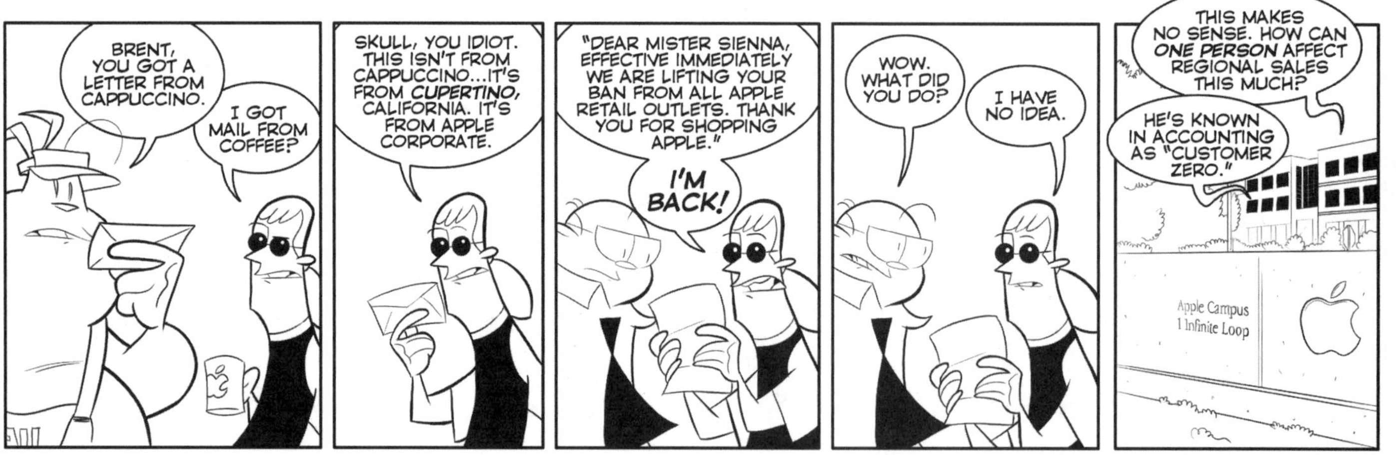
BRENT, YOU GOT A LETTER FROM CAPPUCCINO.
I GOT MAIL FROM COFFEE?
SKULL, YOU IDIOT. THIS ISN'T FROM CAPPUCCINO...IT'S FROM CUPERTINO, CALIFORNIA. IT'S FROM APPLE CORPORATE.
"DEAR MISTER SIENNA, EFFECTIVE IMMEDIATELY WE ARE LIFTING YOUR BAN FROM ALL APPLE RETAIL OUTLETS. THANK YOU FOR SHOPPING APPLE."
I'M BACK!
WOW. WHAT DID YOU DO?
I HAVE NO IDEA.
THIS MAKES NO SENSE. HOW CAN ONE PERSON AFFECT REGIONAL SALES THIS MUCH?
HE'S KNOWN IN ACCOUNTING AS "CUSTOMER ZERO."
Apple Campus
1 Infinite Loop

Panel 1: OH, MY. IT'S HALLOWEEN TIME AGAIN, ISN'T IT?

Panel 2: BREAK IT TO ME... HOW BAD DO I HAVE IT THIS YEAR?

YOU AND ME IN MATCHING COSTUMES AT SAM'S PARTY.

Panel 3: NOT MATCHING. THE GUYS ALWAYS GET SHAFTED IN THAT SCENARIO.

I WANT MATCHING.

Panel 4: OKAY, THEN. MATCHING COSTUMES BUT I GET TO CHOOSE THE COSTUMES.

WELLL... OKAY.

Panel 5: THIS WAS A *HORRIBLE* COMPROMISE.

HEY, COMPROMISE IN A RELATIONSHIP IS SOMETHING NOT EVEN *MISTER MIRACLE* CAN ESCAPE FROM.

Panel 6: DUDE, YOU AND YOUR GIRLFRIEND HAVE SOME BAD ASS COSTUMES!

THANKS! SHE'S MY FIANCEE, ACTUALLY.

Panel 7: OH. I SEE YOU GOT WRANGLED INTO THE RAGGEDY ANDY TRAP THIS YEAR. THAT'S TOUGH.

YEAH. SUCKS.

Panel 8: HOW DID YOU CONVINCE HER TO DRESS UP AS THE NEW GODS?

NO WAY!

WELL, IT'S EASY WITH JADE. SHE'S INTO COMICS.

Panel 9: BABY, SAY SOMETHING NERDCORE FOR THIS GUY.

UH...YOUR *BOOM TUBE* MAKES MY *MOTHERBOX* GO "PING-PING."

Panel 10: HEY, SWEETIE. HAVING A GOOD TIME?

WE'RE THROUGH.

Panel 11: HARRY POTTER?

HALLOWEEN PUT ME IN THE MOOD TO WATCH IT AGAIN.

Panel 12: HARRY POTTER CAN KISS MY ASS. IF YOU WANT TO WATCH A REAL WITCH MOVIE, I'LL PUT IN "*BEDKNOBS AND BROOMSTICKS.*"

BEDKNOBS AND WHO'S ITS?

Panel 13: DISNEY, 1971. ANGELA LANDSBURY PLAYS A BRITISH WOMAN WHO TAKES A WITCHCRAFT CORRESPONDENCE COURSE TO AID IN THE WAR EFFORT. BRILLIANT STUFF AND LANDSBURY WAS KINDA HOT.

Panel 14: ANGELA LANDSBURY. THE OLD WOMAN FROM "MURDER SHE WROTE?"

HEY! DON'T KNOCK HER. SHE WAS STUNNING IN HER DAY.

Panel 15: OKAY. THIS IS SPOOKIER THAN HARRY POTTER. PUT IT IN.

SUBSTITUTIARY LOCOMOTION IS FOR ME!

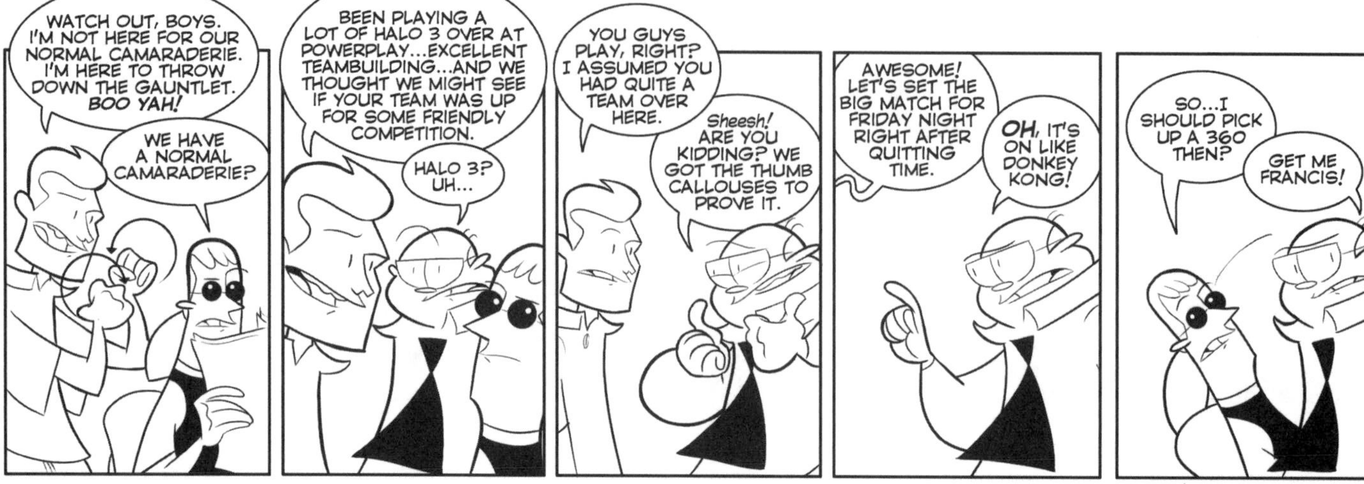
WATCH OUT, BOYS. I'M NOT HERE FOR OUR NORMAL CAMARADERIE. I'M HERE TO THROW DOWN THE GAUNTLET. BOO YAH!
WE HAVE A NORMAL CAMARADERIE?
BEEN PLAYING A LOT OF HALO 3 OVER AT POWERPLAY...EXCELLENT TEAMBUILDING...AND WE THOUGHT WE MIGHT SEE IF YOUR TEAM WAS UP FOR SOME FRIENDLY COMPETITION.
HALO 3? UH...
YOU GUYS PLAY, RIGHT? I ASSUMED YOU HAD QUITE A TEAM OVER HERE.
Sheesh! ARE YOU KIDDING? WE GOT THE THUMB CALLOUSES TO PROVE IT.
AWESOME! LET'S SET THE BIG MATCH FOR FRIDAY NIGHT RIGHT AFTER QUITTING TIME.
OH, IT'S ON LIKE DONKEY KONG!
SO...I SHOULD PICK UP A 360 THEN?
GET ME FRANCIS!

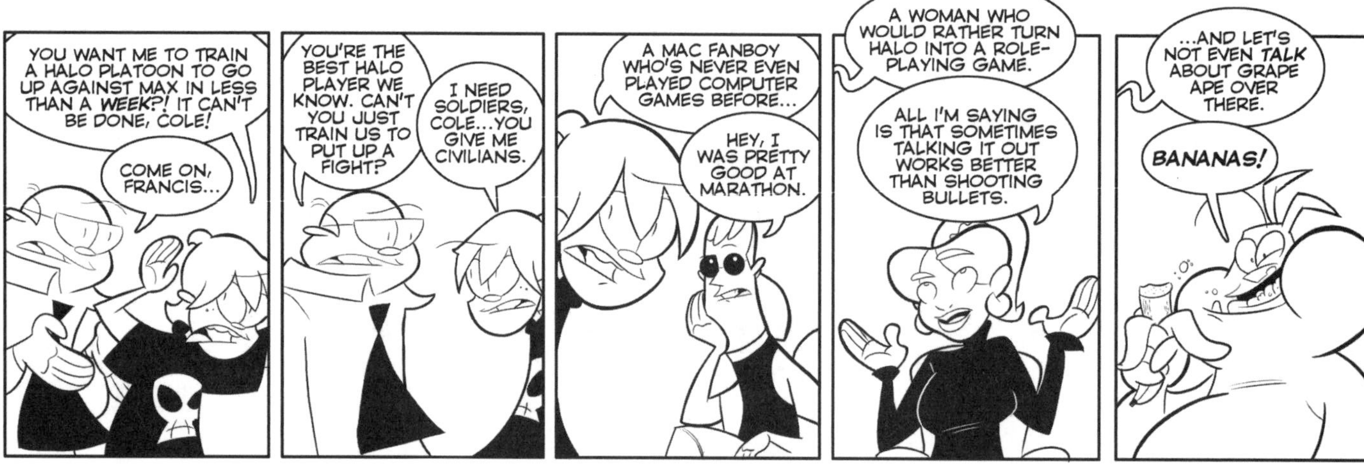
YOU WANT ME TO TRAIN A HALO PLATOON TO GO UP AGAINST MAX IN LESS THAN A WEEK?! IT CAN'T BE DONE, COLE!
COME ON, FRANCIS...
YOU'RE THE BEST HALO PLAYER WE KNOW. CAN'T YOU JUST TRAIN US TO PUT UP A FIGHT?
I NEED SOLDIERS, COLE...YOU GIVE ME CIVILIANS.
A MAC FANBOY WHO'S NEVER EVEN PLAYED COMPUTER GAMES BEFORE...
HEY, I WAS PRETTY GOOD AT MARATHON.
A WOMAN WHO WOULD RATHER TURN HALO INTO A ROLE-PLAYING GAME.
ALL I'M SAYING IS THAT SOMETIMES TALKING IT OUT WORKS BETTER THAN SHOOTING BULLETS.
...AND LET'S NOT EVEN TALK ABOUT GRAPE APE OVER THERE.
BANANAS!

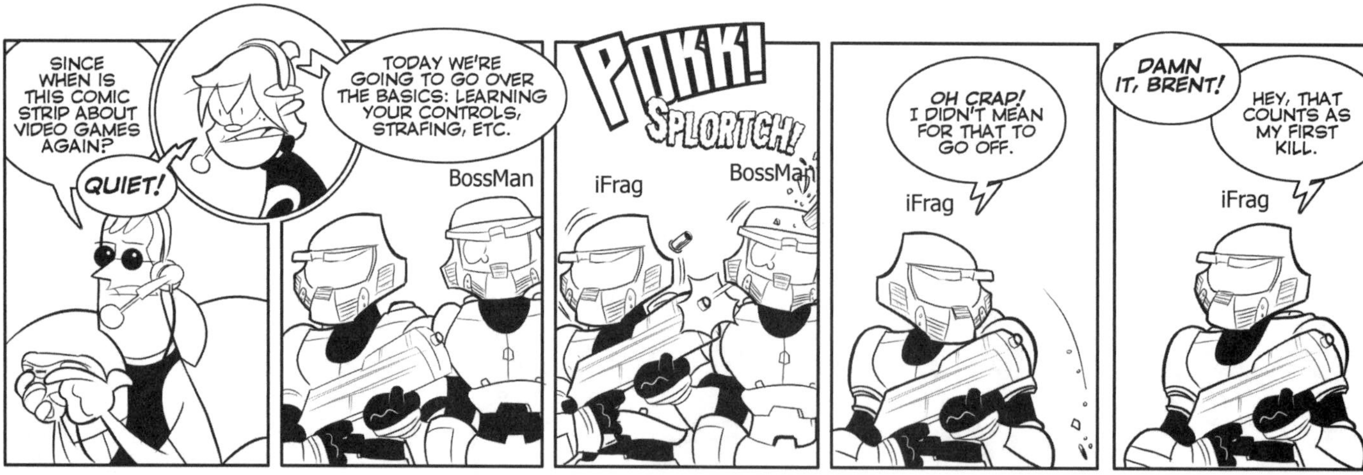
SINCE WHEN IS THIS COMIC STRIP ABOUT VIDEO GAMES AGAIN?
QUIET!
TODAY WE'RE GOING TO GO OVER THE BASICS: LEARNING YOUR CONTROLS, STRAFING, ETC.
BossMan
POKK!
SPLORTCH!
iFrag
BossMan
OH CRAP! I DIDN'T MEAN FOR THAT TO GO OFF.
iFrag
DAMN IT, BRENT!
HEY, THAT COUNTS AS MY FIRST KILL.
iFrag

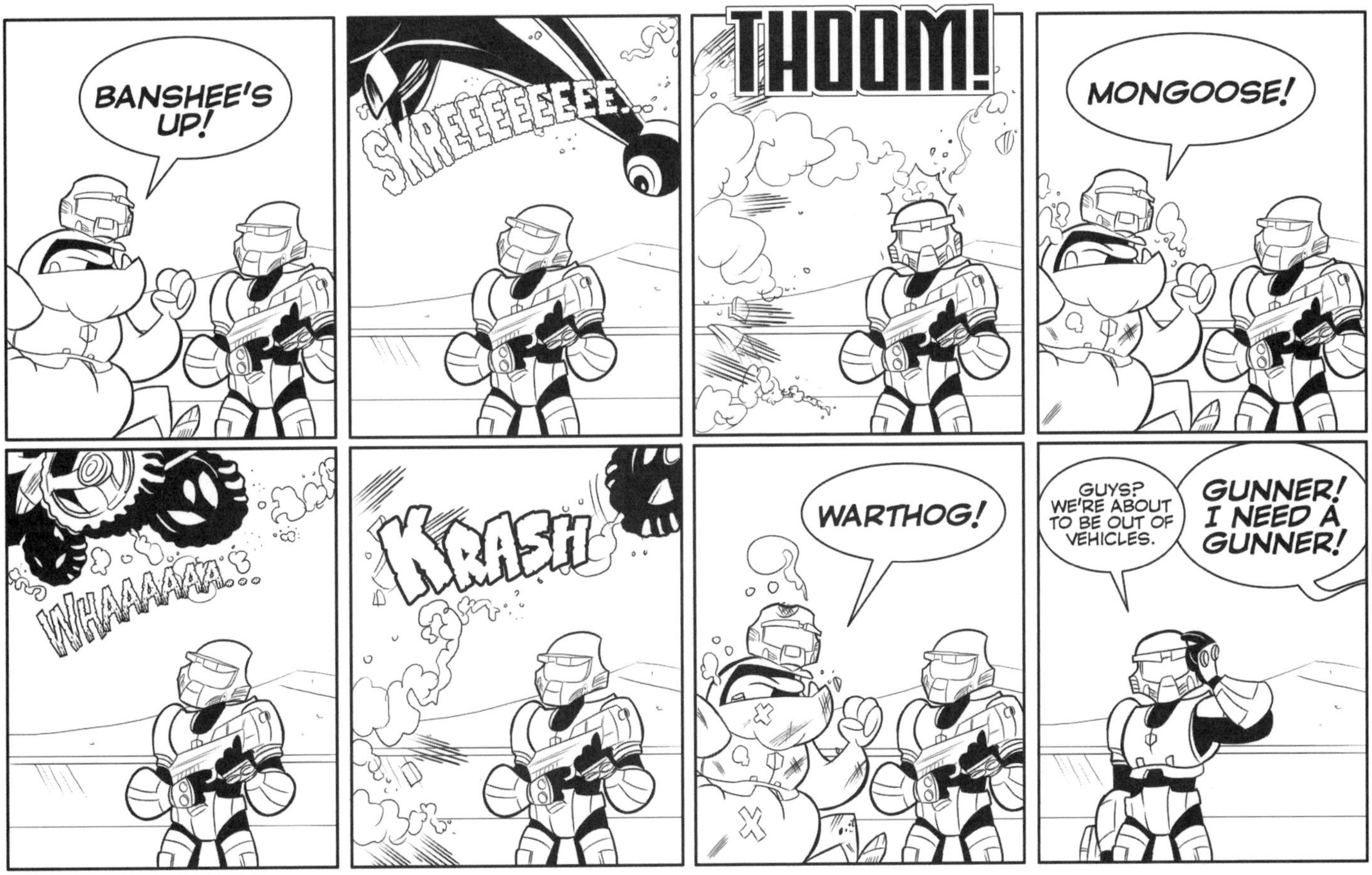
BANSHEE'S UP!
SKREEEEEEEEE...
THOOM!
MONGOOSE!
WHAAAAAAA...
KRASH
WARTHOG!
GUYS? WE'RE ABOUT TO BE OUT OF VEHICLES.
GUNNER! I NEED A GUNNER!

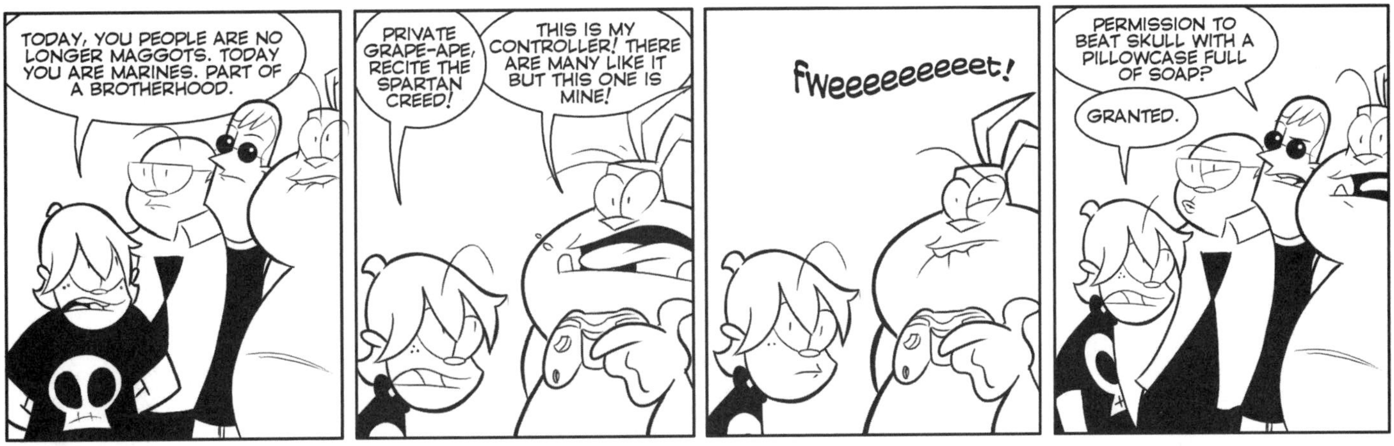
TODAY, YOU PEOPLE ARE NO LONGER MAGGOTS. TODAY YOU ARE MARINES. PART OF A BROTHERHOOD.
PRIVATE GRAPE-APE, RECITE THE SPARTAN CREED!
THIS IS MY CONTROLLER! THERE ARE MANY LIKE IT BUT THIS ONE IS MINE!
fweeeeeeeeet!
PERMISSION TO BEAT SKULL WITH A PILLOWCASE FULL OF SOAP?
GRANTED.

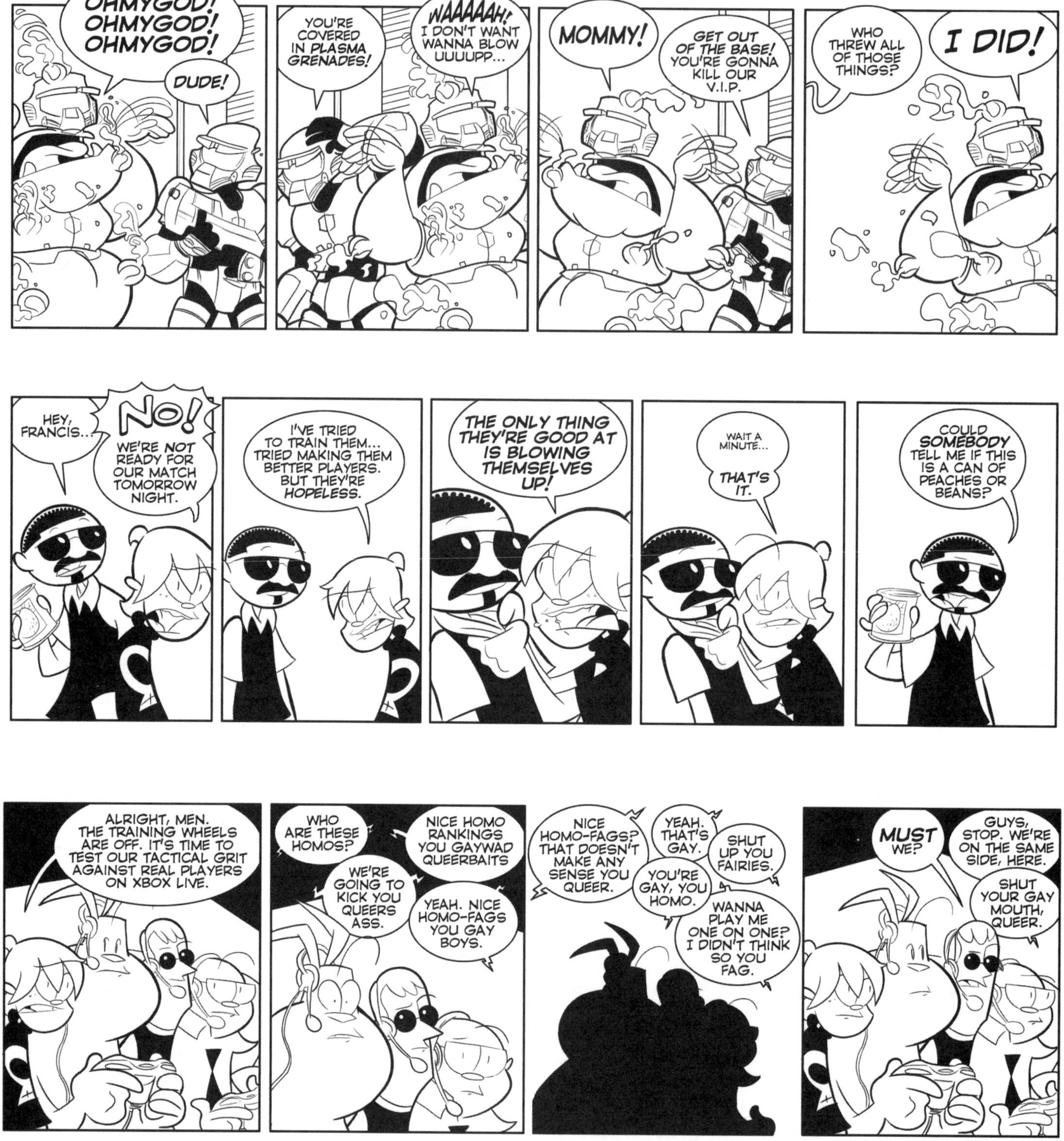
OHMYGOD! OHMYGOD! OHMYGOD!
DUDE!
YOU'RE COVERED IN PLASMA GRENADES!
WAAAAAH! I DON'T WANT WANNA BLOW UUUUPP...
MOMMY!
GET OUT OF THE BASE! YOU'RE GONNA KILL OUR V.I.P.
WHO THREW ALL OF THOSE THINGS?
I DID!
HEY, FRANCIS...
NO! WE'RE NOT READY FOR OUR MATCH TOMORROW NIGHT.
I'VE TRIED TO TRAIN THEM... TRIED MAKING THEM BETTER PLAYERS. BUT THEY'RE HOPELESS.
THE ONLY THING THEY'RE GOOD AT IS BLOWING THEMSELVES UP!
WAIT A MINUTE...
THAT'S IT.
COULD SOMEBODY TELL ME IF THIS IS A CAN OF PEACHES OR BEANS?
ALRIGHT, MEN. THE TRAINING WHEELS ARE OFF. IT'S TIME TO TEST OUR TACTICAL GRIT AGAINST REAL PLAYERS ON XBOX LIVE.
WHO ARE THESE HOMOS?
NICE HOMO RANKINGS YOU GAYWAD QUEERBAITS
WE'RE GOING TO KICK YOU QUEERS ASS.
YEAH. NICE HOMO-FAGS YOU GAY BOYS.
NICE HOMO-FAGS? THAT DOESN'T MAKE ANY SENSE YOU QUEER.
YEAH. THAT'S GAY.
SHUT UP YOU FAIRIES.
YOU'RE GAY, YOU HOMO.
WANNA PLAY ME ONE ON ONE? I DIDN'T THINK SO YOU FAG.
MUST WE?
GUYS, STOP. WE'RE ON THE SAME SIDE, HERE.
SHUT YOUR GAY MOUTH, QUEER.

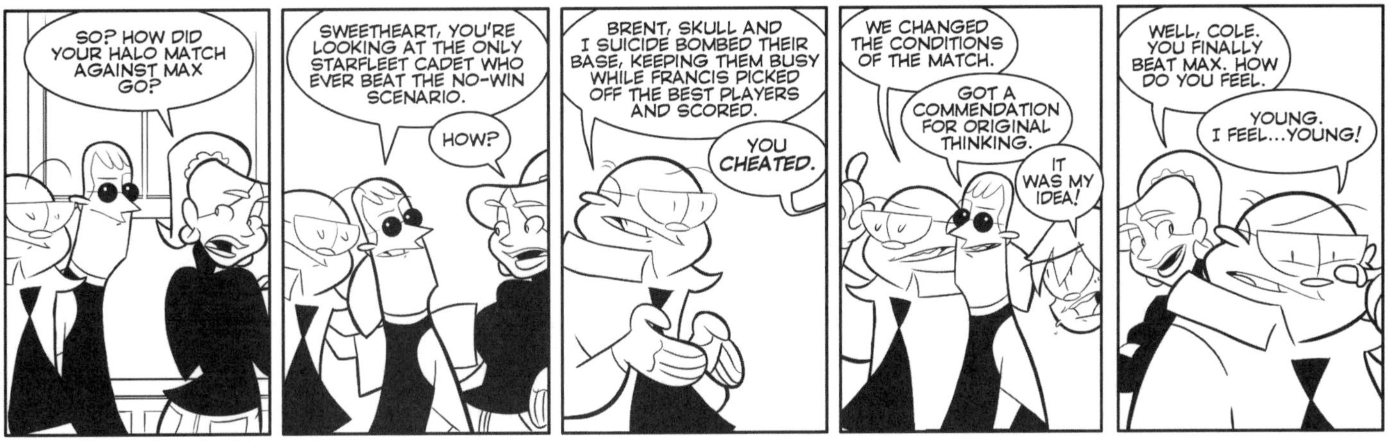
SO? HOW DID YOUR HALO MATCH AGAINST MAX GO?
SWEETHEART, YOU'RE LOOKING AT THE ONLY STARFLEET CADET WHO EVER BEAT THE NO-WIN SCENARIO.
HOW?
BRENT, SKULL AND I SUICIDE BOMBED THEIR BASE, KEEPING THEM BUSY WHILE FRANCIS PICKED OFF THE BEST PLAYERS AND SCORED.
YOU *CHEATED.*
WE CHANGED THE CONDITIONS OF THE MATCH.
GOT A COMMENDATION FOR ORIGINAL THINKING.
IT WAS MY IDEA!
WELL, COLE. YOU FINALLY BEAT MAX. HOW DO YOU FEEL.
YOUNG. I FEEL...YOUNG!

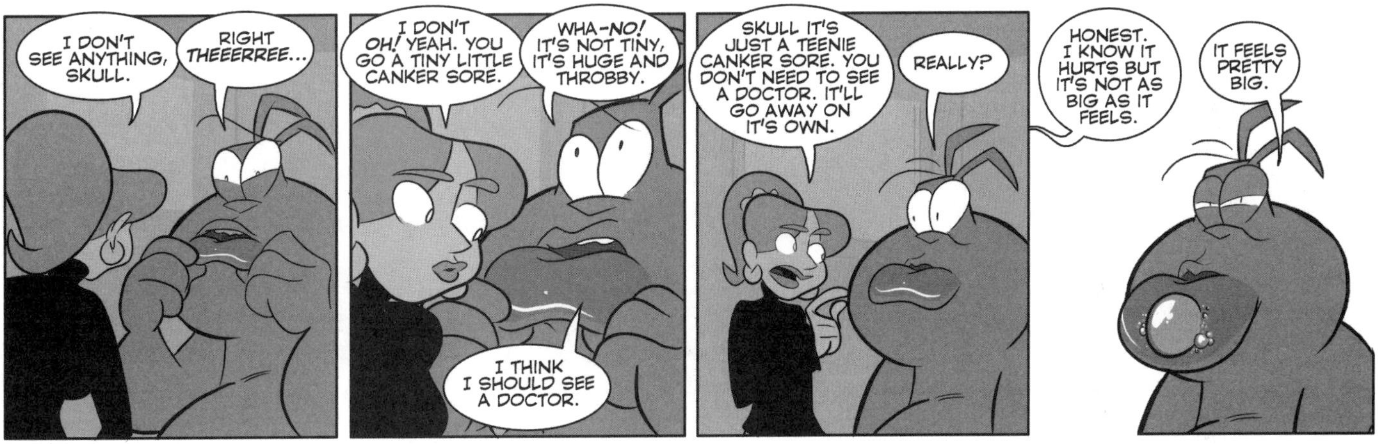
I DON'T SEE ANYTHING, SKULL.
RIGHT *THEEERREE...*
I DON'T *OH!* YEAH. YOU GO A TINY LITTLE CANKER SORE.
WHA-*NO!* IT'S NOT TINY, IT'S HUGE AND THROBBY.
I THINK I SHOULD SEE A DOCTOR.
SKULL IT'S JUST A TEENIE CANKER SORE. YOU DON'T NEED TO SEE A DOCTOR. IT'LL GO AWAY ON IT'S OWN.
REALLY?
HONEST. I KNOW IT HURTS BUT IT'S NOT AS BIG AS IT FEELS.
IT FEELS PRETTY BIG.

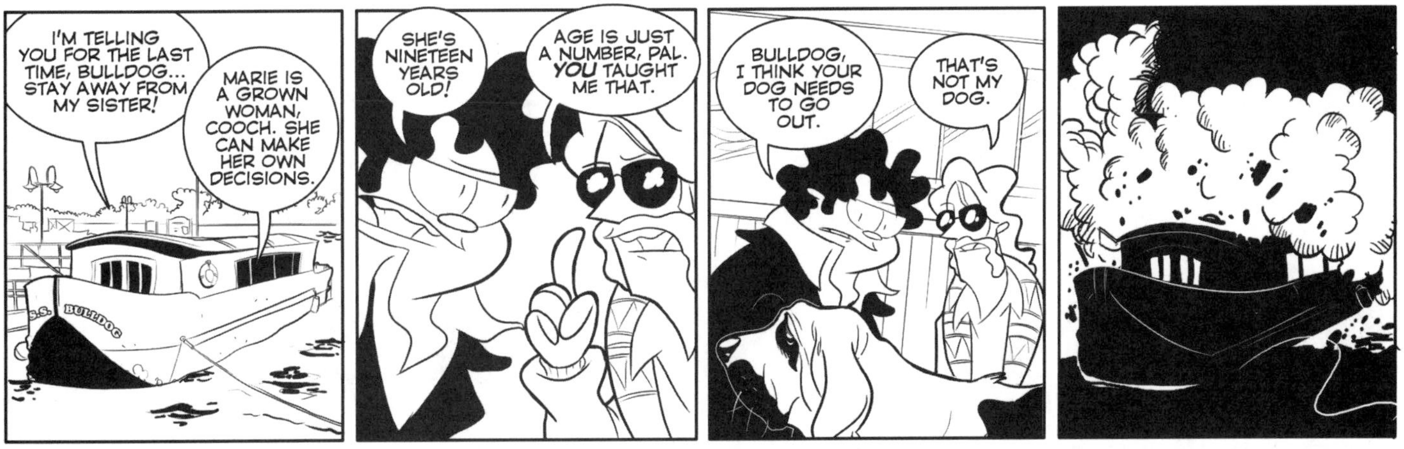
I'M TELLING YOU FOR THE LAST TIME, BULLDOG... STAY AWAY FROM MY SISTER!
MARIE IS A GROWN WOMAN, COOCH. SHE CAN MAKE HER OWN DECISIONS.
S.S. BULLDOG
SHE'S NINETEEN YEARS OLD!
AGE IS JUST A NUMBER, PAL. *YOU* TAUGHT ME THAT.
BULLDOG, I THINK YOUR DOG NEEDS TO GO OUT.
THAT'S NOT MY DOG.

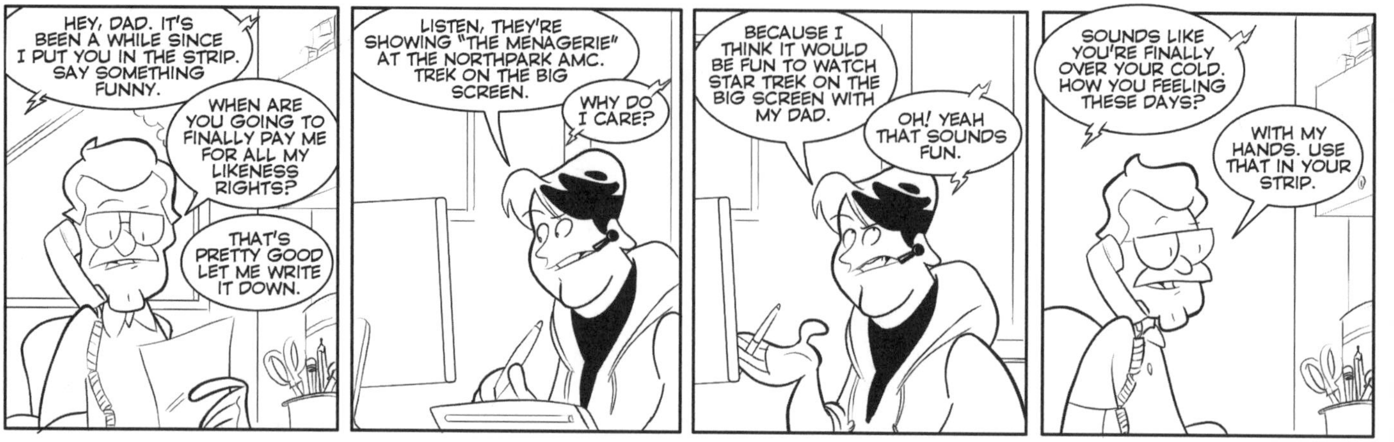
HEY, DAD. IT'S BEEN A WHILE SINCE I PUT YOU IN THE STRIP. SAY SOMETHING FUNNY.
WHEN ARE YOU GOING TO FINALLY PAY ME FOR ALL MY LIKENESS RIGHTS?
THAT'S PRETTY GOOD LET ME WRITE IT DOWN.
LISTEN, THEY'RE SHOWING "THE MENAGERIE" AT THE NORTHPARK AMC. TREK ON THE BIG SCREEN.
WHY DO I CARE?
BECAUSE I THINK IT WOULD BE FUN TO WATCH STAR TREK ON THE BIG SCREEN WITH MY DAD.
OH! YEAH THAT SOUNDS FUN.
SOUNDS LIKE YOU'RE FINALLY OVER YOUR COLD. HOW YOU FEELING THESE DAYS?
WITH MY HANDS. USE THAT IN YOUR STRIP.

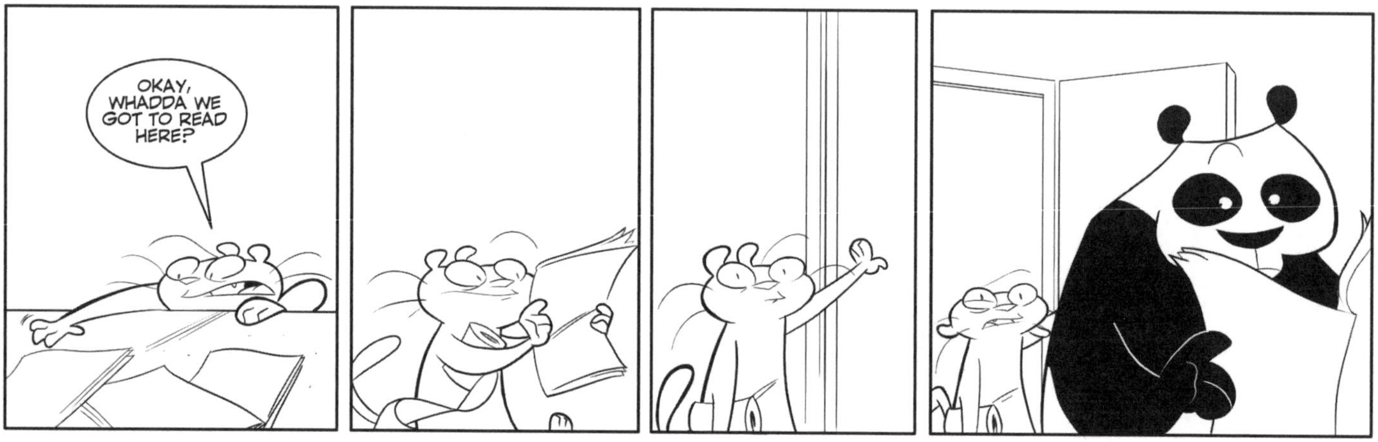
OKAY, WHADDA WE GOT TO READ HERE?

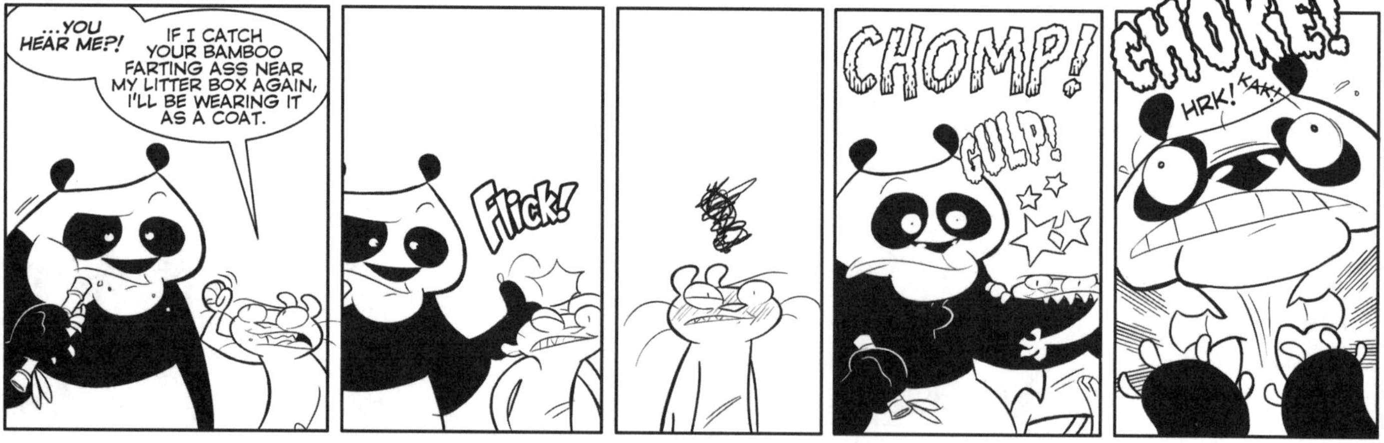
...YOU HEAR ME?!
IF I CATCH YOUR BAMBOO FARTING ASS NEAR MY LITTER BOX AGAIN, I'LL BE WEARING IT AS A COAT.
FLICK!
CHOMP!
GULP!
CHOKE!
HRK!

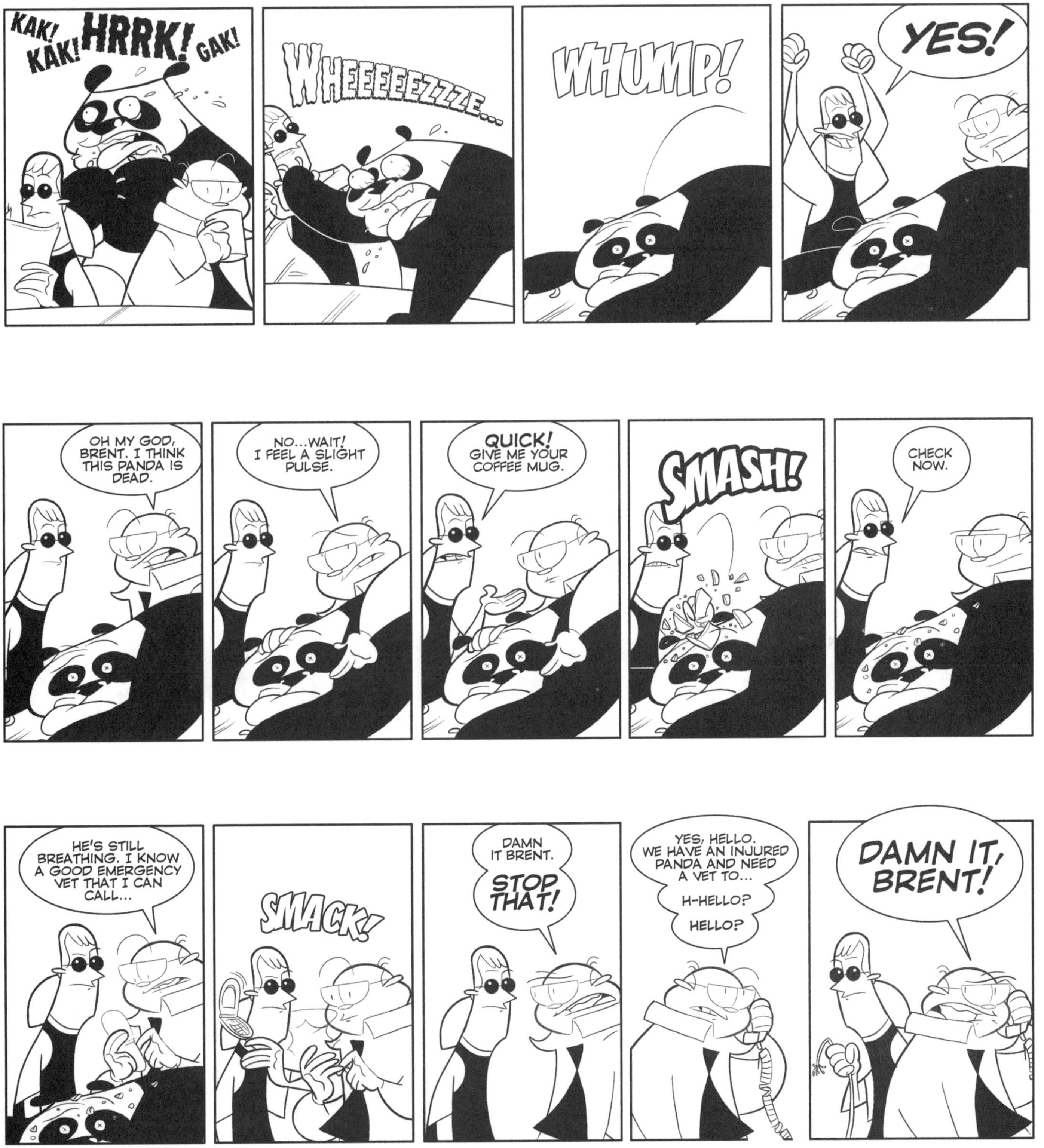
KAK! KAK! HRRK! GAK!
WHEEEEEEZZZZE...
WHUMP!
YES!
OH MY GOD, BRENT. I THINK THIS PANDA IS DEAD.
NO...WAIT! I FEEL A SLIGHT PULSE.
QUICK! GIVE ME YOUR COFFEE MUG.
SMASH!
CHECK NOW.
HE'S STILL BREATHING. I KNOW A GOOD EMERGENCY VET THAT I CAN CALL...
SMACK!
DAMN IT BRENT.
STOP THAT!
YES, HELLO. WE HAVE AN INJURED PANDA AND NEED A VET TO...
H-HELLO?
HELLO?
DAMN IT, BRENT!

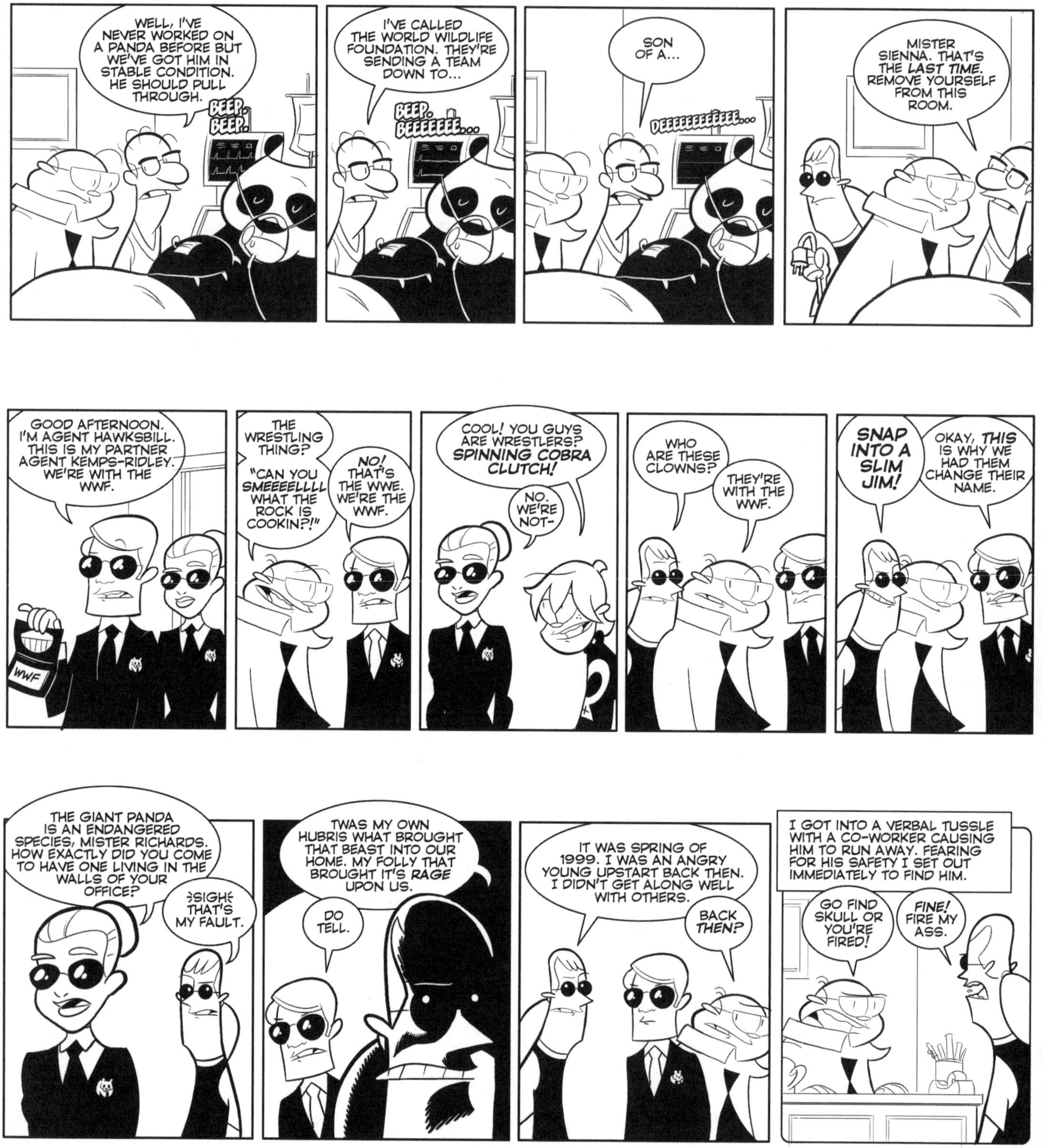
WELL, I'VE NEVER WORKED ON A PANDA BEFORE BUT WE'VE GOT HIM IN STABLE CONDITION. HE SHOULD PULL THROUGH.
BEEP. BEEP.
I'VE CALLED THE WORLD WILDLIFE FOUNDATION. THEY'RE SENDING A TEAM DOWN TO...
BEEP. BEEEEEEE...
SON OF A...
DEEEEEEEEEEEE...
MISTER SIENNA. THAT'S THE LAST TIME. REMOVE YOURSELF FROM THIS ROOM.
GOOD AFTERNOON. I'M AGENT HAWKSBILL. THIS IS MY PARTNER AGENT KEMPS-RIDLEY. WE'RE WITH THE WWF.
WWF
THE WRESTLING THING? "CAN YOU SMEEEELLLL WHAT THE ROCK IS COOKIN?!"
NO! THAT'S THE WWE. WE'RE THE WWF.
COOL! YOU GUYS ARE WRESTLERS? SPINNING COBRA CLUTCH!
NO. WE'RE NOT-
WHO ARE THESE CLOWNS?
THEY'RE WITH THE WWF.
SNAP INTO A SLIM JIM!
OKAY, THIS IS WHY WE HAD THEM CHANGE THEIR NAME.
THE GIANT PANDA IS AN ENDANGERED SPECIES, MISTER RICHARDS. HOW EXACTLY DID YOU COME TO HAVE ONE LIVING IN THE WALLS OF YOUR OFFICE?
SIGH THAT'S MY FAULT.
TWAS MY OWN HUBRIS WHAT BROUGHT THAT BEAST INTO OUR HOME. MY FOLLY THAT BROUGHT IT'S RAGE UPON US.
DO TELL.
IT WAS SPRING OF 1999. I WAS AN ANGRY YOUNG UPSTART BACK THEN. I DIDN'T GET ALONG WELL WITH OTHERS.
BACK THEN?
I GOT INTO A VERBAL TUSSLE WITH A CO-WORKER CAUSING HIM TO RUN AWAY. FEARING FOR HIS SAFETY I SET OUT IMMEDIATELY TO FIND HIM.
GO FIND SKULL OR YOU'RE FIRED!
FINE! FIRE MY ASS.

Panel 1 (circle): I WAS TIRELESSLY SEARCHING FOR SKULL WHEN IT DAWNED ON ME...

Panel 2: PERHAPS I SHOULD CHECK THE LOCAL SHELTERS TO SEE IF THE SPAZ HAD BEEN PICKED UP...

LIBERTY MEADOWS ANIMAL SANCTUARY

Panel 3: WOW. NICE ESTABLISHING SHOT.

MY SEARCH FOR SKULL HAD LEAD ME TO THE MOST UNSUSPECTING OF PLACES...

LIBERTY MEADOWS ANIMAL SANCTUARY? HMMM...

JUST WHAT THIS TOWN NEEDS: A COMMUNE OF HIPPIES WHO LOVE ANIMALS MORE THAN PEOPLE.

BING!

BRANDY CARTER: CARETAKER. EESH! SHE PROBABLY EATS NOTHING BUT WHEATGRASS AND NEVER SHAVES HER LEGS.

HELLO! CAN I HELP YOU?

YES. I'M LOOKING FOR A RACK OF MINE NAMED JUGGS.

SORRY ABOUT THAT. I MEANT TO SAY THAT I WAS LOOKING FOR MY BREAST FRIEND.

BEST! BEST FRIEND. HE, UH...RAN AWAY AND WE'RE ALL WORRIED SICK 'CAUSE IT'S SO NIPPLY OUTSIDE.

NIPPY! SORRY.

ANYWAY...I THOUGHT I WOULD CHECK TO SEE IF HE ENDED UP HERE AT YOUR BEAUTIFUL TITS.

I MEAN, ANIMAL SANCTUARY.

HEH. ANIMAL SANCTUARY DOESN'T EVEN SOUND LIKE

PLEASE LEAVE!

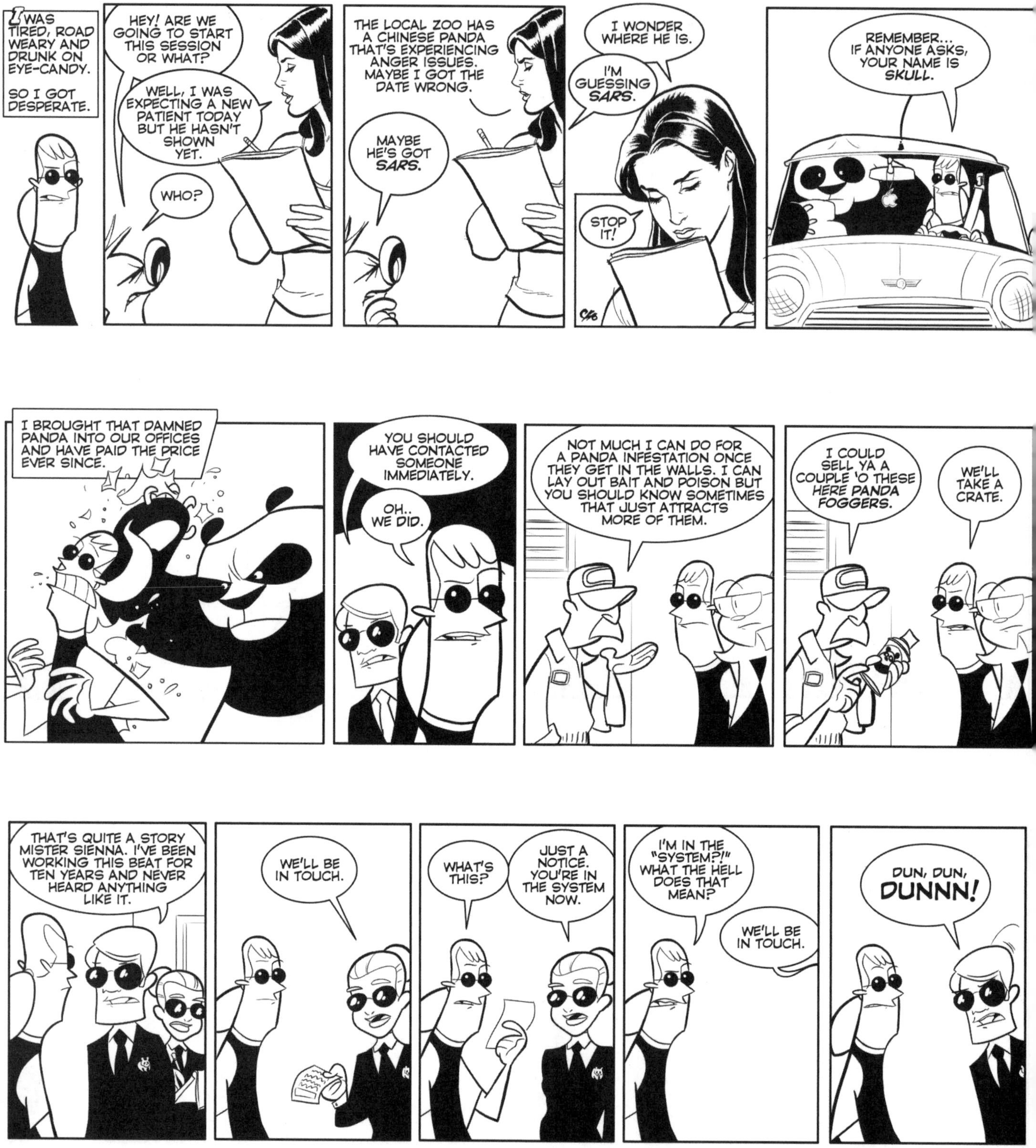
I WAS TIRED, ROAD WEARY AND DRUNK ON EYE-CANDY.
SO I GOT DESPERATE.
HEY! ARE WE GOING TO START THIS SESSION OR WHAT?
WELL, I WAS EXPECTING A NEW PATIENT TODAY BUT HE HASN'T SHOWN YET.
WHO?
THE LOCAL ZOO HAS A CHINESE PANDA THAT'S EXPERIENCING ANGER ISSUES. MAYBE I GOT THE DATE WRONG.
MAYBE HE'S GOT SARS.
I WONDER WHERE HE IS.
I'M GUESSING SARS.
STOP IT!
REMEMBER... IF ANYONE ASKS, YOUR NAME IS SKULL.
I BROUGHT THAT DAMNED PANDA INTO OUR OFFICES AND HAVE PAID THE PRICE EVER SINCE.
YOU SHOULD HAVE CONTACTED SOMEONE IMMEDIATELY.
OH.. WE DID.
NOT MUCH I CAN DO FOR A PANDA INFESTATION ONCE THEY GET IN THE WALLS. I CAN LAY OUT BAIT AND POISON BUT YOU SHOULD KNOW SOMETIMES THAT JUST ATTRACTS MORE OF THEM.
I COULD SELL YA A COUPLE 'O THESE HERE PANDA FOGGERS.
WE'LL TAKE A CRATE.
THAT'S QUITE A STORY MISTER SIENNA. I'VE BEEN WORKING THIS BEAT FOR TEN YEARS AND NEVER HEARD ANYTHING LIKE IT.
WE'LL BE IN TOUCH.
WHAT'S THIS?
JUST A NOTICE. YOU'RE IN THE SYSTEM NOW.
I'M IN THE "SYSTEM?!" WHAT THE HELL DOES THAT MEAN?
WE'LL BE IN TOUCH.
DUN, DUN, DUNNN!

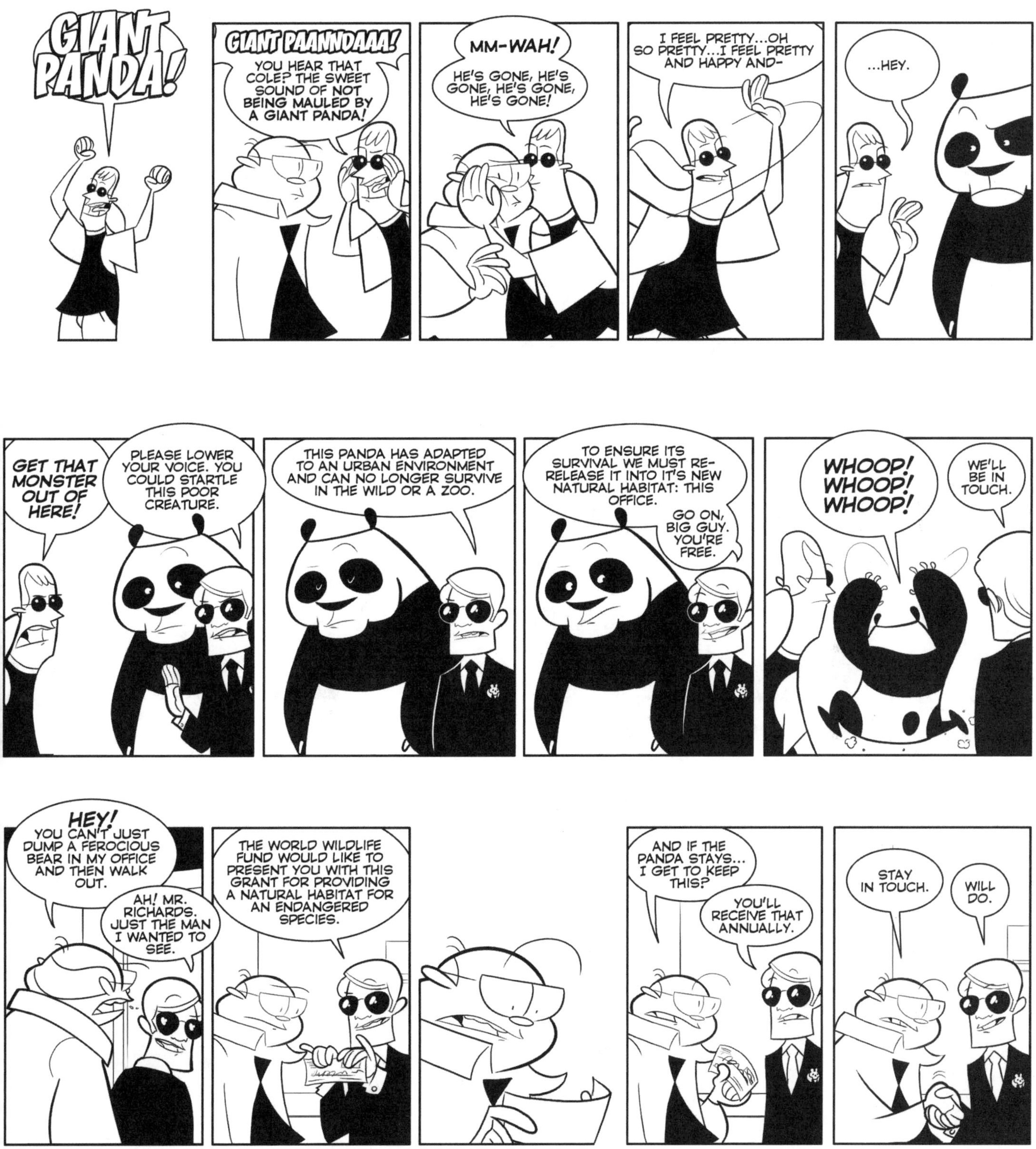

GIANT PANDA!
GIANT PAANNDAAA!
YOU HEAR THAT COLE? THE SWEET SOUND OF NOT BEING MAULED BY A GIANT PANDA!
MM-WAH!
HE'S GONE, HE'S GONE, HE'S GONE, HE'S GONE!
I FEEL PRETTY...OH SO PRETTY...I FEEL PRETTY AND HAPPY AND-
...HEY.
GET THAT MONSTER OUT OF HERE!
PLEASE LOWER YOUR VOICE. YOU COULD STARTLE THIS POOR CREATURE.
THIS PANDA HAS ADAPTED TO AN URBAN ENVIRONMENT AND CAN NO LONGER SURVIVE IN THE WILD OR A ZOO.
TO ENSURE ITS SURVIVAL WE MUST RE-RELEASE IT INTO IT'S NEW NATURAL HABITAT: THIS OFFICE.
GO ON, BIG GUY. YOU'RE FREE.
WHOOP! WHOOP! WHOOP!
WE'LL BE IN TOUCH.
HEY! YOU CAN'T JUST DUMP A FEROCIOUS BEAR IN MY OFFICE AND THEN WALK OUT.
AH! MR. RICHARDS. JUST THE MAN I WANTED TO SEE.
THE WORLD WILDLIFE FUND WOULD LIKE TO PRESENT YOU WITH THIS GRANT FOR PROVIDING A NATURAL HABITAT FOR AN ENDANGERED SPECIES.
AND IF THE PANDA STAYS... I GET TO KEEP THIS?
YOU'LL RECEIVE THAT ANNUALLY.
STAY IN TOUCH.
WILL DO.

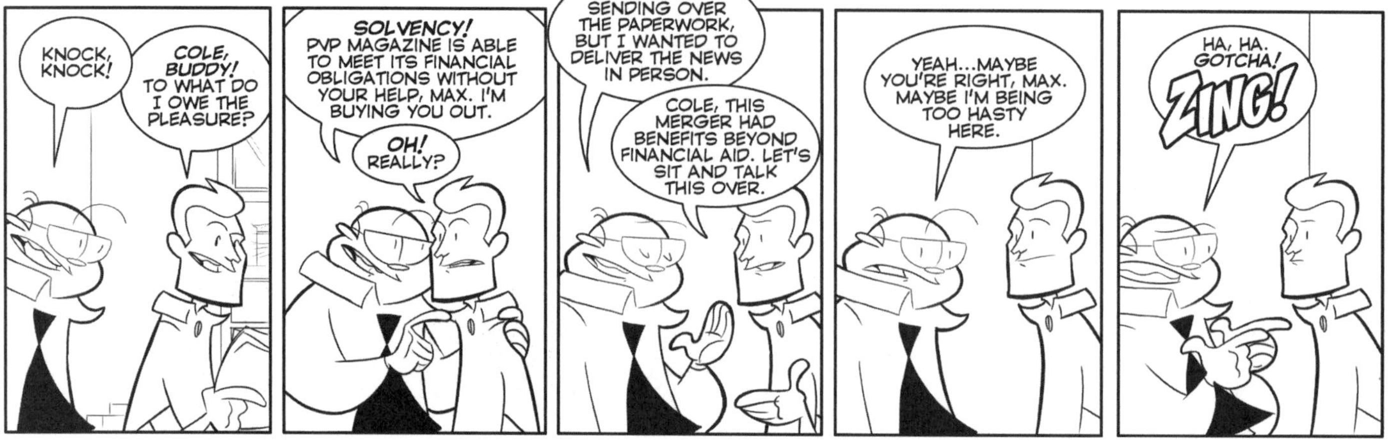
KNOCK, KNOCK!
COLE, BUDDY! TO WHAT DO I OWE THE PLEASURE?
SOLVENCY! PVP MAGAZINE IS ABLE TO MEET ITS FINANCIAL OBLIGATIONS WITHOUT YOUR HELP, MAX. I'M BUYING YOU OUT.
OH! REALLY?
MY LAWYER'S SENDING OVER THE PAPERWORK, BUT I WANTED TO DELIVER THE NEWS IN PERSON.
COLE, THIS MERGER HAD BENEFITS BEYOND FINANCIAL AID. LET'S SIT AND TALK THIS OVER.
YEAH...MAYBE YOU'RE RIGHT, MAX. MAYBE I'M BEING TOO HASTY HERE.
HA, HA. GOTCHA!
ZING!

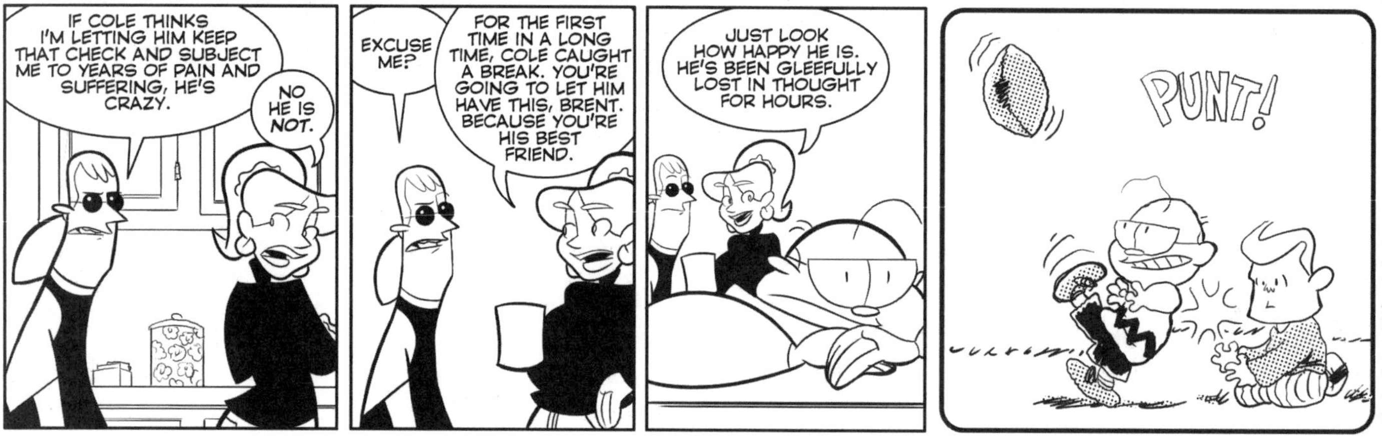
IF COLE THINKS I'M LETTING HIM KEEP THAT CHECK AND SUBJECT ME TO YEARS OF PAIN AND SUFFERING, HE'S CRAZY.
NO HE IS NOT.
EXCUSE ME?
FOR THE FIRST TIME IN A LONG TIME, COLE CAUGHT A BREAK. YOU'RE GOING TO LET HIM HAVE THIS, BRENT. BECAUSE YOU'RE HIS BEST FRIEND.
JUST LOOK HOW HAPPY HE IS. HE'S BEEN GLEEFULLY LOST IN THOUGHT FOR HOURS.
PUNT!

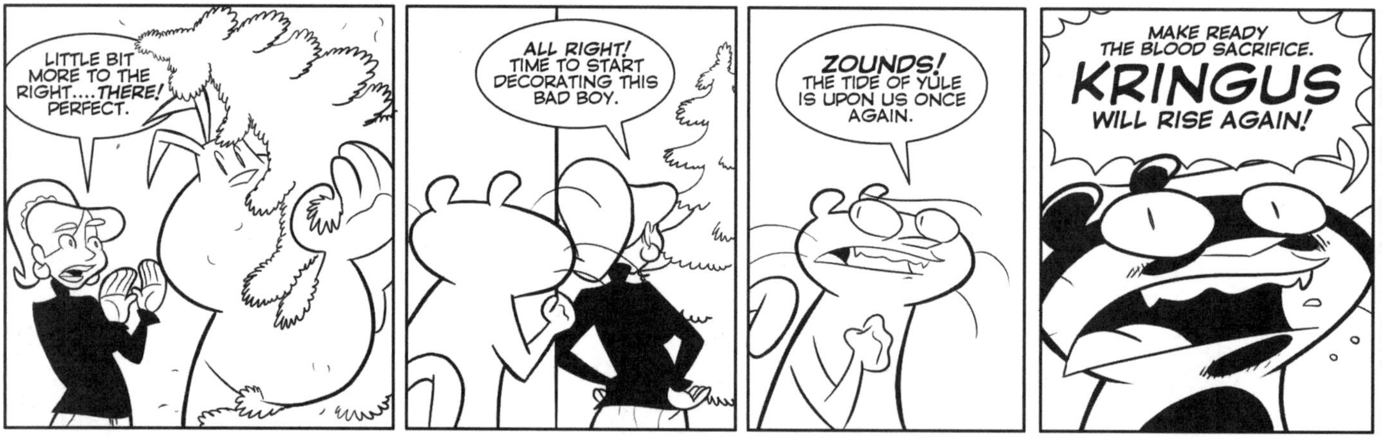
LITTLE BIT MORE TO THE RIGHT....THERE! PERFECT.
ALL RIGHT! TIME TO START DECORATING THIS BAD BOY.
ZOUNDS! THE TIDE OF YULE IS UPON US ONCE AGAIN.
MAKE READY THE BLOOD SACRIFICE. KRINGUS WILL RISE AGAIN!

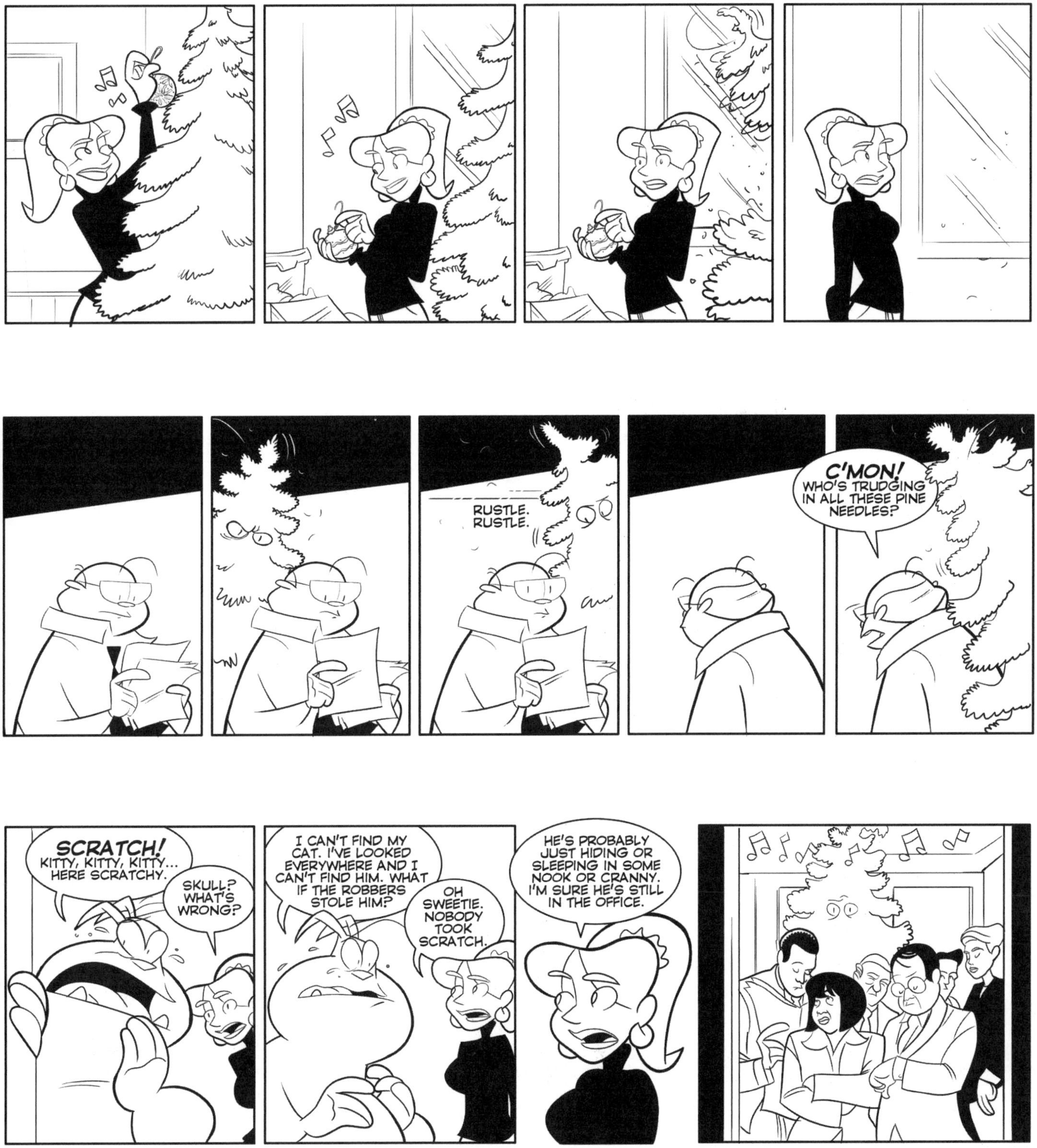
RUSTLE. RUSTLE.
C'MON! WHO'S TRUDGING IN ALL THESE PINE NEEDLES?
SCRATCH! KITTY, KITTY, KITTY... HERE SCRATCHY.
SKULL? WHAT'S WRONG?
I CAN'T FIND MY CAT. I'VE LOOKED EVERYWHERE AND I CAN'T FIND HIM. WHAT IF THE ROBBERS STOLE HIM?
OH SWEETIE. NOBODY TOOK SCRATCH.
HE'S PROBABLY JUST HIDING OR SLEEPING IN SOME NOOK OR CRANNY. I'M SURE HE'S STILL IN THE OFFICE.

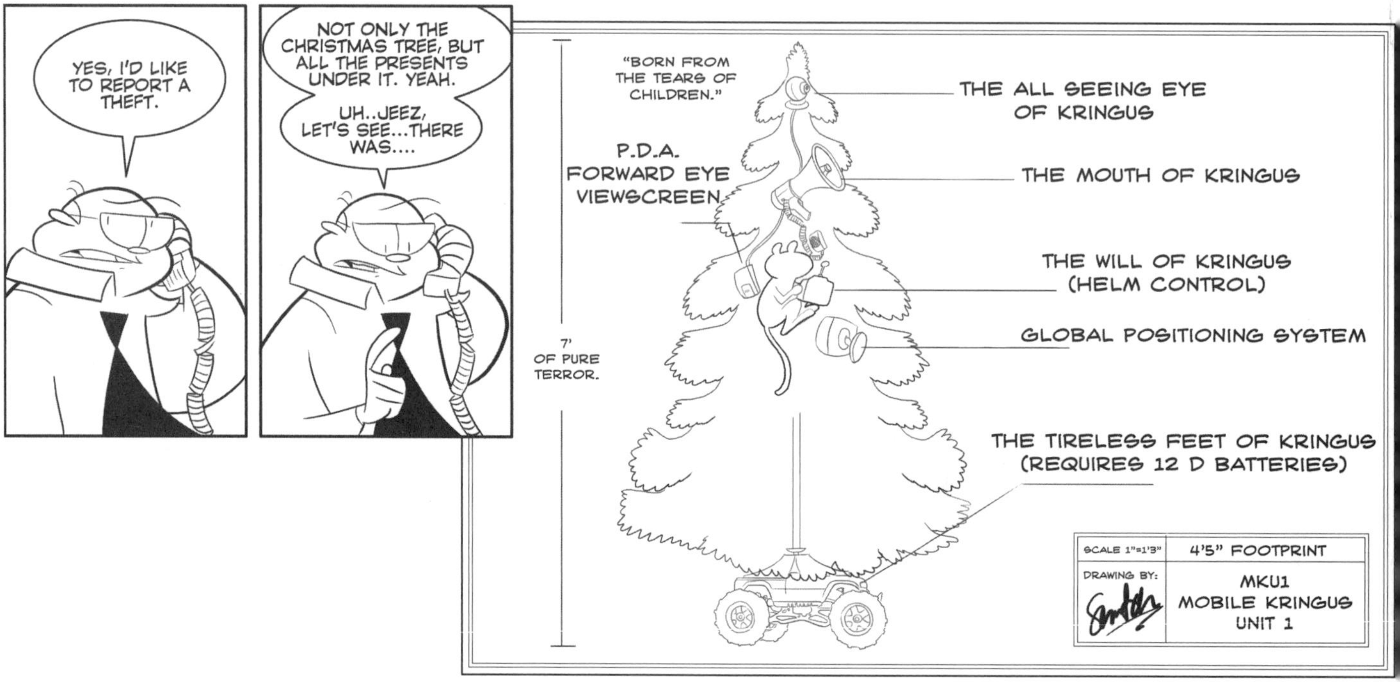
YES, I'D LIKE TO REPORT A THEFT.
NOT ONLY THE CHRISTMAS TREE, BUT ALL THE PRESENTS UNDER IT. YEAH.
UH..JEEZ, LET'S SEE...THERE WAS....
"BORN FROM THE TEARS OF CHILDREN."
THE ALL SEEING EYE OF KRINGUS
P.D.A. FORWARD EYE VIEWSCREEN
THE MOUTH OF KRINGUS
THE WILL OF KRINGUS (HELM CONTROL)
7' OF PURE TERROR.
GLOBAL POSITIONING SYSTEM
THE TIRELESS FEET OF KRINGUS (REQUIRES 12 D BATTERIES)
SCALE 1"=1'3"
4'5" FOOTPRINT
DRAWING BY:
MKU1 MOBILE KRINGUS UNIT 1

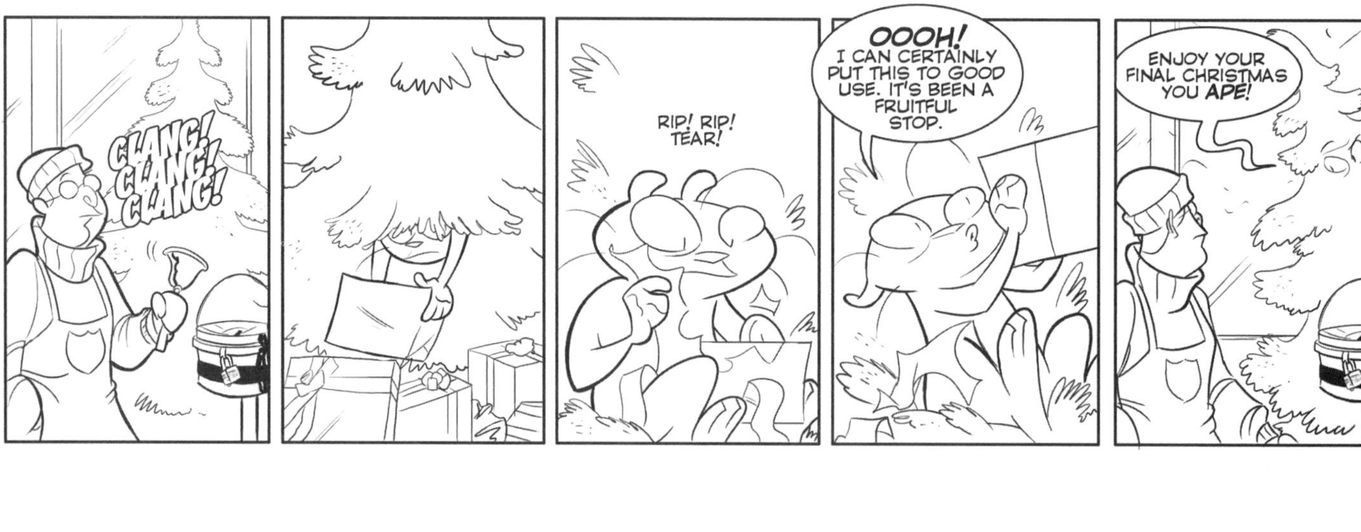
CLANG! CLANG! CLANG!
RIP! RIP! TEAR!
OOOH! I CAN CERTAINLY PUT THIS TO GOOD USE. IT'S BEEN A FRUITFUL STOP.
ENJOY YOUR FINAL CHRISTMAS YOU APE!

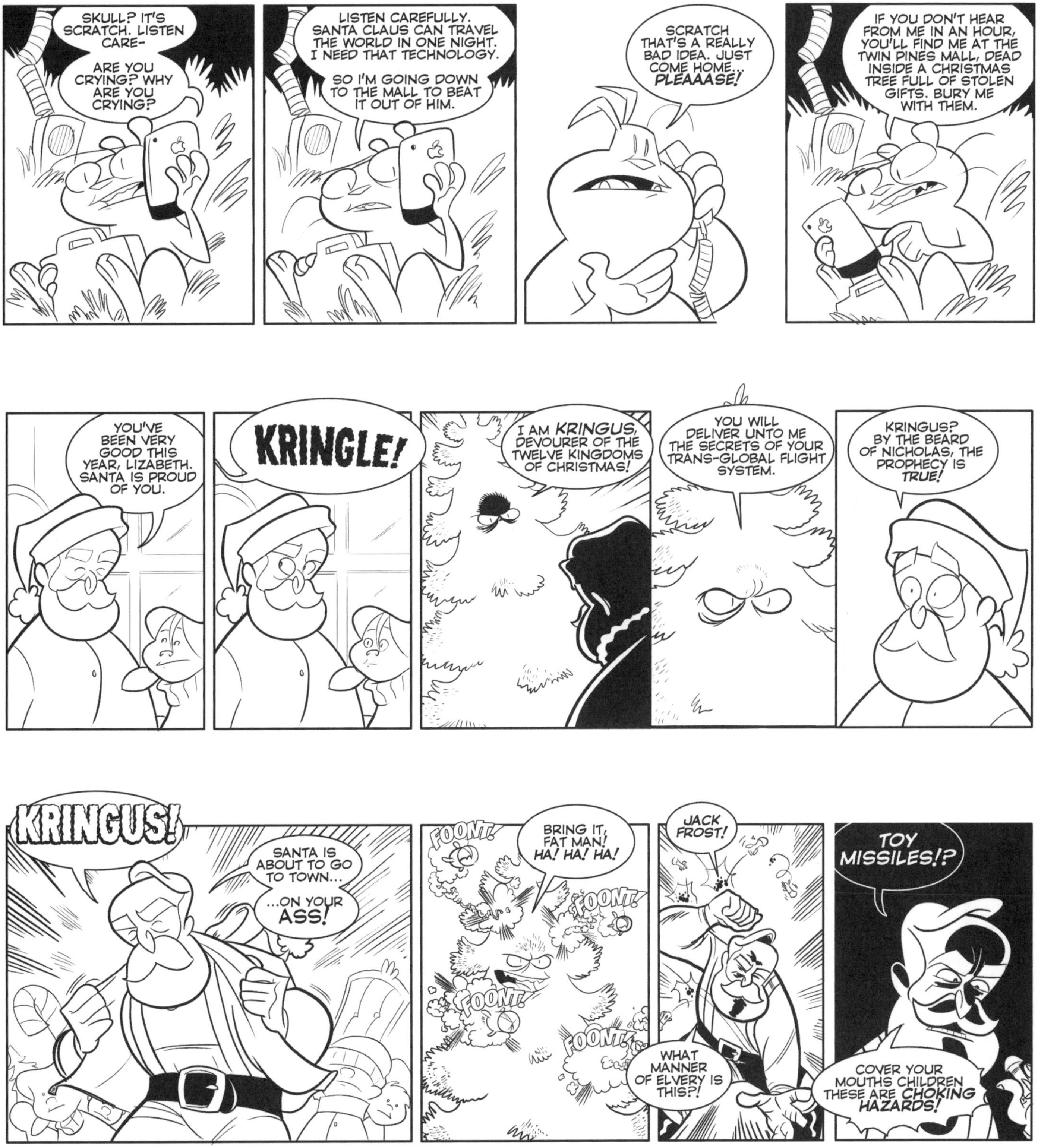
SKULL? IT'S SCRATCH. LISTEN CARE-
ARE YOU CRYING? WHY ARE YOU CRYING?
LISTEN CAREFULLY. SANTA CLAUS CAN TRAVEL THE WORLD IN ONE NIGHT. I NEED THAT TECHNOLOGY.
SO I'M GOING DOWN TO THE MALL TO BEAT IT OUT OF HIM.
SCRATCH THAT'S A REALLY BAD IDEA. JUST COME HOME... PLEAAASE!
IF YOU DON'T HEAR FROM ME IN AN HOUR, YOU'LL FIND ME AT THE TWIN PINES MALL, DEAD INSIDE A CHRISTMAS TREE FULL OF STOLEN GIFTS. BURY ME WITH THEM.
YOU'VE BEEN VERY GOOD THIS YEAR, LIZABETH. SANTA IS PROUD OF YOU.
KRINGLE!
I AM KRINGUS, DEVOURER OF THE TWELVE KINGDOMS OF CHRISTMAS!
YOU WILL DELIVER UNTO ME THE SECRETS OF YOUR TRANS-GLOBAL FLIGHT SYSTEM.
KRINGUS? BY THE BEARD OF NICHOLAS, THE PROPHECY IS TRUE!
KRINGUS!
SANTA IS ABOUT TO GO TO TOWN...
...ON YOUR ASS!
FOONT!
BRING IT, FAT MAN! HA! HA! HA!
FOONT!
FOONT!
FOONT!
JACK FROST!
WHAT MANNER OF ELVERY IS THIS?!
TOY MISSILES!?
COVER YOUR MOUTHS CHILDREN THESE ARE CHOKING HAZARDS!

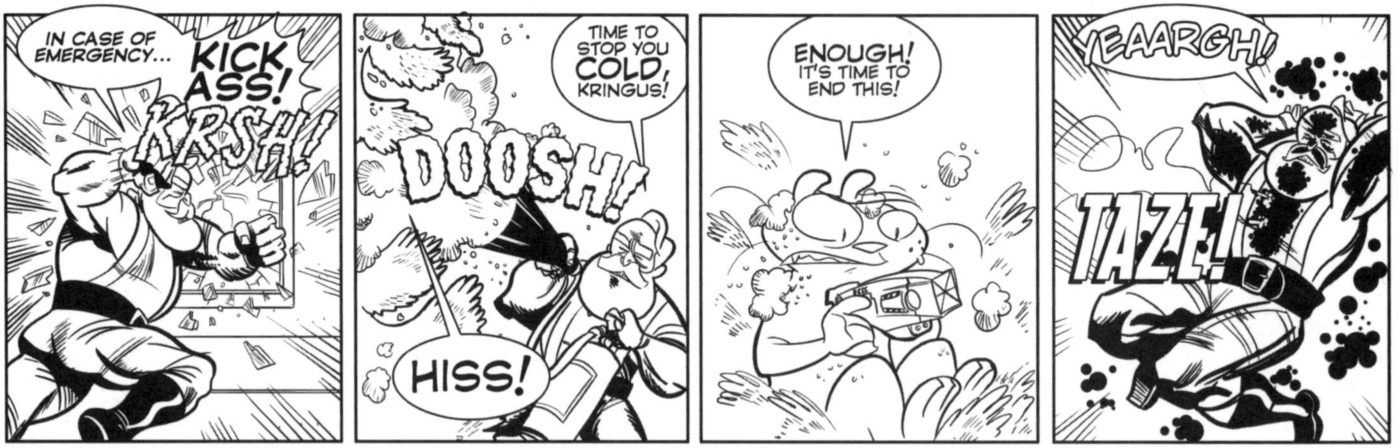
IN CASE OF EMERGENCY...
KICK ASS!
KRSH!
TIME TO STOP YOU COLD, KRINGUS!
DOOSH!
HISS!
ENOUGH! IT'S TIME TO END THIS!
YEAARGH!
TAZE!

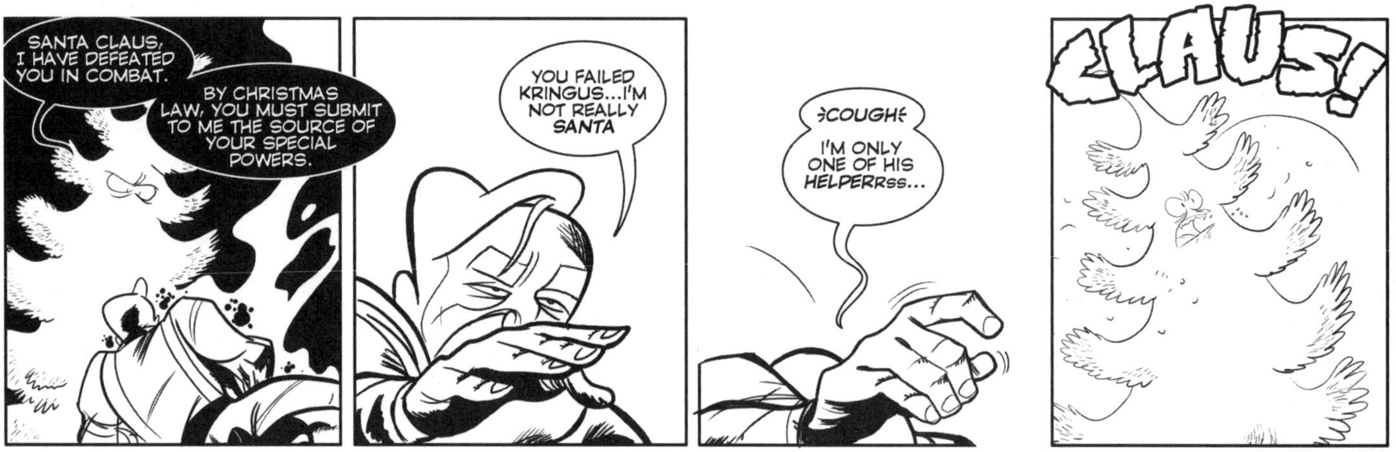
SANTA CLAUS, I HAVE DEFEATED YOU IN COMBAT.
BY CHRISTMAS LAW, YOU MUST SUBMIT TO ME THE SOURCE OF YOUR SPECIAL POWERS.
YOU FAILED KRINGUS...I'M NOT REALLY SANTA
COUGH
I'M ONLY ONE OF HIS HELPERRss...
CLAUS!

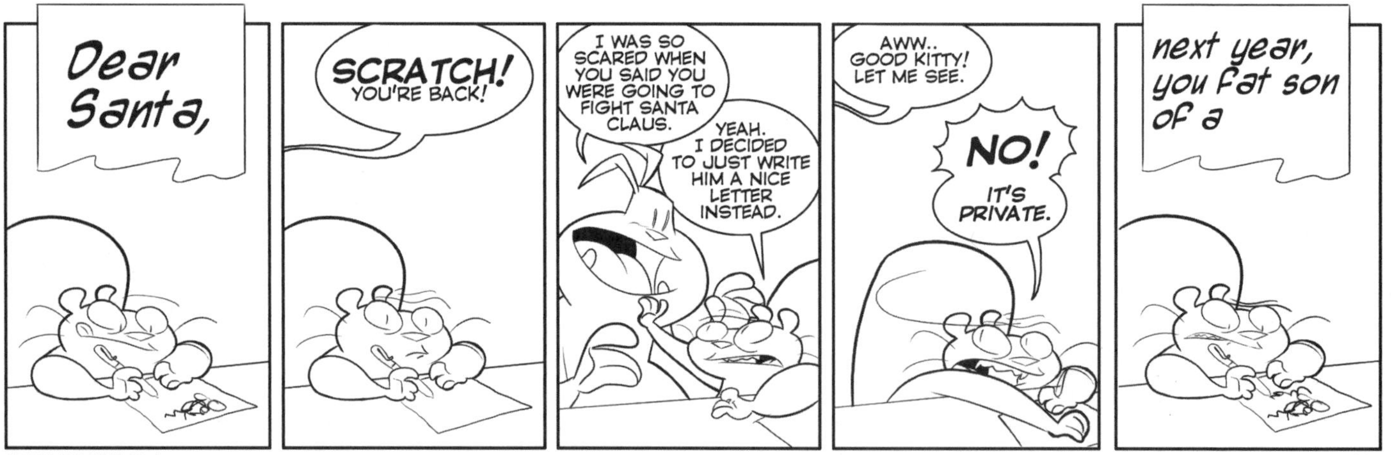
Dear Santa,
SCRATCH! YOU'RE BACK!
I WAS SO SCARED WHEN YOU SAID YOU WERE GOING TO FIGHT SANTA CLAUS.
YEAH. I DECIDED TO JUST WRITE HIM A NICE LETTER INSTEAD.
AWW.. GOOD KITTY! LET ME SEE.
NO! IT'S PRIVATE.
next year, you fat son of a

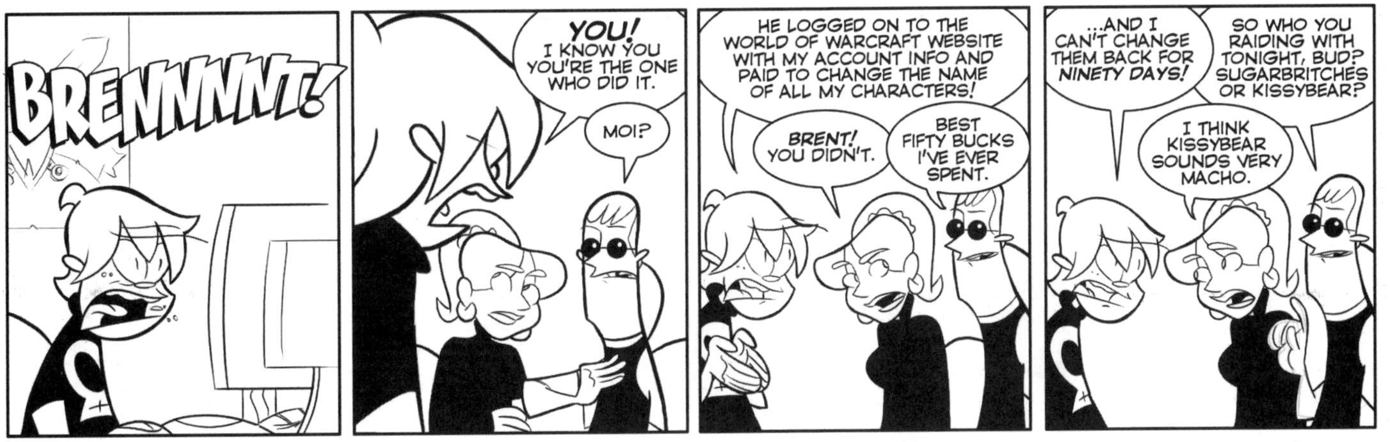
BRENNNNNT!
YOU! I KNOW YOU YOU'RE THE ONE WHO DID IT.
MOI?
HE LOGGED ON TO THE WORLD OF WARCRAFT WEBSITE WITH MY ACCOUNT INFO AND PAID TO CHANGE THE NAME OF ALL MY CHARACTERS!
BRENT! YOU DIDN'T.
BEST FIFTY BUCKS I'VE EVER SPENT.
...AND I CAN'T CHANGE THEM BACK FOR NINETY DAYS!
SO WHO YOU RAIDING WITH TONIGHT, BUD? SUGARBRITCHES OR KISSYBEAR?
I THINK KISSYBEAR SOUNDS VERY MACHO.

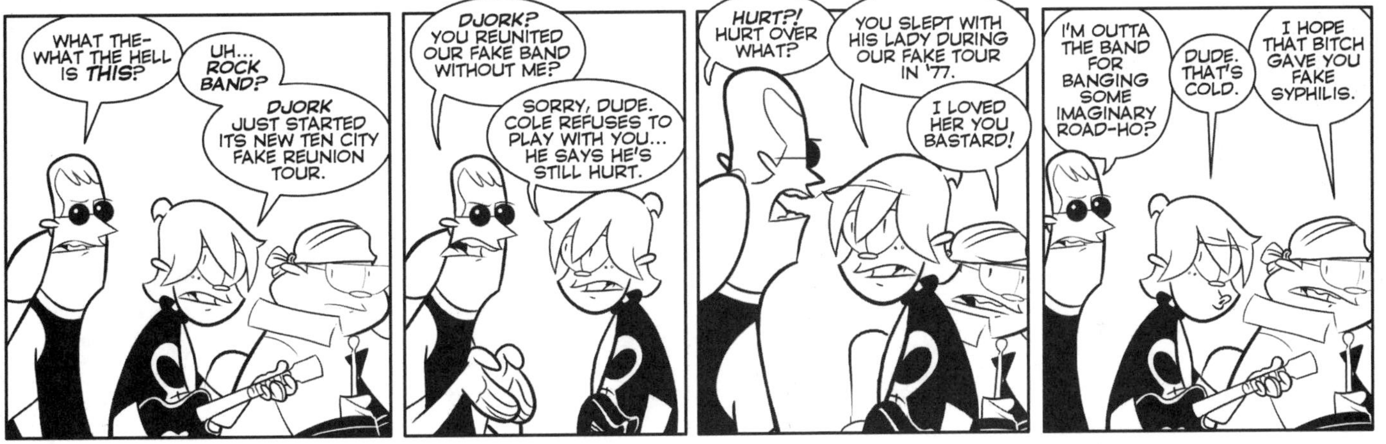
WHAT THE- WHAT THE HELL IS THIS?
UH... ROCK BAND?
DJORK JUST STARTED ITS NEW TEN CITY FAKE REUNION TOUR.
DJORK? YOU REUNITED OUR FAKE BAND WITHOUT ME?
SORRY, DUDE. COLE REFUSES TO PLAY WITH YOU... HE SAYS HE'S STILL HURT.
HURT?! HURT OVER WHAT?
YOU SLEPT WITH HIS LADY DURING OUR FAKE TOUR IN '77.
I LOVED HER YOU BASTARD!
I'M OUTTA THE BAND FOR BANGING SOME IMAGINARY ROAD-HO?
DUDE. THAT'S COLD.
I HOPE THAT BITCH GAVE YOU FAKE SYPHILIS.

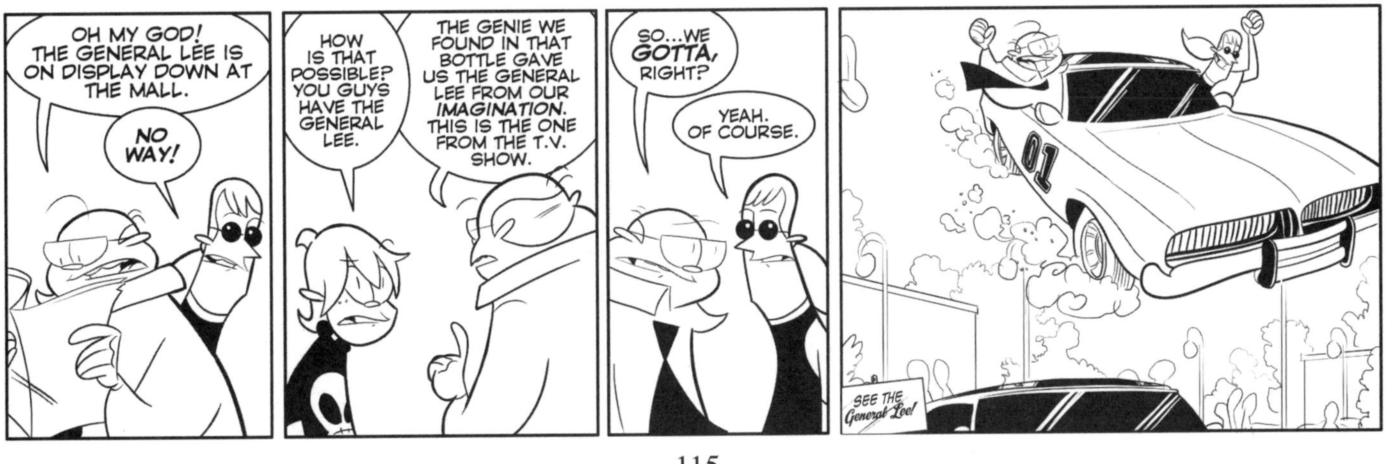
OH MY GOD! THE GENERAL LEE IS ON DISPLAY DOWN AT THE MALL.
NO WAY!
HOW IS THAT POSSIBLE? YOU GUYS HAVE THE GENERAL LEE.
THE GENIE WE FOUND IN THAT BOTTLE GAVE US THE GENERAL LEE FROM OUR IMAGINATION. THIS IS THE ONE FROM THE T.V. SHOW.
SO...WE GOTTA, RIGHT?
YEAH. OF COURSE.
01
SEE THE General Lee!

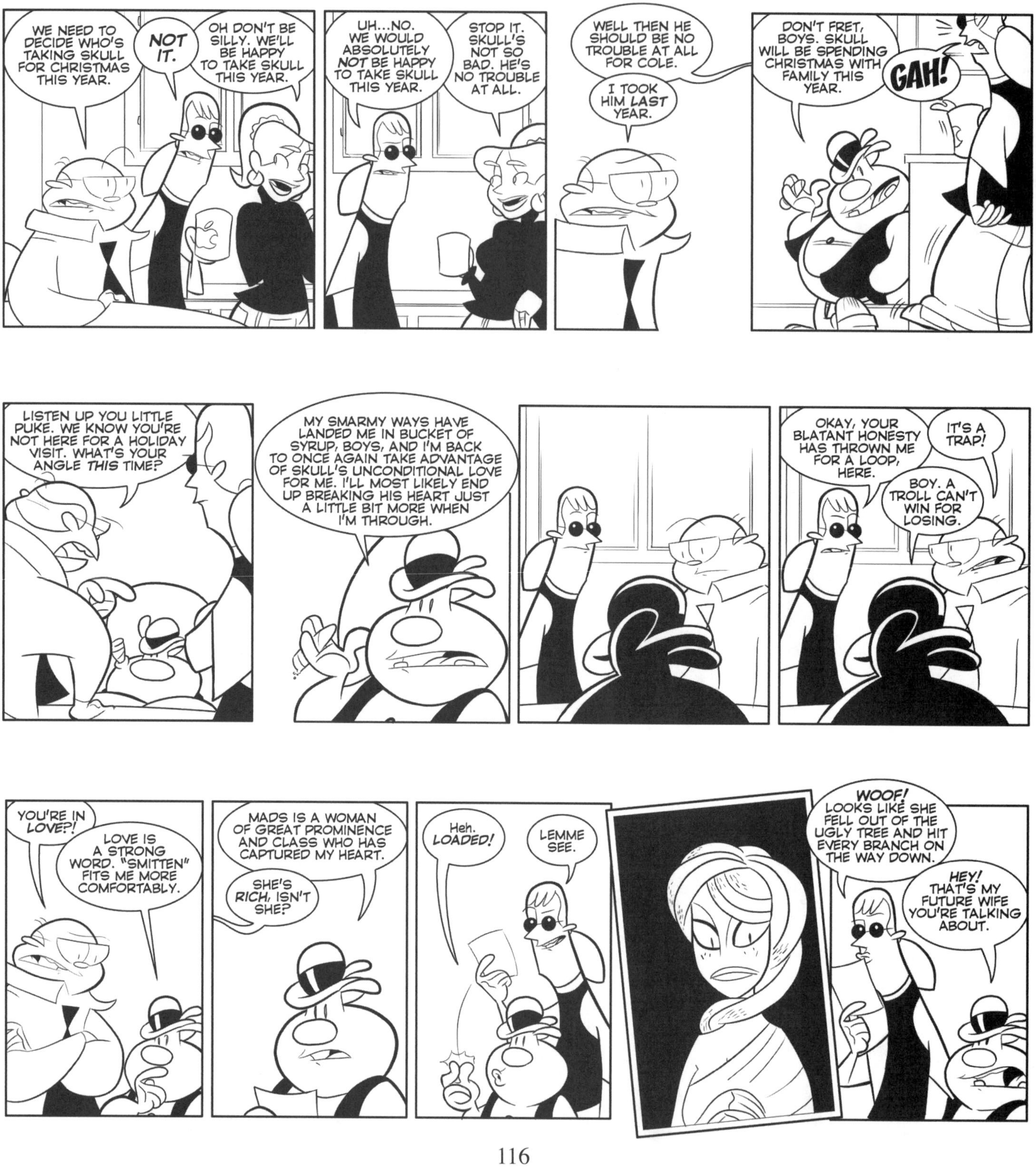
WE NEED TO DECIDE WHO'S TAKING SKULL FOR CHRISTMAS THIS YEAR.
NOT IT.
OH DON'T BE SILLY. WE'LL BE HAPPY TO TAKE SKULL THIS YEAR.
UH...NO. WE WOULD ABSOLUTELY NOT BE HAPPY TO TAKE SKULL THIS YEAR.
STOP IT. SKULL'S NOT SO BAD. HE'S NO TROUBLE AT ALL.
WELL THEN HE SHOULD BE NO TROUBLE AT ALL FOR COLE.
I TOOK HIM LAST YEAR.
DON'T FRET, BOYS. SKULL WILL BE SPENDING CHRISTMAS WITH FAMILY THIS YEAR.
GAH!
LISTEN UP YOU LITTLE PUKE. WE KNOW YOU'RE NOT HERE FOR A HOLIDAY VISIT. WHAT'S YOUR ANGLE THIS TIME?
MY SMARMY WAYS HAVE LANDED ME IN BUCKET OF SYRUP, BOYS, AND I'M BACK TO ONCE AGAIN TAKE ADVANTAGE OF SKULL'S UNCONDITIONAL LOVE FOR ME. I'LL MOST LIKELY END UP BREAKING HIS HEART JUST A LITTLE BIT MORE WHEN I'M THROUGH.
OKAY, YOUR BLATANT HONESTY HAS THROWN ME FOR A LOOP, HERE.
IT'S A TRAP!
BOY. A TROLL CAN'T WIN FOR LOSING.
YOU'RE IN LOVE?!
LOVE IS A STRONG WORD. "SMITTEN" FITS ME MORE COMFORTABLY.
MADS IS A WOMAN OF GREAT PROMINENCE AND CLASS WHO HAS CAPTURED MY HEART.
SHE'S RICH, ISN'T SHE?
Heh. LOADED!
LEMME SEE.
WOOF! LOOKS LIKE SHE FELL OUT OF THE UGLY TREE AND HIT EVERY BRANCH ON THE WAY DOWN.
HEY! THAT'S MY FUTURE WIFE YOU'RE TALKING ABOUT.

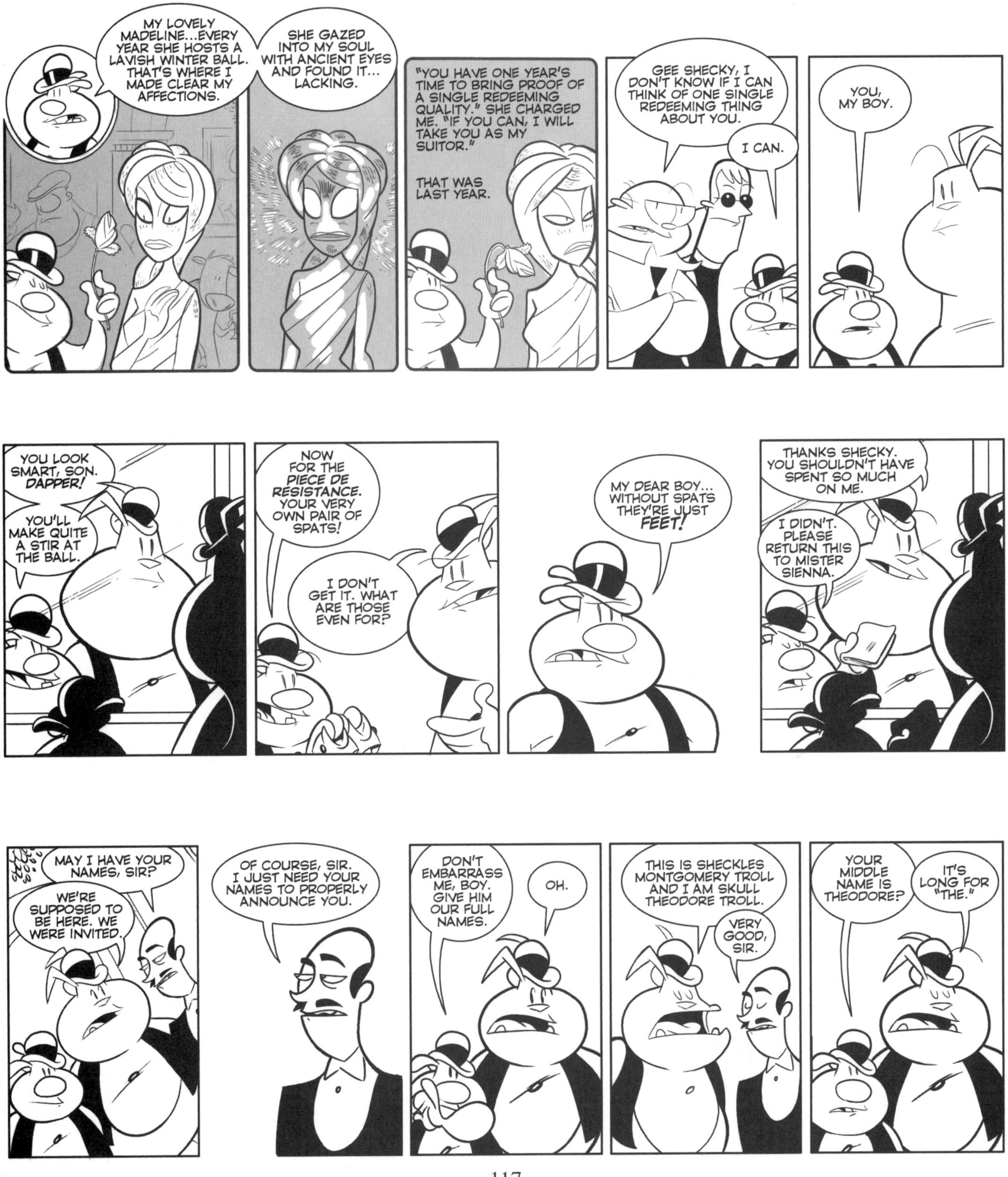
MY LOVELY MADELINE...EVERY YEAR SHE HOSTS A LAVISH WINTER BALL. THAT'S WHERE I MADE CLEAR MY AFFECTIONS.
SHE GAZED INTO MY SOUL WITH ANCIENT EYES AND FOUND IT... LACKING.
"YOU HAVE ONE YEAR'S TIME TO BRING PROOF OF A SINGLE REDEEMING QUALITY." SHE CHARGED ME. "IF YOU CAN, I WILL TAKE YOU AS MY SUITOR."
THAT WAS LAST YEAR.
GEE SHECKY, I DON'T KNOW IF I CAN THINK OF ONE SINGLE REDEEMING THING ABOUT YOU.
I CAN.
YOU, MY BOY.
YOU LOOK SMART, SON. *DAPPER!*
YOU'LL MAKE QUITE A STIR AT THE BALL.
NOW FOR THE *PIECE DE RESISTANCE*. YOUR VERY OWN PAIR OF SPATS!
I DON'T GET IT. WHAT ARE THOSE EVEN FOR?
MY DEAR BOY... WITHOUT SPATS THEY'RE JUST *FEET!*
THANKS SHECKY. YOU SHOULDN'T HAVE SPENT SO MUCH ON ME.
I DIDN'T. PLEASE RETURN THIS TO MISTER SIENNA.
MAY I HAVE YOUR NAMES, SIR?
WE'RE SUPPOSED TO BE HERE. WE WERE INVITED.
OF COURSE, SIR. I JUST NEED YOUR NAMES TO PROPERLY ANNOUNCE YOU.
DON'T EMBARRASS ME, BOY. GIVE HIM OUR FULL NAMES.
OH.
THIS IS SHECKLES MONTGOMERY TROLL AND I AM SKULL THEODORE TROLL.
VERY GOOD, SIR.
YOUR MIDDLE NAME IS THEODORE?
IT'S LONG FOR "THE."

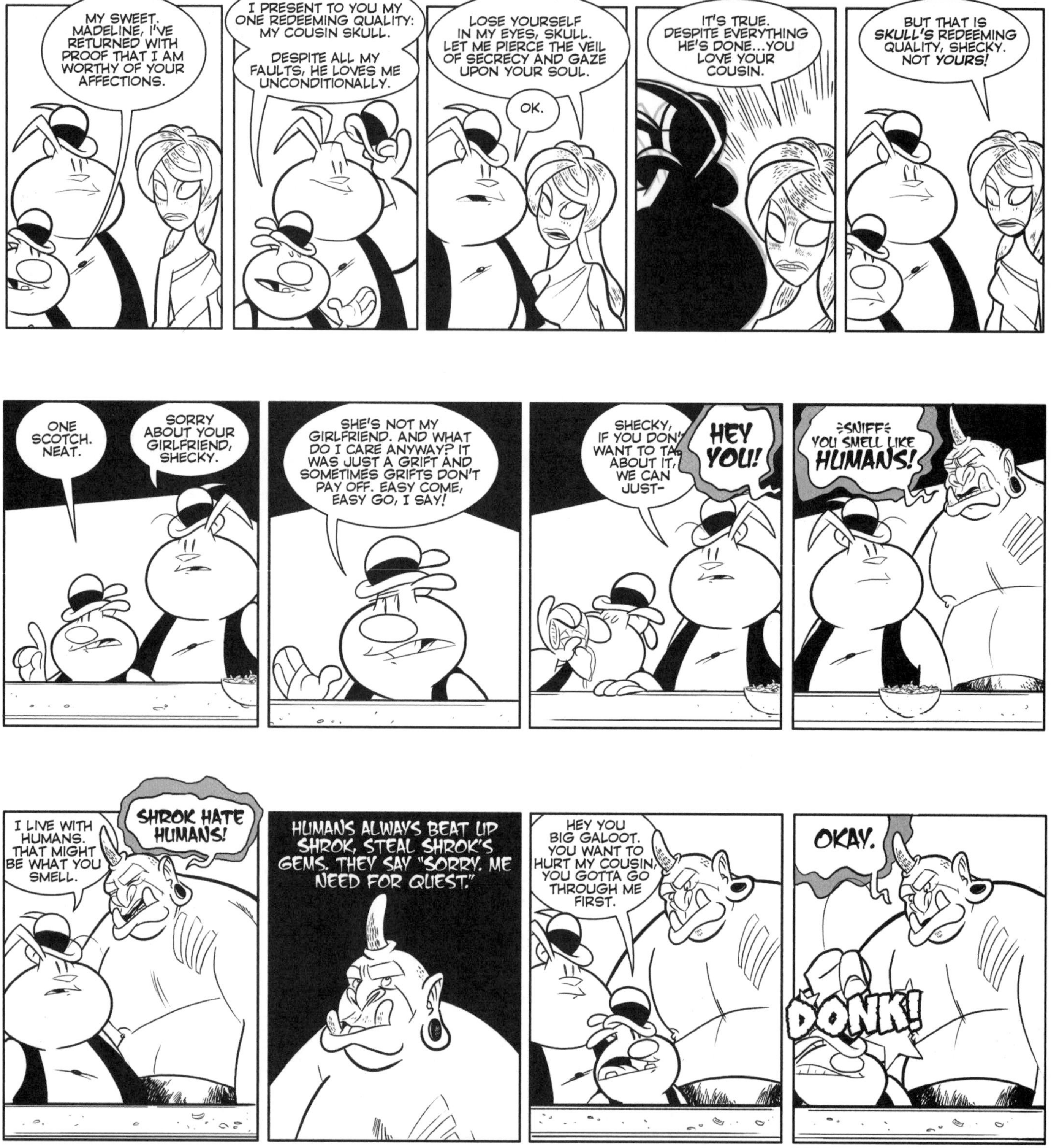
MY SWEET. MADELINE, I'VE RETURNED WITH PROOF THAT I AM WORTHY OF YOUR AFFECTIONS.
I PRESENT TO YOU MY ONE REDEEMING QUALITY: MY COUSIN SKULL.
DESPITE ALL MY FAULTS, HE LOVES ME UNCONDITIONALLY.
LOSE YOURSELF IN MY EYES, SKULL. LET ME PIERCE THE VEIL OF SECRECY AND GAZE UPON YOUR SOUL.
OK.
IT'S TRUE. DESPITE EVERYTHING HE'S DONE...YOU LOVE YOUR COUSIN.
BUT THAT IS SKULL'S REDEEMING QUALITY, SHECKY. NOT YOURS!
ONE SCOTCH. NEAT.
SORRY ABOUT YOUR GIRLFRIEND, SHECKY.
SHE'S NOT MY GIRLFRIEND. AND WHAT DO I CARE ANYWAY? IT WAS JUST A GRIFT AND SOMETIMES GRIFTS DON'T PAY OFF. EASY COME, EASY GO, I SAY!
SHECKY, IF YOU DON' WANT TO TA ABOUT IT, WE CAN JUST-
HEY YOU!
SNIFF YOU SMELL LIKE HUMANS!
I LIVE WITH HUMANS. THAT MIGHT BE WHAT YOU SMELL.
SHROK HATE HUMANS!
HUMANS ALWAYS BEAT UP SHROK, STEAL SHROK'S GEMS. THEY SAY "SORRY. ME NEED FOR QUEST."
HEY YOU BIG GALOOT. YOU WANT TO HURT MY COUSIN, YOU GOTTA GO THROUGH ME FIRST.
OKAY.
DONK!

SHROK!

HRR?

YOU WILL ACT CIVILIZED IN MY HOUSE!

NO NEED FOR YOU TO GET INVOLVED, MY DEAR. I HAD EVERYTHING UNDER CONTROL

MONTGOMERY, ARE YOU RESPONSIBLE FOR THIS? DID YOU ORCHESTRATE IT FOR MY BENEFIT?

MADELINE, I ASSURE YOU THAT I HAD NOTHING—

ASSURANCE IS NOT NECESSARY. LOOK INTO MY EYES.

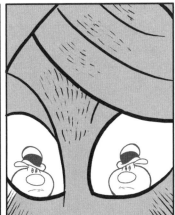

OH! FORGIVE ME, MONTGOMERY. IT WAS RUDE OF ME TO ACCUSE YOU AN ANY IMPROPRIETIES.

IT'S TIME TO CELEBRATE! BARTENDER...ONE ROUND FOR EVERYONE ON ME!

UH...IT'S AN OPEN BAR, SIR.

WHAT HAPPENED?

MADELINE LOOKED INTO MY SOUL AND SAW MY TRUE AFFECTIONS FOR HER.

WE'RE OFFICIALLY AN ITEM.

GET READY TO RING IN THE NEW YEAR THE RIGHT WAY, SON!

BUT FIRST, 'OL SHECKY HAS TO SEE A MAN ABOUT A CENTAUR.

MASTERFULLY PLAYED, MY BOY. BRAVO!

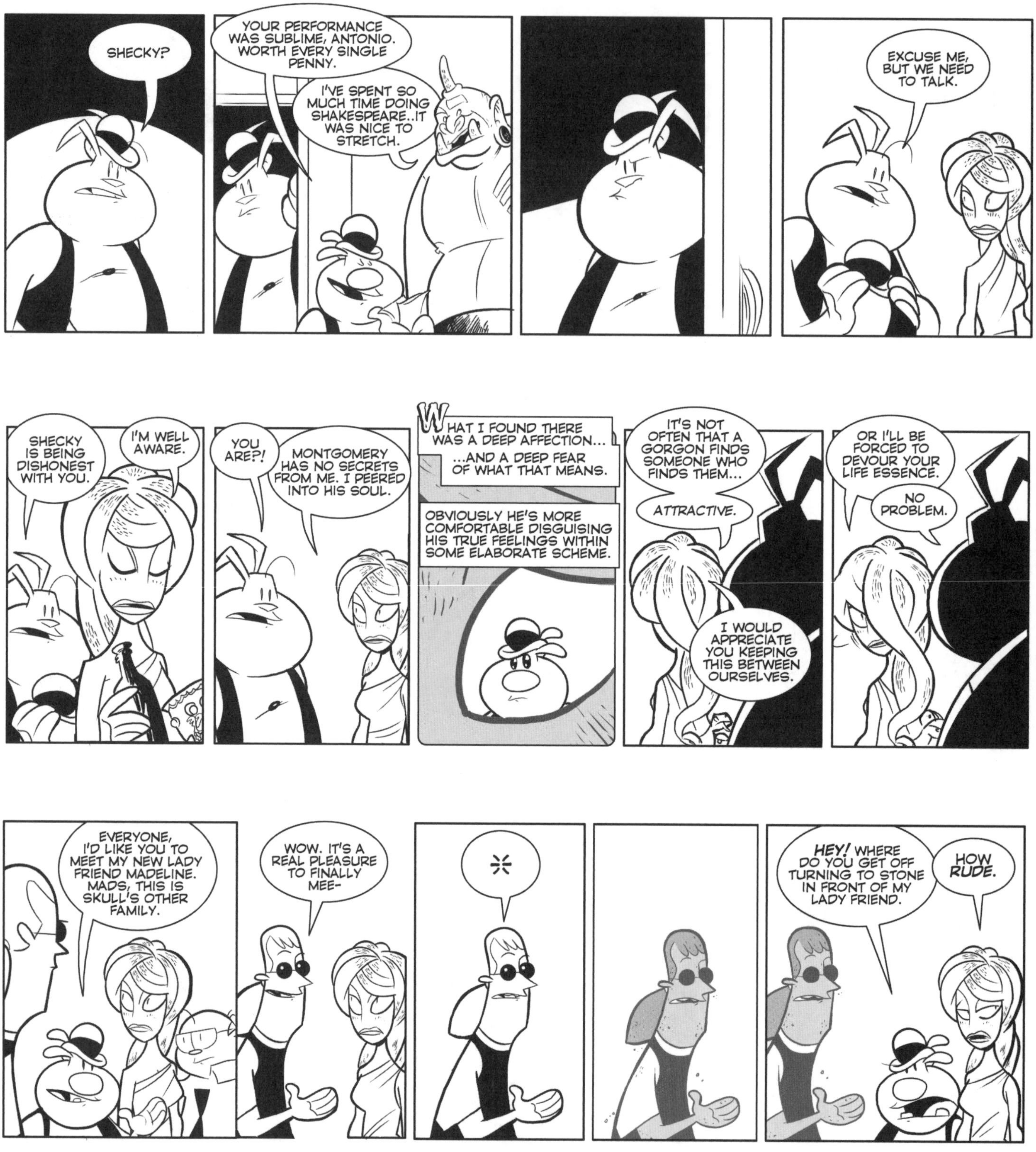
SHECKY?
YOUR PERFORMANCE WAS SUBLIME, ANTONIO. WORTH EVERY SINGLE PENNY.
I'VE SPENT SO MUCH TIME DOING SHAKESPEARE..IT WAS NICE TO STRETCH.
EXCUSE ME, BUT WE NEED TO TALK.
SHECKY IS BEING DISHONEST WITH YOU.
I'M WELL AWARE.
YOU ARE?!
MONTGOMERY HAS NO SECRETS FROM ME. I PEERED INTO HIS SOUL.
WHAT I FOUND THERE WAS A DEEP AFFECTION...
...AND A DEEP FEAR OF WHAT THAT MEANS.
OBVIOUSLY HE'S MORE COMFORTABLE DISGUISING HIS TRUE FEELINGS WITHIN SOME ELABORATE SCHEME.
IT'S NOT OFTEN THAT A GORGON FINDS SOMEONE WHO FINDS THEM...
ATTRACTIVE.
I WOULD APPRECIATE YOU KEEPING THIS BETWEEN OURSELVES.
OR I'LL BE FORCED TO DEVOUR YOUR LIFE ESSENCE.
NO PROBLEM.
EVERYONE, I'D LIKE YOU TO MEET MY NEW LADY FRIEND MADELINE. MADS, THIS IS SKULL'S OTHER FAMILY.
WOW. IT'S A REAL PLEASURE TO FINALLY MEE-
HEY! WHERE DO YOU GET OFF TURNING TO STONE IN FRONT OF MY LADY FRIEND.
HOW RUDE.

Outtakes

It takes a village to make a daily comic strip. Our writers, producers, cast and crew work tirelessly to bring the funny five days a week.. But we don't always get it right on the first take. Here are our favorite bloopers from the year 2007.

Roll it, Ed!

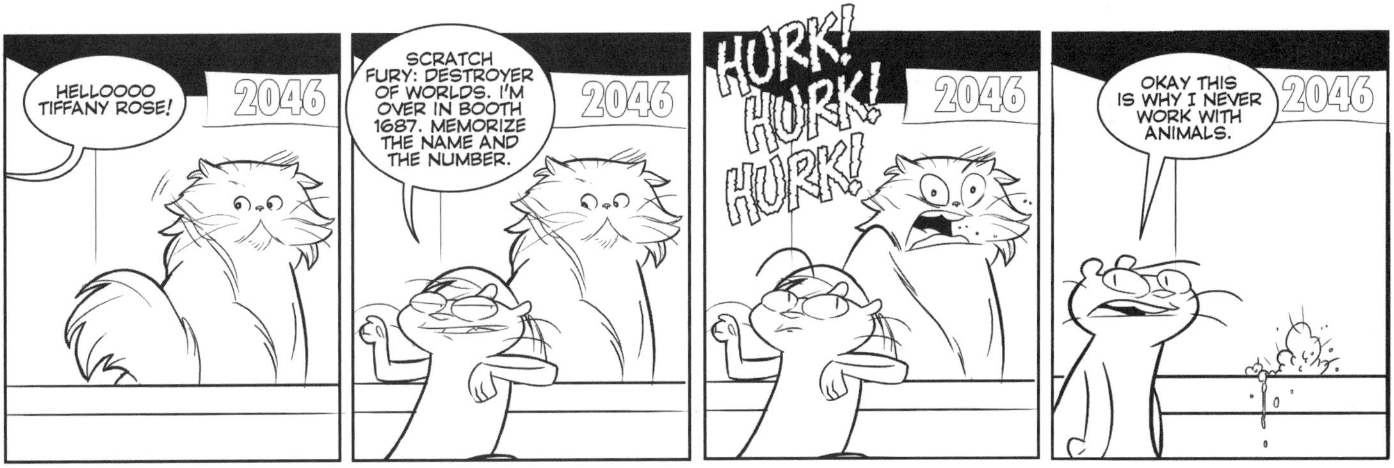
HELLOOOO TIFFANY ROSE!
2046
SCRATCH FURY: DESTROYER OF WORLDS. I'M OVER IN BOOTH 1687. MEMORIZE THE NAME AND THE NUMBER.
2046
HURK! HURK! HURK!
2046
OKAY THIS IS WHY I NEVER WORK WITH ANIMALS.
2046

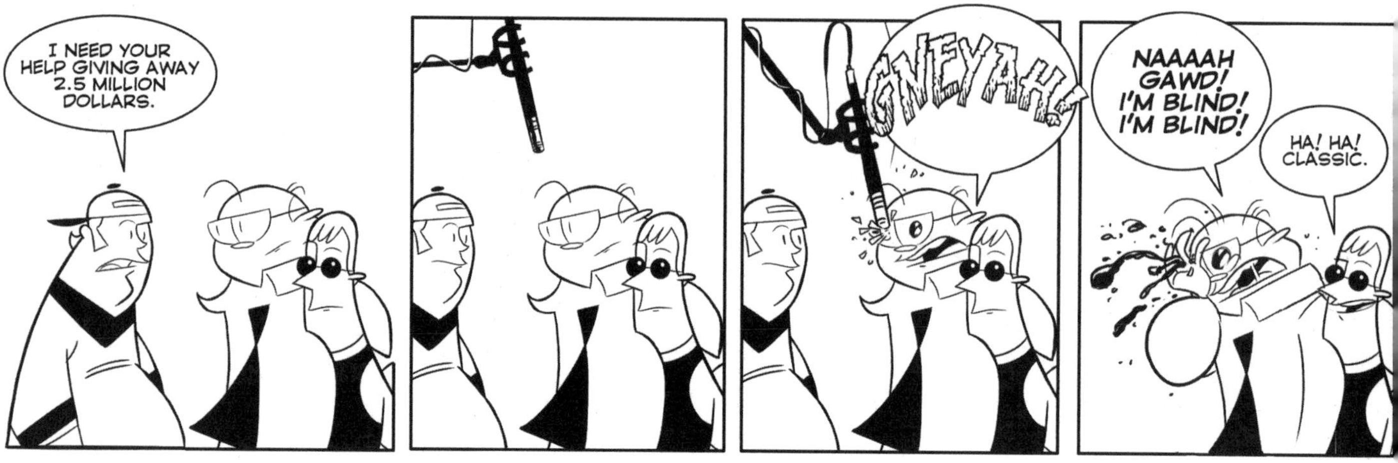
I NEED YOUR HELP GIVING AWAY 2.5 MILLION DOLLARS.
GNEYAH!
NAAAAH GAWD! I'M BLIND! I'M BLIND!
HA! HA! CLASSIC.

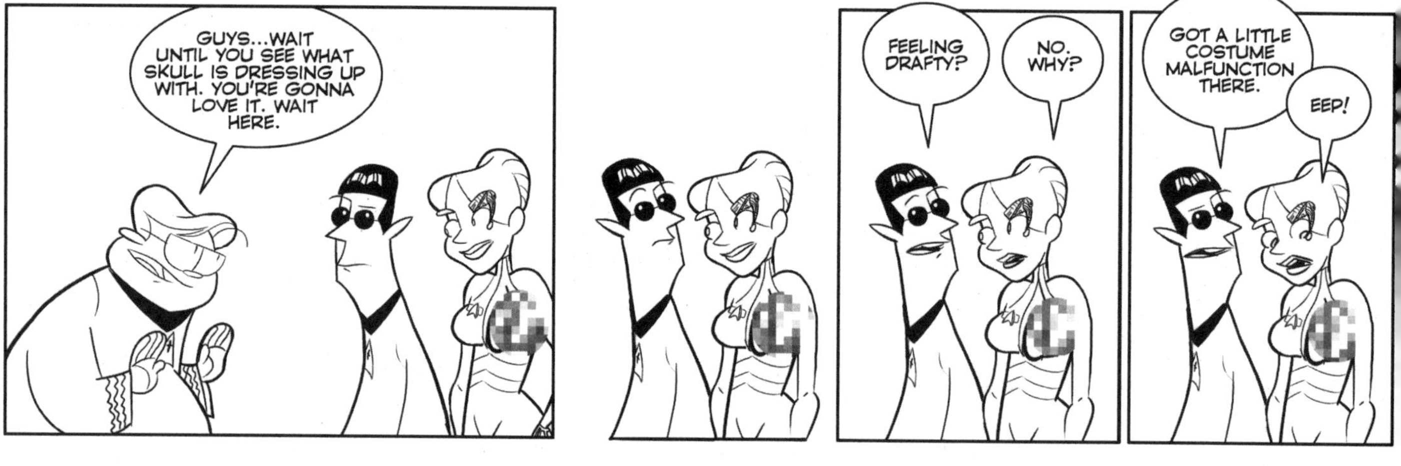
GUYS...WAIT UNTIL YOU SEE WHAT SKULL IS DRESSING UP WITH. YOU'RE GONNA LOVE IT. WAIT HERE.
FEELING DRAFTY?
NO. WHY?
GOT A LITTLE COSTUME MALFUNCTION THERE.
EEP!

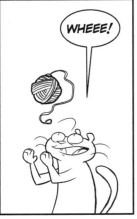

WHEEE!
WHEEE!
UH....
PROPS!

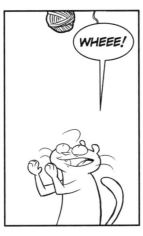

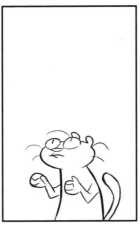

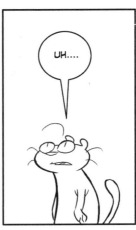

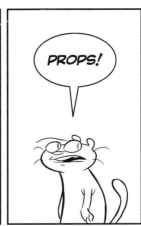

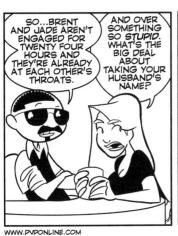

SO...BRENT AND JADE AREN'T ENGAGED FOR TWENTY FOUR HOURS AND THEY'RE ALREADY AT EACH OTHER'S THROATS.
AND OVER SOMETHING SO STUPID. WHAT'S THE BIG DEAL ABOUT TAKING YOUR HUSBAND'S NAME?
LINE!
OH MY GOD.
HEY. IT'S HARD TO MEMORIZE LINES WHEN YOU'RE A BLIND GUY.
YOU'RE FOR REAL BLIND? I THOUGHT THAT WAS JUST YOUR CHARACTER.
WWW.PVPONLINE.COM
©2007 SCOTT R. KURTZ

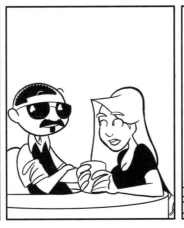

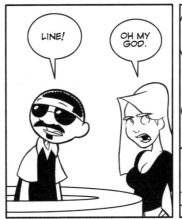

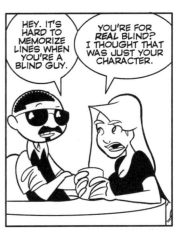

about the author

Scott Kurtz has been self publishing his
comics to the world wide web since 1998.
His work has been nominated for the Harvey Award
and in 2006 won the prestigious Eisner Award
for best digital comic.

He co-founded the new webcomics.com with his
peers to help promote and develop the independent
work of online cartoonists.

Mr. Kurtz lives in Dallas, TX with his
wife Angela, their basset hounds Bella & Butler
and their cat...the REAL Scratch Fury

PvP is read globally by over 200,000 daily readers.

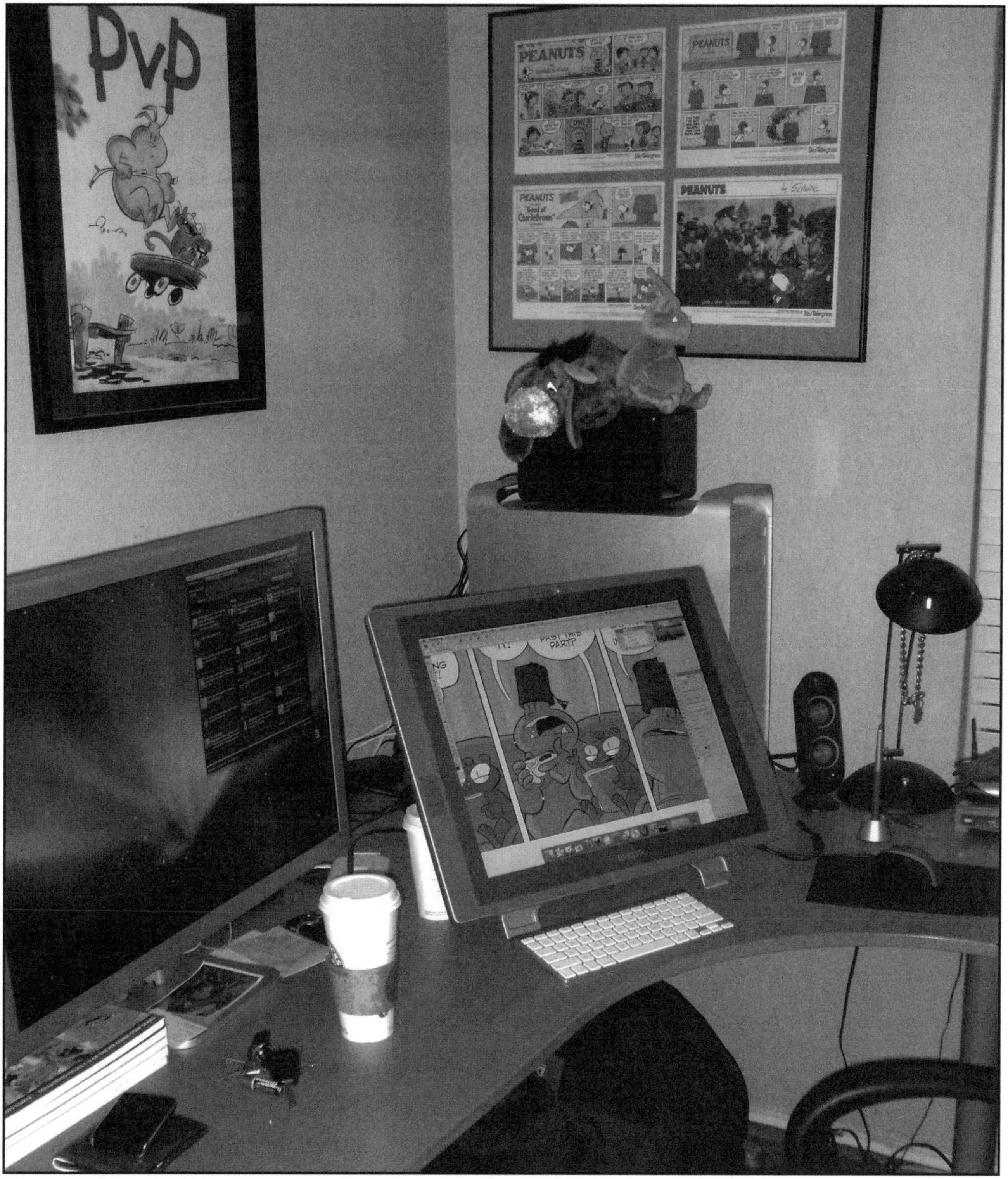
PvP
PEANUTS
PAST THIS PART?

other stuff by scott

PvP AWESOMOLOGY HARDCOVER
ISBN# 978-1-58240-818-7

PvP STRIPTEASE

HOW TO MAKE WEBCOMICS
ISBN# 978-1-58240-870-5

TRUTH, JUSTIN AND THE AMERICAN WAY TP
ISBN# 978-1-58240-705-0

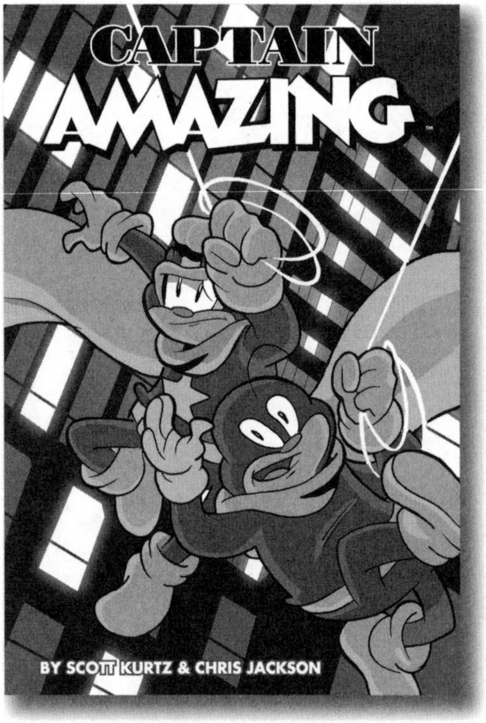
CAPTAIN
AMAZING
BY SCOTT KURTZ & CHRIS JACKSON

CAPTAIN AMAZING
ISBN# 978-1-58240-653-4

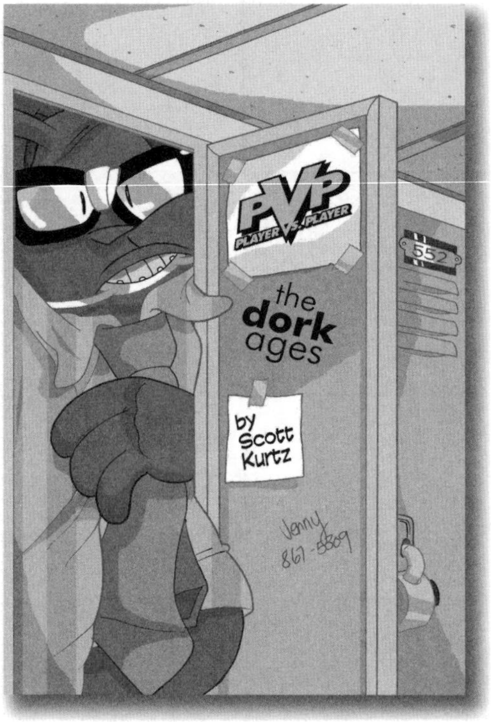
PVP
PLAYER VS PLAYER
552
the
dork
ages
by
Scott
Kurtz

PvP: THE DORK AGES
ISBN# 978-1-58240-345-8

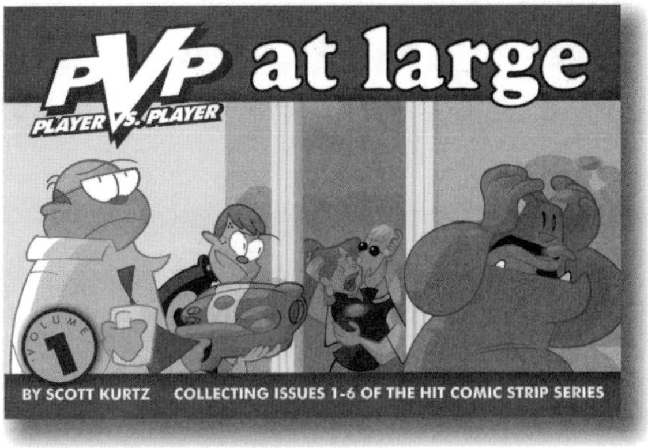
PVP at large
PLAYER VS. PLAYER
VOLUME 1
BY SCOTT KURTZ COLLECTING ISSUES 1-6 OF THE HIT COMIC STRIP SERIES

PvP, VOLUME 1:
PvP AT LARGE
ISBN# 978-1-58240-374-8

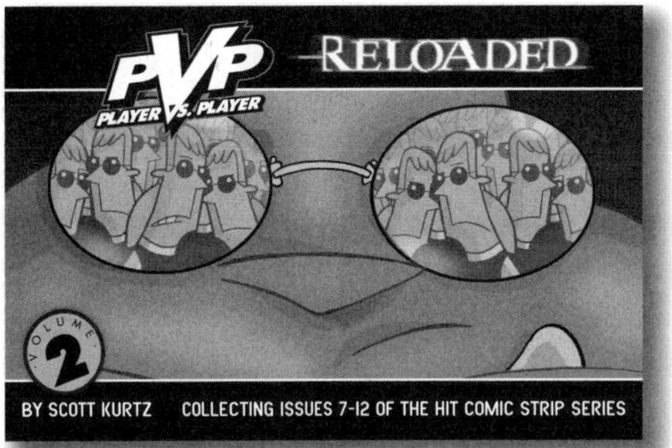
PVP RELOADED
PLAYER VS. PLAYER
VOLUME 2
BY SCOTT KURTZ COLLECTING ISSUES 7-12 OF THE HIT COMIC STRIP SERIES

PvP, VOLUME 2:
PvP RELOADED
ISBN# 978-1-58240-777-7

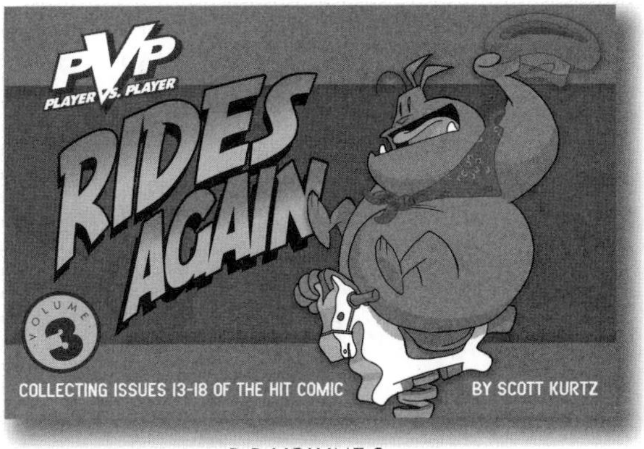
PVP
PLAYER VS. PLAYER
RIDES AGAIN
VOLUME 3
COLLECTING ISSUES 13-18 OF THE HIT COMIC
BY SCOTT KURTZ

PvP, VOLUME 3:
PvP RIDES AGAIN
ISBN# 978-1-58240-553-7

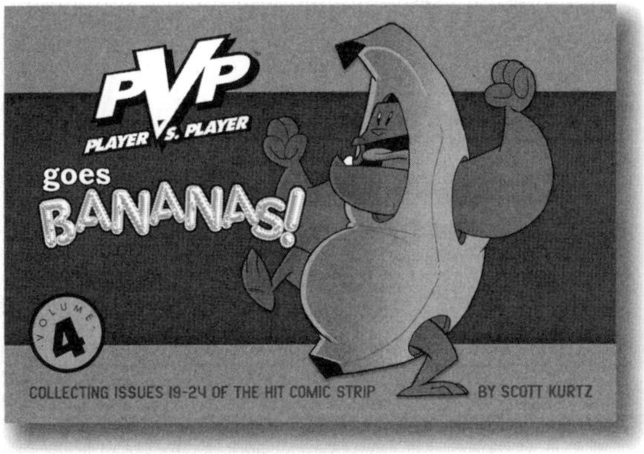
PVP
PLAYER VS. PLAYER
goes BANANAS!
VOLUME 4
COLLECTING ISSUES 19-24 OF THE HIT COMIC STRIP
BY SCOTT KURTZ

PvP, VOLUME 4:
PvP GOES BANANAS!
ISBN# 978-1-58240-722-7

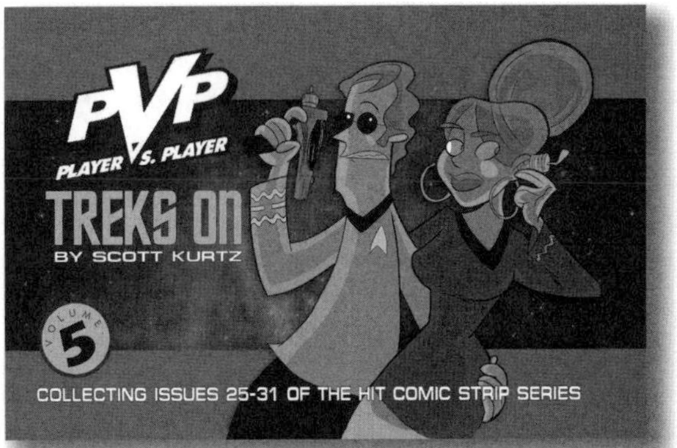
PVP
PLAYER VS. PLAYER
TREKS ON
BY SCOTT KURTZ
VOLUME 5
COLLECTING ISSUES 25-31 OF THE HIT COMIC STRIP SERIES

PvP, VOLUME 5:
PvP TREKS ON
ISBN# 978-1-58240-932-0

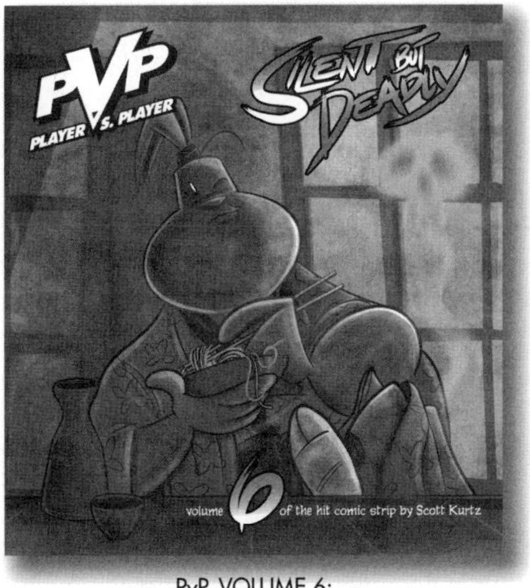
PVP
PLAYER VS. PLAYER
SILENT BUT DEADLY
volume 6 of the hit comic strip by Scott Kurtz

PvP, VOLUME 6:
SILENT BUT DEADLY
ISBN# 978-1-60706-135-9

MORE GREAT BOOKS FROM IMAGE COMICS

For a comic shop near you carrying graphic novels from Image Comics, please call toll free: 1-888-COMIC-BOOK

THE LAVA IS A FLOOR:
THE MAGIC OF A MONSTER'S
IMAGINATION HC
ISBN: 978-1-60706-123-6
$12.99 USD

EVIL & MALICE SAVE THE
WORLD! TP
ISBN: 978-1-60706-091-8
$14.99 USD

T-RUNT HC
ISBN: 978-4-60706-074-1
$16.99 USD

TIMOTHY & THE
TRANSGALACTIC TOWEL HC
ISBN: 978-1-60706-021-5
$16.99 USD

TIFFANY'S EPIPHANY HC
ISBN: 978-1-60706-110-6
$12.99 USD

BRUCE: THE LITTLE BLUE
SPRUCE HC
ISBN: 978-1-60706-008-6
$9.99 USD

DEAR DRACULA HC
ISBN: 978-1-58240-970-2
$7.99 USD

MISSING THE BOAT GN
ISBN: 978-1-60706-015-4
$18.99 USD

THE SURREAL ADVENTURES
OF EDGAR ALLAN POO
BOOK 1
ISBN: 978-1-58240-816-3
$9.99 USD

THE SURREAL ADVENTURES
OF EDGAR ALLAN POO
BOOK 2
ISBN: 978-1-58240-975-7
$12.99 USD

PX! BOOK 1: A GIRL AND HER
PANDA TP
ISBN: 978-1-58240-820-0
$16.99 USD

PX! BOOK 2: IN THE SERVICE
OF THE QUEEN TP
ISBN: 978-1-60706-018-5
$14.99 USD

FIREBREATHER VOL. 1:
GROWING PAINS TP
ISBN: 978-1-58240-380-9
$13.95 USD

FIREBREATHER, VOL. 2:
ALL THE BEST HEROES ARE
ORPHANS GN
ISBN: 978-1-58240-971-9
$16.99 USD

FIREBREATHER, VOL. 3:
HOLMGANG TP
ISBN: 978-1-60706-010-9
$12.99 USD

THE IRON SAINT ONE-SHOT
ISBN: 978-1-58240-446-2
$6.95 USD

CEMETERY BLUES, VOL. 1:
UNEARTHED
ISBN: 978-4-58240-982-5
$16.99 USD

G-MAN VOL. 1
LEARNING TO FLY TP
ISBN: 978-1-60706-087-1
$9.99 USD

LIBERTY MEADOWS
COVER GIRL HC
ISBN: 978-1-58241-640-4
$24.99

LIBERTY MEADOWS
BOOK ONE: EDEN 10TH
ANNIVERSARY EDITION HC
ISBN: 978-1-58241-929-0
$24.99

LIBERTY MEADOWS
BOOK ONE: EDEN TP
ISBN: 978-1-58241-624-4
$14.99

LIBERTY MEADOWS
BOOK TWO: CREATURE
COMFORTS TP
ISBN: 978-1-58241-625-1
$14.99

LIBERTY MEADOWS
BOOK THREE: SUMMER
OF LOVE TP
ISBN: 978-1-58241-650-3
$14.99

BOOK FOUR:
COLD COLD HEART TP
ISBN: 978-1-58241-720-3
$14.99

LIONS, TIGERS AND BEARS
VOL. 1: THE FEAR AND PRIDE
ISBN: 978-1-58240-657-2
$12.99 USD

LIONS, TIGERS AND BEARS
VOL. 2: BETRAYAL
ISBN: 978-1-58240-930-6
$14.99 USD

ROCKETO VOL. 1: JOURNEY TO
THE HIDDEN SEA, PART 1 TP
ISBN: 978-1-58240-585-8
$19.99 USD

ROCKETO VOL. 2: JOURNEY
TO THE HIDDEN SEA, PART 2 TP
ISBN: 978-1-58240-735-7
$19.99 USD

TELLOS COLOSSAL, VOL. 1 TP
ISBN: 978-1-58240-940-5
$17.99 USD

TOMMYSAURUS REX GN
ISBN: 978-1-58240-395-3
$11.95 USD